POLICE FIELD OPERATIONS

Third Edition

THOMAS F. ADAMS

Chair, Criminal Justice Department,
Rancho Santiago College
Santa Ana, California

Former Lieutenant of Police
Santa Ana, California

Prentice Hall Career & Technology
Englewood Cliffs, New Jersey 07632

Library of Congress Cataloging-in-Publication Data

Adams, Thomas Francis, 1927–
    Police field operations / Thomas F. Adams. — 3rd ed.
        p.   cm.
    Includes bibliographical references and index.
    ISBN 0-13-057415-5
    1. Police patrol—United States.   I. Title.
HV8080.P2A397   1994
363 . 2 ' 32 ' 0973—dc20   93-47378
                                                     CIP

Acquisitions editor: *Robin Baliszewski*
Managing Editor: *Mary Carnis*
Production editor: *Adele M. Kupchik*
Editorial assistant: *Rosemary Florio*
Manufacturing buyer: *Ed O'Dougherty*
Director of Production & Manufacturing: *David W. Riccardi*
Cover photo: *Spectra UV*
Cover Design: *Yes Graphics*
Keyboarding: *Calligra-Type Graphics, Jill Baez*
Electronic production and design: *Adele M. Kupchik*

©1994, 1990 by Prentice Hall Career & Technology
Prentice-Hall, Inc.
A Paramount Communications Company
Englewood Cliffs, New Jersey 07632

Printed in the United States of America

10   9   8   7   6   5   4   3

ISBN 0-13-057415-5

Prentice-Hall International (UK) Limited, *London*
Prentice-Hall of Australia Pty. Limited, *Sydney*
Prentice-Hall Canada Inc., *Toronto*
Prentice-Hall Hispanoamericana, S.A., *Mexico*
Prentice-Hall of India Private Limited, *New Delhi*
Prentice-Hall of Japan, Inc., *Tokyo*
Simon & Schuster Asia Pte. Ltd., *Singapore*
Editora Prentice-Hall do Brasil, Ltda., *Rio de Janeiro*

Dedicated to my son Tom,
who courageously earned
the Peace Officer Medal of Valor
as a member of the Orange,
California Police Department

CONTENTS

PREFACE xi

LAW ENFORCEMENT CODE OF ETHICS xiii

1 INTRODUCTION TO PATROL 1

Introduction   1
Objectives of Police Field Operations   4
Activities of the Patrol Division   10
Private Police Activities   22
Distribution of the Patrol Force   24
Proactive versus Reactive Patrol   30
Types of Police Patrol   31
The Woman as Police Officer   35
Police Discretionary Prerogatives   35
Civil Liability of the Field Officer   39
Police Officers' Bill of Rights   40
Summary   44
Exercises and Study Questions   46
References   46

2 BASIC FIELD PROCEDURES 48

Introduction   48
Preparation for Patrol   49
Patrolling the District   55
District Responsibility   64
Inspections on Patrol   64

"Attractive Nuisances," or Patrol Hazards   72
Surveillance and Stakeouts   73
Specialized Patrol   77
Team Policing   79
Summary   79
Exercises and Study Questions   80
References   81

3 OBSERVATION & PERCEPTION   **83**

Introduction   83
Basic Requirements of a Witness   84
Factors in Perception   85
Descriptions of Persons   92
Eyewitness Identification   94
Standard Formula for Describing
    Property   100
Detailed Descriptions of Commonly
    Stolen Items   103
Summary   117
Exercises and Study Questions   117

4 COMMUNICATIONS PROCEDURES   **119**

Introduction   119
Interpersonal Communications   120
Essentials for a Police Communications
    System   122
Intra- and Interdepartmental Communi-
    cations   124
Guidelines for Communications Media   128
Guidelines for Radio Operation   135
Summary   145
Exercises and Study Questions   145
References   146

5 REPORTING AND RECORDS   **148**

Introduction   148

*SECTION 1 – FIELD NOTETAKING
AND CRIME SCENE RECORDING   149*

Introduction   149
What Constitutes Field Notes?   150
Notetaking   150

SECTION 2 – REPORT WRITING   *160*

Introduction   160
Purposes for Police Reports   163
Preparation of Reports   165
Construction of the Report   169
The Miscellaneous Incident Report   175
The Arrest Report   175
The Crime Report   177
Special Reports   181
Discussion   181

SECTION 3 – GETTING THE MOST OUT
OF RECORDS   *183*

Introduction   183
Use of Records   183
Basic Records and Their Uses   184
How to Use the Files   187
Summary   188
Exercises and Study Questions   189
References   191

6   INTERVIEWING TECHNIQUES   **192**

Introduction   192

SECTION 1 – INTERVIEWING   *193*

The "Art" of Interviewing   193
General Techniques in Interviewing   197
Interviewing the Suspect of a Crime   198

SECTION 2 – FIELD INTERVIEWS   *205*

Introduction   205
Objectives of Field Interviews   205
Legality of the Field Interview   208
When to Conduct a Field Interview   210
Field Interview Procedure   211
Summary   217
Exercises and Study Questions   217
References   218

7   THE "ROUTINE" ASSIGNMENT   **220**

Introduction   220
Lost Child   221

Missing Persons   223
Intoxification Cases   224
Civil and Domestic Disputes   225
Alcoholic Beverage Control Investigation
    and Enforcement   232
Abandoned Vehicle Abatement   234
Nuisances   235
Parades and Special Events   237
Fire Scenes   237
Rescue and First Aid   238
Courtesy Services   239
Assisting Public Utilities and Service
    Agencies   241
Handling Animal Calls   242
Exercises and Study Questions   243
References   244

8   CRIMES IN PROGRESS   **245**

Introduction   245
"In-Progress" Communications Pro-
    cedure   246
Field Unit Response   247
Tactics by Types of Crimes   250
General Coordination and Search   261
Methods of Cover and Search   262
Plainclothes Assistance   263
Summary   264
Exercises and Study Questions   265
References   266

9   PRELIMINARY INVESTIGATIONS   **267**

Introduction   267
Prelude to the Investigation   268
Deductive and Inductive Reasoning   271
The Investigation   271
Types of Evidence   273
Marking Evidence   282
Chain of Evidence Custody   282
Photographs   284
Accident and Crime Scene Sketching   285
Investigation of Specific Crimes   288
Traffic Collision Investigation   299
Summary   300

Exercises and Study Questions   300
References   302

10   UNUSUAL OCCURENCES   303

Introduction   303
Disaster Response   304
Unlawful Assembly and Riot Control   313
Aircraft Crashes   326
How to Use Access Hatches, Rescue
    Points, and Exits   327
Checklist: How to Report   328
Bombs and Bomb Threats   329
Crisis Intervention   332
Mentally and Emotionally Disturbed Indi-
    viduals   334
Summary   337
Exercises and Study Questions   338
References   339

11   PURSUIT DRIVING, CAR STOPS, & THE DUI   341

Introduction   341
Pursuit and Emergency Driving   342
Car Stops   352
Driving Under the Influence: The DUI   361
Exercises and Study Questions   368
References   369

12   ARREST, SEARCH, & CUSTODY   370

Introduction   370
Laws of Arrest   370
What Constitutes an Arrest   373
Arrest Procedures   374
Searching Techniques   382
Prisoner Control and Transportation   392
Summary   395
Exercises and Study Questions   395
References   396

13   OFFICER SURVIVAL   398

Introduction   398
Stress   399
Officer Survival   404

Rules of Self-Defense   406
Choice of Weapons   411
Use of Firearms   413
Exercises and Study Questions   418
Answers to Scenarios   418

14 THE COMMUNITY & THE POLICE   **419**

Introduction   419
The Field Officer and the Community   420
Police Department Community Relations
    Activities   423
Community–Police Partnership   427
Community-Oriented Policing   430
Summary   436
Exercises and Study Questions   436
References   437

INDEX   **439**

PREFACE

As a peace officer it is your responsibility to preserve the peace and tranquility of your community and to protect the lives and property of the people who live in—and visit—that community. There are few individuals in society who have a more sacred trust than yours. There will be times when you will have to decide whether or not to arrest a suspected offender, and that decision will have a profound influence on many lives and reputations. In less than a second, you may have to decide whether or not to use deadly force, to take the life of someone who you believe is presenting an immediate threat to your life or that of someone else. You will make wise decisions, and you will make mistakes as well. There will be times when you will have overwhelming support and other times when you will be all alone, with no one willing to give you moral or physical support. Because of these considerations, service as a peace officer is one of the most selfless and courageous career choices you could make.

Police Field Operations, Third Edition, has been developed for your guidance. Literally hundreds of sources have been drawn upon, including several dozens of the training bulletins and course outlines that I have used in 20 years of teaching in police academies, 14 years as a police professional and 35 years as a part-time, and then full-time, college instructor. We have been where you are, and it is my hope that the work that my colleagues and I have done in developing the tactics and techniques covered in this book will aid you in becoming a better professional peace officer. We all learn through the wisdom and experience of others.

We have attempted to present those techniques necessary for you to function as an effective field officer. You will, no doubt, decide that you and your fellow professionals have a better way to handle some of the situations discussed in this book. There are valid arguments why you should or should not—depending on your own perspective—follow the guidelines presented in this text. In the absence of a better way, may I suggest that you start with the data presented here and then improve upon it in your own way as you progress. Each one of the tactics and techniques included in the pages that follow has been field tested and has proven successful under the circumstances at various times over the past 30 years. Please look upon this material as a compilation of guidelines rather than as a collection of arbitrary rules to follow.

Once in a while you will read or hear offhand remarks such as "we are going to each you how police work should be, and not how it has been for many years"—obviously not spoken or written by someone who has been "in the trenches," so to speak. Although it is true that many procedures have changed and many new scientific instruments and techniques have been introduced in recent years, many of the old ones still work. Change just for the sake of change is fruitless; changes must be for improvement of the system. As a former vice-chancellor of the college where I teach said more than once, "If it ain't broke, why fix it?" One of the temptations for the professor and the author who are no longer in the field is to change procedures in one's own special environment far removed from reality. I, too, have been tempted to present the ideal solution to many of our unsolved problems only to find that the problems continue to be unsolved despite my brilliant attempts to set the world right. What I aspire to do in this book is to present what I believe to be the best techniques in the real world of police work today.

Sources of information and ideas for this book number literally in the hundreds, and most of the credit should go to those individuals in the profession whose unselfish devotion to our dream of professionalization has motivated them to share their "trade secrets" with their fellow professionals. None of this material has been taken verbatim from any source. you will note the limited use of footnotes and references, the reason being that this is a procedures book, not a compendium of information sources or a survey of the literature, as are some academic publications.

To you, my fellow professionals, I present this material. I challenge you to improve upon it, even render it obsolete, if you must.

I wish to express my special thanks to two very fine gentlemen—Jack Pritchard and Bob Howland—who were responsible for getting me involved in writing for Prentice Hall in the first place, and to the many colleagues in the teaching and policing business who have inspired and mentored me for more years than I would like to admit.

T. F. Adams, Santa Ana, CA

LAW ENFORCEMENT CODE OF ETHICS

As a *Law Enforcement Officer*, my fundamental duty is to serve mankind; to safeguard lives and property; to protect the innocent against deception, the weak against oppression or intimidation, and the peaceful against violence or disorder; and to respect the Constitutional rights of all men to liberty, equality and justice.

I will keep my private life unsullied as an example to all; maintain courageous calm in the face of danger, scorn, or ridicule; develop self-restraint; and be constantly mindful of the welfare of others. Honest in thought and deed in both my personal and official life, I will be exemplary in obeying the laws of the land and the regulations of my department. Whatever I see or hear of a confidential nature or that is confided to me in my official capacity will be kept ever secret unless revelation is necessary in the performance of my duty.

I will never act officiously or permit personal feelings, prejudices, animosities, or friendships to influence my decisions. With no compromise for crime and with relentless prosecution of criminals, I will enforce the law courteously and appropriately without fear or favor, malice or ill will, never employing unnecessary force or violence and never accepting gratuities.

I recognize the badge of my office as a symbol of public faith, and I accept it as a public trust to be held so long as I am true to the ethics of the police service. I will constantly strive to achieve these objectives and ideals, dedicating myself before God to my chosen profession . . . law enforcement.

Courtesy Detroit Police Department.

1 INTRODUCTION TO PATROL

INTRODUCTION

The uniformed field officer of the local police or sheriff's department is the personification of law enforcement in the United States. To many people in the community, uniformed field officers are the *government*, or the *establishment*. To many, they alone *are* the criminal justice system, as the one judge they encounter becomes *the courts*. These are the people who cannot see the mayor, or the council members, or the prosecuting attorney, or a judge. Field officers thus become the representatives of those individuals because they are highly visible. The majority of the people in the community who are served by the police and who come in contact with them on a day-to-day basis respect the officers they know and respect them as their protectors. Others, however, see the uniformed officer as a nuisance; and still others look upon them as the *enemy*. It is the officer's responsibility to serve all members of the community with equal dedication, respect, and with a sense of justice.

Approximately one-half of all the local police departments in the United States employ fewer than 10 officers, nine hundred eighty-seven of those departments have only one officer. About 90 percent of all departments serve populations of less than 25,000 persons and employ fewer than 50 officers. The sheriffs of the thousands of counties and parishes (Louisiana is divided into parishes) are similarly made up primarily of small departments. Half of the sheriffs and their deputies serve populations of less than 25,000, and their sworn ranks number less than 25 in two-thirds of all departments, with about one-third of that number employing 10 or fewer deputies. These numbers indicate the complexity of training and any efforts to standardize procedures, much less their opportunity in these small agencies to specialize.

At the other end of the spectrum, we have 34 police departments and 12 sheriff's departments that are quite sophisticated and highly specialized, employing more than 1000 officers and deputies each. These are the agencies that we see represented in movies and television, with each officer assigned a specific line of duty, such as detective, juvenile detective, burglary detective, auto-theft and accident investigator, crime scene investigator, fingerprint expert, photographer, and on without end to the list.

The smaller departments will assign all but a few to the task of patrolling and responding to calls for service as well as doing most of the investigative work. In the smallest departments, all officers are on patrol, with some assigned the added responsibility of taking on a specialty, such as identification, or dealing with juvenile victims and offenders, performing those duties on an as-needed basis. Consider the one-officer department, with that officer performing every one of the duties performed by dozens of different specialties. In addition to investigating crimes and traffic collisions, responding to all types of calls for service, and running the administrative responsibilities, the chief must find spare time to make the necessary speeches on the "rubber chicken circuit" to all the local service clubs to fulfill community relations obligations. He or she will spend the greatest amount of on-duty time on patrol assignments, of course.

As the department grows to keep up with the increasing population, expanding geographical boundaries, and growing diversity of the jurisdiction, the chief will begin to add on to the force of officers, then will hire office personnel to take over the secretarial and record-keeping functions to free the officers for their field responsibilities. As the department continues to grow, officers are taken out of the field to specialize in traffic investigation and control, juvenile victims and perpetrators, plainclothes detective activities, and all the other specialized functions, each time adding to the patrol force to replace the specialists. All the while, the patrol force continues to be the principal functioning unit of the department.

Many years ago police and sheriff's departments were made up exclusively of sworn male officers with full police authority. Office and communications duties were performed by uniformed officers, who could be called into the field for full service should the need arise. The prevailing attitude was that only police officers could do police work, no matter what type of work it was. This also assured the administrators that officers could be pulled off the desk or away from the typewriter to pick up a shotgun or a nightstick and go out into the field when necessary. Women were added to do "woman's work," such as searching and guarding female arrestees, dealing with juvenile problems, and doing clerical jobs around the stationhouse, but not what their supervisors considered "real," or confrontational police work. As time passed, that too passed, and women officers are now doing the same tasks as their male counterparts. Office and other nonconfrontational duties are now assigned to nonsworn, or civilian, personnel.

In this chapter we take a look at the basic field unit, which is usually known as the patrol division. What are the objectives of the police or sheriff's department? Whatever they are, so are the objectives for the patrol unit, which is the primary operating unit for the entire organization. We list those objectives and discuss each one briefly; then we describe the many activities that the officers perform to meet each of those objectives. Next, distribution of the patrol force is explained, along with the administrative considerations that influence such distribution.

Administrative evaluation of the field activity reports of patrol officers included a goal of *absence of activities* amounting to the optimum of 50 percent of each officer's duty day. Minutes devoted to arrests, transporting prisoners, answering calls for service, and conducting routine and special investigations were tallied and subtracted from the 550-minute day (8 ½-hour day, including lunchtime) with the goal of having each officer's log show 200 to 300 minutes *not* accounted for. This was interpreted as *patrol time*, when the officer ostensibly was checking out the neighborhood, looking for crimes in progress—or recently committed—and being visible to the public and ready to take whatever action a situation called for. Of course, this never has been verifiable; perhaps an officer was just simply *doing nothing,* sleeping, reading, or visiting a friend.

With ongoing austerity programs brought on by budget constraints, expensive fuel, skyrocketing criminal activity related to the drug epidemic, rapid urbanization, cutbacks on personnel, and cost-effective analyses, there must be some hard decisions made as to whether "reactive patrol" (driving around the district waiting for something to happen, which is not too different from the old-time movie stereotype police officers who sit around the squadroom playing cards waiting for their calls) is still affordable, or sensible. The alternative is "proactive patrol," which puts the field units in their districts with prescribed objectives and verifiable tasks scheduled for the day to augment the calls and other on-sight activities that round out the officer's day.

During those times between called-for services when the officer would otherwise be "patrolling," the proactive officer would be making burglary prevention inspections of businesses and residences, going to the residence or workplace of known drug dealers or burglars and "tailing" them for a while to see if they are plying their unlawful trades, making follow-up contacts with victims and witnesses of crimes and traffic collisions previously reported and currently under investigation. We shall come back to proactive patrol from time to time throughout this chapter, and it will pop up elsewhere whenever "routine patrol" comes up.

The entire book is directed to the people who make up the police department, both men and women of all races and all origins. However, because of the more recent emergence of the woman officer as a viable member of the department, we discuss that development briefly. Three additional topics are addressed in this chapter: civil liabilities, discretionary prerogatives of the field officer, and the Peace Officer's Bill of

Rights. All three go hand in hand, because an officer's use of discretionary powers involves risks and liabilities and the officer is entitled to rights of defense and other constitutional guarantees provided any other person.

OBJECTIVES OF POLICE FIELD OPERATIONS

Defense of Life and Property

The phrase inscribed on police car doors and department stationery—"To protect and serve"—is intended to express the police objectives of protecting lives and property and providing all those other services you as a police officer will be expected and required to provide. Essentially, this objective is met by obtaining an open line of communication between the people and the officers who serve them. Included in this category are the functions of "community relations" and "public relations." "Public relations" may be viewed as a series of programs to educate the public through speeches and public appearances at civic and school functions, keeping people informed on department attitudes and policies concerning law enforcement and crime prevention. "Community relations," an expansion of that concept, emphasizes establishment and maintenance of open lines of communication between the people and their police officers for the purpose of improving police services and communication channels with the public. Community-oriented policing would fall in this category.

Participative Law Enforcement

Attitudes of the people about how effective the police are in protecting them in their homes, on the streets, and wherever they may go in the city or county are extremely important. Opinion polls taken by media such as television or national magazines tend to take on the appearance of contests, listing which city is most dangerous for shopping in the malls—which has the greatest number of thefts from autos. Many people are impressionable and pay heed to what they read in those reports, making decisions about where to move the home office of their major corporation, or their drug laboratory, and where they want to raise their children. Although the surveys may accurately reflect the exact results the reporters wish to report, people may be misled because they not only want security, but want to be told that the security is better than the city from which they are moving. For example, a gate, a high fence, and a security guard at the gate do not necessarily assure absolute safety. Rather, they create an *illusion* of security. Also, you are going to be hard-pressed to convince a family that has just been tied up in their home and robbed by a bunch of thugs that the city they live in is actually safer statistically than any of six other cities in which they might choose to live.

In a letter written to me by Police Chief C. R. Meathrell of Salem,

West Virginia, dated April 27, 1992, we get a glimpse of small-town community policing that appears to work:

> *Both of your books could be written right here in our city. Police Field Operations and Police Community Relations are one and the same if you are a police officer in Salem, W. Va.*

> *We are the typical small city police agency. While we do have crime and investigation, it is . . . small in scope. As you doubtless know, West Virginia ranks very low in the crime rate. I am forced to believe that there are some solid reasons for that.*

The Chief goes on to say in his letter:

> *People have a way of looking after one another. We had a form of the Crime Watch long before it was a national deal. It came of general concern for their neighbors. If your neighbor was gone for vacation, then you watched his place. If someone was seen near the place that did not belong, then you called the police.*

> *As Police Chief of what is now a 3 man department, I have become a clearinghouse for everyone's problems. It doesn't matter if the question is on the law or not, they bring the problem to me. If I don't have an answer, then I find someone who does, or at least send that person in the right direction. . . .*

Teamwork between the public and the police is not a luxury; it is mandatory if we are to perform effectively. It is not a new concept. The teamwork concept just seems new to those of us who have forgotten the basics. In the small, intimate community, there is a constant interchange of ideas and vocalization of needs between the police and the people. In our drive to "professionalize," the police service has, in many respects, removed itself from the people you are to serve. Get back to the basics, and make a constant and deliberate effort to know your district and the people in it. Some people have called this "community-oriented policing" or "basic car plan." What they have done is to break the large and impersonal police departments into small units, creating a series of small "hometown" police departments that are responsive and responsible to smaller parts of the city as though they were separate cities. The citizens and the police work together to reduce crime, prevent delinquency and criminal behavior, maintain the peace, and reduce local problems that are the *mutual* responsibility of the police and the people.

The field officer's responsibility is to ensure that this one-on-one relationship between themselves and the public yields maximum results. There must be a constant effort to use every available opportunity to allow the people personally to know the officers and their enforcement philosophy and to become familiar with the overall attitudes of the department toward its general and specific responsibilities.

Unfortunately, far too many people have formed attitudes based on their impressions of certain motion picture and television police personalities, or on what they have read in biased newspaper and magazine stories about the police, or on what they may have personally observed in isolated or unrelated incidents on occasions when certain police officers did not exemplify the professional image. There is no better opportunity for the police officer to cultivate attitudes toward the police—positive, it is hoped—than through personal and informal contacts.

Prevention of Criminal and Delinquent Behavior

This police objective is particularly aimed at ways and means of reducing the desire to commit crime. Sometimes you will succeed, but most of the time when you are influential in causing someone to "go straight," or decide not to commit a crime, you will probably never know it and will have no way to measure how much crime you prevent. It is going to be virtually impossible for you to convince the successful burglar who nets thousands of tax-free dollars per month that crime does not pay and that a job in a fast-food restaurant at the minimum wage is the better way to go. Nevertheless, it is worth the effort. One objective must be to cause the burglar's net income to diminish through careful planning and effective law enforcement.

Rehabilitation and redirection of the criminal offender is the responsibility of parole and probation officers after those offenders have been identified and brought to trial by the police. The police responsibility is to identify those offenders, delinquents, and near-delinquents before an arrest becomes necessary. This is more regularly carried out by the field officer in contacts with juveniles whose behavior patterns are not so indelibly impressed and who might be amenable to change. Through keen observation and diligent investigation, the officer attempts to locate and detain the first-offending juvenile either before or during the commission of a criminal act and then take steps to help the child to redirect energies into lawful and socially acceptable channels.

Repression of Criminal and Delinquent Behavior

Repression of crime is generally accomplished either by having police officers present at specific locations maintaining a highly visible profile or by publicizing a highly active undercover operation. In both cases, the objective is to cause people to decide not to commit crimes for fear of being caught in the act. The theory is based upon the assumption that people will not commit crimes if they believe they are certain to be arrested when they do. Uniforms and distinctively marked vehicles immediately and unquestionably identify the police. As a field officer, your repressive activities are accomplished by making your presence known in such a way that, even when you are not at a specific location, the would-be miscreant will refrain from misbehaving because of the likelihood that you will suddenly pop out from nowhere and nab him, or her. We usually refer to this phenomenon as *police omnipresence*.

Actually, the uniformed police comprise only a small percentage of the overall force of individuals responsible for enforcement of public health and safety laws. Fire marshals, building inspectors, occupational safety and health investigators, health officers, fish and game wardens, the Coast Guard, harbor police, agriculture investigators, weights and measures examiners, investigators for the multitude of licensing agencies, and all types of referees and umpires and other investigators are constantly looking into the behavior of the people in the community. Other people responsible for the enforcement of police powers include social welfare investigators, probation and parole officers, prison guards, school principals and attendance officers, college administrators, driver's license examiners, highway patrol and animal control officers, customs inspectors, airport security, border patrol, secret service, the various federal and state investigative units. The list goes on. But it is you, the uniformed field police officer, who represents them all.

For the crime and delinquency repressive objective of the police to be successful, it is imperative that the vast majority of the people comply with the law, be it out of fear of being caught or simply a desire to do what is right. Your role is to help those people continue to obey the law. Crime repression by police patrol is to try to create an impression of total and continuous presence without creating an air of oppressive dominance. In New Amsterdam (now known as New York), the night warden walked down the streets and alleyways shaking a noisy staff that sounded like a rattle, warning any criminals that he was in the area and that they should behave, at least while he was in the neighborhood. This "rattle watch" was less sophisticated than our present methods of using distinctively painted vehicles with light and siren bars extending across the roof and wearing readily recognizable uniforms. A continuous and unpredictable patrol by the field officer is an attempt to create this feeling of omnipresence. This repressive patrol activity may become a luxury that cannot be justified on the basis of cost-effectiveness because of the increasing cost of fuel for the vehicles and the higher salaries of the officers.

One of the most effective activities of the crime repressive role of the police is the field interview program, which consists of making actual field contact with individuals you encounter in your district when their presence causes you to have reasonable suspicion as to their identity and motive for being where they are under the circumstances that call for further inquiry. The program has proven to be highly effective.

Identification and Apprehension of, and Conviction of, Offenders

This objective is addressed by the field officers knowing their districts and the behavior patterns of the people in them. As one of those officers, you will be in a position to readily identify obvious or suspected violations of the laws and to take immediate enforcement action when possible. When you are assigned to investigate a complaint of a crime in your jurisdiction, it is first your responsibility to know what is a crime and what is not. You must initiate the investigation immediately, locate and question victims and witnesses, protect the crime scene against further contamination, and make every effort to locate and apprehend the suspect.

For misdemeanors not committed in your presence, and for other crimes requiring further investigation, it is your responsibility to make the decision *not* to arrest at that time, but to carry through with the investigation as fast and as far as you can before taking the case to the prosecutor for a warrant, or turning it over to your investigation unit in the department for follow-up and completion.

Your responsibility also extends to include exoneration of the wrongfully accused, as well as conviction of the guilty. Your participation in this process does not end until you have presented evidence and testimony in court as required by the prosecution and have gained the eventual outcome of the case: conviction of the accused when that person is guilty, or freedom of the innocent.

The *due process* provisions of the Constitution of the United States and the respective states have been interpreted by the various courts, and their decisions have served as controlling influences on such police procedures as field interviews, stop and frisk, arrest, search, seizure of evidence, impounding contraband, storing vehicles, interviewing the suspect, use of force, and various other activities. It is your duty to work within the framework of the many laws and guidelines and to assure fair presentation of evidence in court to assure a conviction that will withstand the test of constitutionality.

Traffic Flow and Collision Reduction

Pedestrian and vehicle traffic must be free-flowing and collision-free so that people may move safely from one place to another in your jurisdiction. The police objective is to determine the causes of congestion and to relieve it, which involves investigation and the Three E's: education, engineering, and enforcement. Enforcement is the most highly visible aspect of these three aspects of the police traffic responsibility, and engenders the greatest amount of antipathy from traffic law violators. Intelligent enforcement of traffic law violations, focusing attention on those violations that cause the most number of injuries and property damage and citing according to a set of priorities designed to significantly reduce those violations and corresponding collisions does yield significant results that even the most severe critic cannot dispute.

Engineering at first does not strike one as a police responsibility, but it is. For example: analysis of the collision statistics show that an inordinate number of unlawful left turns at a certain intersection are listed as the cause of collisions. Officers issue a lot of citations to the violators of those violations at that location and the collision rate goes down. But did they solve the problem? The reason for the collisions may be that many drivers are frustrated because there is no left-turn lane and traffic is so heavy that they cannot make a left turn without taking a chance and cutting in when they see a break in opposing traffic. What they need is a left-turn lane and a traffic signal with a left-turn green sequence so that the people turning left can do so without having to play "chicken" with opposing traffic. Officers in the field can recognize this problem because they are dealing with it on a daily basis, and they should pass this information on to the city traffic engineer or public works department.

The education aspect of traffic control can significantly reduce collisions by requiring violators to attend classes where their specific types of violations are discussed and they may go through a retraining process to reduce their citations and lower their insurance rates. During the past few years we have seen a revolution by the outraged public against drivers who operate their vehicles while under the influence of alcohol and other drugs. Education of the driving public is aimed at changing the behavior and attitude of people who use those drugs and have been driving motor vehicles as a matter of routine, but who are now changing their behavior to avoid arrest and tragedies that they might cause.

Maintenance of Order and the Public Peace

This is one of the broadest, most variable, and sometimes most misunderstood of all the police objectives. It is in the "all other" category, because this category includes not only those activities that have been legally delegated to the police but also those that have been traditionally assigned, and sometimes those that your department may have assumed simply because there was no one else to do them. A free society such as ours is characterized by its relatively small number of controls when compared with other forms of governed society. Yet to permit the majority of the people in the country to enjoy their own pursuit patterns for comfort and happiness, certain controls are necessary. One person's freedom to listen to loud music must be restricted when the sounds interfere with another person's freedom to enjoy the absence of sound. To balance the two, the police must maintain a constant and vigilant patrol, frequently making direct contact with a number of people to demonstrate their presence in a peacekeeping role and responding to called-for services to referee disagreements in family and neighborhood situations that would erupt into full-scale combat situations without their presence.

You will be required to attend places where large numbers of people congregate, such as meeting halls, stadiums, theaters, and places of political rallies and demonstrations to maintain order and prevent violations of the laws. At the same time, you will be required to enforce the people's rights to assemble peaceably and express their opinions and beliefs. Most people are peaceable. You will be called upon to deal with the unusual situation, such as the boisterous party, loud radio or television, or the public gathering that grew into a riot.

The "order maintenance" process includes many other responsibilities, such as directing traffic at fires or collision scenes, controlling crowds and preventing panic at disaster scenes, and providing a stabilizing influence in times of emotional upset. Most breaches of the peace are settled merely by firmly suggesting that the violators desist and comply with the law. In those cases when the violators do not comply, you must take immediate and decisive action, which may lead to arresting and prosecuting the violators.

ACTIVITIES OF THE PATROL DIVISION

Routine Patrol and Observation

Basic patrolling activities are usually referred to as "routine," although even the most mundane of your tasks should never be taken so lightly as to be considered routine. As a matter of fact, it should be your "routine" not to patrol your district the same way twice. Once you establish any sort of pattern or schedule for your patrolling duties, your effectiveness in repressing any sort of criminal or delinquent behavior is virtually eliminated. Many intelligent and wealthy criminals have attributed their phenomenal successes to their ability to work around the time schedules of the field officers. They learn the shift hours, district assignments, and number of officers on patrol at any given time, and then they analyze the patrol methods employed by the officers working the districts where they intend to commit their crimes. Look at your own patterns. Do you always drive the same route in the same sequence when you leave headquarters? Do you spend the first hour making a one-time sweep of the district and then devote specific times to the same activities day after day?

When you do not have a fixed pattern for patrolling your district, the criminals must take greater risks when attempting to commit crimes while you are on duty. The routine of patrol, therefore, should be one of *routine avoidance*.

Preventive Attendance at Public Gatherings

Wherever people gather in sizable numbers, the police should be visibly present. This presence should alert anyone inclined to break the law that there would be a greater probability of arrest. This presence will also assure a peaceful assembly and provide protection for those who wish to exercise their rights to peaceful assembly and free speech. There should be no indication that you intend to control or dominate the people who are in attendance. Your purpose is to prevent—if you can—any unlawful activity by individuals or by the crowd as a whole. Riot *prevention* is much better than riot *control*. Once a riot begins everyone loses. Freedom of assembly is a basic freedom assured by the First Amendment to the Constitution. Your first duty when arriving at the scene of an assembly is to determine that it is lawful. Your responsibility is then to remain present to assure everyone that you are going to ensure that the assembly continues to be peaceful. Although it is true that you must remain on location where there is a continuing need for police presence, such as an organized demonstration attended by opposing interest groups, congregations of opposing street gangs, open-air concerts, a county or state fair, or any event where violence or other criminal activity is anticipated, it is good police practice to leave once you determine that your energies could be better spent elsewhere.

There are times and places where anything more than a casual police presence and departure could be misinterpreted as oppressive. Consider the polling place on election day. Officers standing around for the purpose of keeping the peace could be perceived as government intervention into the free-election process, not unlike elections in a native country from which our new voters escaped to become citizens of this country where they may vote as they choose.

Benevolent and Community Services

Because the police are always available and on duty, they are often called upon to perform many services that do not appear on any list of job specifications for police officers, but they perform them nevertheless. Although not required by any law or ordinance, many of these tasks have become traditional simply by the officers' own willingness to do them as a service to the people who ask for them, or they may have become a social custom in a particular community. You will be called upon to perform midwife duties at childbirth or to render first aid to collision or disaster victims, even though those activities are generally the responsibility of paramedics and other medical service personnel who are far better trained and qualified to perform the task. There will be times when you must arrange for emergency shelter and subsistence for the homeless and destitute, getting them in touch with welfare and social service people who provide them the means and services they so desperately need. Sometimes officers have been known to dip into their own pockets to help less fortunate people on their beat.

You will be called upon to referee neighborhood or family quarrels when they have probably reached the violent stage, and people there will look to you for spiritual or psychological counseling, which you must avoid doing because you are not licensed to do so. Nevertheless, you still have to defuse the situation to avoid later having to take someone to the hospital or to jail. You will deliver death messages when the appropriate spiritual counselors cannot be located. There are times when you will be called upon to help people get into their homes or autos when a locksmith is not available. Be careful when playing good samaritan. I know of a time when a beat officer helped a citizen push his car to get it started, then found out later that he had actually helped a thief steal that car, not knowing he was doing so.

A dilemma is created and perpetuated by the traditional acceptance of various duties that should not be provided by the police. There seems to be no other agency that is geared to cope with the unusual and unexpected. One of the more blatant misuses of police personnel and equipment is the ego-boosting practice of providing chauffeur service for visiting dignitaries and local officials. If the transportation is for the purpose of providing protection, then it is a police responsibility. Usually, however, it is transportation that should be provided by a local taxi service. Even a limousine would be more economical than would taking the officer and the police unit out of service for that period of time. In the absence of a realistic evaluation as to what constitutes police work, you will probably continue to perform these services as though they were required of you.

Business and Property Security

Security of personal and business property is the responsibility of the people who have legal custody of that property. It is also your responsibility to protect that property. Therefore, it becomes a joint responsibility of both owner and the police. Since this is a partnership, you should take it upon yourself to advise your so-called "partners" on how they might make their property as secure and crime resistant as possible. It is not unusual for property owners to install elaborate alarm systems and expensive locks to protect against intrusion through flimsy doors and windows, and their walls are so thin that they may be penetrated by a mere kick and a well-placed foot. Sometimes, in the interest of "economy" property owners will shortchange themselves in the area of security. Another serious problem is that even after installing elaborate protective devices and alarm systems, one of the occupants will leave for the weekend without activating the system or will leave doors and windows open and unlocked.

As a field officer, your responsibility is to check out thoroughly the security of residential or commercial buildings and properties as best you can within the constraints of time and your other responsibilities. If it were possible to educate successfully all these would-be victims of the need for security, you would make your job much easier. Frequent and unscheduled visits to the property for security checks will further reduce the likelihood of criminal activity at those locations.

Inspection Services

Inspections for security against theft are obvious responsibilities of the patrol force. But there are additional types of inspections that you perform. One of the more important is to look for fires and fire hazards at the same time you check for security against crimes. It is not feasible for local government to provide another patrol force that would duplicate the police patrol and that would travel the same routes as the patrol units. Since the officer is already on the streets, it is most efficient to extend the inspection responsibilities of the police and then require the officers to report the law violations or unsafe conditions to the appropriate agencies.

Included in the various types of inspections the field officer performs are utility outages, streets and sidewalks in need of repair, building code violations, health and safety violations, unsanitary conditions in restaurants and grocery stores and butcher shops, obscured traffic signs and signals, professional and business license violations, and leash law violations. Your initial action might include issuing citations or making arrests for criminal violations and/or submitting a comprehensive report to be forwarded to the responsible agency for further investigation and follow-up to correct the problem.

Responding to Calls for Service

The great majority of calls for police service do not involve matters that lead to an on-the-spot arrest or any other action beyond what the officer handles at the scene. Neighborhood children damage fences or border plants along property lines, or the children get involved in a fight that eventually leads to a squabble between their parents; then the police officer arrives and everyone agrees to shake hands and make up. A husband and wife begin to fight over finances, which leads to a bitter debate about each other's in-laws and an airing of previous arguments that had never been settled; the police arrive, and all grievances are postponed until the next argument. The ritual is quite common in many families, and the postponement is sometimes the best the officer can hope for. Sometimes you will be called upon to scold a neighbor child for some sort of real or imagined misconduct. There are other times when you may convince the combatants that fighting is no way to settle an argument. On several occasions in neighborhood and family disputes, a relative or neighbor will demand that the police officer "beat up the husband and teach him a lesson." Eventually, nothing will surprise you when it comes to the variety of demands as to what action you are expected to take, many of which will be inappropriate. In these civil disputes, your presence is legal principally because you have been invited or because the disturbance is in public and your primary responsibility is to preserve the peace and ascertain whether anyone has broken the law. Most of the time, your action will consist of reminding the participants that their problem is a civil one and that they will have to seek a solution to their problem through one of the many services that you will refer them to and of advising them to settle their differences amicably so that you may return to your other duties.

The task of responding to calls for service may be regarded as a matter of disposing of *minor complaints*, although none of them is minor to the participants. The problems confronting these people are obviously beyond their capacity to cope with by the time they call for police intervention. It takes a tremendous amount of tact and diplomacy to handle these so-called "minor" problems. The child who fails to respond to a parent's discipline in a demonstration of contempt for an authority figure may be a family problem today but a police problem tomorrow unless some solution can be worked out today. The unethical, though legal, business transaction in which the unsuspecting consumer buys a $5 burglar alarm for $400 may not in itself be a violation of any criminal code, but if the consumer's complaint is reported correctly and there are sufficient other such complaints, an investigation may ensue that will reveal false representation and fraud.

Many matters involving repossession and property rights, landlord-tenant arguments, employer and employee relations, arguments about property lines, poorly constructed dikes and levees resulting in floods, late garbage collections, and a multitude of "gripes" about various government services will be laid in your lap. Although you have little or no authority over any of the principals in these matters, you will be expected to solve the problems, whatever they are. You must deal with them intelligently and with diplomatic persuasion.

People commit suicide. The police are called. A woman is having a baby. The police are called. An elderly bedridden person falls out of bed and needs help getting back into the bed. The police are called. An explosion destroys the three lower floors of a hotel. The police are called. A sonic boom causes windows to rattle as though a burglar were trying to get in. The police are called. A distraught student who has just received a report card with three F's climbs up on top of a clock tower and threatens to jump unless the professors reconsider. The police are called. You respond to each of these calls. You take appropriate action, whatever it is, prepare the ubiquitous report, and then resume patrol.

Animal Control

There is probably a separate agency in your jurisdiction that handles problems of lost, stray, abandoned, or injured animals. It is either a government-supported agency or a privately funded organization, such as the Society for the Prevention of Cruelty to Animals. The police department will be called in to investigate and enforce violations of animal abuse. Because of the constant availability of a police patrol unit, it will not be unusual for you to have to round up an occasional dog or cat or panther that strayed away from its home. As if you did not have enough problems with domestic pets, there are those people whose ideas of pets are somewhat diverse (or perverse) and who insist on keeping exotic—often dangerous—pets on their premises which are either unlawful to keep, or at least unwanted by the neighbors. You may have to take some action based on your own judgment before you are able to consult wildlife specialists on the best way to handle the critters. You will also be called upon to provide for the treatment of injured animals and disposal of those less fortunate ones that are killed in traffic or by backyard hunters.

Traffic Direction and Control

The police field unit may have both patrol and traffic responsibilities, but even when there is a separate traffic unit, your responsibility as a field officer is to assure safe and efficient movement of vehicular and pedestrian traffic in your district (see Figures 1–1 and 1–2). Traffic control and collision prevention require constant vigilance. In addition to responding to collisions and protecting the scene from further damage and injury, you will frequently be called upon to provide traffic control services at scenes of fires, large crowds and gatherings at public events, rush-hour traffic in school and business zones, and traffic tieups caused by inclement weather or unusual road conditions. Whatever the problem, you will be expected to take the initiative to address the problem the best way that you can and to call for whatever assistance is necessary to protect the scene and restore it to normal.

Information Services

You—the field officer—and your department are expected to be the wellspring of information about everything in your jurisdiction: where everything is and whatever is happening, and where it is happening. You should know the street-numbering plan for your city: even numbers on the north and east sides of the streets and houses numbered in multiples of 10, so that you will know that 1940 is the fourth house from the south cross-street on the east side of the street. This will obviate the need for you to search for the house at night when responding to a "burglary in progress" call and you will probably be able to describe the house to an inquirer about the location of 953 West Pine Street.

Figure 1-1   Traffic control is an important function of police patrol, whether it is in North Dakota or Hawaii. (Courtesy of the Police Department, Bismarck, North Dakota.)

Figure 1-2   (Courtesy of the Police Department, Hilo, Hawaii.)

It should be in your personal encyclopedia where the all-night service stations are located, which pharmacies stay open late and provide emergency all-night services to the ill, and the locations of the variety of ethnic restaurants in the area. If someone asks you where one may get the best lobster dinner for the money, or the best steak or fajitas, be prepared to recommend more than one lest you should be accused by competitors of playing favorites. Of course, if there is only one Chinese restaurant within 10 miles of your town, that's the one you're going to name. People will ask about the old-fashioned ice-cream shop, rare book store, sheet music store, bicycle repair shop, a "respectable" tavern where one may take an out-of-town guest, or a place to have film developed while they wait. You should be prepared to give directions and at least know where to look to help these people. As the most visible representative of your local government, you should be prepared to answer such questions as what is the population? the altitude? the average year-round temperature? What are the names of local politicians and famous residents? You are the weather bureau, the chamber of commerce, but hopefully not the local gossip. You will be expected by your department to be the community's goodwill ambassador.

You should also be the best source of information for your fellow officers and other emergency services as to the location of road closures and other hazards, street parties, hotly disputed athletic events, and other occasions where it appears there will be trouble later if you let it get out of hand during the evening.

Developing Contacts

This is a departmentwide activity. Actually, if a community-police partnership is to succeed, there should be open and free-flowing lines of communication between the police and all segments of the community. The department should zealously guard against showing any favoritism for any particular segment of the community, either in actuality or in the eyes of others. That would only lead to more bitterness and rivalry within the community. You should not be satisfied with just doing a good job. The public should know that you are. If there are effective lines of communication open to all segments of the community, it will make your job so much easier. People outside the department must know enough about the police responsibilities and methods of operation that they may observe and judge for themselves whether their police officers are doing the excellent job they say they are. Then you will have the enthusiastic support that you need to be a successful field officer. Such openness will tend to squelch unfounded rumors, reduce friction, and enhance support.

As a field officer, you are responsible for the development of informants. We are not talking about the character who talks out of the side of his mouth and looks over his shoulder while giving you the information you are seeking in return for a "fiver." Of course, that character will probably be among your reservoir of informants. But we are talking about certain "fringe" businesspersons—those who are operating just inside or outside the law but who seem to conceal their criminal behavior successfully—who will give you information that will be intended to put their competitors out of business. There are the violators you catch but cannot prosecute because of some technical difficulty with constitutional exclusion of evidence but who will willingly provide you with information concerning narcotics traffic or stolen property operations either to get themselves off the hook or to divert attention away from themselves.

When developing leads from informants whose own prosecution was hampered because of contaminated evidence, keep in mind that any evidence emanating from these sources may likewise be inadmissible ("poison tree" doctrine discussed later in this book). Although vice and narcotics detectives are credited with their success in relationship to the volume and quality of their informants, officers in all divisions develop informants, including the newest rookie in the department. When developing these informant relationship, be careful to keep them at arm's length if they are involved in the criminal world and avoid compromise. To understand how a dog behaves, you do not have to sleep with them and share their fleas.

Sometimes you will actually encounter the patriotic person who will provide you with information because "it is the right thing to do." There are others who have served their time for previous violations but as a part of their rehabilitation believe that they must inform on other criminals. You should seek out people from a wide variety of occupations and professions and cultivate them as sources of information.

Jewelers are the best source of information as to actual value of diamonds and other precious stones. They also hear through their own channels which jewelers are honest and which ones will buy stolen merchandise, and they can recognize each other's work in cutting and setting stones and repairing jewelry. People in the construction industry are the best source of information concerning individuals and companies involved in legitimate and illegitimate dealings in the construction industry. Doctors know about other doctors, pharmacists know about other pharmacists, cooks know other cooks, and so on. Everyone who sincerely believes that honesty and ethical practice are the only way to conduct one's business may voluntarily assist you in your investigations of other people in their respective fields who are making "a bad name" for the legitimate practitioners.

Establishing rapport with citizen participants (or informants) in law enforcement should yield mutual benefits to the police department and the participants. Gratuities should not be involved in any of these information-seeking relationships. There are exceptions, of course, as when certain information is rewarded according to established procedures or when a cash reward has been advertised. You may repay the debt in other ways, such as suggesting ways in which the informant may burglarproof his office. Your irregular and unannounced visits to shops may discourage would-be shoplifters and robbers. Using taxicab and truck drivers and their own commercial or citizens band radio networks as an extension of the police radio network may cause a more satisfactory working relationship, and you may, in turn, make a little extra effort in educating them on how to avoid committing so many traffic violations. When dealing with informants, consider their motivations.

Preliminary Investigations

Field patrol officers are constantly available and on the street, ready to take immediate action, and such action involves performing preliminary investigations of traffic collisions and criminal law violations. Providing that the field officers are adequately trained and that there are sufficient officers to perform the work, the patrol division is actually in the better position to handle these initial investigations. There are certain exceptions, such as continuing investigations and those that involve undercover work over a period of time in matters involving narcotics or vice or intelligence gathering. That does not mean that uniformed field officers are not involved in those types of activities. Quite the contrary. In many departments, the majority of arrests for narcotics and vice activities are made by the patrol officers.

As the first officer on the scene, you must look after the safety of the victim and witnesses, and you will apprehend the suspect if one is at the scene. You will be required to take immediate steps to protect the scene from any further contamination and then immediately establish communication with headquarters to broadcast information about wanted suspects and vehicles and request whatever additional assistance that you need.

As the first person on the scene, no one is better prepared than you to take immediate action. While the scene is still fresh and victims and witnesses still caught up in the spontaneity of the situation, your job is to observe carefully all evidence before anyone has had a chance to contaminate it—to reflect or to change their stories or to fabricate alibis. You will probably be assigned to continue with the investigation until all leads are exhausted and any further investigation would take you out of your district for too long a period of time. You will question the victim, the witnesses, and any suspects that you may encounter. You will collect the evidence and catalog and file it; then you will prepare the reports. At some point, the follow-up work on the investigation may be continued by an investigator and other specialists. At other times, you will handle the entire case on your own with no follow-up being necessary. The key to the success of any follow-up investigation is usually attributable to your skill as the one who handles the initial investigation.

In many agencies, initial response and investigation of traffic collisions is the responsibility of the field patrol unit, with the follow-up handled by traffic specialists from a traffic division. Some departments have merged traffic and patrol into a single uniformed field unit. Regardless of the category in which your department belongs, you as the first field officer at the scene will be the first to protect the scene from further collisions, check for injuries and administer first aid, locate and identify drivers and witnesses, and handle the initial phases of the investigation. You are probably the most logical person to perform the initial investigation for the same reason that you would perform the initial criminal investigation. You are in a position to observe the scene before it has been contaminated, see the vehicles before they have been moved, observe short-lived evidence that might be destroyed before the arrival of other police units, and talk with the participants while the incident is fresh in their minds, free of fabrication or exaggeration.

Somewhere along the way in the traffic investigation, as with the criminal investigation, you will have to complete your records and get back to your district, and a follow-up investigator will continue and "wrap up" the case. The *primary* consideration as to just how far you investigate and how long you continue before turning over the investigation to others is *time*. You have other responsibilities and must move on to provide the entire spectrum of services to the people in your district.

As a field patrol officer, you will also conduct investigations into alleged unethical or unlawful business transactions, suspicious persons such as door-to-door canvassers and salespersons (not all these street people are criminals, but daylight residence burglaries go up when there are more of them around, particularly those who move from city to city), and other persons whose presence calls for some sort of explanation.

Additionally, you will investigate vagrants, loiterers, street walkers, and suspected vice operants. You will conduct field interviews with people whose presence in a particular place and under certain circumstances cause you to have a reasonable belief that they should be checked out. You will investigate vehicles that appear to be abandoned and conduct literally thousands of other investigations into matters that pose real or imagined threats to the health, welfare, and safety of the people and property in your district.

Collection and Preservation of Evidence

Inherent in the investigation process is the proper handling of evidence for the purpose of assuring a fair trial of the accused. From the moment you arrive on the scene until you complete your testimony and presentation of evidence in court, you will be directly involved in this process. You must be careful to avoid contaminating any more evidence than is necessary. Your responsibility is to assess carefully the situation when you arrive and then methodically collect and prepare the evidence for transportation and storage and laboratory analysis. After storing the evidence, or forwarding it to the laboratory, you will be required to prepare the necessary reports. When the time comes for the court appearance and presentation of the evidence, you will usually be the same person to withdraw the evidence from storage and account for its continuity of custody. This should be standard department procedure.

For many of the investigations you conduct, you will be required to prepare sketches and diagrams, using them for more effective coordination of the information you put in your reports and for orientation purposes. You may be one of those officers who will be specially trained in the collection and preservation of evidence and carry the added responsibility of being assigned as a crime scene investigator (CSI). Whenever the need arises, these specialists are taken out of their regular field patrol assignment and are dispatched to the scenes of crimes and collisions to collect evidence, dust for latent fingerprints, take photographs, and generally provide a little more expertise to assist in the initial investigation.

Some departments have selected and trained permanent nonsworn men and women to perform CSI as Police Service Officers, or Community Service Officers. Many have found that people who aspire to make a career of this job with no visions of advancement into—and out of—this assignment as a career step do an excellent job, although they are not classified as police officers.

Arrest of Offenders

Second only to caring for the injured or wounded, the field officer's primary responsibility at the scene of a crime is to locate and arrest the offender. Once you effect the arrest, you may use one of several alternative methods to introduce the arrestee into the criminal justice system. The alternative methods are described by the laws, the courts, and the procedural manuals prepared by your department.

In virtually every felony case, you will take the arrestee to jail, where the "booking," or processing, begins. Except when provided for by law, every arrestee is entitled to post bail, which is a guarantee assuring his or her later court appearance after release. In some situations, the arrestee may be taken directly before a magistrate in lieu of booking and bail, although such procedure is not routine. In misdemeanor arrests, the violators are booked into jail, or they are issued a citation and are allowed to sign a promise to appear in court on or before a specified date. The citation method has been used extensively in traffic cases for many years, and in some states more recently, it has been extended to cover most misdemeanor violations when immediate release poses no threat to life or property.

Roll call training sessions and various publications constantly disseminate information about current crimes and wanted criminal offenders. It is your responsibility to search diligently for those wanted persons and to seek information as to their whereabouts and get them into court to answer the charges against them. In many cases of minor violations, you will issue written and oral warnings rather than make arrests and issue citations. Most of those cases will relate to traffic violations.

Traffic laws—as with criminal laws—are separated into felonies, misdemeanors, and (in some states) infractions. The felonies and misdemeanors we have already discussed. The infraction usually carries no punishment other than a fine. The recipient is sometimes required to correct an equipment failure, such as replacing a tail light. When the individual fails to correct the equipment violation and/or appear in court to show that the situation has been resolved, the infraction becomes a misdemeanor violation for failure to comply.

Preparation of Reports

Nearly everything you do while assigned as a field patrol officer will be committed to some sort of a written or printed report. It may consist of merely checking a box or two or recording the names and addresses of the principals involved and adding a cryptic phrase such as "miscellaneous service." However, you will also be required to prepare a detailed report on precisely who was involved in an incident, what were the circumstances, and when and where did the crime or incident occur and provide sufficient information so that the reader will know exactly what took place and what further action, if any, is warranted. Preparation of reports is one of the most time-consuming of all police activities and one of the most demanding. The reports that you will prepare are used as the basis for determining whether to charge an individual with a crime and, if so, what specific charge will be made. In many cases, the reports that you prepare will be the only source your supervisors have to determine your decision-making ability and to evaluate your performance. Your reports must be complete and accurate, since they are usually the only written record of what transpires.

The importance of accuracy, honesty, and efficiency in reporting cannot be overemphasized. In addition to the prosecuting attorney, the defendant and defense attorney have a right to review the reports under the rules of *discovery*. Judges and juries—if the report is placed into evidence—all read the reports. Not only do they evaluate accuracy but they will not resist the temptation to assess the intelligence of the writer of the report. A poor report will be interpreted as a poor job.

Testifying in Court

This is the final step in the investigation process. Your responsibility is to present your evidence and testimony factually and without bias. The final determination of guilt or innocence is the responsibility of the judge or jury.

PRIVATE POLICE ACTIVITIES

Although this text is primarily directed toward field procedures for the public police agency, it would be negligent to overlook the valuable services provided by private patrol and investigative agencies. Because of the limitations on time and resources available to city and county police agencies, many private companies and individuals have security needs that exceed those provided by the services of the government's police. They employ private police agencies to provide those services, which include the following:

Perimeter and Access Control

To protect the premises against intrusion of thieves or spies (of the international or local variety) and to slow down the incidence of theft, guards are posted at various places of ingress and egress and around the perimeter of the property involved. This is accomplished by continuous patrol, or spot inspection, or with the aid of electronic surveillance equipment, such as remote video cameras operated from a central control room. Only authorized persons with specific clearances are allowed access to those locations where patent secrets or secret government information is located. This may actually be required by a government-contracted manufacturer.

Asset Protection and "Inventory Shrinkage"

Theft from the business establishment goes out both the front door and the back. Dishonest "shoppers" are matched in skill and ingenuity by dishonest employees. Spotting and surveilling shoplifters require special training and skills, and the successful store detective learns that one must think the way a thief does in order to catch a thief. One-way mirrors and connecting "catwalks" above the ceiling provide observation platforms from where the investigator may watch and photograph suspected activities by shoplifters and dishonest employees. Strategically placed video-cameras are also utilized for observation of several locations simultaneously by a single operator, who can radio to a fellow investigator on the floor where to go and what (and whom) to look for.

Catching the employee who steals includes many of the same surveillance techniques, plus the use of undercover operatives who fit in as fellow workers, utilization of informants, and professional "shoppers" who act as spotters to look for discrepancies in sales procedures. Use of the polygraph has lost favor during recent years, but it is still an effective tool.

Personal/Executive/Celebrity Protection

The bodyguard business utilizes men and women who have had extensive training and demonstrated skills in weaponless defense, as well as some specialists with weapons, and many agencies have combined forces with limousine services, providing both the means of transportation and the personnel. Escort vehicles are utilized when there is an enhanced anticipation of a kidnap or assault attempt. Sometimes evasive maneuvers are necessary, which may give the protected person the feeling of being transported via a Magic Mountain ride. This has become almost routine of late, because a ransom for a kidnapped superstar of sports or television or some corporations would finance a small war, and terrorism acts are not uncommon.

Location and Recovery of Stolen Children

Children who are the victims of kidnapping receive the full attention of all segments of the police system: federal, state, and local. The probability of a homicide following the kidnap is great. Although private investigation agencies may be hired by the victim's family in kidnap cases, they are utilized more extensively in child-stealing cases, where the noncustodial mother or father violates a court order and takes the child to lavish their own form of love and care, with less likelihood that they will harm the children. In these cases, the matter is both civil and criminal, sometimes involving conflicting laws among nations. The role of the private investigator in these types of cases is to locate the child, then do whatever possible to protect the child and parent by having court papers verifying legal custody, and to manage the retrieval of the child. Investigators without government affiliations are sometimes more effective than the local police because there are fewer restrictions on their professional behavior and their financial resources are restricted only by the parent's ability to pay the tariff.

Disturbance Prevention and Crowd Control

At large athletic or entertainment functions, the promoters of the event and the property owners are concerned with keeping the peace as well as protecting their investment in property and equipment. Security is principally provided by the promoters within the perimeter of the event and by the local police outside the perimeter. Labor-management disputes usually involve heavy reliance on private police agencies. Shopping centers and colleges are equally concerned with protection of people and property and will augment local police protection with their own police forces.

Special-Purpose Police

There is yet another type of police agency that is neither public nor private, or is both. Special quasi-governments such as park districts or housing authorities are created. To protect their property interests and the people who live in, or traverse over, their properties, special police forces are created. Depending on the conditions, these agencies are public or private.

Private agencies would be employed by large residential communities operated by a corporation or association of owners, an industrial park, or large private recreational parks such as Disneyland and Disney World. Government agencies in this category would include public college districts or universities and state colleges, which have their own government-sanctioned police officers with authority restricted to students, properties, and personnel of such institutions.

DISTRIBUTION OF THE PATROL FORCE

No one knows exactly how many crimes are actually committed every year, but it is generally agreed that considerably more are committed than are reported. How many crimes the patrol force will prevent, if any, is another figure that we can only speculate about. Of the crimes that are reported each year, the numbers that are cleared by arrest are much lower than we care to acknowledge. It is apparent that whatever the patrol forces are doing is not enough to show a statistical improvement. The police department is charged with prevention, repression, and solution of crimes within the framework of limitations of funds, human resources, and equipment.

Selectivity of assignment and referral to other agencies seem to be the only realistic approach to the problem of distributing the patrol force so that it may do the most good. Even if two police officers were placed on every one-block square area of the jurisdiction, it would not assure any better patrol results than we are getting at the present time. As a part of participatory management of the police department, in which the citizen representatives take part in making critical decisions as to which calls for service will be designated greater priorities, there must not only be some agreement on priorities but, eventually, a recognition that some of the traditional police services will be given lower priorities or no priority at all.

Policy Decisions Concerning Distribution

When developing a priority sequence on field assignments, certain questions must be answered. For example,

1. Which calls for service will be handled completely by telephone, and which ones will require an officer to be sent to the caller's address? The guiding factor in answering this question is: What can or should the officer do following arrival? Is a suspect still at the scene, or is there evidence available that might lead to conviction for a criminal law violation?

2. Which calls will be "counseled out" by advising the calling party that the matter can better be handled by another agency? Many types of calls fit into this category. A referral directory could be used with the complaint operator providing the appropriate telephone numbers or dialing and diverting the call directly.

3. To what extent will the patrol officers become involved in neighborhood quarrels and family disputes; advise children regarding their school attendance and other behavior patterns; give advice on interpersonal relationships; and undertake peacekeeping functions? While some of these situations call for some sort of police intervention, many could probably be handled better by psychological counselors.

4. What portion of the crime investigations will be handled by patrol officers, and at what point will cases be turned over to the specialists? One factor to consider is that there is often a natural inclination for the specialist to start at the beginning and reinvestigate, which is a flagrant waste of time and resources.

5. What is the patrol officer's role in traffic accident investigation and traffic law enforcement? Will the officers be solely responsible, or will there be supplementary assistance and coordination by traffic specialists? There is also the option of utilizing civilian specialists in taking reports, thereby costing less and freeing police officers for other assignments. Many reports can be taken at the police building.

6. To what extent will the officers be responsible for building security in their districts that will necessitate their being away from their patrol units for extended periods of time? Perhaps the police have spoiled the property owners by doing some of their security checking for them. Flourishing private patrol operators usually sell this service on the grounds that the local police either cannot or will not perform well in this area.

7. How much of the public relations function of the department will directly involve the patrol officers? Will they be required to eat lunch and play basketball with the children? Will the field officer be assigned to crime prevention activities, such as inspecting buildings for burglary security, or will that be done by civilian specialists and volunteers? There must be a limit. The question is: Where is that limit?

8. What will be the reporting responsibilities of the field officers? How detailed must their reports be? Where will they go to make the reports—to headquarters? to a telephone? Or will they carry portable dictating units? What forms will be used—fill-in, checklist, or all prose? Will the officers be required to type or print out their own reports? How often must the officers return to headquarters to turn in their reports? This entire area is very important. In the author's opinion, many departments require far too many reports, many of which could be disposed of by checking a box indicating that the matter was handled and that no further action is warranted—two checkmarks at the most instead of two or three paragraphs. Perhaps many can be closed out by computer from the car.

9. How will priorities be established to give precedence to certain types of calls over others? If units are not available, which calls will not be assigned? Each type of call could be given a weighted point value, such as 5 points for a robbery in progress and 1 point for a burglary that occurred last night. A citizen advisory committee would be invaluable when it comes to making this list.

10. How are the supervisors and administrators used for management of the field officers? Are they going to provide field supervision and leadership? Are they going to handle calls? Are they going to be augmented by senior officers or training officers? Are they going to be used to perpetuate a lot of unnecessary administrative paperwork?

11. What types of forms and other documents must be maintained as supervisory control devices over the patrol officers—daily logs? tally sheets? Are only necessary forms going to be required? Many in use today have no value other than tradition.

Once your department has developed a manual of procedures concerning all anticipated police activities and attached priorities, which should be developed by representatives of all levels of the department, not just management personnel, it should be presented to the people in the community. Your department head will, no doubt, discuss it with the council or board of supervisors and the city or county administrator, but the final discussions should be held with various citizen groups throughout the jurisdiction. Expectations of your services will affect the perception of your effectiveness by the public.

This is where proactive patrol takes place. Your department may have decided that whenever a caller reports that his or her home was broken into sometime during the owner's absence between 7:30 and 5:30 P.M. and that a suspect is not in sight, the police response to the call will be on an appointment basis at the mutual convenience of the victim and a nonsworn crime scene investigator. Many calls for service may be handled just as well by having the victim drive the vehicle into the police station to be dusted for prints when a stereo has been removed from the car sometime during the weekend. By scheduling report taking and crime scene investigations that do not require urgent response, personnel work-load schedules both in the field and in the office may be equalized somewhat.

Factors That Determine Patrol Deployment

How to make maximum use of human resources and equipment is the responsibility of the police chief, particularly when deploying the patrol force. There are never enough people authorized to accomplish all the police objectives. When arranging work days and hours, vacations, holidays, days off, and the unexpected sick or injury days, the object is to meet realistically the community's demands of their police department for service when needed. When planning deployment of personnel, the chief and administrative staff must take into consideration a great many variable factors, some of which are listed here. You as a field officer should be aware of these considerations as well so that you will better understand the reasoning behind the assignments that you receive.

1. Resident and transient populations, particularly in business and tourist centers. A beach community may be 100 times its resident population during the daytime. The county seat or industrial center may have a daytime population a dozen times its nighttime population, whereas a "bedroom community" may be virtually empty of people during working hours on weekdays.
2. Numbers and types of crimes and arrests.
3. Locations of crimes and arrests.
4. Traffic collision statistics and patterns.
5. Locations of "frequent incidents" or hazards requiring concentrated police coverage. Such places as sports arenas, stadiums, popular night spots, singles bars, theaters, transportation terminals, or other gathering places.
6. Disproportionate concentrations of population, such as widely separated single-family residences versus heavily concentrated high-rise multiple-family dwellings. A small area comprising one-tenth of the geographical size of your city might house one-half the population.

7. Socioeconomic factors. Higher-income families may seek their recreation outside the area, whereas those less fortunate must stay home. Some people never stray more than a mile or two from where they live for an entire lifetime, whereas the average person today is considerably more transient. Vehicle ownership also leads to greater mobility.

8. Zoning plan of the city (relative locations of business, industrial; residential, and other types of zoning). By their very nature, certain types of businesses and industries call for higher volumes of police service.

9. Size of the jurisdiction (in square miles) and shape.

10. Geography and topography. Are there widely separated strips and islands in your jurisdiction? Mountains, bays, ravines, rivers, lakes, or various other barriers may make it impossible to patrol both sides of the barrier at the same time.

11. Parks and recreational facilities. Consider locations, size, proximity to residences, access roads, and special characteristics, such as a forest area versus rolling, grassy hills.

12. Streets and highways. Consider total mileage and configurations, traffic flow patterns, state of repair and construction.

13. Locations and number of "attractive nuisances," including abandoned wells and mines, deserted buildings, swimming pools, open holes, woods, sandpits, rock quarries.

14. Age ratios of the population. Consider juveniles versus adults and the various age categories: preschool, adolescent, teenage, young adult, middle-aged, and seniors.

15. Male-female ratios and married couples versus unmarried population.

16. Homogeneity and/or mixture of various ethnic-cultural populations.

17. Modes of transportation and locations of transportation terminals.

18. Restaurants and theaters; volume and types of clientele, hours.

19. Known locations where criminal offenders live and go for recreation.

20. Number and qualifications of officers available for field duties.

21. Amount of trust and confidence of the people in their department, which may influence the frequency and types of calls for police service.

Designation of Districts

Taking into consideration all the preceding factors, the chief must apportion the jurisdiction into patrol districts that can be equitably handled by the assigned officers. With the aid of electronic data processing methods, it is now possible to separate the jurisdiction into very small segments known as "reporting districts," to maintain complete records on each district, to group the reporting districts into contiguous "patrol districts," and then to assign the officers proportionate to the indicated proportionate needs of the districts. Frequent evaluation conferences may cause fluid and frequent changes in the district boundaries to assure maximum utilization of personnel. The days are gone when a city or county can be divided into equal sections, just as a pie is cut, as a basis for work-load distribution.

Police patrol is a serious game of chess. The district officers must be armed with current and valid information concerning the crime and other police activity potentialities in their respective districts and then attack each problem through a systematic patrol approach by being at various places in their districts at unpredictable and irregular times. The goal is to minimize the successes of criminals through strategy based upon knowledge and experience.

Rotation of Assignments

In municipal law enforcement, assignment to administrative duties has been traditionally a promotion in exchange for some years of devoted service. Once assigned and given the title "detective," the officer could then plan on spending the remainder of a career in that assignment. The only alternative was to be promoted to a higher rank, which necessitated a return to uniform or some other assignment. Many detectives chose not to seek promotion specifically to avoid having to return to uniformed patrol duties.

Lately, however, administrators have begun to realize that many of their better patrol officers are lost forever from the patrol division through this promotion policy. And some forward-looking administrators have started to experiment with planned rotational assignments similar to those used in business management programs, in which young business employees are rotated throughout the organization. When certain police officers are rotated throughout the various divisions of the police department and eventually are returned to patrol duty to serve as senior officers, or instructors, to the newer officers in departments where this procedure is followed, it is recommended that those senior officers be proportionately assigned to assure the most advantageous use of their talents.

Rotation of working hours may cause serious health problems if changes are made too frequently. Sleep cycles cannot be changed on the spur of the moment, and other bodily functions also need some stability to sustain good health if officers are to maintain peak efficiency. For special types of assignments, such as vice and narcotics, there is a high rate of burnout if officers stay on the assignment too long. In addition to the tremendous drain on family relationships are the constant temptations regarding "monopoly money" profits and the proverbial offering of the "apple" in the Garden of Eden, which destroy officers who yield to the temptations.

PROACTIVE VERSUS REACTIVE PATROL

The police can no longer indulge themselves in nonproductive and meaningless patrol. The cost of the vehicles, their maintenance, and other operational expenses has pushed into history the days when patrol time was considered correctly proportioned only when the officers could show 50 percent of a watch as being "on patrol." Cruising and looking for the unexpected and unusual is no longer a legitimate agendum.

There has been a trend toward development of a closer working relationship between the police and the public, such as Neighborhood Watch or Community-Oriented Policing programs. Residents and merchants are expected—and encouraged—to watch more closely the activities that are going on around them and to report any suspicious persons or activities to the police department. There has been an increased awareness that the so-called "omnipresence" of the police simply does not prevent and repress crime. The police patrol cannot be everywhere or see everything, and the police administrators and the press must make the public aware of that reality. There must be a working partnership between the police and the people they serve.

Rather than stake out 847 drugstores because there is a very active drugstore burglar operating in town, it makes more sense to stake out the burglars suspected of working drugstores. Investigators and patrol officers make use of the records division data on past and present drugstore burglars. They then locate the burglar and maintain surveillance on the individual. They may watch him or her continuously for a while, or their surveillance might only be during those times when the burglaries are occurring. Then, if the burglar appears to be "reformed" or inactive at the time, the officers drop that burglar and pick up surveillance on another. The officers do not harass anyone. They make contact with the burglar only if they observe a criminal act. A great many officers are highly successful in investigating crimes this way instead of randomly patrolling and hoping to be at the right place at the right time. This is proactive patrol.

Proactive patrol may reduce the occurrence of serious traffic collisions if officers visit the various drinking establishments in a district and greet the patrons as they leave. The obviously intoxicated and disorderly individuals may require arrests or some other alternative for their safety and continued prosperity. Those who appear to have impaired ability to walk will probably be in no condition to operate motor vehicles. A gentle reminder that they should, perhaps, have someone drive them home or take a taxicab may prevent a collision later. Bartenders and cocktail waitresses should be encouraged to pay more attention to their customers when they appear to be drinking beyond the limits of good judgment and to encourage them to slow down and not drink for a while before leaving the establishment. By making occasional bar checks, you will also be in a better position to observe the potential hazards and call them to the attention of the manager or bartender. Such proactive patrol might save some lives, not to mention the loss of property and the humiliation of DUI (driving under the influence) arrests.

Analysis of problem locations and neighborhoods and more realistic selective enforcement practices may aid you in knowing where to be at certain times of the day and night so that your presence may have more effect in prevention and repression of criminal activity. Identify the problem locations; then direct a proportionate part of your patrol time to the places where the problems are.

Reactive patrol involves getting to the scene of the crime or collision after the fact. Through proactive patrol you might actually be there when the event unfolds before your eyes. Although it might be less exciting, you might actually be able to prevent the incident altogether.

TYPES OF POLICE PATROL

Police patrol should involve as much ingenuity and innovation as possible for it to be effective in the aggressive attack on crime. Regardless of how sophisticated it may become, however, its most important function is to serve as the police department's actual field contact with the people—law abiding and criminal alike—on a personal one-to-one basis. The types of patrol refer to the various means of getting from one place to another in the district. None of them are intended to isolate the patrol officers from the people they serve and protect.

Foot Patrol

Foot patrol is probably the original type of police patrol. Although it confines the officer to small areas and limits the scope of activities, foot patrol is still among the most effective of the various types of patrols. The methods of foot patrol consist of the fixed post, line beat, and random patrol. Foot patrol is restricted to small areas and is used to deal with special problems of prevention and repression that cannot be adequately handled by the officers in radio cars. Fixed foot patrol is usually used for traffic, surveillance, parades, and special events. Moving foot patrol is used where there is considerable foot traffic, as in business and shopping centers, bars and taverns, high-crime areas, and special hazard areas and on streets where there are many multiple-family dwellings.

Horse Patrol

Horses may be used for certain patrol problems in jurisdictions that contain large park areas or similar places where automobiles either cannot go or may be forbidden. Motorized officers cannot be expected to race across lawns, wooded areas, or pedestrian malls. Horses fulfill the need for greater mobility in these situations (see Figure 1–3). They also work quite well for moving crowds of people, hostile and otherwise. Search and rescue in wild, undeveloped terrain is accomplished with considerable success by a well-trained team of officers on horseback.

Motorcycles

Primarily used for traffic control and enforcement, the two-wheeled motorcycle has been implemented at times by some agencies as a fair-weather patrol unit. Speed and maneuverability are outstanding characteristics of the motorcycle that make it a valuable police vehicle.

Bicycles and Small Vehicles

The bicycle has been used in many countries as a simple and inexpensive means of silent transportation to carry police officers throughout their

Figure 1-3   Horses are used by many agencies for various types of patrol. This officer is equipped with two-way radio for constant contact with headquarters. (Courtesy of the Police Department, Detroit, Michigan.)

districts. Other, newly developed, small motorized vehicles have been employed by various police agencies for whatever needs they meet. Small vehicles may be used for routine patrol to replace or augment foot or automobile patrol under conditions when such a vehicle is more practicable than more conventional modes of travel. Officers may wear casual street clothing and patrol hazardous areas using these vehicles to provide coverage without being identified as police officers until the moment arises when an arrest is imminent.

Bicycles and other small vehicles permit the foot patrol officer to carry radio equipment, foul-weather gear, and miscellaneous items that would otherwise be carried in an automobile. The versatility of the small vehicle makes it an indispensable patrol unit for covering such places as shopping malls, pathways and trails, and other places where automobiles cannot travel.

Other vehicles are utilized by police departments in jurisdictions with special problems of mobility, such as snowmobiles and dog sleds in the northern states and Alaska, gliders for silent overhead observations of suspected farming of illegal crops, balloon tire motorcycles for the beaches, and boats for the waterways.

Helicopters and Fixed-Wing Aircraft

Fixed-wing aircraft are excellent for patrolling long stretches of highways or expanses of undeveloped or wild land, for transportation of people and equipment, for surveillance, and for search and rescue. The disadvantage, of course, is lack of landing and takeoff spots in urban areas. Some departments have been experimenting with ultralight planes with very short takeoff and landing capabilities, but they still need places to land where they do not interfere with normal air or surface travel.

The first airborne police unit in the United States was created in New York City in 1930, when daredevil pilots were flying and doing stunts above the city, sometimes crashing into densely populated areas. The New York City "Air Police" were put into operation to catch and arrest these daredevil violators[1]. The fleet started out with one amphibian plane and three biplanes and operated well into the 1950s, when the airplanes were replaced with a fleet of helicopters. The helicopter has been added to complement the air capabilities of the airplane, but it has the advantage of being able to travel at slower speeds, to hover when necessary, and to land in otherwise inaccessible places because of its vertical takeoff and landing capabilities. It is a virtual platform in the sky (see Figure 1–4).

The helicopter may also be flown at lower altitudes than can the fixed-wing airplane, and it may be used when marginal visibility conditions exist. A true champion as a police vehicle, the helicopter is used for

[1]Joan Potter, "Aviation Units: Are They Worth the Money?" *Police Magazine*, Vol. 2, No. 4, July 1979, p. 22.

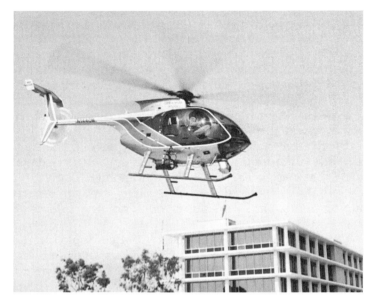

Figure 1-4 Helicopters provide excellent moving "platform in the sky." (Courtesy of the Police Department, Costa Mesa, California.)

rescue, medical evacuation, traffic control, general patrol, criminal apprehension, crime prevention and repression, emergency transportation, surveillance and searches, and other activities.

Automobile Patrol

The automobile is the most extensively used and the most effective means of transportation for police patrol. On the beach it may be a Jeep with four-wheel drive and balloon tires. Usually, for general street patrol, it is an efficient late-model car with high-performance capabilities. It may be designed like a dune buggy for desert patrol or like a safari-type vehicle for mountains and forest areas. In the urban community, the vehicle is the distinctively marked late model automobile.

For all practical purposes, the police car is a mobile police station. Equipped with the latest in radio gear and various types of rescue and restraining devices, it provides a rapid, safe, and efficient means of transportation under average operating conditions. All modern law enforcement agencies use the automobile as a patrol vehicle and many of them use no other means of transportation.

Boats and Amphibian Vehicles

In jurisdictions that patrol beaches, shorelines, and inland waterways, various types of deep-water and shallow-water boats are put into service. In many areas, a separate harbor or waterway patrol unit may be utilized, or field officers may be assigned to boat patrol on a rotational basis. Smuggling of people and contraband from coastal waters into inland harbor areas is a constant problem. Investigation and apprehension can be accomplished only with the aid of boats and helicopters.

Fixed Surveillance

Although not a means of transportation, when we are discussing various types of patrol we cannot overlook fixed surveillance. This is accomplished in person or with the aid of television cameras or stop-frame photography. The occasional stakeout at the place where a crime is anticipated is less likely to turn up a suspect than is installing surveillance on a permanent or semipermanent basis. With the use of monitors at a central location, it is possible to watch several locations at the same time and dispatch a field unit to whichever location is in need of immediate response. At one time used almost exclusively for intelligence operations and by the various governments spying on each other from their respective embassies, various types of listening and viewing devices are now being used to supplement routine patrol. This is in line with the proactive patrol concept.

THE WOMAN AS POLICE OFFICER

As you will find throughout the book, we do not refer to the police field officer as a male. Since the sex barrier has been broken, police administrators and supervisors have been discovering that the addition of women to the field forces has enhanced police service (see Figure 1–5). Certainly, there are a few differences in techniques used by men versus women because of anatomical differences, but police patrol is generally being performed equally well by officers of both sexes. Chivalrous qualities of the male officers who work with their female counterparts tend to appear in times of danger and stress, but their effectiveness is not likely to suffer any more than one officer's sense of responsibility to aid, comfort, and protect a comrade in police uniform, regardless of gender.

POLICE DISCRETIONARY PREROGATIVES

In its 1967 report, *The Police*,[2] the President's Commission on Law Enforcement and Administration of Justice reported that there is considerable variance in police practices throughout the United States, particu-

---

[2]The President's Commission on Law Enforcement and Administration of Justice, Task Force Report: The Police (Washington, D.C.: U.S. Government Printing Office, 1967).

Figure 1-5 "You've come a long way, lady." The woman police officer has justifiably made her way in professional law enforcement. (Courtesy of the California Highway Patrol.)

larly in tactical field problems and arrest situations. It was the consensus of that group of observers that police agencies exercise little or no control over the discretionary decision-making process in the form of operational guidelines.

In 1973, the *Report on Police* by the National Advisory Commission on Criminal Justice Standards and Goals[3] recommended that every police agency

> *should adopt comprehensive policy statements that publicly establish the limits of discretion, that provide guidelines for its exercise within those limits, and that they eliminate discriminatory enforcement of the law. . . . Every chief executive should establish policy that guides the exercise of discretion by police personnel in using arrest alternatives. . . . Every police chief executive should formalize procedures for developing and implementing the foregoing written agency policy.*

With all due respect to those observations and recommendations, there are some problems. As we have discussed elsewhere in this book, it

---

[3]National Advisory Commission on Criminal Justice Standards and Goals, Report on Police, Standard 1.3 (Washington, D.C.: U.S. Government Printing Office, 1973), p. 21.

may be possible to provide the field officer with general guidelines, but specifics are difficult. Some problems in enforcement, for example, include the following:

- The investigator locates the assault suspect, but once the suspect is in custody, the victim refuses to talk about the assault and no witnesses are available.
- Three separate traffic violations are committed in the presence of an officer, but the officer can only get to two of the violators and not the third. The officer alone must decide which ones to stop and cite.
- An officer arrests a suspect for a crime for which the police chief has demanded full enforcement, but every time such a case comes before the local judge, it is dismissed, which indicates that someone in the system does not agree with the police chief.
- The officer knows that the suspect is guilty of a crime but also knows that there is not sufficient cause to justify an arrest, even though the guidelines state that the officer should make the arrest. Only the officer will know exactly when there is sufficient evidence to make that arrest.
- A crime violation occurs at the same time as an incident requiring an immediate rescue.

Consider these situations as being similar to surgery being performed in the hospital. The attending physician-surgeon examines the patient and takes the case to a meeting with a staff of other doctors. A consensus is reached that the surgery is necessary. Later, when the surgeon is operating, a complication arises that makes the removal inadvisable because of certain facts known only to the surgeon. The ultimate decision can rest only with the surgeon on the scene. In police work, too, there are many field situations in which the field officer with the total picture is the only person who can make the critical decision.

Use of discretion in field police work is absolutely essential. There is a continual development and modification of priorities, depending on availability of time, department strength, demands for service, and activities of the public. We are continually reacting to changing situations. A decision to clean up a parking problem can suddenly be changed by an airplane falling out of the sky. Ask a police chief about law enforcement. Is there any truth to the rumor that only certain laws are enforced with greater diligence than others? You will be told that all laws are enforced with equal vigor. Ask a fellow officer about total enforcement and you are likely to receive a similar response. But when a number of laws are violated and only some of them receive attention, ask the investigating officers and the answer you will get is, "We can't be every place at once." What is happening, of course, is the exercise of discretion in which cases to work and which to postpone. It is as predictable as popcorn at the movies.

Within the organized structure of law enforcement agencies, each of the thousands of individual officers functions as a virtually independent agent when it comes to routine as well as extraordinary police activities. The chief and top staff of the department may develop policies as to what will be done and in what manner, but they are not in the field when the time comes to make the critical decisions. Personal value systems as well as training and enforcement policies determine the actual parameters of law enforcement practices of the police as a professional body of individuals.

The broad discretionary powers entrusted to you as a field officer include such matters as dealing with traffic law violators, handling disturbances of the peace involving lone individuals or hundreds of people, enforcement of the criminal laws, apprehension and detention of juvenile delinquents and near-delinquents, regulation of private morals through enforcement of vice laws, and the performance of myriad other duties in the course of a normal day. You will function with little guidance except for the laws and the department manuals of procedure. You will have some field supervision, but when the time comes, most critical decisions—when to arrest, when to pursue, and when to shoot—will usually be left for you alone to decide.

Operational Guidelines for Discretionary Decision Making

The system of criminal justice abundantly provides for broad use of discretion by its law enforcement officers and all others similarly involved in the system. Setting the standard when the California Penal Code was introduced on February 14, 1872, the legislature provided for such discretion by the wording of Section 4:

> *The rule of the common law, that penal statutes are to be strictly construed, has no application to this code. All its provisions are to be construed according to the fair import of their terms, with a view to effect its objects and to promote justice.*

A leading case that further elucidates the intent of law and those who enforce it has been described in the California Supreme Court's ruling in *People* v. *Alotis*, 60 Cal. 2d 698 (1964):

> *When language reasonably susceptible to two constructions is used in a penal law, that construction which is more favorable to the defendant will be adopted. The defendant is entitled to the benefit of every reasonable doubt as to the true interpretation of words or the construction of language used in a statute.*

As a police officer you have the responsibility and authority within existing laws to act in a variety of ways when you encounter what, in your opinion, constitutes a violation of the law or other action requiring your official intervention. You may contact the violator and admonish with no arrest, or you may arrest and release the violator because you believe there is not sufficient evidence or other cause for further action. You may merely issue a citation and release the offender when he or she signs a written promise to appear later in court, or you may take the arrestee directly to jail. Once you have introduced the offender into the system by arrest and booking or by citation, other individuals in the system will make their own discretionary decisions, such as prosecuting attorneys and judges. A large percentage of the cases you handle will be disposed of informally, with no charges filed. Regarding the decision to arrest or not to arrest, you must be judicious in your use of discretionary power.

Specific sections of the criminal codes involving police discretion include such wording as "searching for weapons on *reasonable cause*," "*reasonable* restraint when making an arrest," "*reasonable* force to effect an arrest, prevent escape, or overcome resistance." The basic arrest laws state that the officer *may* arrest when there is *reasonable cause* to believe a person is committing a crime in the officer's presence or there is *reasonable* cause to believe a person has committed certain crimes, although not in the officer's presence, *whether or not such a crime has in fact been committed.*

Wording of other criminal code sections indicates that the use of discretion is in order. Examples of these words are "specific intent," "reasonable" or "probable cause" (again), "malicious," "unsafe," "too close," "unfit," "unnecessary," and "reliable." Each of these words involves value judgments by individual officers.

CIVIL LIABILITY OF THE FIELD OFFICER

In today's lawsuit-conscious society, it is not unusual for you as a police officer to report to work one day and be formally notified that you are being sued. Financial support for the suit is provided by false arrest and other types of insurance carried by your agency. The prospect of an award of some of those funds, however, often encourages people with weak cases to sue.

Police work is an adversary occupation in many respects. Very few people will thank you for arresting them. Even fewer will thank you for using force on them, even if you did believe that it was necessary to prevent injury to yourself. "After all, a police officer has to expect to get hurt once in a while. It goes with the territory. Right?" Wrong, but who are you going to convince? Whenever you arbitrate a dispute, both sides cannot win. Someone is going to be unhappy about whatever you do in such matters. Who is to blame? In other words, lawsuits are a real part of your work, and you might as well expect them and be prepared to present a defense if and when you are sued.

Another aspect in the defense of a lawsuit is money. Even for defense against a false or spurious charge, it will cost your department and its insurance carrier several thousands of dollars before the case ever gets to court. If there is any possibility of your losing, there may be a decision to settle out of court even though you are not at fault.

Bear in mind the fact that you are personally responsible for everything you do in the line of duty. You—and not a fellow officer or your supervisor—will ultimately stand alone in the lawsuit. Constantly evaluate and reevaluate your performance, particularly in the sensitive areas of arrest and the use of force, and remember to be your own counsel. The ultimate test will be the "reasonableness" of your actions and the propriety of your official conduct. Carefully record for future reference any incident that you believe might someday become a contested issue. Your constant awareness might well be the deciding factor in the court's deciding that you were right or wrong.

You are not always left out on a limb with no support. Many agencies have review committees, who evaluate reports, interview witnesses, investigate all aspects of the case, and make a concerted effort to get to the truth of a situation to determine if an officer's actions are defensible and "reasonable." Prosecuting attorneys have roll-out teams to investigate all police-involved shootings for the purpose of determining civil and criminal liability. Officers' unions and associations also come to the aid of their members when there is need for moral or financial support, even in some cases of criminal prosecution of the officer.

There is another side to the coin: There have been some successful cases where wrongfully accused police officers have sued their accusers. Turning the other cheek is sometimes okay, until you run out of cheeks to turn. A police officer must expect to take some "flak," but there is no rule that says the officer should be a masochist.

POLICE OFFICERS' BILL OF RIGHTS

Within the past few years, legislators have been asked to look at the rights of the police officers who selflessly serve their communities, sometimes at great personal and financial risk. In an effort to address some of the concerns of their officers in California, Government Code sections 3300 through 3309 were enacted. We have quoted the sections verbatim in this chapter, citing what is known as the Public Safety Officers Procedural Bill of Rights Act (enacted 1980).

Sec. 3300

This chapter is known and may be cited as the Public Safety Officers Procedural Bill of Rights Act.

Sec. 3302

a. Except as otherwise provided by law, or whenever on duty or in uniform, no public officer shall be prohibited from engaging, or be coerced or required to engage, in political activity.

    b. *No public safety officer shall be prohibited from seeking election to, or serving as a member of, the governing board of a school district.*

Sec. 3303

When any public safety officer is under investigation and subjected to interrogation by his commanding officer, or any other member of the employing public safety department, which could lead to punitive action, such interrogation shall be conducted under the following conditions. For the purpose of this chapter, punitive action is defined as any action which may lead to dismissal, demotion, suspension, reduction in salary, written reprimand, or transfer for purposes of punishment.

    a. *The interrogation shall be conducted at a reasonable hour, preferably at a time when the public safety officer is on duty, or during the normal waking hours for the public safety officer, unless the seriousness of the investigation requires otherwise. If such interrogation does occur during off-duty time of the public safety officer being interrogated, the public safety officer shall be compensated for such off-duty time in accordance with regular department procedures, and the public safety officer shall not be released from employment for any work missed.*

    b. *The public safety officer under investigation shall be informed prior to such interrogation of the rank, name, and command of the officer in charge of the interrogation, the interrogating officers, and all other persons to be present during the interrogation. All questions directed to the public safety officer under interrogation shall be asked by and through no more than two interrogators at one time.*

    c. *The public safety officer under investigation shall be informed of the nature of the investigation prior to any interrogation.*

    d. *The interrogating session shall be for a reasonable period taking into consideration the gravity and complexity of the issue being investigated. The person under interrogation shall be allowed to attend to his own personal physical necessities.*

    e. *The public safety officer under interrogation shall not be subjected to offensive language or threatened with punitive action, except that an officer refusing to respond to questions or submit to interrogations shall be informed* *that failure to answer questions directly related to the investigation of interrogation may result in punitive action. No promise of reward shall be made as an inducement to answering any question. The employer shall not cause the public safety officer under interrogation to be subjected to visits by the press or news media without his express consent nor shall his home address or photograph be given to the press or news media without his express consent.*

f. *The complete interrogation of a public safety officer may be recorded. If a tape recording is made of the interrogation, the public safety officer shall have access to the tape if any further proceedings are contemplated or prior to any further interrogation at a subsequent time. The public safety officer shall be entitled to a transcribed copy of any notes made by a stenographer or to any reports or complaints made by investigators or other persons, except those which are deemed by the investigating agency to be confidential. No notes or reports which are deemed to be confidential may be entered in the officer's personnel file. The public safety officer being interrogated shall have the right to bring his own recording device and record any and all aspects of the interrogation.*

g. *If prior to or during the interrogation of a public safety officer it is deemed that he may be charged with a criminal offense, he shall be immediately informed of his constitutional rights.*

h. *Upon filing a formal written statement of charges, or whenever an interrogation focuses on matters which are likely to result in punitive action against any public safety officer, that officer, at his request, shall have the right to be represented by a representative of his choice who may be present at all times during such interrogation. The representative shall not be a person subject to the same investigation. The representative shall not be required to disclose, nor be subject to any punitive action for refusing to disclose, any information received from the officer under investigation for noncriminal matters.*

This section shall not apply to any interrogation of a public safety officer in the normal course of duty, counseling, instruction, or informal verbal admonishment by, or other routine or unplanned contact with, a supervisor or any other public safety officer, nor shall this section apply to an investigation concerned solely and directly with alleged criminal activities.

i. *No public safety officer shall be loaned or temporarily reassigned to a location or duty assignment if a sworn member of his department would not normally be sent to that location or would not normally be given that duty assignment under similar circumstances.*

Sec. 3304

a. *No public safety officer shall be subjected to punitive action, or denied promotion, or be threatened with any such treatment, because of the lawful exercise of the rights granted under this chapter, or the exercise of any rights under any existing administrative grievance procedure.*

Nothing in this section shall preclude a head of an agency from ordering a public safety officer to cooperate with other agencies involved in criminal investigations. If an officer fails to comply with such an order, the agency may officially charge him with insubordination.

b. *No punitive action, nor denial or promotion on grounds other than merit, shall be undertaken by any public agency without providing the public safety officer with an opportunity for administrative appeal.*

Sec. 3305

No public safety officer shall have any comment adverse to his interest entered in his personal file, or any other file used for any personnel purposes by his employer, without the public safety officer having first read and signed the instrument containing the adverse comment indicating he is aware of such comment, except that such entry may be made if after reading such instrument the public safety officer refuses to sign it. Should a public safety officer refuse to sign, that fact shall be noted on that document, and signed or initiated by such officer.

Sec. 3306

A public safety officer shall have 30 days within which to file a written response to any adverse comment entered in his personnel file. Such written response shall be attached to, and shall accompany, the adverse comment.

Sec. 3307

No public safety officer shall be compelled to submit to a poly-

graph examination against his will. No disciplinary action or other recrimination shall be taken against a public safety officer refusing to submit to a polygraph examination, nor shall any comment be entered anywhere in the investigator's notes or anywhere else that the public safety officer refused to take a polygraph examination, nor shall any testimony or evidence be admissible at a subsequent hearing, trial, or proceeding, judicial or administrative, to the effect that the public safety officer refused to take the polygraph examination.

Sec. 3308

No public safety officer shall be required or requested for purposes of job assignment or other personnel action to disclose any item of his property, income, assets, source of income, debts, or personal or domestic expenditures (including those of any member of his family or household) unless such information is obtained or required under state law or proper legal procedure, tends to indicate a conflict of interest with respect to the performance of his official duties, or is necessary for the employing agency to ascertain the desirability of assigning the public safety officer to a specialized unit in which there is a strong possibility that bribes or other improper inducements may be offered.

Sec. 3309

No public safety officer shall have his locker, or other space for storage that may be assigned to him, searched except in his presence, or with his consent, or unless a valid search warrant has been obtained or where he has been notified that a search will be conducted. This section shall apply only to lockers or other space for storage that are owned or leased by the employing agency.

SUMMARY

In this chapter you have been introduced to the world of police patrol and the overall responsibilities of that unit referred to in this book as the police field unit. There are several objectives of field operations, which include (1) defense of life and property, (2) participative law enforcement, (3) prevention of criminal and delinquent behavior, (4) repression of criminal and delinquent behavior, (5) identification, apprehension, and conviction of offenders, (6) traffic flow and collision reduction, and (7) maintenance of order and the public peace. To accomplish those objectives, the many activities of the police field unit are described as follows:

1. Carrying out routine patrol and observation
2. Performing preventive attendance at public gatherings
3. Engaging in benevolent and community services
4. Maintaining business and property security
5. Providing inspection services
6. Responding to calls for service
7. Providing animal control
8. Performing traffic direction and control
9. Providing information services
10. Developing contacts
11. Conducting preliminary investigations
12. Collecting and preserving evidence
13. Arresting offenders
14. Preparing reports
15. Testifying in court
16. Saving lives and maintaining the quality of life of a free society

Private police and special-purpose police and some of their activities were covered as well in this chapter because of their close working relationship with public police.

Next, we covered distribution of the patrol force and factors that determine patrol deployment as well as some of the administrative decisions that go into distribution of the field patrol unit by times, days of the week, and district distribution. Although the types of patrol vary from one department to another, many are universal, and these were outlined for your consideration.

Although not new on the police scene, the woman police officer has become accepted on an equal basis and is seen more regularly as part of the field units. We offered only a short commentary on that subject, because the entire book has been written to reflect the equality of women in police service.

When the time comes to make the decision of whether to arrest, or to use force, or to use your weapon, that decision will be yours. You will be guided by your department's rules and regulations, by the laws, and by your training as well as by your supervisors and administrators. As we discussed in this chapter, your ultimate guidance will be within yourself. As a companion to that discussion, we followed discretionary prerogatives with a commentary on civil liability, which expands on the concept that you are ultimately going to be held responsible for your own actions. The ultimate test of your actions will be whether or not those actions were reasonable. Finally, the chapter concluded with the Public Safety Officers Procedural Bill of Rights Act, which is designed to clarify police officers' rights vis-à-vis those of the citizens they serve.

EXERCISES AND STUDY QUESTIONS

1. Read and explain the purpose of a Law Enforcement Code of Ethics.
2. Describe routine patrol as you think it should be practiced.
3. List at least five routine services that your department provides that you believe could be performed better or more economically by agencies other than the police.
4. Define proactive patrol.
5. Define reactive patrol.
6. What is the author's explanation of the difference between community relations and public relations?
7. There are six objectives of field operations listed in this chapter. List at least five of those objectives.
8. What part do the residents of a police district play in *participative law enforcement?*
9. What is the difference between crime *repression* and crime *prevention?*
10. What are the Three E's of the traffic function of the police?
11. What is the primary police responsibility upon arrival at the scene of a large gathering of people?
12. List at least five *benevolent services* performed by the field officers.
13. List some of the hazards an officer should look for when inspecting the premises of a business, a residence.
14. What is the role of the field officer at the scene of a marital dispute?
15. What is the police responsibility for animal control in your department?
16. What is the basic purpose for traffic enforcement?
17. List at least five *information* items that will be expected of the field officer by the public.
18. What is the value of developing a network of informants?
19. Describe the procedure for a peace officer to respond to an adverse comment entered into his or her personnel file, according to the Officers' Bill of Rights.
20. List and discuss at least 10 of the factors that determine patrol deployment.

REFERENCES

ADAMS, THOMAS F. *Law Enforcement: An Introduction to the Police Role in the Criminal Justice System*, 2nd ed. Englewood Cliffs, N.J.: Prentice Hall, 1973.

_____. *Introduction to the Administration of Criminal Justice*, 2nd ed. Englewood Cliffs, N.J.: Prentice Hall, 1980.

ADAMS, THOMAS F., GERALD BUCK, AND DON HALLSTROM, *Criminal Justice Organization and Management*. Pacific Palisades, Calif.: Goodyear, 1974.

CHAPMAN, SAMUEL G. *Police Patrol Readings*. Springfield, Ill.: Charles C Thomas, 1964.

NATIONAL ADVISORY COMMISSION ON CRIMINAL JUSTICE STANDARDS AND GOALS. *Proceedings of the National Conference on Criminal Justice*. Washington, D.C.: U.S. Government Printing Office, 1973.

PRESIDENT'S COMMISSION ON LAW ENFORCEMENT AND THE ADMINISTRATION OF JUSTICE. *Task Force Report: The Police*. Washington, D.C.: U.S. Government Printing Office, 1967.

2

BASIC FIELD PROCEDURES

Patrol and observation are two words that probably most comprehensively explain the function of the police officer. Your assignment will probably consist of patrolling a district or "beat" in a distinctively marked automobile with the word POLICE emblazoned on the top, the sides, and the rear trunk, and you will be wearing the traditional uniform of your department. As with any occupational uniform, the design is distinctive to separate you immediately from everyone else not in the same line of work and thereby avoid confusion and assure others of your authority and your presence. This is actually no different than the distinctive uniform worn by opposing baseball teams, or the uniform worn by the airplane pilot, or the cruise ship captain, or the waitress, or any number of other individuals whose uniforms make them immediately recognizable and thus make it easier for them to provide the service you are seeking.

Assuming that the great majority of the population is honest and law abiding, the mere presence of the police officers as they appear at various places throughout their jurisdiction will remind those people that the officer is present and will protect them as well as arrest the law violators. The would-be violators theoretically will not continue with their criminal intentions, at least not while in the officer's presence. The active criminal is less likely to ply his or her criminal trade if the police are also active and seemingly always present.

In this chapter we cover the so-called "routine" aspects of police patrol. In the preparation section of this chapter, we discuss the process of getting ready for your tour of duty as well as the psychological aspects of that tour, which include going out on patrol with a positive and nonjudgmental attitude. This is followed by some rudimentary pointers on patrolling your district, your district responsibilities, and the various inspections that you will perform while on routine patrol. A section is devoted to crime prevention follow-up, which should help the crime victim avoid being the victim again. Other topics addressed in this chapter are patrol hazards, the processes of surveillance and stakeouts, specialized patrol, and the concept and practice of team policing.

PREPARATION FOR PATROL

General Preparation

There are many intangible factors related to an officer's preparation for patrol duty. First and foremost is that of attitude preparation. Your attitude must be positive. So many things that happen and so many of the people around you will be so negative that you will find yourself becoming negative and depressed, which will destroy your personal life if you let it. Attitudes will be affected by your social and psychological maturity, the nature and quality of your education, and physical conditioning. Your personal value system must be in harmony with the objectives of law enforcement and a sense of fair play. You must go to work each day with an attitude of confidence in the honesty and decency of most of the people you will encounter in the course of your work (see Figure 2–1). Because of the nature of your assignments, you may encounter only that small percentage of individuals who are dishonest and hence may judge everyone in those terms. For example, if you associate with only 100 people in your entire lifetime and all hold the same views, you may believe that the whole world thinks as you do because you do not encounter anyone who disagrees. You cannot believe that everyone is a thief just because all you see are thieves. To counteract this feeling, you must get involved in your off-duty hours with other people like yourself who are not violating the law. With this "anchor" in reality and the normal pattern of society, you will be better able to maintain a more accurate perspective on life and your fellow human beings.

A broad base of experiences in education, occupations, and social interaction will prove to prepare you better for the role of police officer than if you were to have lived a one-dimensional cloistered life. As a child, you probably had no choice but to live and grow according to the plans of others. Now that you have had a choice prior to and following your entrance into police work, you should seek out and communicate with people who fill the entire spectrum of social standards, educational and occupational backgrounds, political philosophies, and moral and religious codes. You must be objective, empathetic, and friendly, yet nonjudgmen-

Figure 2-1 Formal inspections are morale builders. The uniform is to be worn with care as well as pride. (Courtesy of the Police Department, Costa Mesa, California.)

tal. As a police officer, you may enforce certain behaviors, but you may not force your personal beliefs on the people you encounter, whatever their views. Your role is that of diplomat and protector of all the people you serve, a public servant who does not serve with obsequious servitude but who firmly and fairly enforces the laws and rules of the society you serve. You will be a servant to the *public*, not to individuals or their personal whims and desires. Although you deal directly with individuals on a personal basis, your responsibility is to handle each situation for the overall good of the community. To function intelligently and effectively, you must continually assess your role as a police officer in this dynamically changing society.

Prepatrol Preparation

Prior to going out on patrol, you must arm yourself with both knowledge and equipment. Only a few of the essentials are covered in this chapter because they vary from department to department and from day to day.

As for the knowledge to do your job each day, there is usually some type of "roll-call training," which is devoted to providing you with specific assignments, such as your vehicle and partner (if any), break and meal times, and district in which you will be working. Other items of information will include changes in laws and court decisions affecting field activities, new tracts and streets, changes in jurisdictional boundaries, such as the addition of a tract to a city, or formation of a new city, thereby reducing the size and changing the shape of the unincorporated county jurisdiction, general and special orders from administration, and new techniques for improvement of your field performance.

Keep in touch with current events in your own community and the world around you by reading the newspapers, news magazines, and watching television news programs on the national networks and cable news. No matter where we are, we are affected by what we see and hear around us, and attitudes toward the police may change because of what happens on the streets or in the courts anywhere in the country. Although the officers in Wichita had absolutely nothing to do with the car stop and beating of a young black man in Los Angeles in 1991, or the state or federal trials and riots that followed, my bet is that the Wichita officers were affected in more ways than one by those events many hundreds of miles away. People will make comparisons between your actions and those hyped by the media to enhance their ratings and advertising revenue.

"Hot sheets" listing stolen and/or otherwise wanted vehicles and people, information about certain robbers and thieves who may be working in your district, modus operandi of street criminals, and descriptions of stolen property and missing persons are presented during the briefing session. Many departments encourage investigators from robbery, theft, burglary, and other details to visit with the field officers frequently and discuss the cases they are working on, the individuals they believe are responsible but cannot yet arrest, and other types of behavior officers might look for while on patrol. Representatives of other agencies may spend a few minutes discussing topics of mutual interest.

Frequently, when new laws and ordinances are passed, some interpretation as to their intent is necessary for the field officer. Following passage of a new law, except when there is an emergency clause calling for immediate enactment, there is usually a 60- or 90-day delay before the legislation is enacted. This is to allow time for publication and for study by the police, attorneys, and judges who will be dealing with it from various angles. In addition to the wording, or the "letter" of the law, there is the additional agenda of the "spirit" or intent of the law. Although the word and spirit should be the same, how many times have you written something and then had to tell someone "let me explain what I meant when I wrote that"? Following passage of new laws, your training will consist of someone—possibly a prosecutor who handles arrests made by your department—discussing with you and your fellow officers the laws as written and as it was intended they should be enforced. The instruction will also include suggestions on what kind and amount of evidence will be required to sustain convictions for those law violations.

Additional facts that you should have available prior to going out on patrol are such items as where streets are closed because of construction or weather, what new hazards are in effect (e.g., power lines down across a street you might use to pursue someone), which business establishments are closed for vacations or repairs and might need some additional protection, who is on vacation and wants a house checked, where special events are taking place, what is the traffic collision and congestion situation, and at what locations have there been family and neighborhood disputes that the officers who responded earlier are convinced will require your attention later. In other words, get to know your district and the people in it, and each day prior to going out on patrol make a deliberate effort to get an update from reports and fellow officers who have just returned from spending the previous several hours in the same district (see Figure 2–2).

While preparing for field duty, you will often receive orders to complete assignments begun by the earlier shift. Jobs that await your arrival

Figure 2-2   Prior to going out on a tour of duty, the officer should compare notes with the officers who have been on duty during the preceding shift. (Courtesy of the Police Department, Detroit, Michigan.)

may include locating and securing additional information from witnesses and victims of incidents that have occurred earlier or relieving another officer on a surveillance or stakeout or conducting special patrol inspections at certain times of day. Warrants may be issued and you will go out and arrest wanted persons on the warrants. You may have to serve subpoenas and notify people whether or not they will be required in court the next day. Because of the heavy case load of the earlier shift, you may have to answer calls that have not yet been assigned.

In-Field Preparation

Whenever possible, one of your first responsibilities when you go out on patrol is to have a "debriefing" conference with the officer whom you are relieving and who has just spent the previous several hours in the district. If you cannot meet the person you are replacing, you should attempt at least a rendezvous with one or more of the officers from the previous shift. Conferences between shifts will tend to assure some continuity in coverage of the district and, it is hoped, more continuity in overall field activities. If you want to know what has been happening, such as pending disturbances, crowds, parties, and traffic conditions, your best source of information will be the officer who has been on top of the situation. It is not unlike the pilot en route to Chicago checking with another pilot who just arrived from Chicago as to weather conditions en route. Military units have used the debriefing process with considerable success.

Some items and bits of information will not be included in the reports, for example, the recent return of a burglar from prison whom the beat officer ran into at the donut shop, observation that two known narcotics dealers just happened to be at the same auto repair shop at the same time, or the family fight that was supposedly settled but the officer has a nagging feeling that nothing was really settled. Officers have "feelings" or "hunches" about certain things they see or hear, but they cannot—and should not be required to in many cases—commit the information to a formalized report that requires documentation. Such nuances of information should be passed on to other officers, however, for follow-through and to see if anything substantial develops.

These are some of the observations that the officer going off duty may share with you so that you may follow-up: a strange station wagon is parked in back of a dress shop and no driver or passengers were observed; two men known to be on parole for armed robbery have been observed loitering near three different convenience stores, which are the types of places they have "hit" before; a middle-aged man sitting in a car with a newspaper on his lap was paying an unusual amount of attention to a junior high school girl's outdoor dancercise class and reluctantly left, but will probably return; there appear to be an unusual number of youths from opposing gangs who are congregating at a park where a "rumble" appears to be in the making.

Vehicle Inspection

At the time you assume control of the assigned vehicle for your tour of duty, inspect it for clean windows and windshield, an adequate supply of gasoline, and correct oil level. Check the tires and the brakes. Start the engine and listen for any perceptible malfunctions. Never overlook special weapons and equipment that are kept in the trunk of your vehicle, including rescue and first-aid equipment and a fire extinguisher. It may sound unimportant to mention such routine items, but my personal experience tells me that it is not unusual to overlook the obvious. Check out all the emergency lights and sound equipment, including the siren. Experienced pilots use checklists prior to flying their airplanes; why not devise and use your own checklist?

During the first few minutes while you are driving the vehicle, other possible problems may become apparent, and you should not hesitate to report the problems. A walkaround should become routine so that you might look for any obvious problems, such as a missing fourth wheel, but also look for structural damage and—using a preprinted diagram of the vehicle—sketch the location and appearance of the dent or other damage. The emergency nature of your work demands that the vehicle you drive be in the best condition possible. Except when absolutely necessary, you should not accept a vehicle for patrol that is not adequate for the demands of both routine and pursuit driving. Since you are responsible for the vehicle, be sure to complete the required faulty equipment forms and follow up to see that the malfunctions and deficiencies are corrected.

District Orientation Tour

Once in the field, take a general familiarization and inspection tour of your assigned district to orient yourself to the sights and sounds and the "normal" patterns that present themselves to you. Use a different route each time you cross the district, and vary your technique so that no one can predict with any accuracy the sequence of your tour or see any resemblance to a timetable. Check for streets closed or under repair and note holes and ruts that may cause traffic accidents or congestion. During a high-speed pursuit later, it will be good to know the condition of the streets you will be traveling.

In the initial cursory tour you may observe many circumstances or people that arouse your curiosity but not your suspicion that there is any criminal involvement. Perhaps there is an automobile parked in an unusual location or a small group of people gathered where such a group has never gathered before. If you believe that you may have stronger suspicions if the situation is unchanged upon your return visit, make notes and plan to return later. Write down license numbers, descriptions of objects, vehicles, and people. These notations may later prove worthless; they may prove priceless.

In addition to noting your existing and potential police problems, be sure to look for—and record—abandoned vehicles, graffiti, and old advertising signs for long-past sales and political campaigns that still fill the fences and walls and utility poles in your district (which, in the opinion of the author, are just as much a blight on the community as those signs and symbols "tagged" by feuding gangs). Be sure to include on your list buildings that have been abandoned and/or have lost their doors and windows, unattended lots that have overgrown with weeds, and other conditions you observe that negatively affect the quality of life in your community. Front and back yards and driveways that have been converted into junkyards should also be cleaned up. Keeping the city cleaned up is not unlike the philosophy of dressing the kids up in clean clothes and watching how careful they are not to get them dirty.

If you use a daily log, and if your department's policy—and form—provides for such a procedure, notations regarding your initial observations during a district orientation tour may be written directly on your log. In any event, make liberal use of the field notebook for information that you believe may be of some value later. During this initial tour, there will undoubtedly also be some items requiring more formal attention and reports. In such cases, take care of whatever demands your immediate attention; then continue the tour.

There are several good reasons for taking an orientation tour of your district. One is that it may allow you to establish time elements. For example, you may note that a particular location appears normal at 10:13 P.M., but when you return at 11:37 P.M., you find a window smashed out. The initial tour of the district allows you to narrow down the times within which the window was broken considerably more than some time between 5:30 P.M. and 11:37 P.M. Another reason for the orientation tour is to acquaint yourself with the entire district in its current condition to gain an impression of what is "normal" and what appears "abnormal." A third reason for this patrol technique is to put the deterrent forces of your presence in the district to work. Any individual bent on committing a crime should know that you are in the district and that you are likely to show up at virtually any unannounced time or place. The optimum result would be that the would-be criminal does not perform his crime.

PATROLLING THE DISTRICT

There are two basic methods of police patrol: foot and vehicle. Both are usually performed in uniform, but either may call for street clothing under unusual circumstances. Use may be made of horses, motorcycles, bicycles, scooters, or aircraft, depending on the individual and special needs of the agency involved. The techniques of patrol are essentially the same regardless of the mode of transportation employed.

The following discussion deals with police patrol from three primary angles: foot patrol, vehicle patrol, and plainclothes patrol. In the discussion of foot patrol, it should be understood that any means of transport may be used to get the officer to the district to be covered on foot. It should also be clear that the discussion of techniques of patrolling a district by automobile may apply equally well to other types of vehicles.

Foot Patrol Tactics

The cop on the beat in the "good old days," whenever that imaginary time existed, seems to be remembered as the sustaining symbol of law enforcement. Depicted in fiction stories and the motion pictures, he was the friendly but firm fatherly type who walked the streets in his small beat, nearly always on duty and always in uniform. He maintained order and control in his district by chiding, scolding, cajoling, and sometimes arresting the violators. He visited the shopkeepers and residents, exchanged anecdotes with the street vendors, and performed numerous benevolent services. Some communities have utilized foot patrol continuously since the beginning of police patrol, but most have discontinued it because of its prohibitive cost and extremely limited use of the work force. During recent years, there has been a trend back to foot patrol in downtown and high-density neighborhoods where there is a lot of pedestrian traffic and at times when officers will have a greater opportunity to deal with the people on the streets on a one-to-one basis. The objective is to establish a bond of trust and respect between the people and the officers on patrol.

In addition to performing your duties as a professional police officer while on foot patrol, you will be performing invaluable community relations tasks for your department. Through your personality and your actions, you will demonstrate to the people what all police officers are like, because you will be the model they can see and touch. By your friendly and understanding attitude, you should make every effort to develop a feeling of confidence and respect in *you and your department* within those individuals whom you encounter. Your assignment to a foot beat might have been without a thought to selectivity, or you may have been assigned because your supervisor believes that you have certain qualities that will enhance the image of the department. Although you should be conscious of the community relations responsibility that you have whenever performing any police task, it will be more demanding when you are on foot patrol and in constant, direct contact with the people.

Whenever you are on foot patrol, take advantage of every opportunity to get to know as many of the people in the district as you can. Make a deliberate effort to meet and talk with people, and use a notebook to keep notes on those contacts. For example, the manager of a dress shop on your beat has a child with a certain medical problem and another in college. You keep notes so that when you stop in to visit the store again you will remember to ask about the children. You and your department will have a friend and supporter for life just for taking a little extra time to show an interest in the people you serve.

At the same time you are getting to know the people, you must also perform all other functions required of the patrol assignment. There will be fewer demands on you because you lack the mobility and other advantages of having a vehicle at your disposal. You will have a portable radio, but you will have greater autonomy to carry out your responsibilities. You may have fewer assignments from headquarters, but you will encounter and handle more "on-sight" incidents while on patrol.

Every district has a distinctive personality, and it is important that the assigned officer get to know that personality. Wanted persons may live in the area. Known felons and narcotics users may habitually loiter around the local disco palace or family recreation center, which is also frequented by many juveniles and young adults who are not criminals or narcotics users. Certain business establishments fall prey to specific crimes, such as armed robberies and burglaries. These locations should be given close attention in an effort to prevent criminal occurrences or reoccurrences. When you are assigned to the foot beat, get to know it and the people in it, then give it personalized service.

When walking through the district, most experts recommend that you walk close to the curb during the day and close to the buildings at night. They reason that the objective of daytime foot patrol is to contact and to be seen by as many people as possible and the objective of nighttime foot patrol is to be seen by as few people as possible and to catch criminals in the act before they are aware of your presence. However, others suggest for nighttime patrol that you consider the time of night and the lighting conditions, evaluate your objectives while covering the particular part of the district in which you find yourself, and then work accordingly. There should be no standard place to walk depending on the relationship of the sun to the earth any more than there should be a standard schedule to follow.

Keeping in mind the fact that police patrol means service as well as protection, never hesitate to take the initiative when practicable to offer your services in whatever way is consistent with the purposes of law enforcement. For example, probably no duty manual will be found that requires an officer to give a distressed motorist a little advice on how to start a flooded car or to call for a tow service for some mother who cannot leave her stalled car containing four preschool children. An elderly lady may have difficulty getting across a busy street because she walks so slowly and no one will allow her to take advantage of a break in a seemingly endless flow of traffic. Stopping traffic to assist the lady across the street would be a typical foot patrol service. These activities are hallmarks of the distinguished police officer who sees the occupation as something more than "just a job."

One of the problems that confronts the foot beat officer, and sometimes comes to the attention of the radio car officer, is the sidewalk showroom. Not having enough room or attention for their products, some merchants move out onto the sidewalk to display their wares. This use of the public walk is unlawful in most cities, and it causes congestion of foot traffic. Maintaining a free flow of pedestrian traffic is just as important as keeping vehicular traffic moving.

Sometimes the street merchant has no vested interest in the neighborhood, and has only the wagon or truck to sell from instead of a store or market. These wandering merchants may have no business license or health department or zoning enforcement agency controls to abide by, and may also be inflicting hardships on the merchants who have to pay rent and follow the rules. Unlike the merchants in the mall who have little wagons or stands placed in open areas, the street merchants do not pay rent and have no reason to take pride in being a part of the community. They simply move to where the money is. You should check on these merchants to be sure that they are in compliance with all zoning, health, and license laws.

When walking the beat, do not develop a routine, yet be sure to give the area adequate coverage. Walk with a purpose and look at the people. Speak with them when it is natural to do so, and encourage them to feel as though they can talk with you. Do not hesitate to smile when the occasion warrants it. Maintain a professional posture by being friendly and firm, not aloof and unapproachable. Never "mooch" by soliciting or accepting special discounts, free merchandise, or free refreshments. One practice that is absolutely intolerable is paying bills or otherwise tending to personal business while on duty, especially stopping to get a haircut. An old-timer once told me "my hair grows while I'm on the job, so I don't see anything wrong with getting it cut while I'm on the job." The entire on-duty time belongs to the department and the people. It should be spent accordingly.

Walk from one place to another so that it appears to the observer that you are patrolling the district, not loitering. Stop frequently to observe the people and the things around you. Change your routine, sometimes retracing your steps, and do not neglect the alleys or areas behind buildings when patrolling your district. When walking, look behind and under things, and inside trash containers. You are looking for safety hazards and stolen property as well as wanted persons and crime incidents. Look for scuff marks on walls alongside telephone poles and drainpipes. As a matter of routine, get to know those buildings that are most vulnerable to attack, such as those with skylights and rooftop entryways. Determine through observation what is normal for the district, then look for the unusual and deal with it accordingly.

At nighttime when you are patrolling for possible burglars, approach each building with caution, assuming the possibility that someone may be inside the building, or hiding in the doorway. Stop momentarily, stand in a darkened area to avoid being seen, and listen for unusual sounds. At nighttime when there is almost absolute silence, it is possible to hear the sounds of breaking glass, or walking, or a dog barking from hundreds of yards away. Sounds seem to be magnified by silence.

When you are satisfied that there are no unusual sounds, continue with the routine. Check the doors and windows, feel the glass for heat that may indicate a fire inside, then move on to the next building. Watch the rooftops and any means of access to the roofs of the various buildings. Roofs are a popular means of entry among some professional burglars. By entering through the roof, the burglar delays the discovery of his crime and is sometimes able to work inside without detection even with an officer standing outside.

Vehicle Patrol Tactics

The vehicles used for patrol should not be used as shells, but merely as means of transportation and protection. When you are on vehicle patrol, one of the first rules to follow is to get out of the car frequently. Never use it as a means of isolating yourself from your patrol duties. In fact, you will probably have few opportunities to remain in the vehicle very long because, due to their high mobility and access to rapid communications, officers assigned to automobiles handle virtually all calls for service as well as the bulk of assigned activities.

For automobile patrol, solo patrols or two-officer teams are used for various times of the day and types of districts, depending on department experiences. When solo patrol is utilized, there is a need for closer coordination of the field officers' activities with communications personnel, and the field units must frequently follow up to other field units. The solo patrol concept is not intended to place lone officers at locations where two or more officers are needed. The patrol officers should work in teams for purposes of field contacts, citations, checking open doors, and responding to most calls. Only the patrolling should be done solo.

Operate the vehicle at normal speeds, consistent with traffic conditions. If the traffic is moving faster than you believe necessary for adequate surveillance of the people and places along the way, stop, turn around, or go around the block and retrace your route. If the traffic is too fast for effective patrol, stop frequently and wait, then move on. Patrolling heavily traveled streets is virtually impossible at times. Move around the district on all the streets rather than just a few. A patrol officer is of no value when driving at high speeds.

Open the windows of the police car whenever consistent with weather conditions, and turn the radio down low so as not to drown out the sounds outside. Patrol the district so that the vehicle will be seen by the greatest number of people, frequently turning corners and covering the side streets as well as the main thoroughfares.

Several types of patrol patterns have been variously described, such as the "zigzag," "quadrant search," and the "clover leaf." The design is meaningless as a technique in itself and merely describes the driving pattern that resembles what the title suggests. Whatever pattern you decide to use should be irregular and unpredictable. Move around the district.

Start at one side and work to the other, or work out from the center, or go across the district, turn around, and immediately retrace your route. The entire district should receive attention with emphasis on those places that require special attention because of the frequency of crimes and arrests. Never develop a time schedule for patrolling your assigned district, and always consider the possibility that a burglar or thief will commit crimes in the most illogical places and at the most unusual times of day.

Patrol Driving

Most patrol driving consists of stop-and-start, slow-speed driving with frequent backing (see Figure 2–3). The majority of accidents involving police units occur during this type of driving, and a large percentage of them involve the backing process. Fatigue and inattention to driving are other patrol accident factors. Seat belts/shoulder harnesses and other safety equipment installed in the vehicle for your safety are absolutely essential. Not only are they installed for your personal safety, but if people who have been cited for failure to wear safety belts and children see that you are breaking the law, your credibility goes out the window!

Keep awake. Driving at nighttime and during the early morning hours often becomes monotonous, particularly when you have not had adequate rest and the patrol routine at that time of the day presents no novelty to you. Open the car window for fresh air, talk out loud occasionally, and move your eyes around frequently while driving along a straight stretch of road. Stop the car occasionally, get out, and flex your muscles. Never use pills or medication to stay awake on the job. It is better to use adequate rest than to use a chemical "crutch" to stay awake.

Figure 2-3 Some agencies, including the Pennsylvania State Police, have comprehensive vehicle operation training for their new officers. Skill development should not be left to chance. (Courtesy of the Pennsylvania State Police.)

Set an example by obeying all traffic laws, including boulevard stops, speed laws, and the general rules of the road. The vehicle operated in this manner serves as much of a purpose as the officer driving it by encouraging compliance with the laws by example.

Special skills are required for driving in rain, snow, and slush. In an article entitled "New Facts about Skidding: They May Save Your Life," E. D. Fales, Jr., outlines some excellent suggestions for driving at times when skidding is possible.[1] Fales points out that studies by various agencies have revealed that the front tires of an automobile moving at higher speeds actually leave the surface, or hydroplane, when moving across rain, snow, or slush. At speeds above 30 miles per hour, the tires begin to lose contact with the road. At a speed of approximately 55 miles per hour on top of a water-covered street surface, there is only slight tire contact with the surface, and at higher speeds there is none whatsoever.

Fales suggests that adding air pressure to the tires and driving more slowly may improve maneuverability. The depth of the tread and the depth of the water on the road surface have a direct bearing on the hydroplaning phenomenon. One other way to reduce the occurrence of hydroplaning in inclement weather is to drive in the tracks made by preceding vehicles, which may be relatively dry because of continuous friction and water displacement.

Skidding occurs under various conditions, and it has been discovered that the skid itself perpetuates the problem. As the vehicle goes into the skid, the tire temperature rises, the rubber melts, and the tire lays down its own thin layer of melted rubber, which makes a slideway. When the vehicle begins to go into a skid, use all the driver training techniques, including braking the vehicle with short, rapid-sequence braking motions instead of the usual steady pushing motion. The brakes are less likely to lock the wheels in a skid when they are applied in this manner.

Parking police vehicles is a frequent problem. Upon arrival in response to an emergency call for service, there may be no readily available space and little time to look for a place to park. The circumstances must dictate the action. There can be no strictly enforced regulations concerning the parking of police vehicles, except that they should always be parked legally unless an emergency condition exists. The vehicle should be parked in a legal manner and the key to the ignition should be removed. Sometimes it is wise to lock the vehicle completely to protect it against vandalism. Instead of taking the ignition key away from the unit, officers working as a radio car team will take the key out of the ignition and place it in a hiding place that is convenient and known to both of them. Either officer thus has immediate access to the unit regardless of his or her partner's location. Better yet would be to

---

[1]E. D. Fales, Jr., "New Facts about Skidding: They May Save Your Life," *Law Enforcement Bulletin* (Washington, D.C.), May 1965, pp. 13–16. Reprinted from *Popular Science Monthly*. Copyright © 1964 by Popular Science Publishing Co., Inc.

assign a key to each officer and avoid the problem of having to worry about where the keys are.

Plainclothes Patrol

Unusual conditions may necessitate patrol officers' special assignment to perform their patrol operations in regular street clothing and to operate department vehicles or privately owned vehicles that are not identifiable as police cars. This type of assignment is particularly effective for "saturation coverage" of high-crime areas. It provides extra coverage without alarming the occupants or signaling the culprits with an unusual number of patrol units. The burglars or robbers may possess a false feeling of security because they lack knowledge of the plainclothes patrol. The result may be successful apprehension of some "long-time wanted" felons and the clearance of many cases.

For plainclothes patrol, dress to fit the occasion and wear whatever clothing is the mode of the day and fits the type of activity you will ostensibly engage in as a "cover" for your presence in the neighborhood. Use a vehicle that similarly matches the occasion. Sometimes it may be wiser to use a rented car or borrowed used car than to use a so-called "undercover" unit belonging to the department.

Situations calling for plainclothes patrol vary with current problems (see Figure 2–4). Within the department, it may be used to supplement any existing or "standing" assignment, such as vice or detective assignments, when a particular situation requires more attention than the responsible division can devote to the problem. At the beach or the amusement park in a resort community, plainclothes patrol may be the most effective way to deal with seasonal problems. In the city, there may be several locations where large numbers of juveniles "just fool around" or seek meaningful recreation, and plainclothes patrol may be used to give those locations extra police coverage without fanfare and without giving the juveniles the impression that they are being "over-policed."

Rallies, sporting events, or other occasions when large numbers of people gather for a variety of reasons may best be patrolled by the police department with an officer or two in uniform and others not in uniform. The latter mingle with the crowd and make themselves available in case of a need for their assistance. A team of plainclothes patrol officers can move about from place to place throughout the city inconspicuously and quite effectively.

Picture this scenario: It is an open-air concert with about 15,000 in attendance. Most of the crowd is orderly and enjoying the performance. Down in front near the stage two young men appear to be under the influence of an intoxicant and are making complete fools of themselves, causing a disturbance and starting to pick fights with half a dozen other people. Unless someone neutralizes the situation, we are soon going to have a riot. There are a couple uniformed officers nearby. If the officers go down and try to arrest the two culprits, they might exacerbate the problem. Out

Figure 2-4   The three people in the foreground are on "plainclothes patrol" covering the uniformed officers on the beach. They also work undercover assignments. (Courtesy of the Police Department, Huntington Beach, California.)

of the crowd emerge four "friends" of the two unruly hoodlums. They take their "buddies" out of the crowd and the rest of the crowd goes back to enjoying the event on stage. Actually, the four "friends" were police officers in plainclothes, but no one was the wiser and what might have led to forcible action by uniformed officers and the inevitable angry crowd getting angrier was defused quickly and effectively. These same officers may be assigned to check on transient vice conditions or virtually any other type of problem not requiring uniformed officers. Plainclothes patrol should be a normal part of the patrol division's repertoire of techniques, and it in no way infringes on the privileges or obligations of the other operating units in the department.

One of the many problems you will encounter in working a plainclothes assignment is that of positively identifying yourself as a police officer once the need for such identification becomes necessary. The less you look like an on-duty police officer, the more effective you are on the detail you are working. Suddenly the need arises for you to identify yourself and state "I am a police officer." A handgun displayed by itself means only that the bearer is armed and may appear to some people as an immediate threat to be overcome. The identification card by itself may look like a driver's license, or a badge carried may have a worn-out appearance and look more like a toy badge than the real thing when presented by an officer in a polo shirt and jeans. Whatever the arrangement made by your agency for your identification when the need arises, you must make it in a positive manner and the credentials and/or badge should have an official-appearing configuration. The person you are confronting in an arrest situation, or some other form of official business demanding proof of your authority, must know that you *really* are the police officer you say you are. Another officer might not recognize you either.

Recognition of an Officer in Plainclothes

Whenever you are working a uniformed assignment and you meet another officer who is not wearing a uniform, wait for him or her to initiate the salutations. Your "Good morning, John, how's the new detail?" may ruin a case that John is currently working that requires that he not be identified as a police officer. In one case some time ago, an officer working in a department's intelligence unit had finally managed to work himself into a position of trust with some high-placed members of an organized crime operation, not an easy task. While in his undercover role, the officer was walking down the street with a member of the syndicate hierarchy en route to meet a contact, who would open up a new avenue for the investigation. As they approached the building and were about to enter, a uniformed officer was standing nearby and recognized the undercover agent. Not thinking, the officer walked up to him with a warm "Hey _____, How're you doin', ole buddy? Haven't seen you since the academy. Heard you were working intelligence. How do you like that 'cloak and dagger' detail?" Needless to say, the old academy friend did not receive a warm response, and the investigation ended at that moment.

DISTRICT RESPONSIBILITY

Your assigned district is the area of the city entrusted to you for a specified period of time to answer calls and to patrol at all times except while otherwise engaged. During your tour of duty, you may leave the district to eat lunch, to go to headquarters for reporting or prisoner transportation, to handle an assigned call outside the district, or to pursue a known or suspected violator. The reason for assigning specific units to designated districts is to assure at least minimum patrol coverage of each district. When you are assigned to a district, give it your full attention and provide its people with the best possible police service.

INSPECTIONS ON PATROL

During a tour of duty, the patrol officer performs a succession of inspections for a variety of purposes and to assist various other agencies and individuals as well as the police department. Fundamentally, the inspections of buildings and other places are for the benefit of the owners and operators themselves, for building security, and for early discovery of fires and other hazards. Additionally, the inspections serve as a crime prevention tool, and there is always an extra deterrence factor during the actual presence of the officer. Other inspections may be for the benefit of building and safety departments, the health officer, license department, public utilities, and environmental protection agencies.

Building Inspections

While you are on patrol, get out of the patrol unit frequently and physically check the buildings. From the front seat of a patrol car with the aid of a powerful spotlight, it is possible to check windows and the ground below for broken glass. Some glass does not reflect.

By getting the right angle of the light on a space between double doors it may be possible to see the locking bolt where it locks the doors together. One technique used by officers for building security is to get out of the car, try the doors and windows of the building, and then place a small piece of paper in the crack above the door. The officer returns periodically during the tour of duty and shines a light on the slip of paper, assuming that the building is secure. Some enterprising burglars have been known to pry open the door bearing the small piece of paper, then tape the paper to the top of the door, enter, commit their crime, and leave. The paper never leaves the doorway, but the building security has been violated.

Other methods of indicating whether someone has intruded are to string thread or fine wires across the entranceway that will be broken on contact; or attach invisible or transparent tape stretching from door to door frame in more than one location in hopes that the intruder will not see any or all of them. Whatever device you use should be creative and be changed from time to time. Burglars are going to be imaginative and resourceful, like the true professionals many of them are.

Plan to check out the entire group of buildings when you approach a shopping center or complex of buildings. Although you may use a spot-check technique, you should be reasonably sure of the security of the entire area. In most districts it is virtually impossible to provide all of the police protection that you should because of the heavy demands on your time and attention. To compensate for this lack of complete coverage, work out some sort of unpredictable spot-check procedure, giving the greatest attention to those places most likely to be subject to burglary or similar crimes.

During your "routine" building checks, it would be wise to plan for the time when you might have to attack the building in a hostile situation, such as a raid, or a barricaded felon and/or a hostage situation. If not on paper, at least have a sketch in your mind of the building's entrances and exits, skylights and windows, and types of locks or latches and locations of the keys or names and addresses and phone numbers of people who can assist you in gaining access. Know where the master switches for electricity and shutoff valves are for the water and gas, and the piping systems for heating and air conditioning. Keep notes also on the proximity of emergency services, such as fire stations and hospitals.

When approaching a location where a suspect may be inside, turn off your headlights and turn the volume down on your radio so as not to signal your arrival. When applying the brakes, use the hand brakes to avoid flashing the brake lights. Park your unit some distance away, and walk, being sure not to slam the car door. When you approach on foot, there is less likelihood that the burglar—if there is one—will hear you. Move silently without keys rattling; walk flat-footed (heels and soles down at the same time) and you will find that your footsteps are much quieter. Take advantage of the natural cover of darkness and the shadows. Do not use the flashlight except when absolutely necessary, and then only when holding it to one side away from your body. Walk close to the buildings and avoid silhouetting yourself in doorways or in front of windows.

Plan your approach so that you are not walking in the glare of headlights or other light or casting shadows that signal your presence. If you work in a team, you and your partner should plan your strategy to complement each other and both of you should know the whereabouts of the other at all times. One effective means of communicating with other officers is by tapping short code signals on the pavement with the police baton. Other methods of communication include flashing a light on a high object that may be visible to officers on two sides of a building or flashing a signal directly toward another officer with the hand covering all but a small "pinhole" of light emanating from the flashlight. Consider carrying a small penlight in your shirt pocket with your writing pens. There are many times when it will be more convenient than your large flashlight. If you must talk, whisper. To reduce the hissing "sibilant explosion" sounds that accompany whispering, first take a deep breath and let out half of your air before making the first sound.

Every building that you approach may have someone inside, either a burglar or someone legitimately there, such as office or cleanup personnel, or the proprietor. Since none of them will be wearing labels, you should expect to find a burglar or two. Using that logic, some training officers recommend that you make every approach with your handgun in your hand ready for immediate use. I recommend against it, because the weapon in your holster is equally accessible to you if you practice drawing and firing your weapon on the range. You are going to have a flashlight in one hand, and the other one should be free to turn doorknobs and push doors open. If both hands are full, you are going to be turning on light switches with your flashlight or the barrel of your handgun, which is not a good idea. It takes very little, if any, more time to draw and fire a weapon than it does to fire it when it is being held in the hand. If an armed culprit is inside and intends to shoot you when you enter, and if you have absolutely no knowledge that he is inside, there is no reason to believe that you would prevent him from shooting at you by holding a gun in your hand. Also, consider your situation if you are turning a doorknob with the gun in the same hand and a burglar on the other side of the door suddenly kicks the door toward you.

While approaching the building, look around for vehicles that seem to be out of place and sacks or suitcases that might have contained burglar tools for roof and safe "jobs." Check for footprints in the mud or loosely packed earth beneath doors and windows that may have been the point of entry or exit. Inspect the sides of the building where it is adjacent to utility poles, piles of boxes, ladders, or some other means of access to the roof. It is possible that the burglar—if there was one—might have scuffed his shoes on the building when climbing.

Make a serious game out of building inspections, varying your technique and starting point each time, and generally causing confusion for anyone who might attempt to analyze your methods. The rear doors and windows are most vulnerable to attack by burglars, but some burglars prefer the front because they may believe officers check only back doors. Never overlook the possibility that there may be some person inside who has a legal and legitimate reason for being there, but consider everyone suspect until you have completely checked them out. Also consider the possibility that a lookout accomplice may be standing, or sitting in a parked automobile, somewhere outside the building and that he or she may appear to have a perfectly logical reason for being at that location. The lookout may have some unique method for signaling your presence to the burglar inside, which may indicate to you possible complicity in some type of criminal activity.

When checking out a door, look first to determine which way it opens. Some burglars close the door just far enough so that when someone carelessly grabs it to see if it is locked, the bolt locks into place. The clicking sound of the bolt serves as a signal device for the burglar. Do not stand directly in front of the door, since the intruder may shoot through the door, Standing directly in front has proven a fatal mistake for many police officers. Hold the door steady, take hold of the knob and turn it to take up any slack that may exist, then attempt to open the door in whichever direction it opens. If it is secure, check for pry marks and then move on to the next door or window.

Whenever you check out the interior of any building that appears to have been forcibly entered and you believe there is a possibility that the culprit is still inside, wait for backup officers and proceed as though it were a crime in progress. Make liberal use of lights, turning them on and leaving them on as you proceed with the search. The eyes adjust to lighting changes that you should use to your advantage. For example, if your eyes are adjusted to the light and you are entering a dark room, reach inside and turn on as many lights as you can find switches for. If there is someone inside the dark room, that person's eyes will take about 20 to 50 seconds to adjust to see in the light. You might check this phenomenon by stepping out into bright sunlight for a few minutes, then walk back into a dark room; or stand in a lighted room, then turn off all the lights. What happens to your vision? It takes quite a while for your eyes to adjust to the change, like going from a positive to a negative photo print. It actually involves a change in functions of the rods and cones in the eyes. In your real-life situation when you are checking out a building and you have turned on the lights, you will have that time to see the culprit and make a decision about what you are going to do about his or her presence. Also, when you are opening the door, give it a firm shove so that it will strike the door stop or a wall. If it strikes something soft, there might be a person standing behind that door. (Figure 2–5 illustrates an alternative to the solo patrol.)

Inspecting windows usually involves first checking for any broken glass, pry marks, or latent prints before touching any portion of the window, to avoid contamination of possible evidence. Make sure that glass is actually in the window. It may have been completely removed by some careful burglar. Touch the glass to feel for any unusual heat inside the building, which may indicate the presence of a smoldering fire or a faulty heating system. Determine the way the window opens; then attempt to open it by applying reasonable pressure. If there is some evidence of entry, check the wall below for scuff marks and the sill for dust disturbance. Sometimes the window may prove to be one that was broken earlier but never repaired. At first it may appear to be a burglar's point of entry, but a closer inspection may reveal a substantial quantity of dust

Figure 2-5 Dogs make excellent partners when performing routine police activities, such as building checks, which can prove to be extremely hazardous. (Courtesy of Lexington–Fayette [Kentucky] Urban County Division of Police.)

and the presence of spider webs, which would have been destroyed if entry had been made recently.

If you find the door and/or window of any building open, consider that it might be the result of a criminal act. Check it out in the same manner whether the person in charge had left the door open and had neglected to lock up for the night or if there had been a burglar inside. Sometimes there is no way for you to determine whether or not a crime has been committed—or is in progress—without investigating further.

Crime Prevention Follow-up

Whenever repeated instances of crime hazards are inadvertently caused by the potential victims, as when doors or windows are carelessly left open or company trucks are parked overnight with the keys left in the ignition, it is your responsibility to encourage the potential victims to correct the situation.

Because your duty hours may preclude your making personal contacts with many of these people, there should be some provision for follow-up contacts by another officer, preferably during the business hours of the places to be visited. If time does not permit personal contacts, an inspection form may be prepared with notations for suggested improvements in security precautions, and it may be mailed to the business in question. This is an excellent job for the community service (nonsworn) people to perform, if your department is fortunate enough to have the luxury of such supplementary personnel. Block captains in your community-oriented policing program or your local community college, or senior citizen programs of the city or county, may choose to assume these community relations-oriented programs.

This follow-up procedure serves two purposes: public relations and crime prevention. It is important that you let the public know of the work that you are doing and the attention that is given to their establishments. By expressing your concern over the security of their property, we hope that those contacted will follow your advice and at the same time have increased confidence in the value of having such an efficient police department. The crime prevention aspect, of course, will tend to reduce your increasing work load. There is always the possibility that the crime rate will increase, but perhaps you may be effective in causing the increase to be less than if you made no effort at all to reduce crime.

House Inspections

As part of an overall crime repression program, it may be wise to institute a house inspection service for people on vacation if your community does not already have such a service. Some people may be absent from their homes for weeks or months, and a crime committed during their absence may go undetected and unreported for all that time. The greater the time between the occurrence of the crime and its discovery, the greater is the culprit's chance of escaping apprehension.

Some burglary victims will remember that they actually provided the burglars with valuable information. A wife may inform the local newspaper that her husband has won an award for being the salesman of the month and that he and his family who live at 1327 Lonely Lane will be on a month-long, all-expense-paid vacation in the Bahamas. A society couple whose home is known for its works of art hanging on the walls may let their friends and suppliers know that they are going on a goodwill mission to a remote Indian village for three months. In both cases, the individuals are indirectly providing burglars with a wealth of information. In either case, the burglars may hire a moving van and take the entire contents of the house.

Residents may be asked to report their anticipated absences to the department so that its officers can instruct them on a few methods of burglary prevention. The officers may request that the people announce their good news to the press upon their return rather than at the time of their departure. Arrangements may be made for "house sitters" to take up residence during an extended absence or to have friends or relatives check the house periodically and report to the police department that they have found it still secure. Some plans should be made to eliminate signs of vacation, such as long grass, dry flower beds, accumulated circulars and sales brochures, milk, newspapers, and other objects strewn about the premises. People should be advised to leave a light or lights on in the house, possibly a radio left playing, and some shades or drapes not drawn all the way; this will leave a burglar guessing as to whether there is anyone inside or not. Timers may be installed to turn electrical appliances and lights on and off at normal times rather than continue to operate during daylight hours. Even electronic equipment goes bad sometimes. I am reminded of the people who left for a month, whose lights turned on and off alternately about every hour for the full month because of a malfunctioning timer, with no friend or relative checking the place. A friend or neighbor should also be given a key and should be present to assist the officer in checking out the residence in the event that a crime has been committed.

During the day, house inspections for those on vacation should include a thorough check of the entire premises for security and freedom from vandalism (see Figure 2–6). Ask the neighbors if they have seen anything at all that might strike them as suspicious and to report to the department if they do see something out of the ordinary. During the nighttime, make occasional and unscheduled inspections. Use your flashlight liberally to avoid injury at the hands of a neighbor who might believe that you are a prowler or burglar. It is also wise to make liberal use of the lights inside the house, turning them all on as you go through the house or business establishment. After all, you are not hiding from anyone.

Figure 2-6   People who leave on vacation often forget such things as locking doors or closing a window. In this case, the family may have forgotten to secure the place, or there may be a burglar inside who forgot to close the door after he or she broke in. (Courtesy of the Police Department, Bismarck, North Dakota.)

I have been told by several officers of larger departments that this service is no longer offered by their departments, and that they recommend the services of private security companies. Another option is to make use of the neighborhood watch program, with neighbors performing these functions. Within the department, the task could be performed by college students who serve without charge as interns in exchange for college credits, or this might be yet another function of community service officers. It may be a trade-off, using time to prevent burglaries in lieu of the time it takes to investigate a burglary.

Miscellaneous Inspections

Each jurisdiction has a widely varied set of regulations and procedures for many other inspection services that are required of the patrol officers in their respective jurisdiction. Some cities require their police officers to make quarterly business license inspections. The building codes in some communities may specify that any building department inspector or police officer who observes a construction job in progress must check for the necessary permits. When they go into cafes or any place where food is served, officers in some jurisdictions are required to look for unsanitary conditions and to forward a report to the health department whenever they observe violations. When venereal disease may result from some promiscuous activities of juveniles, the health department may require that a form be forwarded to them for follow-up treatment.

Depending on the city or county policies, police officers or sheriff's deputies are expected to perform a variety of additional types of inspections, including an examination of all liquor licenses and dancehall or entertainment permits. It is not unusual for certain operators to stretch the limitations of their permits beyond what has been permitted, such as dancing in a place that is licensed for entertainment only, or using a ten-piece band in a saloon licensed for only a three-member group.

"ATTRACTIVE NUISANCES," OR PATROL HAZARDS

The "attractive nuisance" doctrine is that one maintains on his or her premises (business or residential) a condition, instrumentality, machine, or other agency that is dangerous to young children because of children's inability to appreciate peril, which may reasonably be expected to attract children to such premises, and that one therefore has a duty to the children (and society in general) to exercise *reasonable care* to protect against the dangers of such an attraction (*Schock v. Ringling Brothers and Barnum and Bailey Combined Shows*, 5 Wash. 2d 599, 105 P.2d 838, 843).

The doctrine also applies to creating such a condition on the premises of another, or in a public place which may be a source of danger to children, and states that one has a duty to take such precautions as a reasonably prudent man (or woman) would take to prevent injury to children of tender years whom he or she knows to be accustomed to resort there, or who may, by reason of something there that may be expected to attract them, come there to play (*Atlantic Coastline Railroad Company v. O'Neal*, 48 Ga. App. 706, 172 S.E. 740, 741).

One cannot apply this doctrine to a natural condition or common dangers existing as a part of nature (such as a free-flowing creek or stream running through an open field or forest) (*McCall v. McCallie*, 48 Ga. App. 99, 171 S.E. 843, 844). What does apply, however, is that the attraction must be visible from a public place where children have a right to be (*Rokiski v. Polish Nat. Alliance of U.S. of North America*, 314 Ill. App. 380, 41 N.E. 2d. 300).

The term *patrol hazard* is frequently used to describe a specific condition or place that requires the patrol officer's special attention. The hazard may be a bar where gang fights occur frequently. It may be an old dump site that has filled up with stagnant water and is now being used as a swimming hole by the neighborhood children. A hazard location might be an abandoned building, a "haunted house," or a secluded area that a child might consider a "secret place" because it is a place to hide.

Although this may have no direct bearing on the character of the operators, virtually every place that attracts large numbers of people is a patrol hazard because of the potential problems inherent whenever large numbers of people are thrown together for any purpose. Places where tourists stay and congregate are high hazard areas because there is usually a disproportionate number of people on foot, and many of them carry larger than usual amounts of cash on their person.

When you are on patrol, give these "frequent incident" or "hazard" locations more than average attention and attempt to prevent any criminal activity by your frequent and unscheduled attendance. Develop a professional relationship with the owners and operators of the places that require more frequent patrol coverage, and impress upon them the fact that your occasional visits are for their protection as well as that of the other people in the community. Encourage them to call for your assistance if they should need it and generally develop their respect for your ability to perform your duty in a fair and objective manner. Develop informants in the neighborhood, or among the people who work or visit these places, and encourage them to let you know of any potential problems that may be developing so that effective police action may actually prevent the occurrence of any large-scale criminal activity. Maintain a list of these places and continually update your information regarding the names of the owners, operators, and other key people whom you should be able to locate whenever necessary.

SURVEILLANCE AND STAKEOUTS

Surveillance is the process of keeping under observation a place, a person, or an object for the purpose of identifying persons, developing information, discovering relationships between people and places or objects, and discovery of evidence.

The object of surveillance is usually suspected of being related to criminal activity one way or another, either from the standpoint of victimization, or as a suspect. Through the means of a surveillance it is possible to determine who is meeting with whom, who a person's friends and associates are, where certain people go and what they do and for what purposes, where they might be hiding certain things, and what they might be saying to each other. Activities, identities, contacts, and virtually every facet of a person's life are under scrutiny, usually with the purpose of solving a crime and gaining a conviction of the guilty persons.

A loose surveillance is one in which an officer follows or observes a person on an occasional basis, such as after work for a few hours to see if the person may be planning a robbery for this evening. A close surveillance might be an open convoy to protect a person or to let the person being "tailed" know that he or she is being watched very closely. A fixed surveillance is usually referred to as a "stakeout," such as when officer(s) secrete themselves inside a convenience market they anticipate might be robbed at the approximate time the officers are present.

A convoy is a type of surveillance that is performed either to protect the subject or to keep the subject purposefully under observation with his or her knowledge as a means of letting the subject know that he or she is being continually watched. This technique is quite effective when a known organized crime "enforcer" comes into town for what you believe to be a secret visit or to perform a specific task, such as make a collection or pay a debt. Although it may seem to be a form of harassment, the "convoy" technique actually involves no harassment at all. It is merely a form of preventive maintenance. While the subject is being watched, there is little likelihood that he or she will commit any crime, and if the subject commits no crimes, the officers make no attempt to contact him or her or to restrict his or her movements. Sometimes the airport detail of the intelligence unit may even greet an undesirable character on his arrival, greeting him by name and acknowledging his presence. This is usually accompanied by a suggestion that he mind his manners while in town because he will be under constant surveillance.

Objectives of a Surveillance

These are some of the principal objectives for initiating and maintaining a surveillance.

1. Obtain sufficient evidence to make a physical arrest or secure an arrest or search warrant.
2. Locate and apprehend suspects or wanted persons.
3. Locate the residence, hangouts, or other places that the subject of the surveillance and his or her contacts frequent.
4. Identify the relationships between known and suspected criminals.
5. Prevent—or attempt to prevent—the commission of crimes.
6. Check out informants and the reliability of their information.
7. Prepare for a raid of a gambling or vice establishment.
8. Determine the best way to accomplish an arrest or to rescue a person being held as a hostage.
9. Locate missing persons or runaways, adult and juvenile.
10. Obtain background information for an interview or interrogation.
11. Locate hiding places, fences, unethical businesspersons, relay points for criminal transactions, or headquarters for various criminal or espionage activities.
12. Protect persons, places, or objects.

Preparation for Surveillance

Prior to starting surveillance, secure as much information about the subject as possible. Check the files of your own records system and every other available source of information to help you get to know the subject, his or her habits, and acquaintances. If available, secure a copy of a recent photograph of the subject and familiarize yourself with his or her general appearance as well as distinctive features.

If you have any advanced information concerning the specific location or general area where you will be maintaining surveillance on the subject, thoroughly familiarize yourself with that area. Get to know the street names, their relative locations, and the tract configuration. Check records and other officers to identify the people in the area who may assist you in the surveillance or who may assist in the transmission of information to headquarters when regular means are not available.

Foot Surveillance

For an effective surveillance operation, more than one officer must be used. It will be necessary to alternate the sequence and relative locations of the surveillants, or "tails," so that the subject does not become aware of their presence unless they intend that the subject know they are there. When the subject turns a corner, the surveillant immediately behind the subject should continue across the street at the intersection, then turn and walk parallel to the subject down the same street. The next surveillant in line should turn the corner and take the lead position immediately behind the subject. If there are three surveillants, the third officer can be used for relief or can assume the lead if one of the other officers is identified, or "made" by the subject. This "leap-frogging" technique should continue so that a single officer is not continually following the subject.

When on surveillance, you should work out a signal system with your partner so that it will not be necessary to get together in frequent huddles, or to make obvious signals to each other. If you are conducting a surveillance in street clothing, avoid chameleon disguises. Minor changes in appearance can work wonders at times, such as a baseball cap that can be worn or removed and placed in a pocket, a reversible jacket, or removing a necktie or jacket somewhere (and returning later to pick it up). Look natural while operating a "tail." You may find it to your advantage occasionally to wear eyeglasses or sunglasses and to vary the distance between yourself and the subject, but avoid any "private eye" melodrama. The key to your success as a surveillant is to look as inconspicuous as possible and to fit into the surroundings naturally.

Watch out for the subject's methods for testing whether he is being "tailed." Avoid eye-to-eye contacts or any other direct confrontation. There must always be some plausible explanation for you to follow the subject for an extended period of time. Frequent alternation of surveillants will ensure that no solo officer is following the subject for too long a period of time.

When turning a corner, walk naturally and continue moving at the normal rate of travel. The subject may have stopped immediately after turning. If this is the case, your sudden appearance around the corner should not be followed by a sudden, obvious stop. Keep on walking, even though it necessitates walking past the subject. If the subject makes a telephone call, you or your partner should also do something natural during the same period of time. There is little likelihood that you will find adjoining phone booths. If you do, perhaps a call of your own would be in order. When the subject enters a building or an elevator, follow if it is natural to do so. Otherwise, it may be better to wait until the subject returns to the street before resuming the surveillance.

Testing for surveillance is executed in many ways. The subject may stop suddenly for no apparent reason and look around or may suddenly reverse direction of travel and meet his or her surveillants head-on. If either of these things happens, the first officer has been "made" and should be replaced, if a replacement is available. The subject may take a short taxi ride, or get on a bus for a block or two, then get off just before it starts to move after a stop. The subject may watch a "tail" in store windows. To bait the surveillant, the subject may discard some unimportant piece of paper and then watch to see whether the person following stoops to pick it up.

Auto Surveillance

Before beginning an auto surveillance detail, be sure that you have plenty of gasoline. As with the foot method, it is best to have two or more surveillants (vehicles) so that you may use the same leapfrog technique discussed in the previous paragraphs covering foot surveillance. Be sure not to follow the subject's vehicle too closely. If possible, try to keep a "cushion vehicle" between yourself and the object vehicle. Keep the headlights on low beam, and drive naturally without arousing the suspicions of the subject by attempting to maintain a constant interval between your unit and the subject's. The subject may "test for a tail," as described earlier and may also drive alternately fast and slow to watch the car following. The subject may slow down as if to stop at a changing signal, then speed through the intersection just at the moment the light changes to red, leaving the surveillant behind. The subject may make frequent U-turns or take other types of evasive action.

The Stakeout

A stakeout is usually for the purpose of waiting for the anticipated arrival of a suspect who is either wanted for investigation or who is expected to commit a crime at the location being "staked out." When working such an assignment, be sure to preplan carefully. Get adequate food and rest before entering the place, and take a sufficient quantity of food with you in case it is necessary to spend some time. Arrange for efficient communications with other units and with headquarters.

Deliver your equipment, such as a shotgun, binoculars, or other special equipment, inconspicuously to avoid arousing suspicion. Dismantle the gun, and carry it in a case or container that would normally be carried by someone who works at that location. Wear the same type of clothing that would be natural for the establishment.

When working a stakeout in a place of business where other types of crimes may occur that are not related to your purpose, be sure to advise the store owner or other people in charge that they are not to reveal your presence to handle the matter. For example, a stakeout for an anticipated armed robbery will be rendered ineffective if the manager observes a shoplifter and calls to the officer to arrest the petty thief at just about the same time the potential armed robber steps into the store. The manager or others could also destroy the value of the stakeout by announcing to some of the customers that an officer is protecting the place.

Basic Guidelines for a Stakeout

1. Operate in a businesslike manner.
2. Be natural and avoid melodrama.
3. Do not use phony disguises.
4. Be on the alert for a subject "testing for a tail."
5. Be adequately prepared for surveillance, particularly a fixed post where you may have to stay for some time.
6. Prepare a "cover" reason for being in the area while on a surveillance.
7. Keep sufficient money and supplies on hand.
8. Avoid direct eye to eye contact with the subject.
9. Prepare for adequate communications with other officers and with headquarters.

SPECIALIZED PATROL

At one time or another, your department may have to create a specialized patrol unit that is separate from the regular patrol force. The everyday demands of routine calls for service and all other activities of the patrol unit make it virtually impossible to address special problems. Using a great amount of ingenuity and imagination, a separate unit will be able to concentrate on one problem at a time or perhaps on several different activities. Some of the types of special problems include street muggings, sexual assaults, burglaries in a concentrated area or of a certain type, narcotics trafficking, theft and fencing on a wide scale, pilfering from autos, prostitution, and street walking.

For the unit to enjoy any degree of success, the officers must have the freedom to develop their own skills and techniques while working within the framework of good police practice. They should be relieved of any responsibility for generalized patrol, follow-up investigation, and regular crime prevention and repression activities while assigned to this special unit. Another factor that helps such a unit to succeed is to publicize its existence and success rate but keep the actual identities of the officers anonymous. Publicizing the existence of a special team of officers working as decoys in the downtown area to combat the problem of sexual assaults on the streets may reduce the number of such crimes because the responsible offenders know that they run a higher risk of getting caught.

Specialized patrol may or may not acquire some title, such as "Metro," or "Spec. Enf. Bureau," or saturation patrol, or "the sting," and the officers will be assigned to wear uniforms or special equipment for some assignments, plain clothes for others, sometimes costumes and special makeup, and disguises for other assignments. Male officers may be dressed as females and serve as decoys. Negative effects of specialized units include jealousy among officers who are not accepted in the program, an "elitist" attitude among assigned officers, credit being given to the special unit at the expense of the work of the regular patrol, empire building by the assigned officers, hostility from citizens, and problems of coordination and cooperation between specialized details and regular units with a drain on human resources from the regular units.

Advantages of specialized units may overshadow the negative aspects, however. There is a specific designation of responsibility on the special team to get a certain job done effectively. The officers seeking assignment would have something to strive for, and the officers assigned would have the special feeling of being part of the "elite" group. Training and skills development in certain areas, such as special weapons or techniques, will give the officers goals to work for. If all goes well, and the specialized unit is successful, the publicity and positive reactions from the public will greatly enhance the image of the department.

The decision whether to create specialized patrol units depends on such factors as nature and volume of certain crimes, the current effectiveness of current patrolling methods, history of success with special units in saturation patrol or decoy operations, or special methods of surveillance. Some officers might have to change their physical appearance and length and amount of facial and head hair, adjust their mannerisms and speech patterns, and isolate themselves from the police department so that they are not known as police officers while performing special assignments. Deployment of the specialized units would depend on need, and those needs might change daily. For example, the recent release of an unusual number of burglars who have served their time in prison and have returned home on parole, many of them to return to burglarizing, would cause the department to want to maintain close surveillance on those individuals to determine which ones were truly rehabilitated.

TEAM POLICING

Team policing is approached differently by different departments, but essentially it means that the city or county is broken down by area and officers are assigned on a permanent or semipermanent basis to those areas. The large department is broken down into several smaller departments, and the local teams work more closely with the people in their respective areas, on the grounds that the police can be more effective if they have the support, confidence, and assistance of the people they serve. The administrators and supervisors in these team areas are given more autonomy and local responsibilities for field activities, investigation, community relations, and overall police performance.

Team policing is not for every department. As a matter of fact, if your department is one of the smaller ones, with fewer than 50 to 75 officers, you already have team policing. In the larger police jurisdictions, this grassroots approach is undertaken to bring the people and the police closer together in a more cooperative situation. The local substation or storefront headquarters is a place the local citizens can visit to meet with the local police commander and staff to discuss mutual problems. In team policing, a greater effort is made to involve the assigned officers in participative management, identifying problems, setting objectives, and developing methods to meet those objectives. There is more flexible scheduling and flexibility in assignments, and the officers have more opportunity to follow up investigations they have started. The officers are also encouraged to develop and work with neighborhood "watch" groups and encourage the people to report suspicious circumstances and to take a greater interest and more responsibility in preventing and repressing crimes.

In a team policing environment, you may find that supervision is somewhat less formal because you are working closer with your team, but the operation must have discipline if it is to operate effectively. You cannot have four drivers in the same car, all going different directions. Discussion and negotiation will have to be undertaken to determine the direction in which all are to go. So it is with team policing. According to Whisenand, the role of the team policing supervisor is to (1) support subordinates, (2) facilitate interaction, (3) emphasize goals, and (4) facilitate work.[2]

SUMMARY

This chapter has been designed to introduce you to the basics of police patrol, beginning with attitude preparation and going on to actual preparation and the preliminaries prior to commencing patrolling activities. In

---

[2]Paul M. Whisenand, *Police Supervision: Theory and Practice* (Englewood Cliffs, NJ: Prentice Hall, 1971), p. 394.

the sections on patrolling the district, district responsibility, and inspections on patrol, we outlined the many functions and responsibilities of the field officer. A constant and alert as well as imaginative officer is required for this task, and one's principal responsibility is to maximize one's efforts by seeking the willing cooperation of the constituents, the people in the district.

Crime prevention follow-up should be directed toward educating victims on ways in which they might prevent a reoccurrence of the crime. Inspections of houses of people on vacation should be handled conscientiously, recognizing that this gives you an opportunity to ply your skills as a community relations specialist. Patrol hazards include attractive nuisances that may involve criminal and civil liability, but they also include any place or activity that requires more of your attention than other aspects or areas of your duties.

The topics of surveillance and stakeouts are sometimes thought of as the responsibility of more sophisticated police officers, such as the more experienced follow-up detectives. Actually, these are more often assigned to field patrol officers. There are some aspects of the "cops and robbers" game to these activities, but there are hazards and there are rules.

Specialized patrol involves assignment of officers with special talents and skills to units that may be temporary or permanent, their major objective being to address a problem that for some reason cannot be handled successfully through the more traditional police methods. Team policing also involves specialized assignments, but the objectives are to accomplish the police task through perhaps a greater variety of activities. Participative management and public cooperation are the secrets of successful team policing.

EXERCISES AND STUDY QUESTIONS

1. Why does the police officer wear a distinctive uniform?
2. Why is attitude preparation so important to field service?
3. What is the relationship between your personal value system and the law enforcement philosophy of your department?
4. List the personal qualities you believe to be essential to success as a peace officer.
5. Why is it important that the officer cultivate social relationships outside the circle of police friends and other people you encounter during working hours?
6. Describe the public servant role of the peace officer.
7. List some topics that should be covered during roll-call training.
8. Choose a law in your state. Explain the relationship between the letter of that law and the spirit, or enforcement aspects, of that law.
9. Describe the debriefing process as explained in this chapter.

10. What is the purpose for inspecting your vehicle prior to going out on patrol? Describe the process of such an inspection.
11. What is the purpose for a district orientation tour?
12. What is the value of foot patrol as opposed to vehicle patrol of the same district?
13. Describe the procedure for checking out a building when an open door is encountered on patrol.
14. How would you patrol a residential area? a business-industrial area?
15. List and discuss three purposes for utilization of plainclothes patrol.
16. How would you and your fellow officers cover a building when you suspect a burglar may still be inside?
17. What is the advantage/disadvantage of holding your revolver/pistol in your hand while checking out a building, in your opinion?
18. How would you perform a crime prevention follow-up with the victim of a residence burglary? a commercial burglary?
19. What is the purpose of a "vacation house" inspection, and how would you carry it out?
20. Describe at least five different types of patrol hazards that might also be classified as "attractive nuisances."
21. Describe at least two types of problems for which you would have a stakeout.
22. What is a close surveillance, and how is it done?
23. What is a loose surveillance, and how is it done?
24. Describe the method of carrying out a foot surveillance of one subject using three operants.
25. Describe the team policing concept as it is—or might be—utilized by your department.

REFERENCES

CHAPMAN, SAMUEL G. Police *Patrol Readings*. Springfield, Ill.: Charles C. Thomas, 1964.

HALE, CHARLES D. *Police Patrol Operations and Management*. New York: Wiley, 1981.

IANNONE, N. F. *Principles of Police Patrol*. New York: McGraw-Hill, 1975.

LOS ANGELES POLICE DEPARTMENT. *Daily Training Bulletins*, Vol. 1. Springfield, Ill.: Charles C. Thomas, 1954.

_____. *Daily Training Bulletins*, Vol. II. Springfield, Ill.: Charles C. Thomas, 1958.

McCREEDY, KENNETH R. *Theory and Methods of Police Patrol*. Albany, N.Y.: Delmar, 1974.

WHISENAND, PAUL M. *Police Supervision: Theory and Practice*. Englewood Cliffs, N.J.: Prentice Hall, 1971.

WILSON, ORLANDO W. *Police Planning*, 2nd ed. Springfield, Ill.: Charles C. Thomas, 1958.

Various training bulletins and related materials from the police departments of Glendale, Los Angeles, Riverside, and Santa Ana, the California Highway Patrol, and other agencies.

3 OBSERVATION & PERCEPTION

One of the most critical factors in the police officer's work is the eyewitness's ability to communicate accurately what he or she actually witnesses. Sometimes we don't always see or hear, feel or taste, or smell what we believe we have perceived. At other times we have trouble communicating our perceptions to others because of our differences in understanding what another person means. We are influenced by learning and conditioning, by our ability to interpret what we perceive, and by what others believe about our perceptions based upon their own learning and conditioning, which is different from ours. The statement "As unreliable as an eyewitness" holds in all too many cases.

Most people are not trained observers. They see people, yet they do not actually see them and cannot describe such physical characteristics such as the color of their eyes, shape of a nose, stature, color, and style of clothing. If the observer likes or dislikes or recognizes something in what he or she sees, that observer is more apt to be able to give a better description than if the event or any part of it has no meaning at the time of perception. For example, a jewelry designer might notice the style and design of a necklace worn by another person, whereas a dental technician might see a perfect set of dentures in the wearer's mouth and not even be aware of the necklace.

When you are seeking out and questioning witnesses, bear in mind that most witnesses will describe their observations in their own imperfect ways. You must find out as much as you can about the witnesses and their perceptual abilities, likes and dislikes, and the meanings behind their statements, and then interpret accordingly what they tell you. In this chapter we study some witness characteristics and discuss some of the techniques you may develop to utilize more effectively those witnesses in your investigations.

BASIC REQUIREMENTS OF A WITNESS

When you encounter a witness to any event you must establish four facts about that witness, which must be taken into account when determining whether or not to use that person as a witness in court, or whether you can assign any credibility to the information you glean from him or her.

1. *Was the witness present?* "Presence" may be defined for the purpose of this discussion as being at a place of vantage to gain knowledge of a particular fact through perception with one or more of the senses: sight, sound, taste, smell, touch. Some witnesses have been considered "present" when they have (1) observed a game law violation through binoculars in which the offense occurred across a ravine several miles of walking distance away, (2) smelled marijuana smoke through the cracks in a locked door, (3) heard voices in a bookmaking operation through a thin wall, (4) heard lewd remarks by an individual who was telephoning from several miles across town, (5) felt something that was wet or cold, (6) tasted something that was bitter, and (7) have a murder committed in the same room. All qualify for presence, and the annals of the courts abound with similar examples.

2. *Was the witness conscious and aware of what took place?* Not only must the person have been within range to perceive, but was it a cognitive perception? A person may be present in the same room as an old friend and frequently look in the friend's general direction yet never actually be conscious of the friend's presence because of his own occupation or preoccupation with some other phenomenon that he is observing. Two officers may have been sitting in a patrol car parked near an intersection when one officer said: "Say, did you see that violation? That yellow Oldsmobile went through the stop sign." The second officer may have looked up immediately and seen the yellow Oldsmobile traveling east across the boulevard. Only one element is missing: The officer did not see the actual violation at the moment it occurred and cannot testify to the fact. The officer can, however, testify to the identity of the driver of the car and all other circumstances surrounding the pursuit and citation. As the investigating and reporting officer, it is dangerous to assume that since two people were standing side by side when an event took place, they both saw the same things.

3. *Was the witness attentive as the event took place?* To have been present and to have seen something may not be sufficient for an individual to actually have been cognizant of what took place. A witness may actually observe a man holding a revolver up to another man's chest during the commission of an armed robbery and be so inattentive that the action seems to him to be some form of friendly play among friends. When asked about the event, the man who observed the crime may respond, "Yes, I saw it, but I wasn't aware of what was going on."

4. *Was the witness competent to perceive, and competent to communicate that information to you and to the court at a later date?* What is the person's mental state? Is the person suffering from a disease involving memory loss, or does he or she speak at the maturity level of a small child (which does not mean that your witness is no good in and of itself). Was the witness sleeping or imbibing alcoholic beverages, or suffering from the flu? What temporary state of mind was the witness in at the time of perception? Was he or she angry at someone for being late for an appointment, or enamored by his or her companion? Does the witness wear a hearing aid(s) or eyeglasses, and was he or she wearing it or them at the time of the perceived event?

FACTORS IN PERCEPTION

When considering the perceptive faculties of a witness, many factors must be taken into account. These may be divided into two broad categories: (1) external factors and (2) internal factors.

External Factors

Distance, or Proximity.   The closer an object or event is to the observer, the greater likelihood there is that he will direct some of his attention toward it. Something that occurs nearby more directly involves him than does something that may occur in a remote location.

Phenomena That May Affect Perception, Such as Differences in Lighting, Various Weather Conditions, and Sounds.   The eyes function differently under different lighting conditions through the medium of the cones and the rods, and colors appear quite differently under different kinds of light. Some people are night blind. Artificial lighting in darkness causes shadows, which may appreciably affect an individual's powers of perception. Rain, snow, wind, and fog may cause a significant difference in an individual's perceptive abilities. Distortions of vision are not unusual. Noises directly affect one's perception. Loud and unusual noises may cause distractions that divert the observer's attention completely away from an object he may be looking at. An event may be meaningless without sound, but pleasant or frightening with the appropriate sounds. For an example of this phenomenon, watch a "thriller" motion picture on television with the sound off; then turn it on and compare your reactions. Certain illusions also occur when color is introduced. For example, compare a red object with a blue object of the same size. The blue object will appear smaller. The object that makes more noise will appear larger. An object speeding toward you will appear larger than the same object speeding away from you.

Intensity and Size.   If something is louder and larger than other things about it, it will receive the attention of observers more rapidly and with greater intensity than the things around it.

Contrast.   Something unusual or out of the ordinary will receive more attention than will common or ordinary things. For example, the golfer in a funeral home will receive about as much attention as the tuxedoed undertaker on the golf course.

Repetition.   A person or object that appears—under certain conditions—more than one time will attract much more attention than if he or it appears only once. This factor is probably one of the reasons why an individual who appears to be loitering attracts more attention than the individual who seems to be moving with a purpose and a destination.

Movement.   A stationary object will soon appear as if it belongs where it is and will blend in even with contrasting objects. The moving object attracts and holds the attention. For example, consider the attention that a running man on a downtown street receives as opposed to all of the other walking men.

Similarities.   A woman who looks like Cousin Dalmation is likely to receive more attention than is one who is completely strange. For example, when a witness with missing teeth observes a suspect with missing teeth, that characteristic will probably be the most outstanding one the witness will remember having noticed.

Sounds.   Size perception will be affected by sounds. For example, an attacker who is shouting at the same time is more frightening than is a similar attacker who is silent. The person making the noise will appear to be larger, and numbers of people will appear greater when they are making loud and menacing noises. Depending on weather and other atmospheric conditions, the distance from which a noise is coming may be grossly miscalculated, and the direction may not be accurate.

Odors.   According to William S. Cain, in a Psychology Today article: "When it comes to identifying odors, people are strangely inconsistent and often imprecise. When exposed to a smell whose origins are not obvious, they may feel on the verge of identifying it...but they often cannot come up with the name without prompting."[1] Cain points out that people may improve their ability to identify odors through practice, stating that one of the problems we have in describing odors is that we have trouble finding the correct words to describe our olfactory experiences. Cain reported

---

[1]William S. Cain, "Educating Your Nose," *Psychology Today*, July 1981, pp. 56, 58.

that 80 common substances were chosen and 103 young women wearing blindfolds were asked to identify them. On the average, the subjects were successful in identifying only 36 of them with 10 most often identified (5 by brand name). Among those most identifiable were (1) Johnson's baby powder, (2) chocolate, (3) coconut, (4) Crayola crayons, (5) mothballs, (6) Ivory soap (bar), (7) Vick's Vapo Rub, (8) Bazooka bubble gum, (9) coffee, and (10) caramel. Keeping this information in mind, be careful not to place too much reliance on a statement by a witness that he or she smelled beer or whiskey on a person's breath, while actually it could have been any type of alcohol or might not have been alcohol at all. We have expectations, and sometimes the witness might smell what he or she expected to smell.

Internal Factors

Personal Characteristics about the Witness.   People's perceptive abilities depend on their physical condition. Eyesight is one sense that is relied upon most heavily, and the individual's capabilities with respect to acuity and perception should be the subject of inquiry. Some people should wear corrective lenses but do not for reasons of vanity, as in the following case when an identification depended entirely upon the single eyewitness.

One evening after dark, the witness arrived home and was walking along the corridor of the semidark apartment house approaching his front door. At that particular moment a form that appeared to be a man pushed past the witness and hastily departed down the corridor and down the stairs. The witness only glanced at him for a moment, commenting to himself about the rudeness of some people. As he started to enter his apartment, the lady from the apartment across the hall screamed that someone had been attempting to break down her door. She did not see the culprit.

The witness was the only person who saw the suspect. The woman called the police department and reported the attempted entry, and the gentleman witness described the suspect. Shortly thereafter a young man was stopped for questioning in the neighborhood and he was invited to return to the scene of the crime for a possible elimination as a suspect. The witness looked at the young man and stated that he could not be sure, but that there was a strong resemblance to the suspect he had seen in the hallway. The young man's name and address were recorded and he was allowed to continue whatever he had been doing. Two days later, an investigator contacted the same witness and asked him to look at some photographs of suspects. He replied that he would be glad to and then took out a pair of glasses with lenses that were as thick as soda bottle bottoms, indicating an obvious case of myopia. The man could not help with the identification. The investigator asked him if he had an eyesight problem, and he replied, "Oh, yes, I'm blind without my glasses." The investigator asked him if he had been wearing them on the night of the crime, and he replied, "No, I never wear them when I'm driving. I usually leave them home."

Although the case just cited is unusual, there are many degrees of disability that people experience and do not talk about. Some people have no night or peripheral vision, some have color perception problems, and others have difficulty with depth perception. People who are tone deaf cannot hear some sounds, and even someone who hears well can have his perception of sounds to which he is listening altered by distracting noises. Taste, touch, and smell are similarly affected.

Emotional and Psychological Considerations. Under various types of stress, people react differently from when they are in complete control of their faculties in a relaxed state. Some senses may be sharpened by the increased state of agitation of the body functions; others may be rendered ineffective because of preoccupation with a single incident, such as a suspect pointing a gun at the victim. Exaggeration and elaboration are commonplace. A revolver pointed at the face may actually be a .22 automatic, but take on the appearance of a .45 automatic. A boisterous and belligerent attacker may appear to be taller and heavier than he actually is. A crowd or five people may appear more like ten.

The personal drives of sex, hunger, and comfort may play a part in a witness's perception, as indicated by some events that seem to occur at various times which are described in minute detail. For example, someone who has just eaten a meal may not remember any food odors, whereas a hungry person may recall them more accurately.

Some people who suffer from handicaps such as a malformed or missing finger, harelip, missing teeth, or some congenital birth defect, are naturally more sensitive to similar problems experienced by others and would be better qualified to describe such irregularities. Personal interests in occupations and hobbies stimulate greater attention in objects and events that may be peculiar to those particular interests. Compare the number of errors you see in a police movie or television show with the observations of your nonpolice friends.

Experience and Education. The witness's conditioning to certain observation experiences through learning help him to perceive, remember, and communicate his observations and impressions. Conversely, a lack of experience or training may cause problems in communications, such as difficulty in interpreting what was seen into meaningful symbols and expressions. There may be a language barrier.

Prejudice or Bias. Most people tend to see what they want to see. Strong feelings toward or against an object tend to influence the amount of attention one pays to any particular event or object. In his role as the collector of information from the witnesses, the officer's task is not to change such attitudes, but to be aware of them and their effect on the ability of the witnesses to recount a reasonably accurate and objective picture of what actually took place.

Point of View.   When considering the statements of witnesses, ask yourself this question: Could they actually have observed what they say they have seen from their respective vantage points? Some well-meaning people may actually be lacking bits of information and will sometimes fill in the gaps with what they *believe* happened rather than what they *saw.* All people see things through different sets of eyes and experiences, interpret with different combinations of interpretation processes, and then communicate differently using their own unique methods of conveying thoughts and ideas. Your function is to coordinate all these bits of information and interpret them into terms that are meaningful to your superiors, to the prosecuting attorney, and to the courts to assure the accused of due process of the law.

Moods Affected by Color.   In the July 1982 issue of the *Reader's Digest*, Lowell Ponte reports:

> *According to Swiss psychologist Max Lüscher, lecturer at the University for Artistic and Industrial Design at Linz, Austria...colors arouse specific feelings in people. Blue conveys peace and contentment, but those who favor dark blue are motivated by a need for security. Blue is widely used in the symbols of banks and automobile manufacturers. Yellow, says Lüscher, is associated...with modernity, achievement, and the future. Red conjures up power, an urge to win, vitality...Green and red together stir feelings of strength, reliability and incorruptibility. Greenish-blue invokes a sense of security and self-esteem.*[2]

Ponte further points out that in some tests violent prisoners were put in pink cells. The results showed that a particular shade of pink was "sufficient to tranquilize and to replace aggressive impulses with passivity." Exposure to blue serves as an antidote in that the blue color tends to restore the power drained from the person when in the pink room.[3]

Memory   Bower[4] reported that in one of his studies he found that a person in a sad mood recalls more accurately and vividly their sad experiences and when in a happy mood they recall a greater amount of their happy experiences. If that proves to be true, then it will tend to show that recall will possibly be better if the person at the time of recounting an experience is in a mood similar to that at the time of the experience.

[2]Lowell Ponte, "How Color Affects Your Moods and Health," *Reader's Digest*, July 1982, p. 96.
[3]Ibid.
[4]Gordon H. Bower, "Mood and Memory," *Psychology Today*, June 1981, p. 60.

Returning the witness to the scene of the crime may stimulate both the mood and the memory.

James McGough reported[5] that massive amounts of the hormones epinephrine and norepinephrine "released by the adrenal medulla when the body is excited...appear to enhance the organism's ability to remember." He also reports that memory can also be impaired by drugs, such as amphetamines. Elizabeth Loftus, a psychologist at the University of Washington at Seattle, reports that "booze and pot seem to affect information storage more than retrieval." That is, memory may work well at the time, but some things that occur while a person is under the influence may not be recalled. Senility works in a similar way, eroding ability to store new information.[6]

In the Leo article, he points out other findings made by Loftus:

> *[Loftus] has a sobering message for grownups: their memories are almost as unreliable as children's—so encrusted with experiences, desires, and suggestions that they often resemble fiction as much as fact. In* Eyewitness Testimony *[a book by Loftus],...Loftus made a strong case against the reliability of remembrances of court witnesses. In* Memory *[another Loftus work],...she indicts human recollections in general.*[7]

Leo continues:

> *One problem with many, says Loftus, is that people do not observe well in the first place....People forget some facts and "refabricate" the gaps between the ones they do not remember accurately; they tend to adjust memory to suit their picture of the world....We fill in the gaps in our memory using chains of events that are logically acceptable....Our biases, expectations, and past knowledge are all used in the filling-in process, leading to distortion in what we remember.*[8]

Benderly discusses a phenomenon known as the "flashbulb memory." He states:

> *They are simply there, ready to appear in stunning detail at the merest hint. It's as if our nervous system took a multimedia snapshot of the sounds, sights, smells, weather, emotional climate, even the body postures we experience at certain moments.*
>
> *We remember the exact look, sound, and feel of a traffic acci-*

[5]James L. McGough, "Adrenalin: A Secret Agent in Memory," *Psychology Today*, December 1980, p. 132.

[6]John Leo, "Memory, the Unreliable Witness," *Time*, January 5, 1981, p. 89.

[7]Ibid.

[8]Ibid.

dent, the midnight phone call bringing word of a loved one's death; the voice, manner, and surroundings of the doctors who broke the news of a serious illness, the fleeting twinge of pain that appears on a president's face as he is hit by an assassin's bullet and just before he is pushed to the floor of the limousine by a bodyguard.[9]

According to Benderly, a University of California, San Diego, professor of neuroscience, Robert Livingston, in the late 1960s called this phenomenon "print now" and later changed the term to "now store," as if by a computer.[10] Livingston stated that two criteria determine such a response: (1) novelty and (2) biological significance. If a highly novel event were accompanied by pain and sorrow or some other strong emotion, then the event would be instantly stored.

Benderly states: "The contents of the flashbulb accounts, although apparently random, fall into a handful of categories—place, ongoing event, informant, affect in self, and affect in others—and a residual category of unclassifiable information, such as the weather, the brand of cigarettes just lit up, or the color of a garment.[11] This may explain the problem we sometimes run across when a witness can vividly recall certain events relevant to the crime but has no memory whatever of other events that occurred at the same time.

In personal discussions with memory specialists, I have been told that the sense of smell corresponds closely with one's emotions, and that once you smell something and identify it, you will probably always remember it. For example, the narcotics officer will describe the odor of burning marijuana as "distinctive, like nothing else." Animals and babies find their mothers by using their sense of smell. Since the visual process takes up a large portion of the brain, you are more apt to remember a person's face long after you have forgotten the name. Memory may also be enhanced by involving as many senses as possible, such as by repeating a name out loud, by writing it down, and by looking at the person while using his or her name as often as you can during the conversation.

Forgetting   On the down side of memory is the process of not remembering, or forgetting. Consider these factors in the process:

1. *Passive decay.* This is the "use it or lose it" theory. The information is stored in the memory, but it must be "called up" once in a while. Did you at one time speak a foreign language fairly fluently, and now remember just a few words and phrases? If you want to remember a specific investigation, go back to your reports and review them occasionally.

---

[9]Beryl Lieff Benderly, "Flashbulb Memory," *Psychology Today*, June 1981, p. 71.

[10]Ibid., p. 72.

[11]Ibid., p. 74.

2. *Interference.* The filtering process in remembering can get clogged up by having too many types of input at the same time. Try watching a basketball game while you are studying for a promotional exam and carrying on a conversation with several members of your family.

3. *Storage failure.* For some reason you might have simply forgotten because the event did not get stored, such as a name you did not quite hear and which you did not ask to have repeated.

4. *Amnesia.* This is a medical and/or psychological problem.

5. *Repression.* You might not want to remember the event. It may be something you have done that is out of character, or does not meet your self-image requirements. We sometimes block out very undesirable events.

6. *Motivated forgetting.* Did you ever forget an appointment with a dentist? Sometimes you may say "I have a bad memory for names," or "I know I am going to forget this." Then you do forget them, don't you?

7. *Distortion.* The filtering process involves your prejudices and various other emotions that edit what you remember, and you forget the rest. Everyone's filter is different, and it involves morals, ethics, culture, and many other elements of individual personality.

8. *Chemical interference.* Alcohol, antihistamines, blood pressure medicines, and many other substances contribute to the process of forgetting.

DESCRIPTIONS OF PERSONS

Standard formats have been established and are in general use for the purpose of communicating brief but accurate messages regarding descriptions of people and property. When asking a witness to describe an individual, it is usually a good procedure to ask the person to first describe something about the suspect that "stood out" or to recall some similarity between the suspect and anyone that the witness knows. This technique calls into play the witness's ability to recognize objects that are familiar. After having recalled the familiar features, go back and obtain as much detailed description as possible, using the following format and the outline given in Figure 3–1.

1. *Name, if known.* Include the nickname or "monicker." List also all aliases or "aka" (also known as). Include first, middle, last name, plus any additional designation, such as Jr. or III.

2. *Sex.*

3. *Race and nationality descent, if known.* "W" for Caucasian, "N" for Negro, "O" for Oriental. Except when representatives of other racial origins are indigenous to the area, spell out the origin to avoid misun-

1. **Name**
2. **Sex**
3. **Race**
4. **Age**
5. **Height**
6. **Weight**
7. **Hair**
8. **Eyes**
9. **Complexion**
10. **Physical marks, scars, other identifying characteristics**
11. **Clothing**
    a. **Hat or cap**
    b. **Shirt and tie**
    c. **Jacket or coat**
    d. **Dress or trousers**
    e. **Shoes**
    f. **Jewelry**
       (1) **Ring**
       (2) **Watch**

Figure 3–1   Standard descriptions of persons.

derstanding. The nationality descent tends to reduce the field of suspects by identifying hair and eye color and certain similarities in facial features, and it should be used when known.

4. *Age*. Either an estimate or exact age, if known. If such information is available, list date of birth.

5. *Height*. Exact, if known. A male suspect is short if he is less than 5'6", medium if 5'6" to 5'10", and tall if over 5'10". Women are short if less than 5'2", medium if 5'2" to 5'6", and tall if over 5'6". Victims and witnesses will usually overestimate height.

6. *Weight*. Men are light up to about 150 lb, medium if from 150 to 180 lb, and heavy if over 180 lb. The weight and height ratio largely determines the body build. Women are similarly classified. In addition to the approximate weight, indicate whether "slim," "stocky," or other general build.

7. *Hair.* Color, type of hair style, length, and any baldness.

8. *Eyes.* Color, shape if other than Caucasian configuration, and any distinctive characteristics.

9. *Complexion.* Color and shade, plus any other characteristics, such as freckles, pock-marks, acne, birthmarks, blotches, suntan or burn, skin grafts.

10. *All other features and accessories.* Describe facial hair and side-burns, unusual shape or appearance of some facial feature, any disfigurement, scars, marks, or visible tattoos. Include any unusu-al characteristics about any other visible part of the body.

11. *Eyeglasses and jewelry, if any.* Although eyeglasses may be worn as a partial disguise, the wearer may be required to wear them. Look for any distinctive characteristics about them, such as extra thickness or unusual appearance caused by the way they are ground.

12. *Clothing worn.* Start at the top and work down in the following order: headgear, shirt, tie, jacket, coat, dress or trousers, shoes and socks. Include style, color, material, and any characteristics that will identify the clothing article. On headgear, indicate whether it is a hat, cap, uniform cap, helmet, beret, or scarf. The necktie is usually most distinctive and the shape, style, design, and colors should all be described. The shirt should be described by color and style, such as sport, dress, uniform, and the material should be given if it can be determined. On the coat and trousers, or dress, describe the material, design, and the colors. Sweaters or other overwear are quite distinctive and can often be described in detail. Shoe style and color should be indicated, if known, also any heel pattern, if known, for possible surface prints.

13. *Personal characteristics.* Anything about the subject that will tend to distinguish him from any other person should be listed, such as a speech impediment or accent, or a distinctive tonal quality or pitch of the voice. Note any habits or unconscious movements he may be making, such as twitching, chewing fingernails, scratching the face, cracking knuckles, whistling, making unusual sounds with the teeth, picking at any part of the body or clothing, and generally any other observation about the individual that would aid in later identifying him.

EYEWITNESS IDENTIFICATION

There are essentially three types of lineups commonly used by the field officer: the field identification, the photograph identification, and the for-mal in-station lineup. Each of them has its special place in the process.

Field Identification

A primary consideration when using this method of identification is fairness to the individual whom you are holding for the possible identification. Immediately following any type of crime, when the suspect is probably still nearby, you will search for the suspect. The instant the broadcast is sent out, or immediately following your notification that a suspect is wanted, you will be operating on very vague and uncertain descriptions of the suspect. For a short time until witnesses have been more thoroughly interviewed and a better description is known, virtually anyone you encounter in the proximity and who could logically be a suspect should fall within your scrutiny. In some cases, you will have the true culprit; in others you will have an innocent person whose only relationship to the crime is that he or she just happens to be at a location where a suspect might logically be found.

For the field identification, or "showup," always bring the witness to the location where you are holding the suspect to be identified unless (1) you are sure that there is probable cause to make an arrest without the identification, or (2) the suspect validly consents to the movement to where the witness is, or (3) there is some compelling practical reason why you cannot move the witness to the suspect's location. Your witness may be bedridden or injured, for example.

This one-to-one confrontation is automatically suggestive to the witness because of the fact that the person shown to the witness is in police custody and there is only one person to look at. Despite this problem, the courts make an exception to the general rules concerning line-ups because the field show-up is held within a reasonable time following the crime—not more than one or two hours at the most. and the witness has the suspect's image clearly in mind. The person who is not identified as the suspect is free to go immediately, and the investigation can continue so that the true culprit may be found.

Unless it is necessary for security reasons, do not have the subject to be identified in handcuffs, as it implies that you have more information than you do and the witness might feel compelled to make a positive identification even though he or she is really not sure about the person being presented. If you had probable cause to detain the subject, you no doubt had cause to perform a cursory patdown for weapons, and restraining devices might not be necessary at this point.

Be careful to avoid making the showup too suggestive. Consider the competence of the witness, the circumstances under which the witness observed the suspect, the accuracy of the witness's description, the certainty of the witness in making identification at the showup, and your own conduct at the showup. Never tell the witness that you have caught the right person, that contraband was found, or that the person to be identified has made incriminating statements or a confession. Do not call the person you are showing to the witness the "suspect," and if there is a positive identification, do not state that he or she picked out the right person.

Be sure to tell the witness that he or she should keep an open mind and just because you brought the person to the place for an ID is in no way meant to suggest that the person is guilty. When the witness makes an identification or does not make an identification, follow the same reporting procedure as with a lineup.

When making a field identification, be sure to point out to the witness who is about to make the identification that you are not requiring that the person you have in custody be identified. Attempt to re-create the lighting and visibility as similar to the way they were at the time of the crime. If the witness observed the suspect in a dim light through a window, simulate the same situation for the identification. If the suspect and victim or witness were 15 feet apart, place them an equal distance for the field lineup. Be careful to keep them separated to avoid allowing the witness to make some sort of retaliatory attack on the person in custody in the event that you have the true suspect. At the same time, make your own personal observations and determine whether such an identification actually could have been made under those conditions. For example, at 50 yards at that time of day under those weather conditions, it may have been physically impossible to see a face of any color or shape clearly.

It must not be unnecessarily suggestive,[12] and it must be able to stand the scrutiny of the court afterward. One 1968 and two 1970 cases cited situations in which a "confrontation" or on-the-scene lineup can be performed. Those situations include (1) when the evidence is weak that you have the right person; (2) when several suspects have been collected, and there was only one perpetrator; (3) when a suspect is found near the crime scene within a reasonable time after its commission; (4) when it is necessary to take the suspect to the hospital if the victim witness is in danger of dying and might not live until a more formal lineup is arranged; and (5) when the subject is exhibited without restraints, if practicable, unless the person is combative or uncooperative.[13]

Photographic Identification

Armed with a description of a suspect, you may also have been able to locate other leads by checking the modus operandi file (covered in Chapter 5) and any other source for names of possible suspects. You may have known offender photo collections at your disposal or offender "mug" books. To have a fair selection process, you should have at least six photographs to show the witness. Follow these guidelines:

1. Use the most recent available photo of the suspect. If the suspect is in custody, take a photograph.

---

[12]*Stoval v. Denno*, 388 U.S. 293 (1967); *Gilbert v. California*, 388 U.S. 263 (1967); and *United States v. Wade*, 388 U.S. 218 (1967).

[13]*Bates v. United States*, 405 F.2d 1104 (1968); *Arizona v. Boens*, 8 Ariz. App. 110 (1970); and *Martin v. Virginia*, 7 Cr.L 2147 (1970).

2. Number each photograph by putting the number on the back, and make a list of all persons whose photos you are using. You must keep the photos and the list when an identification is made so that you can present the entire collection in court to show fairness.

3. The photographs shown to the witnesses should be selected to ensure fairness and impartiality to the suspect.

4. Fairness and impartiality of this means of identification depends on many circumstances. As much as practicable, select photographs using guidelines similar to those you would follow in selecting subjects for a formal in-person lineup. Be sure that there are several individuals depicted that have similar facial features, hair color and style, and skin texture and pigmentation. If your suspect is in a group photograph, be sure to include several other group photographs in the collection. Consider the possibility that the witness may be somewhat inaccurate in describing the suspect. In other words, just because the witness states that the suspect had a brown mustache and a mole on his nose does not mean that you should restrict the collection to men with brown mustaches and moles on their noses. Use common sense and be reasonable.

5. Have only one witness view the photographs separately from other witnesses. Do not let them discuss the photographs among themselves—if there is more than one witness—either before or after looking at the photographs.

6. Give these instructions to each witness (unless your own prosecuting attorney has a different set of instructions for you to use):

   I am going to show you (state the number) photographs. Please look at all of them carefully before making any comment about any one of them. The person who committed the crime may or may not be among those in the photographs you are about to see. If you recognize any of the persons in the photographs as the suspect, go back and pick out the person you recognize. If you recognize any of these photos, please do not ask me whether your choice was "right" or "wrong," as I am prohibited by law from telling you.

7. Explain to the witnesses that

   a. Their judgment should not be influenced just by the fact that you are showing photographs.
   b. There should be no inference that the suspect they are looking for will necessarily be among those in the pictures.
   c. There is no obligation to identify anyone from the photos presented for their viewing.

> **d.** It is just as important to clear the innocent who are suspected of crime as it is to identify and convict the guilty.
> **8.** If the witness picks out a photo, have the witness initial the back of the photo, and place your initial alongside.
> **9.** Regardless of which photo the witness chooses, do not discuss the choice with the witness.
> **10.** Place all photos in evidence, and handle as any other item of evidence.
> **11.** When you have several witnesses and one or two of them are able to make positive identifications from the photographs, consider discontinuing the photograph identification phase and have the other witnesses make their selection from the in-person lineup. Whenever you have a physical lineup following a photographic identification, there is always the danger that the witness will identify the suspect from having seen his or her photograph instead of remembering the person from the scene of the crime.

The Lineup

The lineup is the more formal method of identifying a suspect. Although the witnesses should be reminded that just because a person is being displayed, it is not an accusation or a statement that he or she is guilty of any crime. Some people are put through a lineup following an arrest when they were discovered in possession of the loot from a robbery or some other evidence that substantially ties them in with the crime in question. The person may already have been tentatively identified in a field showup or in a photo lineup, or perhaps recognized by an officer with the aid of a composite sketch or videotape taken at the time of the crime. While the *Miranda* rule applies when it involves questioning, a person may or may not have the right to the presence of an attorney during a lineup.

There is some variance from state to state and in the federal rule. In the 1967 *Wade* case[14] a person was arrested and charged with robbery. The court ruled that because he had been charged, Wade was entitled to the presence of an attorney during the lineup. In 1972, the U.S. Supreme Court ruled in *Kirby*[15] that the accused has a right to an attorney only if the lineup occurs *after* formal charges have been filed. But, they added, such presence does not entitle the attorney to do anything but observe.

A suspect may not refuse to stand in a lineup, nor can he or she refuse to speak words or phrases for voice identification, or wear certain articles of clothing, put on a wig, walk, or show tattoos on his or her body,

---

[14]*United States* v. *Wade,* 388 U.S. 218, 87 S. Ct. 1926 (1967).

[15]*Kirby* v. *Illinois,* 406 U.S. 682, S. Ct. 1877 (1972).

provided that the lineup is fair and free of overzealousness on the part of the police. In *Simmons* v. *United States*,[16] the Court stated: A violation of due process occurs if the pretrial identification procedure is "so impermissibly suggestive as to give rise to a very substantial likelihood of irreparable misidentification." It is a violation of the 5th and 14th Amendments to suggest in *any way* to a witness that the suspect to be observed in a lineup or showup is guilty of anything.

Prior to conducting the lineup you must decide whether or not to advise the person of his or her right to have an attorney present, depending on your own state's current requirements. If the person does have an attorney there to observe, you should have a prosecuting attorney or department attorney present to represent the state's interests. You may have a printed form for the suspect to sign, waiving the right to an attorney. The top part of the form would read as follows: "You will be placed in a lineup for identification purposes. You may not refuse to participate in the lineup. You have the right to have an attorney present during the lineup to observe the proceedings. If you cannot afford an attorney and want one, a lawyer will be provided you without cost." The waiver portion would read as follows: "I have read the above statement and am fully aware of my rights. I do not desire the presence of an attorney for the lineup. This statement is signed of my own free will, without any promises or threats being made to me." It would then be signed, dated, and witnessed by you or a disinterested third party, if available.

The lineup procedure should be approximately as follows to assure fairness and effectiveness:

1. At least six persons, including the suspect, should be included.
2. Advise the suspect that any type of noncooperation may be commented on in court as an indication of guilt.
3. All persons should be of the same sex, same general coloring, same racial characteristics, and about the same age. Height, weight, skin color, and hair color should be reasonably close to that of the subject as described. Take into account the possibility that there will be some variance between actual appearance and the description provided by the witness. A suspect described as being of Latin origin might have actually been a dark-haired person of Irish descent.
4. The suspect should choose where in the lineup to stand.
5. All persons in the lineup should be dressed similarly. A suspect in a light-gray three-piece business suit with red necktie should not be in a lineup where everyone else is wearing open-collar knit sports shirts.
6. All persons in the lineup must be strangers to the witness if the suspect had been described as a stranger.

[16]*Simmons* v. *United States*, 390 U.S. 377 (1968).

7. Attempts should be made to duplicate the lighting, visibility, and relative distances between witness and suspect as much as possible to recapture the identification problems as they existed at the scene.

8. Witnesses should be kept separate from each other and not be allowed to compare notes or arrive at a "jury decision" in the identification.

9. Subjects in the lineup should be required to make the same statements, put on the same jacket, and act the same as the others.

10. Make a photographic or videotaped record of the lineup in case of later charges of improper conduct or unfairness.

11. Interview each witness carefully following the lineup, particularly if a positive identification is made, and make a complete report on the interview. Comments such as "I vividly remember that look in his eyes" or "I couldn't mistake that triangular shaped scar on his chin and the little red birthmark beneath the left ear" tend to validate the identification.

12. Keep a list of all participants in the lineup and all other persons present during the event. This will come out later during the trial when laying the groundwork to introduce the results of the lineup.

Always tell the witnesses who are about to observe the lineup (remember that each witness does this as a solo effort):

1. To keep an open mind
2. That the person who committed the crime may or may not be among those present
3. That just because the person is in custody does not mean that he or she is guilty of a crime
4. Not to discuss the identification with any other witness

Never tell the witness:

1. That you have caught the person who committed the crime or whom you believe to have committed it
2. That the suspect had the victim's property in his or her possession
3. That the suspect had made confessions or admissions
4. That the persons to be observed in the lineup are suspects

STANDARD FORMULA FOR DESCRIBING PROPERTY

Many people in law enforcement and its related agencies have devoted considerable time and effort to developing a uniform method for describing property. The following material represents some of their work toward establishing such uniformity. For maximum results in the effort to return stolen property to its owner, the formula presented here should be followed as closely as possible when preparing reports, teletypes, and in any other way describing lost, stolen, pawned, purchased, or sold property.

Number of the article in the list. In each itemized list, use a numbering system to facilitate references to a specific item for teletypes or correspondence.

Quantity of the article. For example,

Interesting Categories [handwritten annotation]

   (3) watches...

   (1) television set...

Kind of article

   Watch (or ring, or tire, or...)

   For whom or for what purpose the article is designed. For example:

     watch, man's (or woman's or child's)

     saw, keyhole

     tire, bicycle

   Trade name and manufacturer

Identifying serial and model numbers

Material or type of metal. For example, yellow metal. Indicate the kind of metal claimed by the victim, such as "WM, platinum claimed." The officer's report does not verify the actual material or its value. His report merely reflects the claims and statements of the victim.

   Gold

     Solid gold is 24-carat gold. Carat, when used to describe gold, is a unit of quality. In 24 carats of gold, there are 24 grains of gold to the pennyweight.

     Filled gold and *rolled gold* are both veneers of gold on a base metal. The processes involved in applying the gold are the same, however, the gold used on a filled gold article is of greater carat value than that used on a rolled gold article. A filled gold article has gold of 0.03 carat or more, and a rolled gold article has gold of 0.015 to 0.03 carat.

     Gold-plated or *gold-washed* articles are electroplated with gold of below 0.015-carat value.

   Other metals or minerals

In the case of jewels, follow the same procedure: red stone, green stone. Indicate the kind of stone claimed by the victim. Diamonds are designated as white stones.

Other materials. It is necessary to question the victim closely to get the correct material.

"Silk" may be rayon, bemberg, taffeta, pongee, shantung, satin, crepe, or nylon.

"Leather" may be artificial leatherette, cowhide, horsehide, sealskin, ostrich, alligator, snakeskin, calfskin, or a number of others.

"Wool" may be all wool, half wool, virgin wool, or reclaimed wool.

Physical description.

Model, size, shape, color, pattern, measurements, style

A picture of the article from a catalog or from advertising material is useful.

A sketch of the article may be drawn by the victim.

Clothing size may be determined from the owner's height, weight, and build.

Identifying marks

These include *initials, marks put on by the owner, dents, scratches, and damage repairs.*

In the case of watches when the numbers are known to the owner, find out what jeweler last repaired the watch. If it has never been repaired, find out where and when it was purchased and whether it was bought on credit. Every jeweler keeps a record book of the work he has done. In the book will be found the date the work was done, a description of the watch, the owner's name and address, the watch case and movement numbers, and the jeweler's own number. If the watch has never been repaired the dealer may have a record of its sale.

Flat silver, or *table silver,* has a pattern name. Specify which company made the set, since there are duplications of names among the various lines. List whether the set is sterling or plate. If the silver was in a chest or box, include a complete description of it as well.

Silver services, silver dishes, and *silver trays* have a number on the bottom and usually a hallmark or trademark. Their patterns will also have a name.

Expensive jewelry will often have a jeweler's scratch mark.

Age and condition

When purchased, whether new or used when purchased

State of repair

Shabby, dirty, worn, mended, patched, clean, new

Market value. The current market value should be determined by an expert in the values of the specific items stolen. The value may distinguish the difference between petty or grand theft.

Order for Listing Items in the Report

1. Articles bearing numbers
2. Articles bearing initials or personal marks
3. Articles bearing identifying marks
4. Articles bearing identifying characteristics
5. Articles without market value

DETAILED DESCRIPTIONS OF COMMONLY STOLEN ITEMS

Jewelry

Novelty Jewelry.   Figures, charms, scatterpins, bracelets, necklaces, rings, etc. Of little value, usually gaudy and set with cheap rhinestones of various colors.

Costume Jewelry.   Generally the same as for novelty jewelry except that the material and workmanship are better and the value is somewhat greater.

Jewelry Such As:

Pins

Breastpins or brooches
Lapel pins
Scatterpins

Clips

Same as for pins, but clip-on rather than pin-on
May be in sets with earrings, necklaces, and/or bracelets

Earrings

Kinds:

Clip
Screw; may be for pierced ears
Hoop; may be for pierced ears

Styles:

Teardrop
Dangle
Petal
Button
Novelty

Cuff buttons, cuff links, and studs

Note difference between cuff links and cuff buttons

Necklaces

Kinds:

Chain (size and design of links)
Snake
Lariat
Pearl (simulated, cultured, seed)
Crystal (artificial, tin cut, rock)
Stones (artificial, synthetic, genuine); note number of stones and space between stones.

Number of strands and length:

Knotted
Choker

Lavalieres (on necklace)

Lockets

On chain, fob, pin, or bracelet

Bracelets

Kinds:

Expansion
Link
Bangle

Settings:

How mounted
Distance between sets
Number of sets
Kind and color of sets

Rings

Parts: shank, mounting, and set
Size

Engraving:

Outside and inside
Trademark and carat designation inside
Scratch marks

Kinds:

Men's, women's, baby's
Emblem (lodge, fraternity, class, school)

Signet (initials and type of letters)
Dinner rings
>   Number, kind, and size of settings
>   Baguettes, chip and cut stones
>   Ornamental colored stones

Wedding rings
Width, engraving inside and out

Styles:

Diamond (how many, size, and spacing)
Antique
Modern
Unusual (chain or two that fit together)

Mountings:

Belcher: an old-type mounting, 8 to 12 prongs, deeply scalloped
Bezel: may extend all around or be on corners or sides only
Gypsy: set directly into ring with bezel
Tiffany: set high on 6 or 8 prongs; named after jeweler who designed it
Claw: any prong set other than Tiffany
Basket: filigree work around the stone

Settings:

Diamonds
>   Color
>   Shapes and cuts
>>   Size has no bearing; may be small, decorative, or the large main stone
>   Facets
>>   58 on brilliant, round full cut, emerald cut marquise
>>   24 to 32 on Swiss cut
>>   18 on single cut
>   Chips
>>   Just what the name implies
>>   Used for decoration

Cameos and intaglios

Cameo is a carved, raised figure, usually a head; intaglio is a figure carved into a stone

Cameos and intaglios are used in earrings, pins, fobs, and cuff links, as well as in rings

Birthstones and other colored stones:

Garnet, amethyst, bloodstone, aquamarine, emerald, moonstone, ruby
May be genuine, synthetic, or artificial.

Gemstone cuts (see Figure 3–2):

Cabochon cuts have a domed top of either high or low curvature, and the base may be the duplicate of the top or it may be concave shaped, or any cut between. This cut is used for emeralds, rubies, sapphires, opals, turquoise, starstones, cat's eyes, and other precious stones.

Rose cuts have a flat base with triangular facets, either 12 or 24, terminating in a point. Small diamonds and pyrope garnets use this cut.

Brilliant cut is the most common cut for the diamond. It has 58

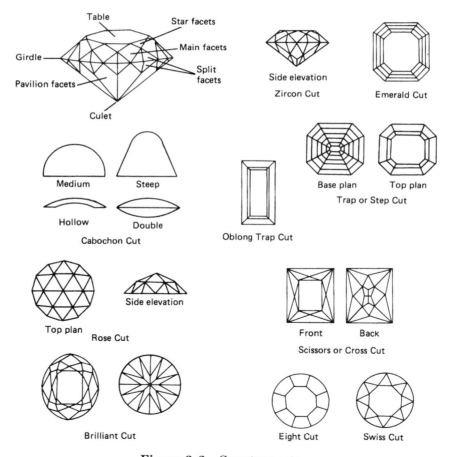

Figure 3–2   Gemstone cuts

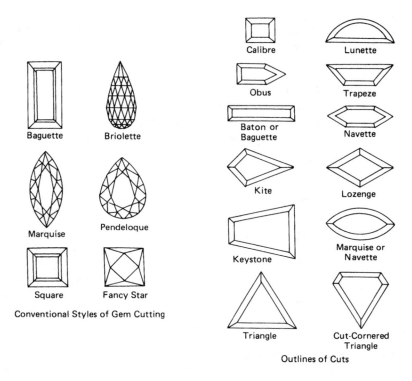

Conventional Styles of Gem Cutting

Outlines of Cuts

Figure 3–2   Gemstone cuts (*Continued*)

facets, with 33 above the girdle and 25 below. The Marquise
and Pendeloque are variations of the brilliant cut.

Zircon cut is similar to the brilliant cut with more facets on the
lower portion of the stone.

Briolette is an oval- or pear-shaped diamond with its entire
surface cut in triangular or rectangular facets.

Step, trap, or emerald cut are cut according to a plan shape of
square, oblong, or baguette and have a series of rectangular
facets arranged parallel to the girdle.

Scissors or cross cut is similar to the step cut with the exception that the side facets are made up of four or more traan-
gular facets.

Other cuts include the kite, lozenge, triangle, and obus.

Clothing

Suits: Women's and Men's.   Women's tailored suits and coats have the
same general identifying characteristics as men's suits and overcoats. The

word "tailored," when applied to any article of women's wear, **means** plain, or without decoration. Men's suits come in three lengths—short, medium, and long—plus a size number. For instance, size 40 will be found in short, medium, and long.

Color and material

Be as exact in color as possible.

Get a description of any pattern in the weave.

Whipcord, serge, gabardine, flannel, tweed, broadcloth. Most other materials are known as worsted.

Labels

Manufacturer's inside of inside coat pocket.

Retailer's outside of inside coat pocket or at nape of neck.

In women's suits and coats, the labels may be any place, so the location would be an identifying feature if it was out of the ordinary. Women's skirts sometimes have labels also.

Tailor-made frequently has the owner's name or initials on the inner coat pocket. Also, many tailors and furriers have the customer sign the inner lining of the coat near the front; it is necessary to loosen the lining to see the name.

Coats (Suit Coats, Overcoats, Topcoats). *There is a difference between a coat and a jacket. Retailers have fallen into the habit of advertising sport coats as sport "jackets." The difference between a coat and a jacket is that the latter is of waist length. Casual or leisure coats are also erroneously referred to as jackets.*

Single or double breasted

Number of buttons

Lapels

Peaked, semipeaked, and notched; wing on women's coats

Cardigan (on men's sport coats and women's suit and top coats)

Shawl (on tuxedos)

Buttonholes in one or both lapels

Pockets

Patch or inset; with or without flaps or piped

Extra cash pocket

Number and locations of inside pockets

Lining

Color and type of material

Full-, half-, or quarter-lined

Back

Box (with or without seam)

Conservative (slightly form-fitting)

Form-fitting

Drape (extremely form-fitting)

Lounge (hangs from shoulders to hips, where it is snug. Wedge-shaped, not form-fitting at waist)

Sport back (half belt with pleats; may or may not have "free swing" or vent; may have two vents)

Stitched or welted edge

Trousers, Men's and Women's Slacks. *Men's trousers and women's tailored slacks, in many cases, are similar even to the front fly.*

Waistband

Regular, with waistband and belt loops at the top

Drop belt loops, with waistband and belt loops, one end of loop on waistband and the other end below

French waistband, with no visible waistband and belt loops below top of trousers

Extended waistband, with waistband continued beyond fly and buttoned

Cuff (or none)

Pleats (number and whether turned in or out)

Men's overcoats, women's tailored topcoats. *Same as suit coats as far as lapels, pockets, linings, single and double breasted are concerned, but with the following additions:*

Slash pockets

Collar (wing lapels, cardigan)

Sleeves

Split

Cuff (adjustable cuff tabs)

Leg-of-mutton (women's only) fitted to elbow or all the way.

1-inch length of sleeves (i.e., short, elbow, three-quarter, or long)

Trim (women's only)

Different material or color from rest of coat, or fur

Collar, cuffs, bottom, tuxedo

Pleats, front or back

Length

Rarely important in men's coats; however, women's coats come in full, three-quarter, fingertip, shortie, jacket, and cape

Fit

Wrap-around in both men's and women's
Flared, in women's only
Full, or "new look," in women's only

Fly front

Vent

Removable lining, zipper or button

Reversible

Raglan shoulders

Hang from shoulders; usually have split sleeves and slash pockets

Chesterfield

Women's Clothes Generally

Size

Labels

Material

Kind
Color (figured, colors and design of figure)

Trim

Color
Buttons
Braid or piping
Embroidery or cut work

Skirts

May be part of a suit
Length
Fit (flared, full, or tailored)
Slashed or slitted (location and length of slit)
Pockets
Number of panels or gores

Jackets, Men's. Waist-length coats. Although a type of man's coat is advertised as a sport jacket, for the purpose of description of property, it should be referred to as a sport coat.

Size

Material

Gabardine, melton, leather (kind)

Color and design of weave

Pockets

Number of (inside and outside)

Kind

Slash, inset, patch, muff type, flap
Fastenings (zipper and button)

Front fastenings (zipper or button)

Collar

Knitted, also cuffs as in leather jackets
Fur, pile
Lapels
Detachable
Parka hood

Lining

Color
Rayon, quilted, sheepskin, blanket

Back

Plain, half-belt, swing shoulders

Sweaters

Man's, woman's, child's (size)

Coat (button or zipper)

Pullover

Neck (crew neck, turtle neck, V neck, roll collar)

Sleeve or sleeveless

Furs. Furs are hard to recover because their appearance can be easily altered. It is necessary to get as complete a description of the piece as possible. Furs are seldom pawned; they are more often sold in the street, in bars, in houses of prostitution, or flown to another part of the country to be sold on consignment.

Kinds:

Generally the name of the animal, but may have a more exotic name to correspond with the price.

Color (dyed or natural)

Lining

Material: dull or shiny, color, bindings or pockets
Pockets

Labels

Wear and repairs

If custom-made or if ever repaired, the owner might have written her name on reverse of skin.

Length

Measured from bottom of collar down back

Three-quarter, fingertip, chubby

Fasteners

Frogs (size)

Hook and eye (size)

Buttons (kind and size)

Snaps (number and size)

If a neckpiece, number of skins

    Heads and/or tails sewn on

    Fasteners

Any repairs, and what furrier used

Hosiery

Kinds:

Brand-new or used

Thigh length

Panty hose

Material

Silk, nylon, rayon, silk and wool, wool

Size

Foot size

Length

Weight

Sheer, medium weight, service weight

Runproof weave (denier or gauge)

Color (clocks or heel decoration)

Cotton tops and/or feet

Support hose

Men's Shirts

Color, pattern, brand, collar style

With or without collars

Size

Collar and sleeve length

Sport shirts come in small, medium, and large

Kind:

Sport, dress, work, cowboy

Material

Cotton, wool, rayon, rayon-gabardine, nylon
Oxford weave

Buttons

Number on cuffs if more than one, as on cowboy shirts
Buttondown collar
Number of buttons down front

Pockets

Number
With or without flaps

Cuffs

Regular
For cuff links (both collar attached and without collar)
French cuffs

Handbags

Style

Women's handbags are of five basic styles: pouch, box, envelope, underarm, shoulder strap
Frame

Handles

Pannier and double pannier, cuff, wrist, plastic, chain

Fasteners

Zipper, turn lock, lift lock, snap lock

Material

Leather

Patent leather, suede, sealskin, ostrich, calfskin, cowhide (any of which might be imitation)
Plastic (may look like patent leather or enamel)
Cloth
Corde, petit point, moire, knitted, metal mesh

Reptile

Alligator, lizard, snake

Inside

Lining (material and color)

Label
Number of divisions
Attached or loose coin purse and / or mirror
Accessories (comb, lighter, lipstick, lipstick holder, address book)

Contents

Complete list

Radios and Televisions

Kind (portable, table model, etc.)
Brand
Dials

Horizontal or vertical slot
Round
Slide
Half-circle

Bands

AM, FM
Short wave, stereo

Number of control knobs
Color and material of case

Measurements

Phonograph
Television

Size of screen
Control knobs
Description of case and cabinet
Portable, console, table
Serial numbers (do not confuse with model numbers)

On small radios and television sets, the serial number is usually inside, out of sight, and on the outside of the carton.

Tools

Tools are frequently the objects of theft. Since there are so many kinds, types, and manufacturers, it is necessary to depend upon the victim for details.

Private marks
Damage
Description of the chest or box if one was taken, and of the tools inside
Serial numbers on certain tools

Electrically operated tools

Luggage

Suitcases
Gladstone (suitcase-size bag that opens flat)
Club bag (box bottom with top the apex of a triangle; closed with zipper or locks)
Two-suiter
Weekend case (may be fitted)
Fortnighter (small trunk carried like a suitcase)

Describe inside
Lining and color
Number of partitions, pockets

Material
Top-grain cowhide, split cowhide, rawhide, plastic, canvas

Handles and fasteners

Trunks
Foot lockers (with or without tray)
Steamer or wardrobe trunk (number of hangers, drawers)
Box trunk
Describe material, inside, fasteners

Briefcases and brief bags
Describe material
With or without straps
Single or double handles
Fasteners
Number of compartments

Cameras

Two numbers appear on the more valuable cameras, one on the lens and one on the camera itself. Camera lenses are interchangeable. Speed of the lens is important. Owner's description is usually dependable.

Binoculars

Power and size. First number indicates magnification and the second number indicates the size of the lens in millimeters (8 × 30).

Type of focusing (central or single eye)

Hinged or solid bridge

Barrels (length and covering material)

Coated lenses

Carrying case

Firearms

Make, caliber, and serial number
Hidden numbers and parts' numbers
Foreign guns without serial numbers; also have proofmarks as a rule
Complete description

Finish
Nickel-plated
Blue
Anodized
Rough or sandblasted

Length of barrel

Grips
Material and color

Condition
Marks
Damage
Repairs
Signs of wear

Loaded or unloaded

Where and when purchased

Musical Instruments

Kind, make, and serial number

Pitch. Most wind instruments are made in varying pitch (e.g., saxophones are in C, E flat, B flat, tenor, and B-flat baritone; clarinets are in A, B flat, tenor, and bass). The same applies to many stringed instruments.

Finish
Brass, silver, or gold
Rough or sandblasted
Gold or brass with silver design or vice versa

; in the case

major topics. First, we studied some of servation and perception and the problems involved, including internalization of perceptions as well as the external factors. Because of the high degree of tentativeness in the qualifications and accuracy of the eyewitness, you must be extremely careful to validate any descriptions of suspects presented by witnesses and victims. The second topic was that of the identification process, be it in the field, by a photograph, or in the more formal in-station lineup. The key to accurate identification is to pay attention to the details and reasonableness in assuring yourself—and the courts eventually—that any positive identification of persons responsible for crimes be made in a fair and objective manner. The third topic was devoted to the actual process of identifying persons and property. Accurately describing items that have been stolen or people you are searching for will enhance your chances of successfully locating either one.

EXERCISES AND STUDY QUESTIONS

1. Describe some of the factors that make an eyewitness unreliable.
2. Considering the examples cited in the text as to who might better describe an item of jewelry or a person's false teeth, who would you expect to give a good description of a person's eyeglasses? make of an automobile? hair style? unusual looking facial feature?
3. What are the three basic requirements of a witness?
4. List and discuss at least five of the external factors that influence perception by a witness.
5. Which will appear to be larger—a blue object or a red one—considering the fact that they are actually the same size?
6. Of the perceptive senses of a witness, which one is considered the least reliable?

7. Can a trained witness distinguish between the odors of whiskey and beer?

8. Test yourself by choosing a dozen edible items. While blindfolded, identify each one by taste. Then identify each by odor. How did you do?

9. If you want to check out the perceptual ability of a witness, what would you do to make sure the witness actually did see an event under certain lighting and weather conditions, and from a specific distance?

10. List and discuss at least three internal factors that influence perception by a witness.

11. According to Ponte, what color would you paint a jail cell that holds violent prisoners?

12. What effect do alcohol and marijuana have on memory, if any?

13. Describe the phenomenon known as "flashbulb memory."

14. Give an example when such an event occurred in your lifetime that you vividly recall in precise detail.

15. When asking a witness to describe another person, which sequence would you follow?

16. What height is medium for a man? a woman?

17. List and describe the three types of lineups described in this chapter.

18. May an attorney legally advise a client not to take part in a lineup? May the client legally take the advice of the attorney and refuse to take part in such a lineup?

19. Describe the wristwatch you are wearing, if any; a ring, a necklace.

20. From memory, describe the following gem stone cuts: brilliant, emerald, cabochon, marquise, baguette.

21. Describe the clothing you are wearing.

22. Describe the clothing of a person of the opposite sex who is in your presence or whom you saw in person today.

23. Describe the television set that is in your living (or other) room.

24. Describe the various parts of a guitar, a trumpet, a sewing machine.

25. What wording would you use to describe a metal that appears to be gold? silver?

26. When you take a suspect to a witness for a full identification, describe how you would go about it and what instructions and/or advice you would give the witness.

4 COMMUNICATIONS PROCEDURES

INTRODUCTION

Some of the greatest strides in improvement in law enforcement have been made in the area of communications. Radio and cellular communications via the airwaves have made it possible for every officer to be in constant touch with headquarters. The cartoon character Dick Tracy and his wrist radio are now behind the times and no longer a futuristic pipe dream. Telephone lines now carry not only voice messages, but instantaneous reams of information from one computer to another, and facsimile can beam a copy of a warrant right into the field officer's car. No longer is it necessary to go off the air while checking an unusual circumstance or open door. Radio tracking also makes it possible to determine the exact location of the officer and /or the vehicle emitting a signal by radio. Not too many years ago, the lone police officer on the beat had no contact with fellow officers or the station except through signals tapped out on the pavement with a nightstick or a flashing light on top of the tallest building in town. Telephone, teletype, and radio communications have made it possible for police field activities to be carried out with increasingly greater efficiency over a larger geographical area.

In this chapter we study police communications from an operational standpoint, beginning with interpersonal communications and departmental administrative communications. We follow with a survey of the department's communications system and how it works. The balance of the chapter is devoted to guidelines for radio operation to ensure speedy and reliable communications.

INTERPERSONAL COMMUNICATIONS

Many of the problems in society today relate to our communicating with one another. Breakdowns in communications, or lack of communications, or misunderstandings in communications are the root of the breakdown of family, marital, social, and a variety of other relationships. As a police field officer, it is imperative that you develop the skills essential to communicate effectively with the people with whom you come in contact. If asked to rank order the skills necessary for effective performance of your job, this author would list the "ability to communicate effectively" at the top of the list.

Through various means of communications, we transmit information and ideas, we change behavior or convince or persuade others, and we generally interact socially. We transmit messages, and with luck, the receiver gets the same message that we sent. Your success in communicating will actually depend on how well your messages are received. We hear what we want to hear, and how we receive the message is influenced by our own interpretative system, which is influenced by our language skills, prejudices, fears, and various emotions as well as through the nonverbal communications that accompany the spoken word, such as facial expressions, gestures, movements, and posture.

Barriers to effective interpersonal communications are language, thinking processes influenced by life experiences, and negative reactions to body language. To overcome those barriers, you must develop a technique in encoding and decoding your messages in language that both you and the person you are communicating with agree upon as being the same. To accomplish that task, it will be necessary to establish some rapport prior to trying to convince or persuade. Look for the areas in verbal communications where there seem to be some difficulty and try to improve, but also devote some time and attention to the matter of body language, or language without the use of words.

In nonverbal communications you might be mouthing the words "I am interested in what you are saying," but your body language is saying "I'm not going to listen to you" or "I really don't care." Gestures indicating openness and a receptive attitude include open hands, unbuttoning or removing a jacket or coat, opening up the body by uncrossing the legs and leaning forward, or outstretching the arms and leaning back, similar to the trusting animal who will lie on his back and spread its legs so that you may rub its stomach. The defensive or nonreceptive person will cross the legs or fold the arms, or both, and physically assume the attitude of "closing up." The person with the folded arms will probably not take your advice. Finally, you are showing a position of authority and will shut off communications by rising to your full height and folding your arms, which means that you are in charge and that you are going to do the talking, not the listening.

People who are interested in each other's conversation look at each other, but not intently. Usually when you see two people gazing intensely at each other, they are more interested in each other than in what each one is saying, as when there is extreme anger or adulation. Depending on cultural differences, the person who looks at another person while telling the truth will avoid eye contact when on the defensive or when telling a lie or when trying to hide something.

Listening is one of the most important facets of the art of communicating. Many of us hear what another person says to us, but we are really not listening to what the person means by what he or she is saying, *how* the words are being spoken, and if there is a hidden agenda. Statements made with a smile and under the guise of feigned sarcasm may actually be hiding intense anger and hatred. Although people who say "I see what you are saying" may not actually understand the significance of that statement, spoken words are accompanied by body language that might reveal the true feelings behind the words.

Most people will look at you while listening to what you have to say, but may turn away and avoid your eyes when answering a question that embarrasses them or to which they are giving an evasive or false response. Sitting with a leg draped over a chair or sitting backwards in a chair with the back serving as a shield, the person may be displaying an attitude of competition or superiority.

Signs of frustration may be rubbing or scratching the hand, taking deep and short in–out breaths, sighing, kicking dirt or sand, making clucking sounds, or wringing of the hands. You can usually tell that a person is nervous when he or she is clearing the throat or locking dry lips, adjusting clothing or picking at imaginary lint, sighing, whistling, humming, or fidgeting. The nervous person may also be picking on the fingernails or picking up and putting down nearby objects for no apparent reason.

Is the person actually listening to you and considering what you have to say? If so, these are some of the signs you may see: hand goes to the cheek, strokes the chin or beard, toying with eyeglasses or other objects in the hand, or leaning back in the chair and putting the arms out on sidearms or back (opening up).

By carefully observing people while they are demonstrating certain emotional involvement, you may be able to determine when in your contact is the best time to shift to another phase in your conversation, such as when the person will probably listen to your advice. You may be getting across to that person if he or she puts a hand to the cheek, or with an elbow on the table puts the chin on a hand, or slightly cocks the head to one side, or the hand begins to stroke some part of the face.

All of these indicators are merely clues to look for, but if you look carefully while you are talking with people, you will be well on your way to enhancing your communicative skills. These are some of the modes of body-language communications:

1. *Facial expressions*. People may show fear, anxiety, love, hatred.

2. *Eye contact*. Determine a person's style, then look for changes.

3. *Motion and gestures*. Walking, standing, tapping a hand or leg.

4. *Touching others and themselves*.

5. *Use of space, or the "body bubble."* Intimate space is usually from 6 to 18 inches. Social space is at least at arm's length, and a hostile distance might be more or less, with the angry argument at nose-to-nose distance, extending outward until the person begins to assume a fighting stance at about arm's length.

6. *Silence*.

ESSENTIALS FOR A POLICE COMMUNICATIONS SYSTEM

The police department is an emergency operation. All forms of communication must be geared for emergency conditions and completely operational at all times. In addition, secondary systems must be ready for immediate implementation without loss of time or human resources. Under most conditions the actual routine of meeting the emergency and routine demand upon the various forms of communication will function smoothly and efficiently. However, plans should exist to cover all of the potential, "unexpected" situations that can be foreseen as well as those situations that occur frequently.

To assure maximum efficiency in carrying out those plans, certain criteria must be met.

1. *Training*. As much as possible, most types of messages should be committed to standard handling procedures. Any conceivable type of situation should be worked out in hypothetical "role play" sessions and communications procedures worked out accordingly. Once standard operating procedures are established, they should be made well known to all operating personnel, and these personnel should be instructed and rehearsed in as many different types of situations as possible. The training must coincide with the planning, and both must be constant in the dynamic environment of the law enforcement milieu.

2. *Dependability*. The police communications systems must be totally dependable under both emergency and routine conditions. Secondary systems must be available on a standby basis, and they must be totally operational. Frequent inspections and tests should be made as a matter of routine. For example, an auxiliary radio transmitter should be occasionally used for a short time to test its efficiency. Backup power systems are essential.

3. *Security*. The police communications system must be secure from attack in the event of any criminal action directed toward destruction or neutralization of any part of the police agency's vital functions. It must also be secure from any foreseeable natural or accidental disaster, such as fire, flood, earthquake, tornado, hurricane, or airplane crash.

4. *Accessibility*. All operational units of the organization must have

convenient access to every type of communications medium that is essential to its efficient operation. Mail delivery, extension telephone systems, and computer terminals usually accommodate most of the basic needs of a police organization, but there may also be a need for radio broadcast and monitoring equipment at remote locations, and for teletype units in locations separate from the battery of units maintained in a communications center. It is also quite feasible to install remote terminals for electronic data processing systems that tie in with centralized information storage banks. Access must be commensurate with utilization.

5. *Speed.* Radio and telephone and interfacing computers provide immediate access to other persons or agencies, assuming that the line or air is clear to transmit the message (see Figures 4–1 and 4–2). One method to assure maximum utilization of all forms of communications for law enforcement agencies is to develop a language that is clearly understandable to all its users but that can appreciably shorten the time it takes to deliver the message. Radio codes are primarily designed for such brevity as well as clarity and, to some small extent, possibly some confidentiality. Redundancy in police correspondence or teletype messages should be avoided.

6. *Confidentiality.* Police communications should not be made public as a matter of course. Much of the information in possession of the police agency is private and personal as it relates to suspects and victims, and it is essential that this information be guarded to protect the innocent. Although radio codes are known by virtually anyone who is involved in law enforcement, there is some degree of privacy in using the codes because they are not universally known. Teletype and computer systems

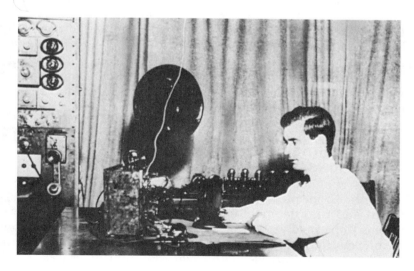

Figure 4–1 The first police radio broadcasting station. (Courtesy of the Police Department, Detroit, Michigan.)

Figure 4–2   One of Detroit's first radio-equipped cruisers. Note the "antenna" on the roof. (Courtesy of the Police Department, Detroit, Michigan.)

used by law enforcement agencies are on private lines with accessibility only through coordinating agency authorization. For some transmissions by radio or telephone, it may be feasible to use scrambler systems that transmit garbled sounds and "unscramble" them at each end. For certain types of unusual police operations, unpublished frequencies may be utilized. It is a simple matter for eavesdroppers to listen in on any unscrambled radio transmission you make with the use of sophisticated scramblers that many amateurs have for personal entertainment. Remember, also, that wireless phones within a building and cellular phones are nothing more than radios, and people with scanners may listen in on those, too. A truly secret message should be whispered into the other person's ear, or at least by telephone line, using a code and a scrambler.

INTRA- AND INTERDEPARTMENTAL COMMUNICATIONS

Two other aspects of police communications that should be defined are intra- and interdepartmental communications. Intradepartmental communications involve the formal and informal transmission and exchange of information throughout the various divisions and subdivisions within the agency. The interdepartmental communications system involves the interchange of information among the members of two or more agencies. Both these systems will be briefly reviewed.

Intradepartmental Communications

With a quasi-military organization such as a police department, there are several methods for the formal transmission of directives, orders, ideas, and information to be conveyed through the various levels of the organizational structure in a downward, upward, or lateral direction. There must also be provisions for an informal interchange of ideas and information in all directions throughout the department. Without this informal flow of communications, there is the danger that incentive will be destroyed, mediocrity will be perpetuated, and eventually the effectiveness of the department will be totally neutralized.

For the purpose of presenting to the public an image of unanimity within the agency, all news releases and general information emanating from the agency should "clear" through the office of the agency head—the chief of police or sheriff or a press relations officer. This increases the possibility of getting out information that is accurate and complete, and reflects the true philosophy of the department. Incoming communications should be received by a central office so that it may be routed correctly. Personal and confidential mail should be so labeled and routed, but mail addressed to a specific person within the department might not get appropriate attention concerning urgent matters if not opened and routed to someone who can give the necessary immediate attention.

General and special orders usually originate in the office of the chief. *General orders* are long-lasting policy statements or standardized procedures that affect all members of the department. *Special orders* have a shorter effective length, or they involve matters of interest to some number of employees rather than the general membership. Time limits should be placed on all orders, whether intended to be long-lasting or not. This will make it mandatory to have periodic review and evaluations of such orders and modifications as necessary.

A variety of other types of directives or information bulletins may emanate from the chief's office or other divisions within the department in accordance with the system established by the chief and the staff. Conformity to some sort of system assures consistency and predictability.

In addition to the written message that the chief or sheriff must continually originate and update, there should be a more informal system for the interchange of ideas as well as the delivery of orders. The chief usually meets with immediate staff on a daily basis, sometimes several times during the day. The immediate staff consists of those ranking officers who are in the direct line of command in the organization and report directly to the chief indicated on the organizational charts. The chief holds less frequent meetings on a formal and informal basis at irregular or scheduled times with command and supervisory officers. The general purposes of such staff and command meetings are to articulate policies, to maintain some uniformity in the interpretation and execution of the department's responsibilities, and to provide for a continual, free flow of communications and feedback essential to the management process.

Following the lead of the chief, all supervisory employees and ranking officers should have both formal and informal meetings with their subordinates to discuss the same general policies, philosophies, and ethics, but also to work out ways and means to perform their jobs with the greatest degree of efficiency. There should also be provisions within the organization at all levels of supervision up to—and including—the chief for an open door into that person's office to discuss any personal matter that directly affects the department. Naturally, it is not possible for the chief of police or the sheriff of a large agency to personally visit with each of the members of the department, or the entire day would be consumed by such visits and the chief could not accomplish the other responsibilities of the office. However, there must be some system of unstifled flow of information to allow feedback and also to provide a safety valve for the officers and other employees to communicate their emotions, their ideas, and their complaints.

Within the ranks and between the various working units in the department there must also be an established system for the free flow of information without the unbending restriction that everyone go through the "chain of command" to exchange information. There is a particularly acute need for such a continuous flow of information between the field officers and the investigators, for example. A field officer may develop some good leads on a case and pass them on to the investigator assigned to the follow-up investigation of that case. It is imperative that the investigator later send back word to the officer who originally uncovered the leads, preferably by telephone or a personal note in a department mailbox, to let the officer know the information helped in the case. The investigators should frequently visit the patrol roll call sessions to discuss their cases and to seek assistance in locating wanted individuals or information that the field officers may be in a better position to find because of their continuous presence in the field.

Accident investigators may ask for patrol assistance in a hit-and-run case in which the only leads they have are that the suspect drives a light-blue car and that he might drive on a certain street every night about the same time. Vice detail officers may request that a particular house be watched for unusual activity or more than the average number of automobiles in the vicinity. These are just a few examples of the many instances when the cooperative efforts of two or more operating units are enhanced by informal communications.

Rumors will usually fill the gaps left by the lack of information, and police departments are not exempt from rumor-passing situations. To counteract the dissemination of rumors, it may be necessary to point out the true facts of a situation, such as the purpose for disciplinary action. Rules and regulations should be published and distributed. Policies, procedures, and other types of information should be passed on to the employees. Additionally, there should be some provision for the release of information that is newsworthy to the many members of the department. Although there are some items of information that must remain confidential, they should be kept to a minimum to keep the air clear of intrigue and rumor-producing conditions.

Interdepartmental Communications

There is an acute need for a free flow of communications between the various law enforcement agencies throughout the country and, in many cases, with other law enforcement bodies in foreign countries. Nonpolitical and non-religious organizations that are directly involved in the law enforcement or investigative process serve as one means of assuring this interdepartmental exchange of information and ideas. Through membership in national and international organizations the chief meets other chief administrators from the United States and the rest of the world. They and their intelligence details and community relations officers also develop valuable contacts outside their own jurisdictions. These contacts facilitate the flow of information that is essential for the successful operation of police units in cases having national and international aspects and far-reaching effects. They may be extremely useful, for example, in cases involving safe burglars or clothing store burglars, who often work many cities across the country.

Another instance of interdepartmental communications is when the officer-specialists in several different departments meet under formal organization meeting situations. Through such organizational relationships they form friendships that facilitate frequent informal contacts for social reasons as well as for discussion of cases in which they are mutually interested. It is not unusual for the officers from several departments in contiguous jurisdictions jointly to solve a series of cases through the medium of their organizational ties. Otherwise, they might solve only those crimes that a culprit commits in one jurisdiction.

External Relationships

Isolation is not a favorable situation for any single segment of society, and you should avoid developing an insulated barrier between yourself and the other members of society. You should make a diligent effort to diversify associations among as many different special- and general-purpose organizations as possible, consistent with your work schedule and other responsibilities. These include school–parent organizations, church clubs, fraternal organizations, youth groups, and others that you encounter in the course of the many roles that you play. If you focus all your attention on those organizations related to law enforcement, you may develop a narrow, ethnocentric outlook.

Politics and religion are often causes for debate when a police officer is involved. As a private individual, you should be encouraged to take an active part in exercising your right to vote and expressing your freedom to worship in any way that you choose. When on duty, however, you should be as objective as possible and remain aloof from intense religious or political discussions so that you do not become identified as one who attempts to foist personal points of view on others under the guise of your official position.

On duty, never be so vocal in your beliefs that it can be said that you arrested an individual, or used your official position to coerce another person to comply with a certain request, because of your differences in religious or political beliefs. A police force should not be used as a tool to extort votes for a particular individual, or the people have a political police force, which is contrary to the American system of government. Keeping this neutral posture while on duty is a must, but if you wish to take an active part in your private life by affiliating with a church and political party of your choice, you have every right to do so as a first class citizen. You also have the right not to affiliate if that is your wish.

GUIDELINES FOR COMMUNICATIONS MEDIA

U.S. Mail

Mail is one of the oldest and most durable forms of communication used by law enforcement. Virtually every type of police business is transacted by mail, from the routine letter of verification for delivery of a shipment of ballpoint pens, to a special delivery, airmail letter to the detective division advising them of the whereabouts of a possible robbery suspect. Individual patrol officers may not be directly involved in the routine use of the mails; but whenever it is necessary to send a letter related to the department's business, it should be in accordance with an established procedure. Outgoing mail should usually be sent over the signature of the chief of police or the division head, and returns should be requested in the same manner. The primary purpose of this procedure is to present the image of a single agency rather than a haphazard conglomeration of individual operators. Also, if an individual has been transferred or is off duty, the mail will be processed immediately.

Whistles, Nightsticks, and Hand Signals

Prearranged signals with either or both of these standard items of police equipment may be used for a variety of worthwhile purposes. At nighttime a nightstick rapped on the sidewalk pavement may be heard with a distinctive sound for several blocks. Short blasts of the whistle may also be heard, yet be considerably less noticeable than an officer's voice shouting a command or call for assistance. Whenever working with other officers under conditions when it will be necessary to be on foot, set up two or three distinctive hand signals. These may be particularly effective when attempting to surround a building to apprehend a burglar who is hiding inside.

Recall Signal Devices

Prior to the advent of portable two-way radios, some police departments set up systems of signal lights located throughout the areas covered by officers on foot beats. The lights were connected directly to the station houses, and messages were sent to the beat officers by means of coded combinations of light flashes. In other cities, small signal lights were installed atop a building in the center of town, and they signaled the officers downtown to report immediately to the station to take out a car for a service call in the outlying areas, or to come in for lunch relief.

The signal light system has been replaced by more sophisticated equipment in large urban areas. However, variations of the signal method are still being used with more modern equipment. One device is a small beeper that the officer can wear inconspicuously on the belt. A sound signal or vibration notifies the wearer to go to the nearest phone and call the office or a base station to receive messages. Another device is the recall light that is affixed to the dashboard of the police car, which is turned on and remains lighted until the officer switches if off and goes to the phone or calls in on the radio. The most popular and widely used recall device today is the portable radio that the officer carries whenever away from the police car. The teleprinter is also gaining wider acceptance, because a printed message is waiting for the officer upon return to the police car.

Telegraph

Before the implementation of the teletype, one of the more common means of police communication was telegraph. Telegraph wires were linked to the police headquarters and the various precinct stations. They were also wired from one police department to another. Telegraphers were employed for the purpose of maintaining communications between stations. One disadvantage to the system was that police officers had to be specifically trained in operating the telegraph equipment and using the Morse code, which consists of combinations of clicks made by activating an electromagnetic key. The alternative was to employ trained telegraphers for the specialized job and to keep them on duty around the clock, which they apparently did. The system was used for many years, but it is now virtually obsolete.

Teletype and Computers

Automatic teletypewriters on telephone lines connecting headquarters with substations in the various precincts and with patrol units in the field, and connecting police departments throughout the various states in a nationwide network, are now fully operational. Most major U.S. cities are linked together through the facilities of the various coordinating agencies. The past few years have seen the marriage of teletype, radio, telephone, and computers to create a highly efficient system of information storage and retrieval, which holds great promise for the future. Centralized records of stolen automobiles, criminal records, pawned and stolen items are maintained in state clearinghouses, and computer networks make it possible to inquire and receive replies regarding whether or not an item is stolen or a person is wanted within a matter of microseconds.

In addition to the statewide networks and information systems, the U.S. Department of Justice established in 1967 a central computerized information clearinghouse that provides instantaneous information retrieval and storage services for virtually every police agency in the country. Known as the National Crime Information Center, or NCIC, the system is operational and functioning as an integral part of the police information system.

NCIC serves all FBI field offices, all of 50 of the United States, the District of Columbia, and Canada. It contains computerized files on wanted persons, stolen vehicles, license plates stolen and related to wanted persons, firearms transactions, stolen identifiable articles, securities files, aircraft, snowmobiles, dune buggies, and stolen boats. The system also contains criminal history files that allow an interchange of information concerning personal descriptions of arrested persons, total times arrested, charges and convictions or other dispositions, the number of times arrested in each offense category, the latest arrest and current status and/or disposition, appeal information, custody status, and change in status, such as probation on parole.

Any person whose name is contained in the NCIC files has a right to see and challenge any of the information contained therein to assure accuracy. The confidentiality and integrity of NCIC is assured in the following manner: (1) terminals are available only to criminal justice agencies, (2) security provisions at the sites of the terminals are required, (3) there is a limit on the number of people who have access to terminals, (4) all personnel who have access to terminals and at the data center are carefully screened, (5) logs and other appropriate records are maintained to identify the users of the file, and (6) there are editing procedures implemented to assure file accuracy.

Secretaries, stenographers, and other clerks regularly employed by the various police departments may be easily trained to use computer equipment. Established uniform message formats should be followed closely to assure brevity, clarity, and maximum benefit from the exchange of information in accordance with a uniform sequence and style.

Facsimile (Fax) and Computer Interface

When we wrote the first edition of this book several years ago, fax and computers were new to criminal justice. Although computers have been around for decades, it was often difficult to get them to talk to each other because of their incompatibility. Now the process is quite commonplace and routine for records and investigative information to be shared throughout the world by computers and telephone connections. The same is true of fax, or "facsimile" as it was called when first used by major communications during the 1940s. Smaller than a copy machine of the portable variety, and connected to a telephone line, the exact duplicate of a document can be sent immediately to any other fax machine in the world.

Investigators are able to compare fingerprints and "mug shots" and to have the new sophisticated fingerprint identification system (in California it is called CAL-ID) search the files and identify the culprit by his or her fingerprints in a matter of seconds. Just a few years ago, the process of identifying some of our more notorious wanted criminals—including some mass murderers—would have taken dozens of experts months or even years to do. Now the same job may take as few as 10 or 15 minutes, including human verification by experts at either end of the line. While a suspect is being booked in jail in Montgomery, Alabama, his or her fingerprints can be sent to the central clearinghouse in Washington, D.C., then on to various other states where the suspect is known to have been. Before the booking is completed, Montgomery will be notified by the Sacramento, California department that they want the suspect for burglary, and Charleston, South Carolina will be sending them a message that the suspect is probably in violation of parole in that state. Sketches, diagrams, composites, ransom notes, and forged checks can all be duplicated and sent via fax. The possibilities are limited only by your imagination.

Television

Sight and sound transmissions by means of television are an excellent adjunct to the other communications media employed by police departments. Television is popular because of its economy and ease of operation. As employed by the field officer in the patrol division, it is possible for the investigating officer at the scene of a crime to record the entire scene by means of videotape.

Use of television makes it possible for lineups to be held at a central location while witnesses who are unable to travel view the suspects at some other location. The chief of police, the sheriff, or other officers may address a maximum number of officers and other employees who are located at various places throughout the jurisdiction either "live" or on videotape, thereby assuring the greatest possible coverage without interfering with normal operations or the off-duty time of the many employees.

Remote television cameras and transmitters carried in a helicopter, or located at various key places in a city, such as a heavily used intersection of two major arterials, make it possible for officers to view many places simultaneously, providing greater patrol coverage. A single officer can visually observe as many places as there are television cameras, and can dispatch a patrol unit to whichever one of the various locations requires the physical presence of a patrol officer. Using television to supplement patrol, it is possible to observe on a continuous basis many high-hazard or high-crime areas that otherwise might be checked only occasionally for a minute or two at a time one or two times a day.

Telephone

The most common means of communication between police departments and the people they serve will always be personal contact. The first contact—and sometimes the only one—usually consists of the telephone call requesting advice or assistance from the police officer. No type of police operation is transacted without frequent use of the telephone. Many members of the department literally spend their entire duty time on the telephone, answering questions for information or advice, questioning people concerning their identities, where they are, and their reasons for calling the police.

The telephone is a convenient, economical, and rapid means of communicating with others. Your department may have a central switchboard (PBX, Private Board Exchange) or Centrex system that allows calls to be made directly between the offices and the public without going through a central operator. This substantially reduces operator time. Because the telephone is so intimately involved with the role of law enforcement in the lives of people during times of great need and tragedy, the department members must be constantly mindful of the sensitive part they play in that role. It is just as important that the representative of the police department answer every call with a pleasant attitude as it is that the representative of an insurance company respond to each call as if it were from a new customer.

Telephone Techniques. Every telephone call must be answered with a pleasant voice, never in such a way that the caller gets the feeling that he or she is interrupting someone's sleep or that the person answering the call would rather be doing something else. The brusque or rough-sounding voice has no place in an operator's methods of response to calls. A good telephone voice should be similar to that of a radio announcer. The voice should be clear, distinct, evenly paced, pleasant, and natural. Speak directly into the mouthpiece. If you wear a headset with a small tube-shaped mouthpiece, be sure it is in front of your mouth when you talk.

Always answer the phone promptly or transfer the call to someone who can answer. Be attentive to the caller and attempt to determine from the tone of voice the urgency of the call for services. Keep the length of all incoming calls short. Be polite, but discourage the marathon conversation. If the caller must talk longer than you have time for, perhaps it may be possible to transfer the call to a clerk who will advise the caller that the officer was required to move on to another call and inquire whether there is additional information that should be passed on to the officer.

Such a tactic should not be designed to discourage callers, but it is necessary if the lines are to be kept reasonably clear for an emergency call that may come in at any moment.

Any incoming phone call to the police department may be a request for help in a life or death situation. It may not be such a call—most calls are not—but law enforcement is an emergency service organization and must be geared for emergency at all times. The next call may be the most important call of the day, and a minute saved may mean the difference between an individual's life or death. The phone must not be allowed to continue ringing unanswered, and there should be a standard procedure for immediate response when the telephone operator is busy. One method for handling all incoming phone calls is to have the principal operator respond to as many calls as possible and immediately connect other calls to other persons who have desk assignments in the building. The call may be handled by that person, or if it is a nonemergency call for service or a request to speak with a particular individual within the building, it can be returned to the operator when the earlier surge of overloading calls has subsided.

One effective method for handling many calls at once is to answer each call with "Police Department. Is this an emergency?" If the person at the other end of the line states "No," go to the next call, handling only the emergency calls. Then go back to the calls that were not in need of immediate attention. By using this method it is possible to give all callers the attention they expect of their police department and at the same time give them priority attention. If you use this procedure, the key to success is to wait for a reply when asking, "Is this an emergency?" Otherwise, the purpose is defeated.

There is nothing worse for the caller with an urgent message to have the police operator open the line and say: "Police Department. Is this an emergency?" followed by an immediate click and to be placed on hold without the operator having listened for answer to that critical question.

Another technique is to utilize a complaint board and tape recorder combination. Any request for service can be switched to the tape recorder on a delayed-action arrangement, which allows you as the operator to switch to an extension after the caller has already begun talking. You can listen to the recorded conversation at high speed and catch up with the slower pace at which the caller is talking. This is a time-delay device that phone-in radio and television talk shows use when taking incoming calls so that they may block out obscene or profane words of slanderous comments before they are broadcasted. When the complaint desk is at normal load, you will answer incoming calls directly. It is good practice to use the tape recorder and record all telephone conversations. There may be a need to study the tapes for voice identification or to establish who said what to whom and under what conditions for a variety of reasons.

However you answer the phone, or when you must put the caller on hold, or if you transfer the call to another station, check back frequently to be sure that the caller gets the call completed as intended.

Incoming calls of an emergency nature should not be referred to another phone number. The operator should take the information and relay it to the agency that can respond to the situation by virtue of jurisdiction or nature of the requested service. If the call is for service or information that does not require immediate attention, the caller should be referred to the correct agency and provided with the correct name, address, and telephone number. "It's in the phone book" is not an appropriate retort.

The 911 telephone system has been a tremendous boon to the emergency services. A free call from any telephone, including a pay phone, immediately links the caller with the service desired and the geographical location of the caller.

Some agencies have an excellent incoming phone call arrangement called the *hot line*. Whenever the telephone operator receives an emergency call that involves several different units within the department, such as an armed robbery in progress, the operator simultaneously rings the hot line on all the phone extensions carrying it as one of their numbers. The operator immediately connects the call and an unusually loud bell or signal sounds. The officer in charge, the investigative unit, dispatcher, and anyone else to whom the call is directed can listen simultaneously. Only one person, usually the dispatcher, carries on the conversation with the caller to get pertinent information. The others listen and handle whatever assignments or other arrangements they deem necessary.

Alarm companies frequently call concerning silent or audible alarms that are triggered in burglary or robbery situations. They are also set off accidentally by tellers and clerks, and by conditions during windstorms, by shorted connections, and a variety of other malfunctions. When an alarm system is activated, the alarm company follows a prescribed procedure to check the system and then calls the police department for response. All these calls must be treated as potentially dangerous "in-progress" crime situations and should be connected to the hot line.

Whenever a private person takes the time to call the police department about some need for police service, it is usually one of the most important events in that person's life at that particular moment. Very few people call for police aid with any regularity, and they are sometimes unfortunately referred to as "chronic complainers." With due respect for the officers who use this term, we would agree that there are some persons who fit that category because their requests are for the police officers to perform false arrests or to "put a scare into" someone. On the whole, however, most callers are sincere and justifiably want the police to perform some action that falls within the purview of our responsibilities. When such is the case, it should be a matter of routine courtesy for you to take a few extra minutes when possible after responding to the call to phone or visit the callers to bring them up to date on the action you took. There is no need to disseminate tidbits of gossip for the rumor-mongers; just state what is sufficient to satisfy the caller that you did perform your duty.

Police Radio

It is difficult to imagine a modern, efficient law enforcement agency without the use of radio. Now it is taken as a matter of course, with little thought to the fact that police radio was nonexistent until about 1929. The first radios were quite cumbersome and considerably different from those in use today. The transmitter was located at headquarters and the police cars were equipped with receivers only. In many agencies there was no transmitter, and it was necessary to send emergency calls to the police cars in the field by using the facilities of local broadcast stations.

By 1938 the use of one-way radios in police cars had become fairly widespread, and it was during that year that some departments began installing transmitters in their vehicles, making two-way radio communication possible. (The newspaper clippings in Figure 4–3 extol the virtues of the police radio.) The system involved use of a common frequency for all transmissions from both the station at headquarters and the mobile units. This simple configuration is called a *simplex system*. The next step was to provide separate frequencies so that the station was using one frequency and the mobile units another. This double frequency system is known as the *duplex system*. As it progressed, police radio added a third frequency for car-to-car transmissions, and the triple frequency system was named the *triplex system*. Variations of all three systems are presently in operation (see Figure 4–4). Some police units are equipped with scanners that allow interception of messages over other frequencies in addition to the "priority channel" they are regularly assigned.

GUIDELINES FOR RADIO OPERATION

Utilization of the radio frequencies for many purposes by hundreds of different types of organizations and individual operations has made it necessary to have very strict limitations on frequency allocations and on the actual use of those frequencies that are allocated. Along the spectrum of sound wave frequencies, only a portion of the frequencies may be used by radio. Other frequencies are used for ultraviolet and infrared transmissions, for X-ray, diathermic, and ultrasonic therapeutic devices and for television and both private and commercial radio. As a result of all of these demands on the existent frequencies, which cannot be expanded, the frequencies are constantly being narrowed and exploited more efficiently through the use of highly sophisticated equipment.

Air time on the police frequency is as valuable to the police officer as the most valuable gem is to the jeweler, and you should use it accordingly. Even though there may be silent gaps during the day, it is just as desirable to save the silent moments as it is for the jeweler to preserve every scrap of the precious gem or metal and get maximum use of the leftovers in producing other items. With the radio, the object is to use only that time that is

Figure 4–3 Examples of the value of the police radio.

necessary to deliver the message, no more. Each transmission must be brief, but not so brief that it must be repeated for explanation or clarification, and it must be accurate. Through the use of standardized radio codes, it is possible to cut sentences down into numbers, such as "code seven at 14," which means, "I am going to stop for a few minutes for lunch at the coffee shop to which we gave the number '14' sometime previously, and I may be reached at that phone number—also listed previously—if you need to get in touch with me while I am eating."

Operating Laws and Regulations

The Federal Communications Commission is charged with the responsibility for the legal and efficient use of the radio frequencies. Profanity,

Figure 4-4 Today's police communications include both voice radio and computer transmissions, with terminals in each patrol car. (Courtesy of the Missouri State Highway Patrol.)

obscenity, and superfluous transmissions are unlawful and are prosecutable offenses. It is your responsibility to follow the recommended procedures discussed in this chapter and to avoid the use of profanity, obscenity, and superfluous transmissions. All other matters will be handled by the engineers and those people who are appropriately licensed as the principal operators for the various radio stations.

Microphone Technique

Prior to broadcasting by radio, depress the button to turn the microphone on and wait for a moment to allow the transmitter to be at full power when you are speaking. Hold the microphone about 2 inches from your mouth and in such a position that the sound is going past the microphone rather than directly into it. Using this technique will reduce the distracting sounds that occur when spitting the P's and hissing or whistling the S's. Some high-quality broadcast microphones filter these sounds out, making it possible to speak directly into them.

Use radio codes as much as possible for clarity and brevity, and speak in an evenly modulated tone of voice, slowly and distinctly. Exaggerate the diction slightly, such as the consonants at the end of the words, and the vowel sounds. For example, the word "police" should sound like "po lees" rather than "plece." As much as possible under the circumstances at the time of broadcast, try to make every transmission free of emotion. Any expression of anger, impatience, rudeness, or excitement may be exaggerated during the radio transmission and its contagion will negatively affect most of the people who are listening to that particular frequency.

Volume control is essential. Keep the volume evenly modulated. Shouting will cause a distorted transmission, and an important request for help may be so distorted by shouting that it is unintelligible. Outside noises from sirens, racing motors, overhead aircraft, and other sources all interfere with the transmissions, but shouting over the noise will not correct the problem. If at all possible, time your broadcasts so that they occur at times of least interference. If there is outside noise and you must transmit, try talking with the microphone directly against the throat at the larynx.

Broadcast Procedures

Listen to the radio for a few seconds before broadcasting to be sure that you are not interfering with another exchange of transmissions. Use this time to quickly think out your message before you say it. Depress the microphone button and begin talking after a brief pause, keeping the transmission "moving." The pause allows time for the transmitter to turn on because there might be a delay from the remote location of the activating switch. If you start talking at the same time you depress the switch, your first word or two might be lost. If you must stop to think or secure additional information, clear the air and return a minute later rather than stutter or stammer as a stall for time. The air time is valuable; use it as if it were gold dust.

If the transmission is long, stop occasionally and secure an acknowledgment of the message so far before continuing. The break will ensure clear communication, and it will also permit another unit with an urgent message to interfere when essential. Wait briefly for an acknowledgment before repeating the message or asking for an acknowledgment. The person at the other end of the message may have received the message, but may have been momentarily called away from the microphone by some other matter. If you do not wait, you may be broadcasting at the same time the station is broadcasting its acknowledgment, and with both transmitters on simultaneously, neither of you will hear the other. Unfortunately, impatience for a response sometimes causes considerable confusion.

Do not repeat messages unnecessarily, as occasionally portrayed on television or in the movies. A well-executed message given once may be sufficient, and usually is. If the receivers did not get it all, they will ask for a repeat of that portion they missed. There is no need to transmit a message and then ask for an acknowledgment in the same manner as the individual who asks after every sentence, "Do you understand?" or "Did you get that?" Whether he is asked or not, the receiver is required to acknowledge a transmission. Therefore, the request for acknowledgment is superfluous.

Pay attention to other transmissions on the radio that do not directly affect you, such as open-door discoveries or car stops. Although the officer may not request a follow-up unit, it should be a matter of course for the nearest unit to follow up to assure adequate protection for the lone field officer. When another unit calls in a license number and auto description when the officers make a car stop, copy it down. In the event that an officer is attacked or the vehicle flees the scene, or both, you already have the essential information and do not have to wait for a general broadcast to take action.

Acknowledgment of Calls

Respond to all calls as quickly as possible to avoid the need for a repeat or a second call to ask you if you received the first one. When acknowledging a call, respond with the appropriate code, but also give your location. The dispatcher and the other units that are listening to your transmission will know the distance you will have to travel to respond to a call and they can estimate your probable route of travel. Follow-up units, if necessary for the occasion, will know how they should proceed. In some cases, it may be possible to reassign a call to a closer unit, which is particularly important for injury accidents and "crime in progress" calls. If you are operating the follow-up unit and intend to respond, broadcast your intentions and the location from where you are responding.

Station Broadcasting

Although the dispatcher at the base station usually may not be a ranking officer, the broadcast is with the authority of the chief of police or sheriff. The operator does not have that power as an individual, but is merely relaying that authority, and should avoid any attempt to assume an attitude of personal control of the authority merely being relayed. The radio is often your only contact with headquarters; the operator is your partner in most field activities that involve use of the radio, and the dispatcher must constantly operate as an efficient partner. The field officer relies heavily on the dispatcher to provide assistance and protection whenever needed.

Most assignments of field officers are by radio. They must be as clear and understandable as possible. Avoid any display of emotionalism to avoid transmitting undue anxiety. The radio is no medium for transmitting a scolding, or impatience, anger, or any other emotion to the field officer. The transmissions must be impersonal. They are station-to-station messages and have no relationship to personal, face-to-face conversations. The radio is not licensed for personal messages. It should be standard operating procedure to limit transmissions only to essential transmissions that are directly related to the official business of the police department.

General Broadcasting Rules

Whenver using the police radio, use the following rules as guidelines for effective broadcasting results.[1]

1. Practice courtesy. It is contagious and will make their work much easier for everyone who uses the radio as well as those who must listen to it constantly during their entire tour of duty.

2. Broadcast station-to-station only. "Mike to Joe" transmissions are not allowed and should be held for personal meetings or telephone calls.

3. Humor and horseplay have no place on the police frequency. Rude sounds and sarcastic comments emanating from anonymous users of the radio frequency may sound funny for the moment, but they are immature, unlawful, and they may someday interfere with a transmission that could mean the difference between whether the officer lives or dies. Leave the humor to the commercial broadcasting clowns, who are employed specifically for the purpose of entertainment.

4. Avoid any use of the radio for personal conflicts, such as "chewing out," arguments, or sarcasm.

5. Keep all transmissions brief and to the point. Use the telephone for lengthy messages.

6. Profane and indecent language are unlawful.

7. Transmit only essential messages. Avoid asking for the time of day just to hear the radio, and secure routine information, such as time to eat lunch and other scheduled matters, either before going out in the field or by telephone.

8. Be completely familiar with your department's radio procedures and the individual items of equipment.

9. Assume a personal responsibility for correct and intelligent use of the radio by your department.

10. Use radio code for brevity and accuracy when practicable.

Radio Codes for Emergency Services

10-1	Receiving poorly
10-2	Receiving well
10-3	Stop transmitting
10-4	OK, or acknowledge
10-5	Relay
10-6	Busy
10-7	Out of service
10-7-B	Out of service at home
10-8	In service

---

[1]Some departments still have a policy of using simple English and perhaps restrict usage of the code to just a few basics, such as "10-4" and "10-8."

10-9	Repeat
10-10	Out of service, subject to call
10-11	Transmitting too rapidly
10-12	Officials or visitors present
10-13	Weather and road conditions
10-14	Escort or convoy
10-15	Enroute with prisoner
10-16	Pick up prisoner
10-17	Pick up papers
10-18	Complete present assignment quickly as possible
10-19	Return or returning to the station
10-20	Location, or what is your location?
10-21	Call your station or dispatcher by telephone
10-21-A	Advise my home I will return at _____
10-21-B	Call your home
10-21-T	Reply via teleprinter
10-22	Cancel last message or assignment
10-23	Stand by
10-25	Do you have contact with _____?
10-27	Check _____ computer for warrants
10-28	Registration request
10-29	Check for stolen or wanted
10-30	No records or wants your subject
10-31	Subject has record, but not wants
10-32	Subject wanted. Are you clear to copy?
10-33	Standby. Emergency traffic only
10-34	Resume normal radio traffic
10-35	Confidential information
10-36	Correct time
10-37	Name of operator on duty
10-39	Message delivered
10-40	Is _____ available for telephone call?
10-40-A	Is _____ available for radio call?
10-42	Pick up officer
10-45	Service your equipment
10-46	Stand by. I am moving to a better location
10-48	I am now ready to receive information
10-49	Proceed to _____
10-86	Traffic check (Do you have any messages for this unit?)
10-87	Meet _____ at _____
10-88	What phone number should we call for station-to-station call?
10-96	Request test of selective call equipment
10-97	Arrived at the scene
10-98	Completed last assignment
NO CODE	Handle calls routinely
CODE 1	Routine, take this call next

CODE 2	Urgent. Expedite, but obey all traffic laws. No red light/siren
CODE 3	EMERGENCY. Proceed immediately, using red light and siren
CODE 4	No further assistance needed
CODE 4-A	No further assistance needed, but suspect at large in area
CODE 5	Stakeout. Other units stay away unless ordered there
CODE 6	Out for investigation
CODE 7	Out of service to eat
CODE 8	Fire box pulled
CODE 9	Jail break
CODE 12	Patrol assigned area and report extent of disaster damage
CODE 13	Activate major disaster plan, or perform major disaster duties
CODE 14	Resume normal operations (used only following CODE 12 or 13)
CODE 20	Notify news media
CODE 20-D	Request department photographer
CODE 99	EMERGENCY situation. The emergency button in mobile unit has been depressed. No voice contact.
901	Traffic accident, not known if there is an injury
901-K	Ambulance dispatched
901-N	Ambulance needed
901-Y	Is ambulance needed?
901-T	Injury traffic accident
902	Accident, not traffic
902-H	Enroute to hospital
902-M	Medical aid
902-T	Noninjury traffic accident
903	Plane crash
903-L	Low flying plane
904	Fire
904-A	Fire alarm
904-B	Boat fire
904-C	Car fire
904-G	Grass fire
904-I	Illegal fire, or incendiary
904-M	Trash fire
904-S	Structural fire
905	Animal information
905-B	Animal bite
905-D	Dead animal
905-H	Animal in heat
905-I	Animal injured
905-L	Loose stock
905-N	Animal noise
905-R	Rabies suspected

905-S	Stray (dog or cat)
906	Rescue
906-N	Rescue unit needed
906-K	Rescue unit dispatched
907-N	Paramedic team needed
907-K	Paramedic team dispatched
907-Y	Is paramedic team needed?
909	Traffic information
909-C	Traffic congestion/control
909-F	Traffic flares needed
909-T	Traffic hazard
910	Can handle call
911-B	Contact the officer
912	Are we clear to/for _____
913	You are clear to/for _____
914-A	Attempt suicide
914-C	Coroner needed
914-D	Doctor needed
914-H	Heart attack
914-S	Suicide
917-A	Abandoned vehicle
918	Mental case
918-V	Violent mental case
919	Keep the peace
920-A	Missing adult (18 and over)
920-C	Missing child (under 14)
920-J	Missing juvenile (14 to 18)
920-F	Found child
921	Prowler
922	Illegal peddling
924	Station detail
924-D	Station detail/desk
924-F	Food for prisoners
924-R	Return to station to file
925	Suspicious person
925-C	Suspicious person in a car
925-V	Suspicious vehicle
926	Tow truck needed
926-A	Tow truck dispatched
927	Unknown trouble
927-D	Investigate dead body
928	Found property
928-B	Found bicycle
929	Investigate person down
930	See the man
931	See the woman

932	Open door
933	Open window
949	Gasoline spill
950	Burning permit
951	Need fire investigator
952	Report on conditions
953	Check smoke
954	Off the air at the scene
955	Fire under control
956	Assignment not completed, but available for another if needed
957	Fire out on arrival
960	Car stop. Request a follow-up
960-X	Car stop. Expedite follow-up, dangerous suspects.
961	Car stop. No follow-up needed
962	Suspect armed and dangerous. Are you clear to copy?
965	Tab for intelligence unit. Full F.I. (field interview)
966	Sniper activity
967	Outlaw motorcycle movement
968	Request record check of person
970	Illegal surfing
971	Boat over
972	Boat speeding
973	Swimmer on boat
974	Boat adrift
975	Wreckage adrift
976	Oil slick
977	Check mooring line
978	Vessel aground
979	Vessel sinking
980	Radioactive materials present or involved
981	Need radiological monitoring team
982	Bomb threat at _____
983	Explosion at _____
995	Riot or major disturbance
997	Officer needs assistance from own agency units only. Urgent
998	Officer involved in shooting
999	Officer needs help. Any units respond. EMERGENCY. HELP!

Video Data Terminals in Field Units

It is now possible to carry on a multilevel communications conversation with field units through traditional two-way radio transmissions, with simultaneous exchange of data on the computer terminal, with a visual display of wanted persons and stolen merchandise, and an officer running checks for records and wants on a suspect. A third function would be a constant signal transmitted on a frequency unique to the individual unit so that a tracking receiver could locate the unit anywhere on the map by activation of a light on the map within a few yards of the present location of the vehicle.

If your vehicle is equipped with a computer, the dispatcher can leave a message on your computer for your return. There is less possibility of misunderstanding the message, and there is greater confidentiality than if the message were transmitted by voice. Outside noise will not interfere with the reception, and you will not have to get out of traffic and park so that you can write down the message.

SUMMARY

In this chapter, we covered basic procedures in telephone, radio, and other communications, as well as a discussion of some of the many types of communications equipment available to the modern police agency, such as computers, television, speed photo and facsimile, the mails, whistles and nightsticks, and recall signal devices, and some of their uses. One of the most important aspects of police communications is how to deal with each other interpersonally. Addressing that aspect, we discussed both verbal as well as nonverbal communications and some of the problems and responsibilities attendant to those ways that you, the field officer, communicate with the people you serve.

EXERCISES AND STUDY QUESTIONS

1. What factors influence how we interpret what we hear?
2. Give two examples of how body language may contradict what a person might be saying.
3. If a person you are questioning sits back on the chair and opens up his arms while answering your questions, would you interpret the body language as that of a cooperative person?
4. How would you shut off a conversation and let it be known by body language that you are in charge?
5. When two people are gazing very intently at one another, what type of conversation are they likely to be having?
6. Describe how a person's body language will say that he or she is nervous.
7. Describe a sign of frustration.
8. Six items were listed as being essential for a police communications system. List and explain all six.
9. Interview one or more of the old-timers in your department, and

write a brief synopsis on how officers handled communications prior to the advent of the police radio.

10. What is the reason for putting a time limit on all orders, including general as well as special orders?

11. What is the purpose for a chief executive officer to have an "open-door" policy?

12. Do you believe that a peace officer should have the freedom to actively practice partisan politics while on duty? Why? (or) why not?

13. What is the basic reason for having official department correspondence addressed to the department rather than to an individual officer?

14. What is NCIC, and what type of information may be found through its use?

15. What is the correct way to answer the police telephone when you are overloaded with incoming calls?

16. Of what value is the tape recorder to the police complaint board operator?

17. What is the "911 system," and how does it work?

18. What is the purpose of a telephone hot line?

19. What is the correct technique for speaking into a microphone?

20. What is the principal purpose for using radio codes?

21. What is the recommended technique for speaking into a microphone when outside noise, such as a wailing siren, makes it almost impossible to be heard over the sound?

22. What does the author say about personal conversations over the police radio?

23. What is the radio code for "received your message"?

24. Using radio code, how would you say "Please repeat your message"?

25. What is Code 1? Code 2? Code 3?

26. How would you report a structural fire by radio?

27. What is the radio code for "everything is OK"?

REFERENCES

ADAMS, THOMAS F. *Training Officers' Handbook*. Springfield, Ill.: Charles C Thomas, 1964, Chap. 5.

FEDERAL COMMUNICATIONS COMMISSION. *Rules and Regulations* (annual).

LOS ANGELES POLICE DEPARTMENT. *Daily Training Bulletins*, Vol. 1. Springfield, Ill.: Charles C. Thomas, 1954, Chap. 9.

_____. *Daily Training Bulletins*, Vol. II. Springfield Ill.: Charles C. Thomas, 1958, Chap. 25.

Los Angeles Sheriff's Department. *Communication Procedure (Daily Training Bulletins 1–8)*, Vol. 1, Los Angeles: Los Angeles Sheriff's Department, n.d.

Morris, Desmond, *Manwatching: A Field Guide to Human Behavior.* New York: Abrams, 1977.

5

REPORTING & RECORDS

INTRODUCTION

As a novice, you may look upon the preparation of reports and the maintenance of comprehensive records as a relatively unimportant part of the total police role. These tasks may not hold much interest. However, as you gain experience and as cases are won and lost in court, personal evaluations are discussed with superior officers, commendations for outstanding performance of duty are awarded, and reports are sent back for rewrite, the tremendously important part played by officer-prepared records becomes quite evident. They are vital to the continued efficiency of any police agency. Their effectiveness is your responsibility.

This chapter covers the subject of reporting and records maintenance in three parts. The purpose of this format is to emphasize the relative importance of each of the three parts with respect to the other two. Basic to all three sections is the premise that no police action is performed correctly unless the report accurately recounts such action exactly as it happened in clear, concise, and objective language. Section One deals with field notetaking. This is where it all begins. Accuracy at this stage will often set the tone for an entire investigation and will be the determining factor in the eventual success in prosecution. Section Two covers basic report writing techniques, including report dictation, which is actually the most logical method for recording reports. It also presents a collection of forms that can be completed by checking the appropriate statements concerning routine calls that have been handled in accordance with standard operating procedures. Section Three, "Getting the Most Out of Records," is intended to stimulate the field patrol officer to do just that:

get the most out of the police records system (see Figure 5–1). It is a gold mine of information providing, of course, that it has been filled previously with "gold" as indicated in Sections One and Two in this chapter.

— SECTION 1—
FIELD NOTETAKING
AND CRIME SCENE RECORDING

INTRODUCTION

Of all the various types of notes you make regarding day-to-day activities, the most important are field notes. They are made specifically for the purpose of compiling facts in the order in which they present themselves to you. As viewed by the observer at some later time, it is apparent that the

Figure 5-1   Computers play an important role in the management of police organizations. Shown here at his PC is Police Chief David L. Snowden. (Courtesy of the Police Department, Costa Mesa, California.)

officer making the notes had no reason, no desire to alter the notes in any appreciable way. They are likely to be highest on a credibility scale if there were to be such a measuring device. It is probably for this reason that the rules of evidence provide that a witness may refer to notes while giving testimony if those notes were made by the witnesses themselves, or by someone under their direction at the time the fact being recorded was actually occurring, or was still fresh in the memory of the person recording it.

Field notes should be limited to names, addresses, and other pertinent data relevant to the identities of persons mentioned in reports and their relationships with the incident, and short succinct statements relating elements of the situation being recorded in the sequence as they occur and come to the attention of the recorder. Any opinions should be clearly explained and substantiated by facts and be kept to an absolute minimum. Departure from facts should occur only when inferences could be made by any other reasonable and prudent person with the same collection of information. *Never* fabricate or fictionalize reports to make a better case or for self-aggrandizement.

WHAT CONSTITUTES FIELD NOTES?

Field notes are actually the index to your memory. They are generally limited to brief notations entered into some type of book, or a collection of notes on cards or papers you carry for the purpose of recording notes. They may include letters or diaries, log books, or complete reports prepared in the field after you complete the call. Principal characteristics of field notes are accuracy and proximity in time to the actual incidents recorded.

NOTETAKING

You may use your field notebook for a general collection of notes concerning the many aspects of your job, such as new orders or policies emanating from the administrative sections of the department, work schedules, court appearance calendars, notices of changes in laws, and any other bits of information that you wish to have at your immediate disposal in your pocket. The key to maintaining a good notebook is to determine what notes *not* to keep. Selectivity is necessary to ensure that only essential data are recorded but it is important not to exclude any information that will later prove to be critical to a case.

When to Take Notes

At the beginning of the workday, it is advisable to start a new page. List the date and time worked, partner—if any, unit number, and district worked. It should be a matter of routine to jot down notes on each incident as soon as possible after arriving on the scene. It would not seem appropriate to approach the calling party with notebook in hand or to approach a suspected law violator with your hands full. You should make your initial approach with your hands free to respond to any immediate need for action, such as rescue or apprehension. Once you have taken whatever action is necessary, it should then be a practice to take out your notebook and start recording brief but succinct notes.

Include the date and time of the incident, weather conditions if relevant, and location of the incident—not only the street address but also the character of the neighborhood (industrial, residential, transitional) if the incident and the neighborhood for some reason should be recorded. You may find it an excellent adjunct to your memory to write down any impressions you may have to indicate reasonable cause to interview an individual at a particular moment. You may later find yourself hard put to define your impressions at the time of the interview. When walking into a crime scene, you may detect a peculiar odor, hear unusual noises, or see something that just does not seem right for that particular place or time of day. Such an impression is a fleeting one and will almost as quickly be forgotten if not recorded as perceived. It is also a factual situation, not mere opinion.

When taking information concerning routine complaints, the notes you enter in your notebook may later prove quite important. For example, in a routine neighborhood quarrel, you respond to the call. After contacting the calling party and serving as a referee while the persons present settle—or at least air—their differences, you determine that no crime is being committed in your presence and that nothing seems to have occurred prior to your arrival but hot debate. You record in your notebook the names and addresses of all the people you contact and jot down a few statements concerning the actions you observed and whatever action you took or advice you offered, and then leave. Some time later you are dispatched to the same scene to investigate an aggravated assault or worse. Armed with the notes you made at the earlier incident involving the same principals, you will be far better prepared to carry the investigation through to a successful conclusion.

When you first arrive on the scene of a crime, it would be ideal to have a portable television recorder with attached microphone. As you walk up to the scene, you simply record the scene visually while simultaneously narrating your observations, pointing out and describing each item of evidence, and generally attempting to reconstruct the crime as it probably occurred. The next best arrangement is to prepare a rough sketch and jot down notes in your notebook in the same manner as if you were going to later narrate the investigation from start to finish. A miniature tape recorder should be a standard item of your reporting equipment. Record all statements made by the victims, witnesses, suspects, and anyone else you question concerning the incident, and generally record brief notes on everything that you will later commit to more formal reports. Tape as much as possible, especially verbatim statements of witnesses as long as they do not refuse to speak into the microphone and object to the recording. It is wise first to ask the person you are talking with: "Do you mind if we record this? I want to make sure that I get it all right." Gather as much information as possible.

Value of Field Notes

There are many valuable aspects to field notes and the notebook, some of which we have already covered. Consider a few more. During your busy day, you respond to many demands for service. It is impossible to remember all that you should about each incident that involves you. Your notebook serves as your memory bank, and the brief entries serve as your index of "landmarks" in your memory.

The notes provide valuable leads to investigations, data about certain items of evidence that should be checked out more thoroughly, and invaluable bits of information necessary to conduct an intelligent interview with witnesses or suspects. The notes actually serve as a self-discipline tool, forcing you to be accurate and thorough and to organize your thoughts in logical sequence.

Because of their admissibility as "past recollections recalled" and "recorded impressions," the set of well-prepared notes provides a medium whereby you may quote exactly entire statements by the principals in the investigation rather than fragments and sometimes inaccurate bits of statements. Good notes thus prepare you to deal in specifics rather than generalities. The notes will "remember," whereas the human mind may not remember efficiently. Needless to say, testimony based upon an excellent set of notes will make a more favorable impression in the courtroom and will be weighed against testimony presented by persons who did not take notes and whose memory on key points may be sprinkled with "I don't recalls" and similar excuses for not having all the facts.

What to Record

Selectivity is essential for field notes. Experience in the field and in the courtroom will be the principal teachers in this important matter; however, both take time. Foremost in your mind should be the elements of the corpus delicti if you are investigating a crime. All of those elements are going to have to be substantiated if you are to lead the case to a successful conclusion. The Five W's and the H of every case—When, Who, Where, What, Why, and How—are

W-1: When? When did the event occur?

When was it reported?

When did the problem begin that is now being reported?

W-2: Who? Who are the principal characters in this scenario?

Who else is present?

Who are all these other people?

Who has information concerning the details of this problem?

Who has information about the background of this problem?

W-3: Where?   Where are the victims?

Where are the witnesses?

Where are the suspects?

Where is the evidence?

W-4: What?   What appears to have happened?

What do the people tell you happened?

What really happened?

W-5: Why?   Why is the informant telling you this?

Why is the story people tell you "too perfect"?

Why did the crime occur? (Look for motive.)

H-1: How?   How did the crime occur? Was it possible?

How did the burglars remove six tons of gold bullion in two hours with a pickup truck?

How did the burglarized store have the window glass smashed from the *inside*?

How could the culprit get in through that little opening?

When you record names and descriptions of victims and witnesses, be sure to use correct spelling as the people themselves spell their names, not as you guess they might spell them. List the names of other officers who are involved in the event, describe their activities, and indicate that they, too, are preparing reports (if, in fact, they are). Describe in detail the chain of custody of evidence that you handle.

Don't be surprised to see more on these items of reporting again and again throughout your instruction. Your job as a police officer includes looking beyond the statements of the witnesses and surface appearances, and to get to the *truth*. Never take anything for granted when investigating any type of police incident. While compiling the information in the field and the courtroom, you will have to attempt to anticipate all the questions that will be asked (and the spaces to be filled out in the report forms) by the supervisors, the prosecutor, and the court; and then you must set about recording the answers to all those questions in your notebook. You may choose to keep a separate notebook on debriefing data and significant impressions that you would rather not make public but need for a convenient reference.

Retention or Destruction of Field Notes?

Department policy may decide this question for you, and require that either you retain or you destroy your field notes once you have committed the information to a formal report. Certain internal affairs and intelligence assignments may require the destruction of all notes to assure that the formal report you submit to the Chief is the only report in existence. My recommendation is that you retain your original notes for at least a year or two except for one or more of the reasons listed above.

The courts have held that it is proper to throw away your field notes as long as (1) you destroy them in good faith; (2) you incorporate them into a formal report; (3) the formal report accurately reflects the contents of the notes; and (4) the prosecutor turns over a copy of the formal report before trial.[1]

The Notebook

Although some departments are quite specific about the type of notebook officers carry, the type of book is secondary to what you put inside (see Figure 5–2). Some "experts" recommend that only loose-leaf books be

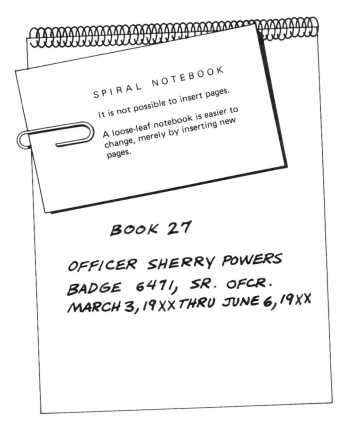

Figure 5-2   Sample notebook.

[1]*Gary, G.* 115 Cal. App. 3D 629 (1981); *Seaton,* 146 Cal. App. 3D 67 (1983); *Angeles,* 172 Cal. App. 3D 1203 (1985); *Trombetta,* 467 U.S. 479 (1984); and *Youngblood* 109 S. Ct. 333 (1988).

used, allowing the insertion or removal of pages in any desired sequence. I prefer the bound or spiral notebook, because it is immediately apparent when a page has been removed. Most legally required log books and ledgers are bound to avoid the problem of "page juggling." The least efficient type of notebook is the standard clipboard with a collection of loose sheets of paper held together only by a spring clip at the top of the board.

The argument against the bound notebook is that when an officer once refers to the notebook in court, the defense attorney may inspect the book, presumably to challenge its authenticity. The argument then points out that the rest of the book is laid bare for the inspection of the attorney and that the attorney will go on a "fishing expedition" reading passages from other cases and perhaps reading aloud in the courtroom some statement that might prove embarrassing to the author, thereby serving as a means to attempt to impeach the officer's reference to the notes in question. If that is the case, where is the prosecutor? The officer who plans to refer to a notebook in court should make that fact known to the prosecutor and show the portion of the book that includes notes relevant to the case at hand. Any other portion of the notebook is "off limits" because it is totally irrelevant and immaterial to this case. Introduction of any of that extraneous material to the case by either side would be inadmissible, as would be any other extraneous material. The judge may order those portions of the book closed, or stapled shut, and inadmissible.

The book should bear some identifying data on the cover, such as the name and badge number of the officer and perhaps a notebook number. After the book has been filled with information, it is a good practice to keep it for a reasonable period of time. The book should be numbered and maintained in some semblance of sequence for quick retrieval in the case of a call to court to testify in some case whenever it comes up for trial, or retrial. To reduce the possibility of any charge of "doctoring," the pages can be numbered.

Format of the Book

The specific style of keeping notes should be a personal matter; notebooks will be distinctively different from one officer to another. As a guide in developing your own style, consider the following formats.

The style of notes will vary with the situation, and several styles may occur while recording facts in a single event. The *narrative* style is a shortened version of the events as they are going to be recounted in the more lengthy report. It may include information that is only indirectly related to the incident and is included because it provides a series of memory "landmarks." For example, when a suspect states that he was attending a motion picture, it may be immaterial to the case at hand, but it will be significant to the investigation if the suspect is asked about the title of the picture and the story line. Other people he saw, or incidents that may have occurred during his attendance at the theater, such as the traffic accident that occurred just outside the theater as he and his date were en route to the ticket booth to purchase tickets, may be necessary for inclusion in a narrative account recorded in the field notebook (see Figure 5–3).

Another notetaking format is the *question-and-answer method*. An excellent example of this format is the advisement of a suspect's constitutional rights against self-incrimination and right to an attorney before and during questioning and the suspect's verbatim responses to both the admonishment and his or her exercise or waiver of those rights. Instead of writing "I advised the subject of his rights," indicate the exact words used and the exact response by the subject to tell the officer that he knows exactly what his rights are and that he still chooses to confess; this may prove quite significant when later referring to those notes in court, leading up to the introduction of the actual confession. Use of the question-and-answer format in this instance may make the case because it demonstrates the professional approach of the officer to a delicate situation involving an individual's constitutional rights in our democratic society.

A third format for recording notes is the *chronological approach*, which may consist of a series of notes, each preceded by a letter or num-

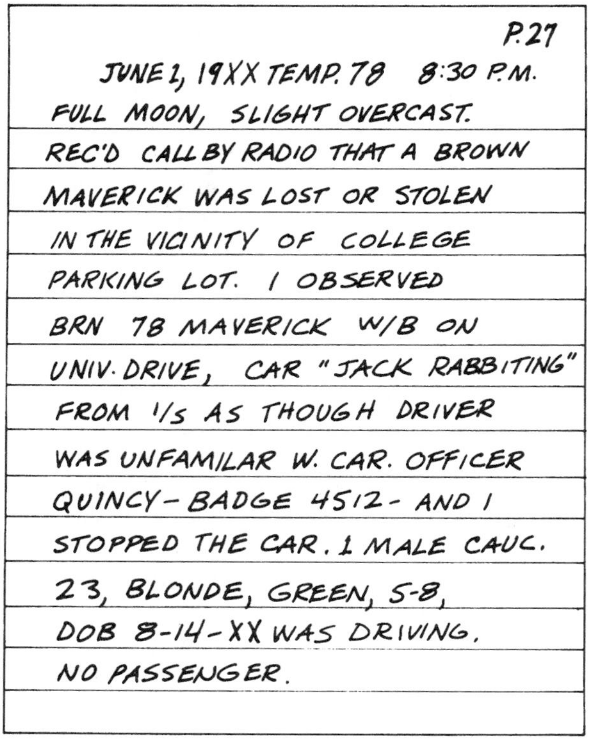

```
                                   P.27
        JUNE 1, 19XX TEMP. 78   8:30 P.M.
FULL MOON, SLIGHT OVERCAST.
REC'D CALL BY RADIO THAT A BROWN
MAVERICK WAS LOST OR STOLEN
IN THE VICINITY OF COLLEGE
PARKING LOT.  I OBSERVED
BRN 78 MAVERICK W/B ON
UNIV. DRIVE,  CAR "JACK RABBITING"
FROM 1/s AS THOUGH DRIVER
WAS UNFAMILAR W. CAR. OFFICER
QUINCY - BADGE 4512 - AND I
STOPPED THE CAR. 1 MALE CAUC.
23, BLONDE, GREEN, 5-8,
DOB 8-14-XX WAS DRIVING.
NO PASSENGER.
```

Figure 5-3   Narrative style. Used to substantiate "probable cause" and to record events in logical sequence.

biographical approach

ber to indicate the exact sequence of events as they occurred and as they presented themselves to the recorder.

Numbering pages in the notebook is a matter of choice for the keeper of the book. The advantages have been pointed out, but there may be no actual need for this extra procedure. As a general guide, when you come to the end of information concerning one case before reaching the end of the page, you should draw a line or several lines from the bottom of that information to the bottom of the pages to clearly indicate that there is no more information to be entered. The lines also show to the observer that nothing has been added since the drawing of the lines.

Each new case or incident should begin on a new page in the book, with the identifying data somewhere on the page. Using a fresh page makes it easier to keep information on several cases separate, and it will also serve to keep the nonrelated material out of the courtroom. The data on each case should include the date and time the notes are being entered, the weather conditions (if relevant), the location, names and addresses of persons contacted or mentioned, and their respective relationships to the incident. It may later be to your advantage if you also write a brief description of each individual named to serve as an additional memory jogger. This description should be followed, of course, by whatever information is provided about or by each individual named.

A word of caution when describing a person: You are not preparing this report to entertain the supervisor or the records clerk who reads it. The purpose of the description is for identification. An officer once described a male Negro whom he believed to be a homosexual by using two derogatory and totally unacceptable words to "enhance" his description. That report was presented in court as evidence and the defense attorney had a field day. Needless to say, the case was dismissed and a civil rights lawsuit followed. Not only was it embarrassing and costly for the department, but it was unnecessarily stupid.

"Creative report writing" is a term you will hear from time to time. A police report is not a novel, nor may you take "literary license" as a novelist and embellish the truth to make the story read better. Boring as it may be, adhere strictly to the truth and the facts.

Techniques in Notetaking

One of the predominant pitfalls in recording statements by various persons contacted during the course of an investigation is to represent paraphrased information provided by witnesses or victims as exact quotations. A simple rule to follow is to identify quotations with quotation marks and then record the verbatim statements in precisely the same words used by the subject. Never violate that rule. If one word is changed or missing, do not use quotation marks.

Whenever you are questioning people, be sure to speak with them separately so as to get individual impressions from each witness. Avoid the "jury description" of people or of events. This is particularly important when securing descriptions of suspects, since the differences between descriptions may lead to a quicker apprehension. The individual with the stronger personality may be wrong and yet be able to convince his fellow witnesses that he is right and they are wrong. Be sure to get facts, not suppositions, about what might have happened.

Too much information in the notebook is usually better than too little, but be careful not to overdo it. If you include too little, your notes may have no value later because you left out information that you later found was important but did not know was important when you were taking notes. Use all the space you need for the notes, but keep the language understandable and the writing legible (see Figure 5–4). One instructor may say that you should make your notes illegible and use a shorthand that is understandable only to yourself, so that you can testify in your own style without having to slavishly stick to your notes. Use of such a system seems foolish and unnecessary. If there is some question as to the veracity of your notes, then perhaps they should not be used at all. Deliberate efforts to keep notes

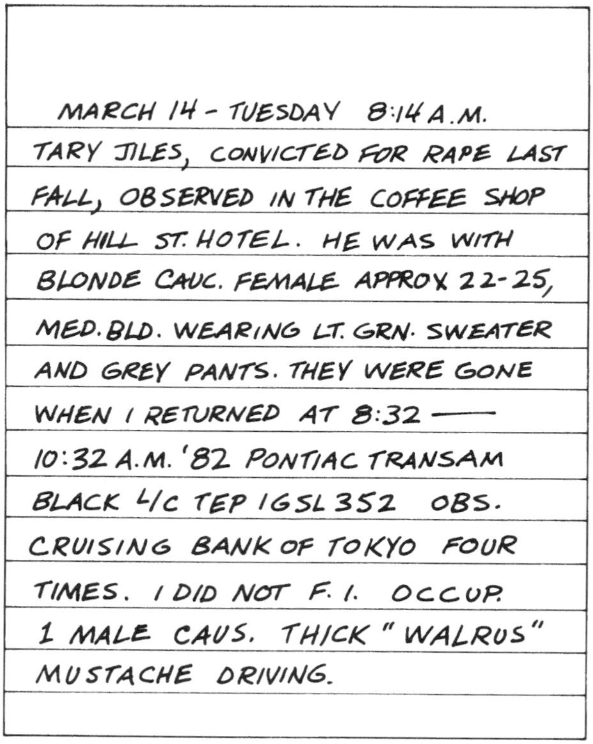

> MARCH 14 – TUESDAY 8:14 A.M.
> TARY JILES, CONVICTED FOR RAPE LAST
> FALL, OBSERVED IN THE COFFEE SHOP
> OF HILL ST. HOTEL. HE WAS WITH
> BLONDE CAUC. FEMALE APPROX 22-25,
> MED. BLD. WEARING LT. GRN. SWEATER
> AND GREY PANTS. THEY WERE GONE
> WHEN I RETURNED AT 8:32 ———
> 10:32 A.M. '82 PONTIAC TRANSAM
> BLACK L/C TEP IGSL 352 OBS.
> CRUISING BANK OF TOKYO FOUR
> TIMES. I DID NOT F. I. OCCUP.
> 1 MALE CAUS. THICK "WALRUS"
> MUSTACHE DRIVING.

Figure 5-4   Recording impressions.

are difficult enough without the added complication of deliberate illegibility. Also, *absolute honesty in reporting is paramount.*

There should be some sort of general uniformity throughout your notebook that will develop as you identify the elements that are essential to good reporting. Consistency in your reporting format and style will make it much easier for you to use your notes intelligently for later testimony and report preparation.

Officer's Daily Log

In addition to the field notebook, it is essential that you maintain a daily log or some form of accounting system to keep track of your on-duty field patrol activities (see Figure 5–5). With a data processing system, it may be possible to maintain accurate records without a log by using "activity record cards" that are made out and time-stamped for every accountable activity in which you take part. In lieu of the computer method, which is standard with law enforcement agencies throughout the country, you must keep a log.

The purposes of a log are manifold. One obvious purpose is that the log actually serves as a chronological diary of the field officer's working day. You may use it for reference at some later date to supply specific information, it may serve as a memory jogger, and it can be relied on to show where you were and what you were doing at particular times of the day. In addition, supervisors use the log as a control device, for guidance in counseling officers on the types of activity with which they concern themselves and to discuss their work in general. The log is good for documentation of

OFFICER'S DAILY LOG

Name _____ Rank_____ Badge_____ Date_____

Day of the Week_____ Duty Hours: Start _____ End _____

Weather_____ Visibility_____ Unit #_____ Partner_____

Assignment_____ Mileage: Begin_____ End_____Total_____

Citations_____F.I.'s_____ Arrests: Fel._____ Misd._____ Open Doors_____

Recov. Veh. _____Calls_____ Reporting Time_____ Patrol Time %_____

Time Start	Time Compl.	Time Cons.	Case No.	Incident	Dispo. & Comments

Figure 5-5   Daily log.

an officer's activities; for example, when a burglary was committed in the officer's area, the supervisor may ask: "Where were you when the burglar was breaking into a building in your district?" The log can also be used for cost accounting, tabulating actual time spent on various types of activities, and interpreting the information in matters of actual cost for each activity. Other uses for the log are as a source for tabulating volume of work and percentages of time devoted to various tasks on the job.

The daily log should contain columns for each of the following entries for each separate activity: source of call (radio, supervisor, private person, or observation by officer), time started, time completed, and time consumed in performing the activity. Next in line should be a space for a brief statement of the nature of the call and names of principals. The disposition is next, and the final space calls for any numbers related to the incident, such as case, citation, or warrant numbers.

If necessary for management or planning purposes, the various amounts of time could easily be totaled at the end of the day. The breakdown would vary with individual department needs, such as criminal versus non-criminal activities, time spent on incidents observed at your own initiative, miscellaneous time spent in delivering or servicing vehicles, actual patrol time, and reporting time. The recapitulation portion at the top of the log could include spaces for tabulating such activities as citations issued, field interviews conducted, open doors investigated, vehicles recovered, and any other type of activity for which a number count would aid in supervision or planning.

Each log should be maintained for a tying up my computerseparate day, headed with your name, district assignment, unit number, and any other pertinent information. If it would serve a purpose, a space for starting and ending vehicle mileage could be provided as well as a place for statements on the condition of the vehicle and any conditions on the beat requiring some attention but not a separate report.

— SECTION 2 —
REPORT WRITING

INTRODUCTION

Reports and other police records provide the basis for the many different activities carried out by the field officers, the investigators, the many specialists in the organization, the supervisors, and the administrators.

Nearly every service you perform, each crime or accident you investigate, and any other police operation you participate in calls for the initiation of a permanent record of some type or other. The record may range from a single terse entry on a line in a daily activity log to a detailed document several pages in length.

Your skills as a police officer are evaluated largely on the basis of your reports. How you do a job or perform a service is of tremendous importance and is actually the real test of your abilities as a police officer. How you report what you have done indicates your skill not only in doing the task, but also in transmitting that information to your readers. To the majority of people affected by your actions, your report is accepted at face value as an accurate account of what you did. A supervisor may have been present when you performed your task, but probably was not (at least during the majority of occasions he or she will not be). The ranking officer in the office who reviews your reports and passes judgment on your abilities through in-office contacts, and through your reports, will not have been present. The various people to whom the report is sent for appraisal, action, or filing will have only the report to go on.

Your supervisor checks the report to make sure that you operated in conformance with department policies and procedures. Follow-up investigators of your department and other agencies determine what you have done on the case to date (based upon what you relate in your report) and what they must do next to bring the case to a successful conclusion. You should include in the report a statement of what you did not do and the people you did not contact, and give the reasons, such as "works nights, home during the day," or "did not have sufficient information to establish that he was the perpetrator."

For example, assume that during a routine crime investigation you collected evidence, interviewed witnesses, and performed hundreds of minor related acts, thoroughly investigating the case. During the investigation, several of the people whom you contacted had nothing of material value to add to the case. Several leads resulted in dead ends. When preparing the report, you omit the information that led to dead ends because it is of no evidential or material value to the case; and you also omit any mention of the names or identities of the many persons you contacted who had no information to offer. By omitting this information you have streamlined the report. However, when the follow-up investigators get the case and set out to wrap up loose ends, they will probably experience many hours of wasted motion. They will retrace your footsteps without knowing it, come to the same dead ends you did, and gain the same lack of information from the many nonwitnesses you had contacted earlier. What a tremendous loss of time! It would have been of far greater value to the investigators if your report had been a page or two longer and had included all the negative information—which is also essential to an investigation—as well as the positive.

In an office far removed from the scene of the crime, the prosecutor reviews the report and the many factors that constitute the circumstances surrounding the crime: dramatic moments of confrontation between officer and suspect, weapons, sounds, and other factors. The prosecutor must use the report as the sole criterion for determining whether the elements of the crime are all reflected accurately and firmly so that the charge will be sustained. "Is there sufficient information to show that the evidence will prove the case?" The answer must be "yes."

Confession or admissions by the suspect are valueless in themselves. If they are to be of value, certain other factors must be shown in the report: Was the suspect admonished regarding his or her rights to remain silent and to have an attorney present while questioned? Were those rights waived intelligently? What language was used to admonish the suspect and what language did he or she use to convey his or her waiver? Were you acting on reasonable cause when you made the stop or conducted the search of the suspect? What were the circumstances? What was the exchange of dialogue between the suspect and you? If you read the *Miranda* admonition from the card, your report should state that you did. (You do use the card, don't you?)

The prosecutor can assume nothing, but must have accurate facts to plan strategy for the courtroom. All decisions concerning the preceding questions must be made in the absence of the reporting officer and be based exclusively on the officer's report. If any questions remain unanswered, the prosecutor must act on the premise that the reporting officer probably did not perform a specific function, such as admonishment of rights, if the report does not indicate that it was done. Absence of information in the report does not indicate that it was done. Absence of information in the report indicates absence of action in the field.

After conviction of a defendant, the judge must determine the most appropriate punishment within the framework of the law. The judge relies upon reports from probation officers who investigate the background of the accused. That background includes information from the many police reports they may review and summarize for the judge. The judge may also review the actual report itself. Even though the defendant may have been found guilty, if the judge finds that the report is an extremely poor one, he or she may determine that the investigation was equally poor. The punishment may then be lessened because of the judge's sympathy for the defendant who apparently was not handled by a professional police officer.

When the guilty party is sentenced to prison in states having the indeterminate sentence, a committee of responsible citizens may review all the facts surrounding the subject and the crime committed, including a copy of the reports, from which they make their determination as to whether or not they will schedule an early date when the subject may apply for parole. The police report may or may not be used. What type of impression would it make upon them if they were to find the report full of misspelled words and grammatical structure reflecting a sixth-grade education, although the officer preparing the report is alleged to have attended college for some time? If the report also lacks critical information about the crime and the criminal, it will be virtually worthless.

Many other situations may present themselves when the officer's reports are reviewed in an effort to know the person preparing them. Transfers into choice assignments may be on the basis of how well you can express yourself in the written and spoken word, and promotions may also take into account your ability to prepare reports. Policies are formed, police action is planned, command decisions are made, and cases are won and lost on the basis of single police reports. Finally, but certainly not to be discounted, is the fact that suspects, witnesses, and victims may have an opportunity to review your reports. If they contain misinformation, or untruthful information, there may be damaging repercussions. Your integrity and reputation of credibility is at stake.

PURPOSES FOR POLICE REPORTS

The report file and all of its related indices serve as the memory bank for the police department. This file provides for the members of the department a compilation of written records of all department transactions for which policy requires that reports be made and maintained. How extensive and detailed the system must be is a matter for the administrator to decide. What you expect to get out of it is, of course, the determinant as to what is going to have to be put into it.

Allocation of Resources

Reports are administrative tools. Budgeting decisions are made through a series of interpretations involving translating personnel and material needs into realistic money amounts. Various types of plans, long and short range, are made on the basis of compiled reports. Most plans involve establishment of a system of priorities for the order in which certain police operations will be performed or the amount of stress to be placed upon each operation. Officers' reports of past experience in performing those various tasks will be used as the basis for planning future activities. In some cases, certain types of police service traditionally relegated to the police for no apparent reason, particularly those involving noncriminal matters, may be discontinued. The decision to discontinue the service will be backed up by a collection of reports involving police officers' actions in that type of situation in the past.

Department personnel will be distributed to the various shifts, or watches, of the day, days of the week, and even the various separate operating divisions, on the basis of the reports compiled by the department and its members. If there is not sufficient personnel to cope with the problems confronting the agency, or if the existing force is performing in substandard fashion because of insufficient personnel, the reports should also indicate a need for a decision as to whether additional workers are to be added or whether certain services are to be discontinued.

Policy Changes

Long-lasting department policies often go unchallenged because of apathy, lack of interest, a desire to avoid conflicts with stronger personalities, or a "don't rock the boat" philosophy. Properly prepared reports recounting department activities utilizing means prescribed by department policies may actually point up the need for revision, or at least review, of those existing policies. In defense of tradition, it might be added that some long-standing policies are still valid and workable; often, however, the officers may have developed habits and actually be performing in violation of the existing policies.

Lack of efficiency may actually be due to the fact that officers are not abiding by policy. Any change in procedures will be long-lasting and will affect a great many people. Such change must be for improvement, not merely for "furniture rearrangement." Statistics and crime trends are indicated through the medium of police reports. Data are compiled as well for annual or semiannual reports.

Investigative Source

The reports serve as an information exchange device between the officers in different divisions and between officers on different shifts in the same division. They provide leads for investigation and a common pool of information available to all who have access to the files. Compare this method of relaying information with a system in which each officer has a separate series of information sources and resources. To find what information each has, you must first guess which officer has the information you are seeking. Once you have found the correct one, you must meet and compare notes at your mutual convenience, considering days off, sick leaves, vacations, holidays, and work schedules. When the reporting system is complete and accurate, the common pool of information is instantly available regardless of all those considerations. The reports, if kept current, will accurately reflect work that has been done and things still to be done. It serves as an aid to preparation for court and prosecution.

Information Resource for Other Agencies

Police reports provide prosecutors and the courts with a ready source of information regarding current or past cases. Probation and parole officers make decisions and recommendations regarding their probationers and parolees using every possible source of information, including police reports. Even innocuous types of reports may have an appreciable influence on their actions. The press makes use of police records to assure accuracy in reporting.

The various media have access to most police files for the purpose of assuring accuracy in reporting. Cases under investigation usually are not open to anyone, but some agencies find that by frankly presenting considerable information to the press concerning a specific case and then pointing out how the release of certain information will hinder the investigation, ethical press people will respect a confidence and are less apt to release critical information.

Although police records are generally private records of a public agency, because much of the information they contain is relevant and useful to other agencies, these agencies may be given access to the information that affects their operation.

PREPARATION OF REPORTS

Background Preparation

Before proceeding with the actual preparation of a report, spend a few minutes gathering and arranging the information in a logical sequence, thus outlining the report before you start. Although it takes more time in the initial stages, preparing a rough outline is more than worth the time and actually results in a net saving of time. Working from an outline reduces the likelihood of your finding it necessary to later insert out of sequence statements such as "It should be noted that..." or "We failed to mention in the preceding paragraph..."

Arrange all your notes, evidence, and exhibits in the same order as you intend to present the information in your report. When you come to the part of the report in which you refer to a certain item of evidence, you will not need to look for it. You can simply pick it up or otherwise examine it, determine how you are going to discuss it in the report, and then continue with the report.

Before starting with the report, also eliminate any superfluous information and excess verbiage. Mere words to fill space have no place in a police report. This does not imply that valuable information should be sacrificed for space purposes, but rather that the report should be used as a medium for transfer of information and not as an entry for a literary award. Include all information that is relevant even if it has a negative effect on the investigation. If you omit negative information, and if it is found later that you withheld it, the court may rule that you suppressed valid evidence.

If there is to be more than one officer taking part in the preparation of the report, in one continuous document, or if you are to prepare a summary of your own part in the case, be sure to correlate the information before beginning your work. In addition, be sure that the reports refer to each other and that they are correlated in such a way that readers will have no difficulty in maintaining continuity of thoughts when reading the reports and taking follow-up action on them.

Report Style

For some reason, normal, reasonably articulate young people who become police officers stop talking in a normal manner; instead of getting out of a car, they "alight from said vehicle." A car becomes a "unit," and "we" becomes "officers" or "undersigned." Instead of running after a suspect, they "pursue the alleged perpetrator." Instead of running west, they "proceed rapidly in a westerly direction." The dead man becomes "the deceased," Jones becomes "victim number one," and whenever an officer watches someone, the officer's report states that he or she "maintained visual control." The possibilities in this strange police language are endless and for the most part do nothing but obfuscate.

What happened to good "olde" English? If the novice and the old hand alike would just write the way they talk, there would be far less trouble with the police reports. As a watch commander, I spent many days and nights in the office discussing reports with officers. They would come into the office and discuss the circumstances and merits of the case, lay out the scenario, and seek advice from the "master." Then they would go off to their chores of wrapping up the investigation, booking the suspect, "lodging the evidence" (which is similar to putting it into the evidence locker), and preparing their reports. By the time the report got to my office, the only similarity between the report and the earlier conversations that I had with those officers were the names and the places. The "gobbledygook" characteristic of the police report would often change the circumstances of the event and result in great confusion for the prosecuting attorneys who had to read the reports and sort out the facts.

A police report should be simple, brief, descriptive, factual, and to the point. Adherence of the Five W's and H are essential. By all means the police investigative report should very clearly enunciate the WHO—who did what to whom or who are the players in this life drama; the WHAT—what happened, what was the means to commit the crime, what was the weapon or tool used to commit the crime, what was the object of the theft or assault; the WHY—the motive or reason for the crime; the WHERE—the location of the crime, where the weapon or tool came from, where the tool or weapon was found after the crime; the WHEN—the time of day, day of week, month, year; and the HOW—how the perpetrator went about committing the crime.

Tell the story as you would tell it to a fellow officer. There are few officers who pass the entrance exams and the academy training without being able to express themselves in at least an average articulate manner. They have little trouble in their daily discussions about their day on patrol and the interesting events. Your report should be written in the same style as your conversation. Explain the events in the report using the same style that you would use to explain it to your sergeant or fellow officer when you take time out from your reports and bring each other up to date on what has been happening. Take a tape recorder to the coffee shop and record your explanation of the incident while discussing it there, then play it back when you get ready to prepare your report, and you will probably discover that your report will be much better than if you succumb to the urge to write in the outdated language of the police reports of 30 years ago when we were told that we must write about the things we do as police officers in a detached third-person language so as to avoid giving our readers the impression that we are egotistical by using the big "I" too often in the report.

Use a free-flowing and uncomplicated reporting style to describe the action and investigation and other information in logical sequence as it presented itself to you. Be sure to write to *express*, not *impress*. If you use the same language you use in normal conversation, and know the meaning of the words you use, there will be little likelihood of confusion. The reporting style should reflect your individual personality. If you are not quite sure of the meaning of a word that you want to use, don't use it.

Resist temptations to exaggerate or to model a report on someone else's work. There is sometimes a desire to prepare an outstanding report on an individual's physical appearance, as when someone is under the influence of narcotics or dangerous drugs. The temptation is also great to memorize the case number of a report that was brilliantly executed by another officer at some time in the past, to refer to it for guidance in preparing similar reports, and then to either consciously or unconsciously plagiarize the material because it reads so well and can be used to apply to the specific case at hand. Incongruity between the officer and his or her reports will indicate whether this may be the case.

Do not copy the reporting style of other officers. If you do resort to such chicanery, consider what happened to one of my officer colleagues. One report in the department was very popular for its description of a suspect while under the influence of an opiate. Several officers had the case number, and whenever they wanted to write a good description of their suspects under the influence of opiates, they used the sample report as a guide. One officer who copied the sample report verbatim to describe the suspect he had just arrested ran into trouble when the report was presented later in court. The defense pointed out that the defendant's eyes could not have reacted to light the way the report said they did because the defendant was *blind in one eye*.

Follow a logical sequence when preparing the report. The sequence of events as reported to you will probably be the most common method of presentation. In a very complicated case, the events that occurred may be presented to you entirely out of sequence through several disconnected accounts from a series of people. If that is the case, it will be necessary for you to reconstruct the information, and the various bits and pieces of information, and report it in logical sequence without showing a lack of continuity in the investigation. It may be necessary to list the many people who provided information, describe briefly what each person had to offer to the case, and then bring together all the information in the report.

If you are reconstructing the crime on the basis of your investigation as it progresses, you may have to step back briefly, look at the entire sequence of events, and attempt to reconstruct the crime as you believe it *probably* occurred. If you use this method, be sure your report reflects a statement to that effect.

Be careful when you do this, and be sure to present the information as "supposition." Your investigation may later turn up evidence and reveal information that discounts your suppositions, making your original and supplemental reports look as though they are contradicting each other.

Use variety in your vocabulary. It will reduce reader fatigue as well as the possibility of each of your reports developing into a carbon copy of each preceding one on a similar matter. A person may state, he may reiterate, retort, reply, say, or do any number of things when he responds to a question. The English language is designed to express many shades of meaning when appropriately used.

Unless your own department head has established a policy that prohibits it, try using the first-person singular when reporting what you did, whom you questioned, what you observed. It seems more sensible to write that "I" did something than for you to write the "undersigned" or "officer" did this or that. Suppose that you and another officer jointly investigate a case and that one discovers a piece of evidence while the other questions a witness. The alternatives might be: "Officer Jones discovered a crowbar with a 2-inch bite under the left front seat of the suspect's car while I was questioning the suspect. The suspect told me that he had used the crowbar to force entry into the drugstore just a few minutes before I had observed him running down the alley." Or "Undersigned and Officer Jones conducted a search. Officer Jones (who is also undersigned, by the way) found the crowbar while the suspect told the undersigned that he had used the crowbar just a few minutes before he was discovered by the undersigned." Which way do you talk when recounting the situation to your supervisor or how will you relate it in court?

There are some proponents of the traditional third-person style who will say that third person makes the case more impersonal and unbiased. They also feel that it reduces the possibility that personal aggrandizement will creep into the account of the story, maintaining that too frequent use of the word "I" does not belong in a police report. I say that this argument is invalid. The personality of the reporting officer, and not his or her style of writing, will determine whether or not bias will creep into the picture. An egotist will not be stifled by mere elimination of the use of the word "I." If the word "I" may be used in court, why not in the report?

If you have prepared in advance and have arranged the sequence of events in the report, it will seldom be necessary to use statements such as "It should be noted" and "We failed to mention" or to preface a statement with "The information gained was substantially as follows." If the information substantially follows, why preface it with worthless words?

CONSTRUCTION OF THE REPORT

Many police reports have been reduced to forms and filling in numbered boxes or spaces with single words, symbols, or checks. This is ideal for the common types of reports, when it is necessary to report only that certain procedural requirements have been met by the reporting officer. The time saved by maximum utilization of this type of form amply justifies the creation of the separate form it may require. If you have put the information in the spaces at the heading of the report, it is not necessary to report it again in the prose portion. Do not include such statements as "on above time and date" or "at above location." It is already there; there is no need to say it again.

Most reports, however, demand that the officer recount the information in prose form and in longhand. As in an essay or other form of written communication, the report should have an introduction, a body, and a conclusion. The introduction usually consists of a synopsis of the report and an announcement of what the reader may expect to find in the body of the report. The conclusion consists of a reiteration of the body of the report in capsule form and some recommendation for further action, or a statement that this particular case requires no further action. The following deals with these basic components in more detail.

The Synopsis, or Introduction

Designate the type of report according to the agency's classification system. List all the names of persons mentioned in the report for whom there are no specific "boxes" in the standardized portion of the form, if there is such a section. Be sure to indicate the relationship to the case each named person plays. Enumerate and describe any evidence, exhibits, or other information you intend to bring in during the body of the report. In a paragraph, summarize briefly the information you are going to recount in more detail in the following paragraphs.

The Body

Use short sentences and short paragraphs in your reports. Describe the sequence of events and information in concise and understandable terms. Either recount the events as presented to you, or, if necessary for continuity and if possible without compromising the authenticity of the report, lay out the body of the report in a logical sequence either as the events occurred or as you believe they might have occurred.

Be *completely honest* and *objective*. Be sure to include all information developed, even though some of it may be detrimental to the case from your point of view. The purpose of the report is to report information accurately as it presents itself, not to distort it to make a more convincing case against anyone named in the report. When taking and recording statements by various informants, bear in mind the fact that victims and witnesses are not always unequivocally correct. Suspects may offer rationalizations and defenses that may be wholly or partly true. Any opinions you may have to advance as the report progresses should be clearly identified as such, and they should be included only when the opinion has a substantial bearing on the case. Never express an opinion as fact. It is more appropriate to label and recite observations and impressions that present themselves to you, and to leave any opinion making to the reader. Whatever reporting method you choose, be sure that you do not employ any device that serves to communicate any prejudice or bias that you may entertain about any of the persons named in the report.

When recording statements made by the many persons in the report, identify verbatim statements with quotation marks and correct punctuation. Never paraphrase a statement and present it as a direct quotation. Identify all sources of information. Avoid statements such as "one of the witnesses stated...." Name the witness. Your police report is not an authentication of fact. A witness states something as "fact," but you are simply recording that statement, which the witness may be required to repeat in court. The court may choose to accept the statement as fact, but at best your report is "hearsay."

Answer all the questions that must be answered in any police report, or at least all those to which you can obtain answers. The Five W's (who, what, when, where, why) and How should be the object of your investigation, and as many as possible should be answered. Sometimes the absence of certain answers are just as significant as their presence. If you observe behavior by a suspect or witness that causes you to believe there is going to be a "diminished capacity" or witness qualification problem at the trial, describe the behavior you observe without making a statement of your opinion or conclusion.

Report all the investigative leads you have followed, including those that did not bear fruit. It is just as important to report that you contacted five named potential witnesses and gained no information as it is to enumerate only the names and information provided by those who present positive leads and information. Without the unsuccessful leads, the follow-up investigator will have to pursue leads that you have already checked out. If you obtain identical information (or lack of it), it is correct to summarize by reporting that witness Jones stated substantially the same as witness Izenthall, if that is the case.

If you have information that tends to point toward the innocence of the suspect although all of your other information points toward guilt, you must include all of the information in the report. While it is true that you are responsible to the prosecutor to aid in the prosecution, it is also your responsibility to clear the innocent.

Explain delays in the investigation. For example, why did you wait three months before interviewing a key witness? If it was because the witness had been out of the country, say so in your report.

Use of Names

The first time you use a name in a report, list it in full, including the title, such as Mr. Jonathan Quincy Forthright. During subsequent references, use the last name only. If there are two or more persons with the same name, such as Mr. and Mrs., or John and Georgia, it will be necessary to use the different first names or titles to continue to distinguish the two different players. Avoid the use of labels, such as "victim number 1" and "witness number 13." Such labeling adds to the confusion that is already prevalent in what is usually a complicated case, and readers have to prepare a cast of characters for themselves so that they can continuously refer to it while reading your report. Use of the names lessens the confusion.

In addition to the names, use date of birth and description of the named person. Two people in the same place of residence may have identical names, such as father and son who do not use the "junior" or "senior" labels. Also, you should include a statement as to any obvious impairment that might alter the value of his or her statements, such as "speech slurred, and odor of alcohol indicates that he is under the influence of alcohol" or "wearing hearing aids in both ears," or "wearing eyeglasses that appear quite thick."

The tenor of your report should indicate the nature of the follow-up necessary. Sometimes the results you achieve will be far more productive if you provide the readers with sufficient information to determine the need for urgent action as a result of their own thought processes rather than tell them that they should perform their jobs in the manner you suggest. The message is the same, but the method is more effective. If there is an urgent reason for following a certain lead, the wording of your report should indicate the priority it should receive. In most agencies, cases are handled in accordance with some system of priorities. The priorities are usually established by the follow-up officers on the basis of the information they glean from the reports, except for those cases that fall into specific report classifications.

The Conclusion

Before preparing the conclusion of the report, go over the synopsis and body at least cursorily, then "wrap it up" with your conclusion. If the case is cleared or closed, indicate that fact so that recordkeeping requirements may be fulfilled. Any unfinished work should be listed and presented in such a manner that the reader can make his or her decision to pursue the investigation according to an independent priority system. Generally summarize what you have done and what is left to be done on the case. In some cases, policy may require that you make a recommendation for further action. If that is the case, any recommendation you make should be based upon information that the reader may find in the body of the report.

Abbreviations

Some standardized forms make it necessary to abbreviate to get all the relevant data in the undersized space provided. Only in that case is it wise to use abbreviations. Too often the time that may be saved by using them is lost in later attempts to decipher some of the abbreviations that may be employed by the economy-minded reporter. If in doubt, do not abbreviate except for use of the very commonly accepted forms that are listed in any standard dictionary, and avoid the use of police jargon.

Avoid Ambiguity

Following is list of words that are commonly used in police reports that cause more confusion and raise more questions than if they had been left out of the report. After each word or phrase, we shall attach a comment or list some of the unanswered questions posed by use of those words. Bear in mind that the readers are not going to be able to have you around when they don't understand what you meant when you wrote the report.

"was contacted"—how? by whom? in person? by telephone?

"She (or he) indicated"—how? by saying something? by a gesture?

"we responded"—was the response in person? an emotional response? did you drive there? or walk? or call back?

"proceeded to"—started to? went to? Better to write: We went…

"observed"—in what manner? by which of the senses?

"detected"—by what means? odor? smell? brilliant police work?

"it should be noted"—an unnecessary statement

"it was determined"—by whom? how?

"we failed to mention earlier"—plan ahead and you will. Delete.

"residence"—what kind of residence? a house? apartment? motel?

"related"—did he or she tell you something?

"articulated"—was this done by word of mouth? by telephone?

"verbally related"—the word "verbal" means either orally or in writing, or by the use of words

"informed"—told? wrote? sent a secret message by telegraph?

"altercation"—why not just say they had a fight?

"verbal altercation"—do you mean to say they had an argument?

"in reference to"—a lot of words to say "…about…"

"at that point in time"—a lot of words to say "…then…"

"utilize"—use?

"the bottom line"—just what does that really mean?

"maintained surveillance over"—did you watch? or listen?

"officer (or undersigned) verbally advised"—I told him...

"a knife was found"—who found it?

"a sound was heard"—by whom?

With a little imagination, your own list could grow extensively. Try to make every word mean exactly what you want it to mean. As you can see from the preceding list, some words may have more than one meaning.

Second only to the video recording of both sight and sound, one of the more accurate methods of assuring accuracy in reporting is to use a tape recorder on the spot and tape everything. That is hardly possible in all circumstances, but you should attempt to make extensive use of such a device whenever practicable. Verbatim accounts of any event are valuable when you are analyzing the activity later and are evaluating what went wrong, or right, and how the situation might be handled better the next time. It also is a tremendous aid when preparing your reports and it is difficult to remember everything that happened and who said what. Once you get away from the scene, immediately record whatever it is that you want to remember. Then review the tape while the events are still fresh in your mind.

Dictating the Report

An encouraging trend during the past few years has been the attempt to reduce the time required for report writing without reducing the efficiency of the reports. Short forms have been developed for many of the "routine" reports, such as miscellaneous service, calling for insertion of a series of X's in appropriate boxes on the form. Other forms have been streamlined and designed so that you may write or print out your report in its entirety while still in the field, and turn it in at your convenience when you return to headquarters for some other purpose. Some reports have been virtually eliminated, and the information they once contained is now recorded in a terse statement as a single line entry on an officer's daily log. Despite such developments, however, many reports cannot be streamlined by use of any of these methods. The crime report must include a detailed narrative account of exactly what took place during the commission of the crime and during the investigation. In cases when the report must recount actual words used and verbatim accounts of things done by the principals, the narrative report is still the only efficient method for recording the necessary information.

Stenographers have been introduced into the police reporting system as have several types of dictating and transcribing equipment to be used by reporting officers and clerical assistants as a team. The results have been rewarding in many cases. Reports have improved, and officers have increased their ratio of field time to report time. In other cases, the results have been tremendously disappointing. I suggest that the concept is sound but that the system must be well planned and executed. The people using it must be willing to sit down together and work out the details of how to make it work.

Individual department needs vary, as do their financial resources and facilities. However, every department must have some provision that will allow you to stop occasionally and listen to a partial playback (or readback in the case of an in-person stenographer), so that you may edit when necessary and maintain continuity in your reports.

Whether you dictate your reports in person to the stenographer in the office, telephone in the reports, use a dictating instrument, or carry your dictating unit in the field with you, there are a few basic rules that must be followed.

1. Organize your thoughts in advance. You should have developed the report from start to finish before you begin dictating. Random notes may suffice, but an outline may prove more useful.

2. Dictate your report while the information is still fresh in your mind.

3. Dictate the report in clear, concise language. Exaggerate the consonants so that they are heard, and avoid slurring words together. Whenever there is any possibility of misunderstanding in the pronunciation of a word, particularly when listing, spell it out. The person transcribing the information you dictate cannot be expected to guess what it is that you meant to say or how a particular name should be spelled.

4. Dictate the report in the same language and style you would use if you were telling it in person. First-person singular reads most naturally, and I recommend its use.

5. Avoid redundancy. Do not ramble, repeating yourself in several different approaches. This is to be avoided when dictating a report rather than typing it yourself.

6. Have all names, addresses, and phone numbers to be included in the report close at hand.

7. Do one thing at a time. While dictating, do not perform other tasks, such as making out a log, shuffling papers, or carrying on a conversation with another person.

8. Make maximum use of your field notes, which should provide a good foundation for accurate and complete reports if they have been compiled as recommended earlier in this chapter.

9. Keep your sentence structure simple and correct.

10. Check the report after it has been typed, and compare it with your dictated tape to assure accuracy. Retain the tapes until you are able to make the comparison.

11. Never expect the person who is preparing the actual typewritten

draft of the report to alter it in any way from the way in which you dictated it.

THE MISCELLANEOUS INCIDENT REPORT

Every agency has a standard procedure for reporting actions and incidents for which there is no specific form. In fact, such a miscellaneous classification may have a standardized form. There are two basic kinds of formats for this type of form. One consists of a series of statements with adjacent blocks for insertion of X's or checkmarks for indicating basic information that is so standardized that no value could be derived from narrative response. For example, you might respond to a call on a family disturbance. Upon your arrival you determine that no law had been broken. You contact the principals in the case, separate them, and get a brief account of the nature of the problem. You determine that the matter is entirely civil in nature and that if you were to give advice, it would be unethical and extralegal. You arbitrate the matter because your role is to prevent crimes. After calming the people down and making sure that the likelihood of a crime occurring after your departure is not apparent, you leave.

In this case, you might use a *forced choice* form. You merely have to fill in the date and time of the incident, the names and addresses of the principals, the identity of the calling party, and the location of the incident. You then go down the list of choices and mark the boxes adjacent to the statements to the effect that the call was (1) a neighborhood dispute; (2) it was noncriminal in nature; (3) the people were advised to contact attorneys in any civil law question; or (4) you kept the peace and advised the parties that someone could be arrested for any law violation.

The second type of form for miscellaneous incidents is more common. It calls for brief statements concerning the nature of the call and any action taken by the officer, a summary of the circumstances leading up to the demand for police service, and a synopsis of any other relevant data that might later be of some value in criminal investigations.

In completing this report, indicate the names of all principals involved in the call, and indicate by a brief statement the relationship of each named individual to the call, such as "our presence was requested to keep the peace" and "involved in neighborhood disturbance." The report should briefly recount the facts in an informative fashion and contain only relevant data. What occurred while en route to the call and the fact that you "resumed patrol" are examples of irrelevant data.

THE ARREST REPORT

Many departments use a form that serves as a combined booking slip and arrest report (see Figure 5–6). The information required is mostly self-explanatory, and only a very small space is reserved for any narrative

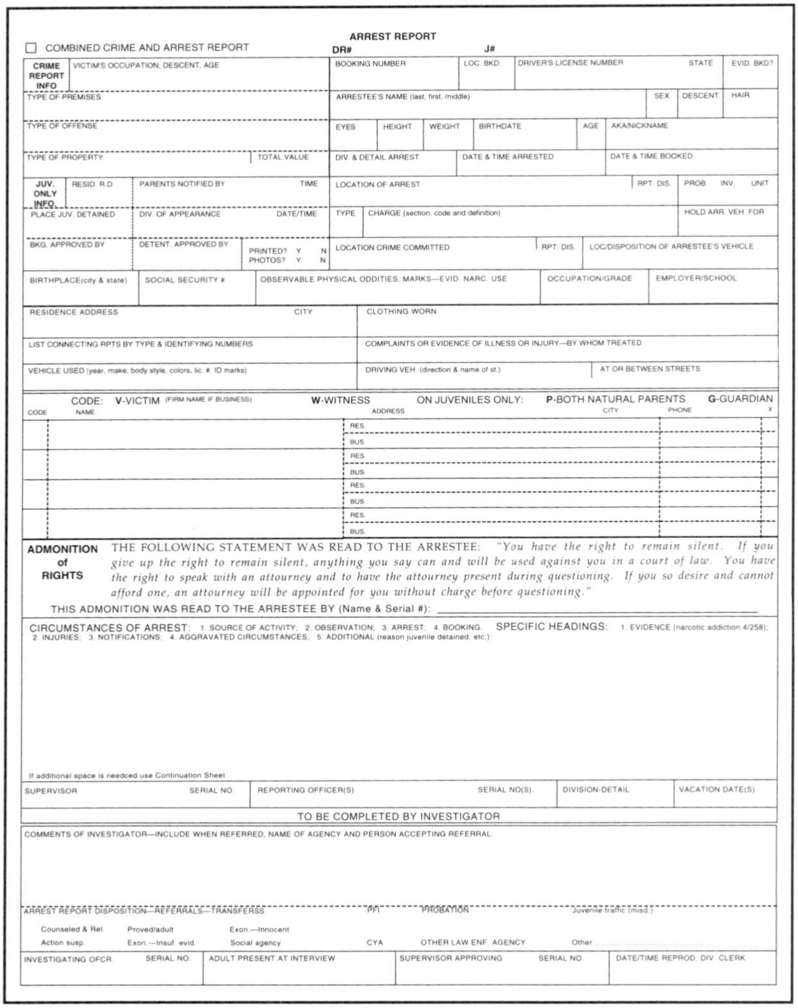

COMBINED CRIME AND ARREST REPORT

ARREST REPORT

DR# J#

CRIME REPORT INFO | VICTIM'S OCCUPATION, DESCENT, AGE | BOOKING NUMBER | LOC. BKD. | DRIVER'S LICENSE NUMBER | STATE | EVID. BKD?

TYPE OF PREMISES | ARRESTEE'S NAME (last, first, middle) | SEX | DESCENT | HAIR

TYPE OF OFFENSE | EYES | HEIGHT | WEIGHT | BIRTHDATE | AGE | AKA/NICKNAME

TYPE OF PROPERTY | TOTAL VALUE | DIV. & DETAIL ARREST | DATE & TIME ARRESTED | DATE & TIME BOOKED

JUV. ONLY INFO. | RESID. R.D. | PARENTS NOTIFIED BY | TIME | LOCATION OF ARREST | RPT. DIS. | PROB. INV. UNIT

PLACE JUV. DETAINED | DIV. OF APPEARANCE | DATE/TIME | TYPE | CHARGE (section, code and definition) | HOLD ARR. VEH. FOR

BKG. APPROVED BY | DETENT. APPROVED BY | PRINTED? Y N | PHOTOS? Y N | LOCATION CRIME COMMITTED | RPT. DIS. | LOC/DISPOSITION OF ARRESTEE'S VEHICLE

BIRTHPLACE(city & state) | SOCIAL SECURITY # | OBSERVABLE PHYSICAL ODDITIES, MARKS—EVID. NARC. USE | OCCUPATION/GRADE | EMPLOYER/SCHOOL

RESIDENCE ADDRESS | CITY | CLOTHING WORN

LIST CONNECTING RPTS BY TYPE & IDENTIFYING NUMBERS | COMPLAINTS OR EVIDENCE OF ILLNESS OR INJURY—BY WHOM TREATED

VEHICLE USED (year, make, body style, colors, lic. #, ID marks) | DRIVING VEH. (direction & name of st.) | AT OR BETWEEN STREETS

CODE: **V**-VICTIM (FIRM NAME IF BUSINESS) **W**-WITNESS ON JUVENILES ONLY: **P**-BOTH NATURAL PARENTS **G**-GUARDIAN

CODE	NAME	ADDRESS	CITY	PHONE	X
		RES.			
		BUS.			
		RES.			
		BUS.			
		RES.			
		BUS.			
		RES.			
		BUS.			

ADMONITION of RIGHTS THE FOLLOWING STATEMENT WAS READ TO THE ARRESTEE: *"You have the right to remain silent. If you give up the right to remain silent, anything you say can and will be used against you in a court of law. You have the right to speak with an attourney and to have the attourney present during questioning. If you so desire and cannot afford one, an attourney will be appointed for you without charge before questioning."*

THIS ADMONITION WAS READ TO THE ARRESTEE BY (Name & Serial #): ______

CIRCUMSTANCES OF ARREST: 1. SOURCE OF ACTIVITY; 2. OBSERVATION; 3. ARREST; 4. BOOKING. SPECIFIC HEADINGS: 1. EVIDENCE (narcotic addiction 4/258); 2. INJURIES; 3. NOTIFICATIONS; 4. AGGRAVATED CIRCUMSTANCES; 5. ADDITIONAL (reason juvenile detained, etc.):

If additional space is needced use Continuation Sheet

SUPERVISOR | SERIAL NO. | REPORTING OFFICER(S) | SERIAL NO(S). | DIVISION-DETAIL | VACATION DATE(S)

TO BE COMPLETED BY INVESTIGATOR

COMMENTS OF INVESTIGATOR—INCLUDE WHEN REFERRED, NAME OF AGENCY AND PERSON ACCEPTING REFERRAL.

ARREST REPORT DISPOSITION—REFERRALS—TRANSFERSS | PFI | PROBATION | Juvenile traffic (misd.)

Counseled & Rel. | Proved/adult | Exon.—Innocent

Action susp. | Exon.—Insuf. evid. | Social agency | CYA | OTHER LAW ENF. AGENCY | Other

INVESTIGATING OFCR. | SERIAL NO. | ADULT PRESENT AT INTERVIEW | SUPERVISOR APPROVING | SERIAL NO. | DATE/TIME REPROD. DIV. CLERK

Figure 5-6 Arrest report.

that may be necessary. Listing the name of the arrestee may seem relatively unimportant because it is so routine. Yet this is probably the most important part of the report. When spelling out the name, be sure to check all the identification materials and documents that the subject has in his or her possession. Ask the arrestee to explain any discrepancies, and be sure to record all different spellings as aliases. Many times a name has not been assumed at all; it has merely been misspelled.

Of the many sources of information about the identity of a subject, the arrest report is—or should be—the best. Take extra care to fill out the form completely. Add any items of information that come to your attention, such as various organizations and unions in which the subject holds membership cards and physical deformities or other distinguishing characteristics, that would help a later identification even under an assumed name or after an attempt at altering his or her appearance.

THE CRIME REPORT

Usually the crime report form consists of a series of standardized, required bits of information to establish jurisdiction for the case, questions that must be answered to reflect all the elements of the corpus delicti—or body—of the offense and all the required data to serve as a base for the investigation and, ultimately, the successful prosecution of the alleged perpetrator (see Figure 5–7).

The heading of each report calls for a title. In a crime report, the title includes the specific law that has been violated. The balance of the report must substantiate that fact. When more than one law violation is listed, the report must also reflect all of the elements of each separate offense.

The date and time of the occurrence and the date it is reported may provide clues to the investigator as to the possible motive of the reporting party, particularly in cases where personal animosity may be involved. The occupation and age of the victim, and the location and type of premises where the crime occurred, might lead to a specific suspect who specializes in some type of crime. Every question has a purpose and should be answered as thoughtfully as possible.

Spaces are provided for the name, address, and phone numbers of the victim, the person reporting the crime, the person who originally discovered its occurrence, and other witnesses. When listing this information, be sure to secure additional information concerning where each of these persons may be contacted when they are not at their places of residence, such as business addresses and phone numbers. If they are planning to be absent from the area for some period of time, be sure to include that information in the summary portion of the report.

The crime report should include a "modus operandi" section for recording in easy-to-locate spaces certain distinguishing characteristics about the crime that provide keys to the investigatory leads and to the possible identification of the culprit. At times the criminal will say and do certain things during the commission of crimes that are almost as effective in identification as fingerprints. The experienced investigator can sometimes compare the reports of two different crimes and see similarities in the "MO" section that indicate that both crimes may have been committed by the same individual. Filling in those spaces in the report should be done very carefully.

In crimes against property, such as burglary (see Figure 5–8) or breaking and entering, and in some crimes against persons, the point of entry and the point of exit must be identified and an effort should be made to reconstruct the crime as it probably occurred. In some cases, the

Figure 5-7   Miscellaneous complaint or crime report.

nature of the force—or lack of it—used to gain entry serves to prove intent. This is particularly important in specific intent offenses.

The weapon or tool used should be identified. If not known, marks made by tools may serve to indicate the type of weapon probably used. Be sure to include in the report a statement that the weapon or tool was *probably* whatever you believe it was if you do not know for sure. A positive statement could be disastrous to the prosecution if it later developed that an error had been made. Only when you have positive facts should you make a positive statement.

The location of the property stolen or damaged is always significant,

BURGLARY REPORT

VICTIM'S NAME (Last-first-middle. Firm name if business)

9

1.

DR

2.

BURGLARY

REPORTING DIST.

POINT WHERE ENTRANCE WAS MADE

METHOD USED TO GAIN ENTRANCE

LOCATION OF OCCURRENCE

INSTRUMENT USED (Describe)

DATE AND TIME OCCURRED

DATE AND TIME REPORTED TO P.D.

WHERE WERE OCCUPANTS?　SUSP(S). NUMBER - SEX- DESCENT

TYPE OF PROPERTY TAKEN

TOTAL VALUE
$

TRADEMARKS OF SUSPECT(S) (Actions or conversation)

TYPE OF PREMISES ENTERED

INVESTIGATIVE DIVISION(S) OR UNIT(S) NOTIFIED AND PERSON(S) CONTACTED

VEH. USED BY SUSP(S): (Yr.-make-body-color(s)-lic. no. & I.D.)

LIST ANY CONNECTING RPT(S) BY TYPE AND DR NO.

CODE: V–VICTIM　**R**–PERSON REPORTING CRIME　**S**–PERSON WHO SECURED PREMISES　**D**–PERSON WHO DISCOVERED CRIME　**W**–WITNESS

VICTIM'S OCCUPATION　DESCENT　CODE　RES. ADDRESS (Bus. add. if firm)　CITY　RES. PHONE　X　BUS. PHONE　X

NAME

ITEM NO.　(1) IDENTIFY SUSPECT(S) BY NO. (Name-address-sex-desc-age-ht-wt-hair-eyes-complex-clothing-identifying characteristics. If arrested, include Bkg. No. and Charge). (2) RECONSTRUCT THE CRIME. (3) DESCRIBE PHYSICAL EVIDENCE, LOCATION FOUND AND GIVE DISPOSITION. (4) SUMMARIZE OTHER DETAILS RELATING TO CRIME. (5) LOCATION WHERE VICT/WIT. CAN BE CONTACTED BY DAY INVEST. IF NO AVAILABLE PHONE NOS. (6) ITEMIZE (only one article to a line). DESCRIBE AND SHOW VALUE OF PROPERTY TAKEN, LISTING ALL SERIAL NOS. & MARKS OF IDENT.　SERIAL NUMBERS

If additional space is required, use Continuation Sheet, Form 15.9.

SUPERVISOR APPROVING　SERIAL. NO.　INTERVIEWING OFFICER(S) - SER NO. - DIV. - DETL.　PERSON REPORTING CRIME (Signature)

X

DATE & TIME REPRODUCED - DIVISION - CLERK　CLEARED BY MULTIPLE

FOLLOW-UP　**DR**

INDEXED　CHECKED

Figure 5-8 Burglary report.

but it is more so when the property had been in a concealed or out-of-the-way location. The apparent ease with which the culprit found the item may indicate familiarity with the place. The nature of the object attacked, such as a safe, may indicate the skill of the thief.

It is not necessary to prove motive to prove the elements of the case or to establish the identity of the culprit, but when you ask yourself "who would have benefited from this?" the motivation may lead to an indication of intent and eventual identification of the suspect. In a property crime, the motive is usually to gain possession of the stolen property. The motive in a sex crime may be revenge, or to inflict serious injury, and is usually not to achieve sexual satisfaction. An attack with a deadly weapon may be for the purpose of committing another crime, such as robbery or rape, or it may be a matter of revenge. When attempting to determine the motivation for the crime, it is sometimes possible to come up with one or more suspects. To know the motive is also an insight into the personality of the perpetrator.

Each crime report calls for a "trademark." Whether it is discernible depends on the case, but most criminals do something that is just a little unusual that distinguishes them from all others. Some individuals make a habit of using exactly the same words each time they assault a victim; others use a specific technique that seems to work each time they force entry into a place of business. The "trademark" thus becomes as distinctive as the persons themselves, and it may immediately identify a known criminal to the follow-up investigator. An example of a burglar's trademark is found in the case of the thief who steals an item of some value from a teacher's drawer in a classroom and then causes so much destruction that it appears to be the act of several juvenile vandals. One case presented such an appalling sight that we immediately approached the investigation from the standpoint of malicious mischief. It was just by accident that we found a pried drawer that was usually kept locked and discovered that some prescribed medication the teacher had kept in that drawer had been stolen. Because of the outrage, the teacher herself had actually overlooked the theft. Several trademarks may be present in the following case of robbery.

The bandit walks into the savings and loan office precisely at 12:15 P.M., walks up to the cashier, hands her a brown paper bag, orders her to place all the money she has in the drawer into the bag, then smiles and apologizes for the inconvenience, and leaves through the front door. Both the time and the brown paper bag may be significant. Another unusual factor is the smile and the apology. The eventual solution in a similar case established that the robber always committed his crimes during his lunch hour and that the bag was actually the one in which he brought his lunch to work. Unusual? So is the idea of committing armed robberies.

Suspect

Whenever you describe, or name and describe, a person in the "suspect" box of the crime report form, there must be a sufficient substantiation of the subject's responsibility for the crime to justify an arrest. If there is enough information in the report reflecting evidence pointing toward an individual as the culprit, and if a judge would issue a warrant on the basis of that information, the individual should be listed as a suspect. If there is some doubt, or if there is no proof but circumstances indicate that a particular individual's possible relationship to the crime is more than casual, list and discuss him or her in the narrative portion of the report as a possible suspect.

Descriptions of Property and Other Relevant Information

Additional spaces in the crime report form call for complete descriptions of the property stolen, the vehicle used by the culprit, and any evidence collected during the investigation. Several spaces are also provided for administrative handling of the report and its accompanying material. In addition to these special information spaces, there is usually a substantial portion of space for the narrative account of the crime as reported to you, as you observe it and as it develops during the investigation. This section often continues on a second page. It is in the narrative portion that the entire case should be explained in prose.

SPECIAL REPORTS

In addition to miscellaneous incident reports, crime and arrest reports, and traffic accident reports, each department has a wide variety of special forms. Some departments create separate forms for every conceivable type of incident, while others have a few basic forms and instruct their officers to adapt the information in each situation to fit existing forms. A few of the items for which special forms are often used are missing persons, dead body, lewd or annoying phone calls, impounded vehicle, evidence report, checks, intoxication, advisement of rights, and abandoned vehicle (see Figure 5–9). Other special forms may be made to fit virtually any need of some unit within the department with a special interest.

DISCUSSION

Every agency has a different set of reporting policies. For a crime report to be prepared, all the elements of a corpus delicti must be evident and reportable. For a traffic accident report, the vehicle must be moving, or there must be a minimum value damage. A missing person report will depend on the person who is missing and any attendant circumstances that indicate some criminal behavior as well. The missing child calls for an immediate investigation and report, and broadcasting the information as quickly and as thoroughly as possible. The errant husband or wife who left work at 5 and has not shown up for dinner at 7, who has a history of stopping at a pub on occasion before going home, will be reported differently from the missing child.

Some people may request that a specific report be made, such as a theft report for the benefit of an insurance or tax deduction claim. Exactly which form you as the reporting officer use is strictly a department matter and should be of no concern to the complaining party. It is of absolutely no value to the overall effectiveness of the department to tell a distraught wife "Sorry but your husband has not been gone long enough for

DRIVING UNDER THE INFLUENCE ARREST REPORT   DR No.

VISIBLE SCARS, MARKS, DEFORMITIES—EVID. OF NARCOTIC USE		ARRESTEE'S NAME (Last, First , Middle)				BOOKING NUMBER	

RESIDENCE ADDRESS   CITY   CHARGE (Section No., Code and Definition)   ☐ MISD. ☐ FEL. ☐ OTHER

EMPLOYED BY   OCCUPATION   LOCATION OF ARREST   R.D.   DIV. & DET. ARREST

NICKNAME, ALIAS   SOC. SEC. NO.   DATE & TIME ARRESTED   DATE & TIME BOOKED   DIV. BKG.   EVIDENCE BOOKED   YES ☐ NO

DRIVER'S LIC. NO.   STATE   BIRTH PLACE   SEX   DESCENT   AGE   HEIGHT   WEIGHT   HAIR   EYES   BIRHTDATE

COMPLAINTS OR EVID. OF ILL. OR INJ.—BY WHOM TREATED   LOCATION CRIME COMMITTED   PROB. INVEST. UNIT

LIST CONNECTING REPORTS BY TYPE & IDENT. NUMBERS   DISPOSITION OF ARRESTEE'S VEHICLE   HOLD FOR

VEHICLE USED (Year, Make, Body Style, Colors, Lic. No., Identifying Marks)   DRIVING VEHICLE (Direction and Name of Street)

AT OR BETWEEN STREETS   CLOTHING WORN

CODE: V–VICTIM   W–WITNESS   P or G–PARENT OR GUARDIAN

NAME	CODE	RES.		CITY	PHONE	X
		BUS.				
		RES.				
		BUS.				
		RES.				
		BUS.				

JUV. ONLY: PARENTS NOTIFIED BY   TIME   PLACE JUV. DET.   DIV. OF APPEAR. DATE/TIME   BKG. APPROV. BY   DETEN. APPROV. BY   PRINTED?   PHOTOS

ADMONITION IF RIGHTS: The arrestee was "warned" that he had the right to remain silent, AND that if he gave up the right to remain silent, anything he said can and will be used against him in a court of law, AND that he had the right to speak with an attourney and to have the attourney present during questioning, AND that if he so desired and could not afford one, an attorney would be appointed for him without charge before questioning.

ADMONITION IF RIGHTS GIVEN BY: FIELD SOBRIETY TEST GIVEN BY: CHEMICAL TEST GIVEN BY:

FIELD SOBRIETY TEST ADM. ☐ YES ☐ NO   ATTITUDE   BREATH   COORDINATION   EYES   FACE   SPEECH

Walking Line Test: ○ R. Foot △ L. Foot   BALANCE   WALKING   TURNING   TURN   PUPIL REACTION RIGHT EYE | LEFT EYE   TIME TEST ADMIN.   ○ Right Index △ Left Index

Are you sick or injured? ☐ Yes ☐ No   Are you under care of doctor or dentist? ☐ Yes ☐ No
Are you diabetic or epileptic? ☐ Yes ☐ No   Are you taking any medicine or drugs? ☐ Yes ☐ No
Do you take insulin? ☐ Yes ☐ No   Do you have any physical defect? ☐ Yes ☐ No
If answer to any of the above is "Yes", explain completely on Continuation Sheet, Form 15.9.

WHAT HAVE YOU BEEN DRINKING?   HOW MUCH?   WITH WHOM?   WHERE?

NAME OF LAST DRINK   WHAT TIME IS IT NOW?   WHERE ARE YOU NOW?   WHERE ARE YOU GOING?

WHAT HAVE YOU EATEN TODAY?   WHERE?   WHEN?   WHEN DID YOU LAST SLEEP?   HOW LONG?

Arrestee was requested to submit to a chemical test of his blood, breath, or urine, and was informed of his failure to submit to such chemical test of his choice would result in the suspension of his privilege to operate a motor vehicle for a period of six months.

CHEMICAL TEST ADMINISTERED ☐ BLOOD ☐ URINE ☐ BREATH ☐ ALL TESTS REFUSED   BREATHALYZER TEST NO.   %   LOCATION   TIME ADMINISTERED   IF NOT BOOKED STATE REASON

In the opinion of the arresting officer(s), arrestee was intoxicated and unable to safely operate a motor vehicle.

Use a Continuation Sheet, Form 15.9, for circumstances of the arrest. Include statements of arrestee's understanding of his rights, manner of operating motor vehicle, unusual actions during field sobriety test, and any other information necessary in the completion of this report.

SUPERVISOR APPROVING   SERIAL NO.   ARRESTING OFFICER(S)   SERIAL NUMBER   DIVISION—DETAIL   VACATION DATES

DATE & TIME REPRODUCED   DIVISION   CLERK

Figure 5-9   DUI arrest report.

us to make a 'missing person' report." What matters is that (1) you have taken the information, (2) you will make some sort of report, and (3) you and the department will take some action on the basis of that report.

— SECTION 3 —
GETTING THE MOST OUT OF RECORDS

INTRODUCTION

The records system is the nerve center, the memory bank, and the control center of the police department. The nerve center characteristic of the records system is seen in the fact that virtually all the functions of the department involve maintenance of records, constant reference to them, and sometimes total dependence upon them. The memory bank aspect is apparent. As with any other memory system, it is only as accurate as the information fed into it, and its indexing system must be as comprehensive and as easy to understand as possible to assure complete and instantaneous access to the contents of the files. The control center aspect is best illustrated by the fact that the personnel responsible for the system will not accept faulty or incomplete records for inclusion in the system—whenever they receive it through channels—because it "does not compute." Reports prepared by field officers constitute the majority of the records for the system. Accuracy is a must. The most useful and efficient system will be the one that receives the most complete and the most accurate bits of information for its files.

USES OF RECORDS

Records information provides the basis for interchange of such information among the various units of the department, and between the department and numerous other individuals and agencies with whom it communicates. Officers working together during the same hours of the day are in a relatively good position to keep each other informed because of their rather frequent contact with each other. Personal contacts provide the major means of communication. But what about these officers and the rest of the department? They have no direct line of communication beyond their own sphere of contacts. Their written reports and related documents serve as their major means of communication with all others.

Other members of the department, or some other agency, who must take follow-up action, such as continuing an investigation or returning to a specific address to verify that a dog that has bitten a child has been correctly placed under quarantine by its owner, must act upon the report on the assumption that all the information has been recorded accurately in its entirety. The information in the initial report provides the base for the follow-up work.

Because all officers are required to complete their reports during the same working day or within a very short time afterward, it is possible for one officer to assume an investigation inaugurated by another in the event that the original officer does not continue for some reason. The reports filed to date, together with their accompanying data from related files, are available for review. They allow the investigation to continue without interruption.

Records of filed reports provide a factual record of work performance: work that has been done and work to be done. The officer who not only performs well in the field but also prepares complete and factual reports accurately reflecting good work is a double threat in the competitive service. In addition to serving as a tool by which the quality of your work may be evaluated, your reports provide a means by which to ascertain the quantity and the nature of the work you have performed.

BASIC RECORDS AND THEIR USES

Every police agency has a different structure for its records system. Special needs and interests of the many persons involved in the evolution and development of the systems have made them as distinctive and original as a set of fingerprints. There are several basic files that are more or less standard, with minor variations of course. They include the master— or alphabetical—index of all named persons, places, and things listed in reports; the report files in which the original reports are maintained; stolen and pawned object files; and several other files.

The Master Index

Originally found in the form of a massive collection of 3- by 5-inch index cards, these magnetic tapes or other forms of storage and retrieval systems are used for an alphabetical listing of all named persons, places, and objects that will be found elsewhere in the system. They are used strictly as an index, although some agencies will actually carry in the "alpha file," as it is sometimes called, some original and complete records, such as field interview cards. By searching through the master index, it is possible to find a wealth of information in the various other files for which it serves as the index.

Some of the many bits of information that will be found on the cards in the master index will be names of victims, witnesses, suspects, wanted felons, and persons who died under circumstances when the police were notified of the death, such as suicides, individuals who have made purchases of concealable firearms from local dealers, and others who have licenses or permits to carry concealed weapons. Some "alpha files" contain nicknames of persons who are known to the majority of their friends and neighbors only by those partial names, or "monickers." The index also includes the names of persons who repossess vehicles and the purchasers from whom they are repossessed, and the names of individuals who have been interviewed under a variety of circumstances in the field. This is only a partial description of the contents of the master index. The only limitations to the extent of the master index in the police department are space and the imagination of the people using it.

Report Files

The originals of all reports are filed for a period of time. In some cases they are microfilmed and permanently stored in compact form; the filmed copies become the originals, and the bulky letter-sized originals are destroyed. The reports may be filed under a single numbering system, in chronological sequence as the incidents were reported to—or came to the attention of—the department, or they may be separated under several different categories with different numbering systems and stored in various places.

The Crime File

Each reported offense is classified according to the Uniform Crime Reports classification system. Since 1930, the Federal Bureau of Investigation has served as the central clearinghouse for crime statistics in the United States. With very few exceptions, virtually every police agency in the country contributes information concerning their statistics to the system. The information is cataloged in a variety of ways and published annually in booklet form. Each contributing agency maintains its own collection of bits of information to satisfy the reporting requirements of the system, usually in the form of a 3- by 5-inch card file or computer cards.

The crime file is an excellent source of leads for an investigation, providing that the modus operandi portion of the original report has been accurately filled out by the reporting officer. The file is separated by crime classification and then is divided into "cleared" and "uncleared" categories. Although the primary purpose of this file in most agencies is statistics, it doubles quite efficiently for a "modus operandi" file.

Crime file information cards contain the case number of each offense, the type of crime, date and time of occurrence, description of the property stolen and its market value, the location of the crime and the type of real estate attacked (market, parking lot, city street, or private residence). The card also gives the name, address, and occupation of the victim, and any "trademark" or unusual circumstance about the case that may serve to identify the culprit. If the name or description of the suspect is known, or if a person has been arrested, that information will also be indicated on the card.

Serial Number File

Serial number files are maintained by local departments and by state agencies that have centralized clearinghouses for criminal information. Whenever the serial number of a stolen item is known, the number is included in this file. The method of filing may vary, but it is usually in numerical sequence according to the last three digits of the number. For example, an item bearing serial number 7Z09253 would be filed in the 253 file. Also filed in the same location are serially numbered items that have been pawned or sold to secondhand dealers, who are required to report such transactions to the police department and a state agency.

By placing both stolen and pawned items into the same file according to serial number, the hope is that the two may meet in the files and thus arm the investigators with sufficient data to investigate the circumstances surrounding the sale or pawn transaction, solve the crime, apprehend the thief, and return the stolen property to its owner. In addition to cards on stolen and pawned items, the serial number file might contain cards on new dealer sales of handguns or any other item bearing serial numbers on which the local jurisdiction requires report of transactions.

Stolen Object File

This is another file that is common to many police departments. Any identifiable object that has been stolen is carded and filed according to its classification. There is considerable dependence upon the thoroughness of the reporting officers for this particular file to serve any practical purpose. A stolen radio, for example, would be filed as a transistor, subfiled again by name of manufacturer, and possibly filed again into another subcategory of style or band name. Watches are subfiled under "man's" or "woman's," calendar, yellow or white metal, manufacturer's name, and popular name. Accuracy in describing the object may be the determinant as to whether it will be recovered and returned to its owner.

Pawned Object File

As in the case of serially numbered items, the local department or a central clearinghouse may classify and file stolen objects in one file and pawned objects, plus others that are sold to secondhand dealers, in another, with the ultimate objective of matching the items in the file and causing an investigation to be conducted that will eventually end in return of the stolen property to its lawful owner. The clerical personnel in the records division should check cards destined for one file against the other, and vice versa, whenever the opportunity presents itself, as a matter of routine. This check is simplified to a great extent when the information is committed to an electronic data processing system that has an automatic matching procedure built into its program.

Location File

The location file may be designed according to either one of two plans: the street and number system or the grid system. Cards are prepared for each crime and/or arrest for any of a number of specified offenses, or they may be made for all crimes and arrests, depending on the administrative decision made by the individual department head. For maximum utilization, the information is cross-referred to the object file, serial number file, and crime file. In the grid system, the police agency's jurisdiction is divided into reporting districts, which consist of square blocks, groups of blocks, specific streets, single locations (frequent incident bars, recreation centers, and other places determined by the operator of the system to require special attention), or the reporting districts may correspond to census tract boundaries. In the street and number system, the file is arranged according to numbered streets and lettered streets in logical numerical and alphabetical sequence. This file can be used quite conveniently in conjunction with spot or pin maps, which show special problems or types of crimes by location.

HOW TO USE THE FILES

The files discussed in this chapter comprise only a small portion of some records systems. Some agencies create separate files for literally dozens of different uses, and they are usually cross-indexed for efficiency. But consider the possibilities of just those files covered in the preceding pages.

Case 1. You respond to a burglary call. While investigating, you discover that the culprit entered through an unlocked back door during daylight hours while the occupants of the house were away. The culprit very carefully ransacked the house, taking care not to destroy any property, and took only money. While in the house, the culprit turned on a different radio station from that ordinarily selected by the owner of the house, indicating that the burglar had a particular desire to listen to a certain type of music while he worked. The investigation reveals no other information. There are no latent fingerprints to be found. Actually, the culprit left behind a trademark although he left very little evidence. There is no known suspect in this crime.

    Probably the first place you should go upon arriving at the office to prepare your report on this case, if time and departmental procedure allow, is the record bureau. Check the crime file for daylight residence burglaries, both the solved ones and those that have yet to be solved. Other crimes with similar circumstances, such as the method of entry and the selection of music on the radio, may indicate the possibility that they have been committed by the same person. Perhaps there is a similar one or two that had been cleared by arrest some time in the past. If the latter situation occurs, you may have at least a possible suspect, because most people—including burglars—are creatures of habit. If there are other cases with similar MOs, you should include this information in the report. The investigator who follows up on the case will attempt to determine whether the burglar follows some sort of pattern, such as always committing his crimes in a specific area, or on a particular day of the week, or at the same time of the day. He will also consider the strong possibility that a firm lead on one crime will result in the eventual solution of all of the similar offenses.

Case 2. You arrest a young man for theft of a stereo tape deck from a car parked on the parking lot at the football stadium. While questioning him, the subject admits to stealing other items of a similar nature, but he cannot remember when or where. A check of the stolen object file may reveal a series of similar thefts of stereo tape decks. By retrieving the original reports and discussing the cases with the subject, you may be successful in clearing up a series of thefts rather than just one. Other sources of information to check while conversing with this willing confessor are a map and the location file. By discussing the various locations where he may have committed theft, you may find that he is a parking lot specialist. Check similar crimes that have occurred on parking lots throughout the city, and again you may strike pay dirt.

Case 3. This case may be a little different. During a routine field interview of a person observed under suspicious circumstances, you discover that he is in possession of several objects, such as transistor radios, household appliances, and a television set. He is unable to provide a reasonable explanation for such possession. By searching the stolen object and the serial number files, you discover that one or more of those items had previously been reported stolen.

The greatest limitation on your imaginative use of your records system will be imposed by the time that may be involved. There are occasions when the pressure of other field responsibilities will prevent your maximum utilization of those records, but there are other occasions when the time is available and should be put to use.

SUMMARY

This chapter is divided into three major sections: field notetaking, basic report writing techniques, and getting the most out of records.

Field notes must be comprehensive and accurate. Many times you will find that incomplete notes will result in incomplete reports and the appearance to all who judge your work that your work was incomplete. We cannot overemphasize the importance of well-prepared reports to the overall effectiveness of a police department. It should become routine for you to take notes on virtually everything you do while on patrol, including casual observations that may seem insignificant to you at the time. For example, when you are called upon to testify in a traffic case, you may be asked to describe the weather and lighting conditions at the time you wrote the citation.

Whenever you are making field notes that will later be typed onto standard forms, be sure to have in mind all the information that the form will require. Later, when you are filling out the report and discover that you forgot to record certain essential information, you will be hard-pressed to explain why you neglected to record that information in your field notes. You may have to go back and reinvestigate the case all over again.

In the report writing section, we placed a heavy emphasis on the importance of complete and accurate reports. Throughout your career you will find that you will be judged by the reports you prepare. Decisions are made by supervisors, investigators, prosecutors, and dozens of other people on the basis of what your reports say you did and saw during your investigation, which should be the same as what you actually did do and see.

In the records section of this chapter, we reviewed many of the various records that are maintained by most police agencies. Effective use of records will result in effective police work, providing that the information contained in those files is accurate and complete.

EXERCISES AND STUDY QUESTIONS

1. What is the value of accurate field notes?
2. What type of information would you include in your field notes?
3. What type of notebook do you believe best for field notes? Why?
4. Give an example of how you might use a portable television recorder at a crime scene.
5. Give an example of how you would use a miniature tape recorder in an investigation.
6. What is the value of field notes as "past recollection recalled?"
7. How do you think a jury would react to an officer's reference to field notes compared with recollection from memory only?
8. What does the author mean by the term *debriefing*? Of what value is it?
9. How would you go about preparing for a trial and assure that only those portions of your notebook related to the case at hand be open for inspection by counsel for the defense?
10. What type of notes would you use to record an interview of a burglary suspect?
11. Give an example of a narrative report, a question-and-answer report.
12. In your notebook, how would you record your conversation with a suspect who waives rights to an attorney and against self-incrimination?

13. When quoting verbatim statements in your notes and reports, how do you distinguish between actual quotes and paraphrasing?
14. What is a *jury description*, and how might you avoid getting one?
15. List and discuss at least three purposes for an officer's daily log.
16. What types of information should you record on a daily log?
17. Why should you report negative leads, or lack of information, as well as those that prove fruitful?
18. Of what value is your report to the prosecutor?
19. For what purpose would a judge review a police report?
20. To what extent is your department's record system computerized?
21. In your opinion, how broad should the access of the press to your department's files be?
22. In the discussion regarding report preparation, how were the H and Five W's explained?
23. What is the advantage, if any, of writing a report in first-person singular?
24. What is the argument against using the pronoun "I" when you are preparing a report?
25. What is the purpose of outlining your report before dictating or typing it?
26. Prepare a list of phrases that confuse, rather than enhance, a report. (Please send a copy to the author.)
27. Into which part of the report will you insert your opinion as to the honesty or integrity of a witness?
28. What is the purpose of beginning a report with a synopsis or summary?
29. What is a good basic rule concerning abbreviations of words in reports?
30. Add at least 10 phrases to the ambiguous list. (Send a copy to the author.)
31. List and discuss at least 10 of the 11 rules presented in this chapter regarding dictating reports.
32. Collect a copy of each type of form used by your department, and make a set of model reports. (You may use the samples included in the text.)
33. List and explain how each of the several types of files are used by your records system.
34. What is the function of an alpha file?
35. In your records file, how are serial numbers indexed for rapid retrieval?
36. When you recover a suspected stolen car stereo, how do you check your department's records to see if it has been stolen?
37. What is the purpose for a location file?

38. Describe how you would check a vehicle and its driver for wants.

39. How would you go about identifying a burglar by his or her modus operandi?

40. If you had the authority and financial resources, what would you change about your department's record system?

REFERENCES

DIENSTEIN, WILLIAM. *How to Write a Narrative Investigation Report*. Springfield, Ill.: Charles C Thomas, 1964.

FEDERAL BUREAU OF INVESTIGATION, *Manual of Police Records*. Washington, D.C.: U.S. Government Printing Office, 1966.

_____. *Uniform Crime Reporting Handbook*. Washington D.C.: U.S. Government Printing Office, 1966.

INTERNATIONAL CITY MANAGERS' ASSOCIATION, *Municipal Police Administration*, 5th ed. Chicago: International City Managers' Association, 1961.

U.S. ARMY. *Criminal Investigation FM 19-20*. Washington, D.C.: U.S. Government Printing Office, 1951.

_____. *Police Planning*, 2nd ed. Springfield, Ill.: Charles C Thomas, 1957.

WILSON, O. W. *Police Records: Their Installation and Use*. New York: Public Administration Service, 1951.

_____. *Police Administration*. New York: McGraw-Hill, 1963, Chap. 18.

6

INTERVIEWING TECHNIQUES

INTRODUCTION

The best sources of information about people are the people themselves. And probably the best means of getting information from people is to ask them for the information. As a police officer, if you expect to be effective and successful, you are going to have to become proficient in the art of interviewing people. Actually, there are two basic methods for getting information: interviewing and interrogating. Since the *Miranda* rule was written by the Supreme Court,[1] the term *interview* has come to mean obtaining information by asking questions, whereas the term *interrogation* seems to have acquired some sinister meaning. When one interrogates, one asks questions in a prying manner, sometimes getting answers that the person being questioned did not intend to provide voluntarily. The *interviewer* is assumed to have a willing respondent, whereas the *interrogator* has an unwilling respondent. Basically, the definitions fit, but that does not necessarily mean that one is good and the other is bad.

You are going to be asking questions of a wide variety of people. Most of them are not criminal suspects. You will be interviewing victims, witnesses, informants, complainants, interested participants, disinterested parties, women, men, children of both sexes, professional people, blue-collar workers, white-collar workers, no-collar workers, people who arouse your curiosity, people who behave in a lawful manner, and people who do not. You will even question an occasional suspect. The purpose of this chapter is to introduce you to the art of interviewing people no matter who they are.

---

[1] *Miranda* v. *Arizona*, 384 U.S. 436 (1966).

The chapter is divided into two parts: one addressing the art and principles of interviewing and the other addressing the propriety and process of the field interrogation, or interview. Using the recommended procedures contained in the pages that follow should enhance your techniques in the art of questioning with the purpose of getting answers and also the art of listening, which is critical to success in interviewing.

— SECTION 1—
INTERVIEWING

THE "ART" OF INTERVIEWING

Of the many police activities you must perform, interviewing truly approaches the category of "art." It takes talent, a natural inclination to perform the task well, study and practice to develop the basic skills, and continual self-analysis and cultivation of the talents and skills involved in the questioning process. To be adept at interviewing, you will first study yourself; then you will adapt your own personality to the various situations and the personalities of the people whom you question. You should develop a style that is distinctive and improve with studied experience. No one is a "born" interviewer any more than one is a born marksman. You must have an intense interest in human nature, a desire to develop the skill, and the ability to learn from each interview experience.

Human beings are gregarious; they like to talk. They like to talk about their successes, their failures, their good and bad luck, their ambitions, themselves and others, and—quite significantly—they feel a compulsion to talk about their crimes when they commit them. Many experts theorize that it is the intense desire to share experiences with others that causes criminal law violators to confess their crimes. Theodor Reik, a student of criminal psychiatry and a protégé of Freud, advanced the theory that an individual who commits a crime is haunted by the guilt feelings caused by violating personal ethical standards, and the terrible truth of the crime begs to be let out through confession. Reik called this the compulsion to confess. This is congruous with the beliefs of many skilled police interrogators, who have often encountered individuals who demand to be heard and who freely and voluntarily confess to atrocious crimes that are so repugnant to the confessors that they must purge themselves of the terrible secrets or suffer a lifetime of torture. Once they tell of their crimes, they show distinct signs of relief, and they seem to look forward to whatever punishment society has prescribed for them. The penance of punishment may help to cleanse them of their crimes.

A key to your development as an interviewer is your ability to see each person that you interview as an individual with a distinct set of values and a personality quite different from that of all other humans. Be constantly mindful of the individuality of the people you question and guard against letting yourself oversimplify a problem by stereotyping individuals into "categories" that may seem to you to be all alike. Once you begin to generalize in this manner, the "artist" fades and the "report taker" emerges. Your responsibility as a professional police officer is to strive to perform as the "artist."

Objectives of the Interview

There are four basic objectives of an interview and of an interrogation: (1) secure complete and accurate information, (2) distinguish fact from fantasy, (3) proceed according to a well-thought-out plan, and (4) have *truth* as your target.

Information. It is important that your investigation reveal the real truth. You may be able to verify the statements of one person by interviewing several other people who witnessed the same event. As we discussed in our earlier discussion of perception, you know that not everyone sees the same things through the same set of eyes or experience, or any of a number of factors that influence perception, memory, and articulation of those observations in a later discussion with a police officer. The fact that two eyewitness accounts differ does not necessarily mean that one person is lying, nor is it impossible for two witnesses to tell stories that sound quite similar. You should also test the information that a witness gives you by actually visiting the scene of the observation and placing yourself at the exact spot occupied by the witness at the time, and then see (or hear, or smell) for yourself if it was possible to perceive what the witness reported.

Fact versus Fantasy. Check out the witnesses for honesty and reliability. Check records and what other people who know them have to say about their sobriety, emotional level, and reputation for truthfulness. Compare statements of the several witnesses and walk-through the event as it had been described to you to determine what *could have happened* and what *could not have happened*. People who remember events have "landmarks" in time because they actually happened. They will remember the sequence, the people present, and attendant items that tend to verify the witness's statements. For example, the witness describes an event, names other people who are present, and may even be able to tell you what show was on television at the time. They will remember these things even if they are asked to recount their observations in reverse, or to skip around and go back and forth to their various observations. A fabricated story will sound different every time and will probably fall apart when the witness is asked to recount certain observations out of sequence.

Plan. If you have examined the crime scene and have learned all that you can about the crime and the person you are about to interview, you will have a fairly good idea as to which questions you are going to ask the witness. Make an outline of your questions, have your reports (if they have been prepared yet), and have a sketch of the crime scene.

Truth. This is the ultimate focus of every crime or collision or other investigation that you are going to conduct. Although you may have certain information that makes you believe that you know what a suspect or witness is going to tell you, it is imperative that you keep an open and nonjudgmental mind. A preconceived notion that certain people are innate liars, or that others speak nothing but the truth, will get you into trouble. As an internal affairs investigator, I have even—on rare occasions—run across police officers who have lied, others who have exaggerated, and still others who have fallen into the habit of being careless with the truth. None of these is acceptable for a police officer, but the fact that they do have such imperfections further illustrates the fact that you are going to have a job on your hands ferreting out the truth from the information you collect during your interviews and interrogations. Do not hesitate to ask people to tell their stories more than once, and challenge them by pointing out discrepancies with their own earlier statements or those of others.

General Interviewing Techniques

Preparation. Whenever possible, arrange to have a private area for the interview to take place, free from outside interference, telephone calls, or interruptions by children or friends of the witness. The best location is a specially furnished interview room at police headquarters. Set aside enough time to conduct the interview, and take into account any time commitments that the person you are about to interview has. It is very distracting to be at a crucial time during an interview when one or both of the participants start fidgeting and looking at their watches. Be sure to have all the facts that are available to you. If you are interviewing the victim or suspect in a crime, it will certainly enhance your effectiveness if you had visited the crime scene and if you have all the facts straight in your mind as to time and location of the event, weapon used, location and nature of injuries, evidence left at the scene, and items removed from the scene. Without this information, you would not even know if the suspect was telling the truth while giving a full confession.

Seating Arrangement. Depending on the effect you wish to create, you may choose to have a table or other barrier between you and the interviewee, with the chair you sit in bigger and better to give you an unspoken psychological advantage. Size and design differences in furniture are traditionally used to indicate relative importance or superiority. Look around the offices of the captains and sergeants in your own department, or the offices of the instructors and the president or chancellor of your local college.

If you want to show the person you are interviewing that you do not intend to take advantage of your obvious position of advantage, move away from your desk to another chair of the same size as the one occupied by your subject. This will have a tendency to indicate an air of openness and trust between the two of you.

Comfort and Social Necessities. You are responsible for the safety, health, and comfort of the person you are interviewing if the interview takes place where you control the environment. Provide for restroom facilities, water, or other refreshments if the interview is prolonged, and food if the interview extends beyond normal limits. When you are interviewing a suspect, it is particularly important that there is no indication of duress or psychological abuse that influences a confession or admission. Treat everyone with the same respect as you would expect yourself. Smoking is not only unhealthy, but it can be a distraction. If you smoke during the interview, you must allow the subject to smoke. A better alternative would be to simply state: "I'm allergic to smoke, so I would rather that you not smoke."

Opening the Interview. Establish some sort of rapport between yourself and the subject of the interview. This is principally to determine that you are both speaking the same language, so to speak, or talking on the same "wavelength." You want to make sure that the words you are using have the same meaning to each other or that at least you know what the differences are. Determine the other person's interests, language level, and value standards as much as possible so that you will be able to communicate. You can determine a person's truth-telling style while going through the preliminaries so that you may later be able to see any differences in style that may indicate an attempt at deception or holding back information. If there is any personality conflict or for some reason you cannot effectively communicate, arrange to have another person conduct the interview. If you are interviewing a suspect, be sure to abide by the *Miranda* rule, which will be covered later in this chapter.

If you intend to get information from the subject, be careful not to take on an adversary role or to show contempt or displeasure with the person. Stay calm and maintain a professional posture throughout the interview. Whether you work alone or not will depend on department policy, but recognize that no one likes to talk to a crowd, especially when relating something embarrassing, or, if you are interviewing the suspect, to confess to a crowd the commission of some cruel or inhuman crime. In addition, some victims feel guilty, particularly in sex crimes. They are not guilty, of course, and they need to be reassured that responsibility for the crime is not theirs.

GENERAL TECHNIQUES IN INTERVIEWING

There are basically two approaches to questioning, which you may use one at a time or simultaneously: the direct approach and narrative approach. The direct approach usually consists of asking questions and getting answers, and the narrative response consists of you asking a question and then allowing the respondent to give an answer by recounting the event with interruptions for new questions, or to get the story-teller back on the subject, or to help the person remember. Your attitude should generally be aloof. Variations may consist of a sympathetic approach and a logical approach.

Sympathetic Approach

The sympathetic approach is usually more effective than the direct approach, because the person who has committed the crime usually feels remorse and guilt for having done something that he knows is wrong. To call him a thief or a liar will surely end the interrogation before it begins. Accidental offenders and first-time criminals respond to this approach most readily. Others who will usually respond to sympathy are sex offenders, persons who have committed crimes of passion involving intense emotional feelings, and people who have sensitive personalities.

The technique in the sympathetic approach is to indicate an interest in the person as an individual. Show him that you can understand why he would have done whatever it is that he did. Be kind and considerate to the person, who is entitled to your respect. His crime may have been indicative of animalistic tendencies, but if you are to gain his confidence and respect, and his confession, it is imperative that you appeal to his human qualities in a rational and understanding manner. Be friendly in a professional way. Your role as the interrogator is not to scold or punish the criminal violator.

Logical Approach

The direct approach is most likely to work with preadolescents, recidivists, and those types of law violators who commit crimes against property, which indicates their disregard for the property of others. Some people commit crimes in defiance of the law or because they do not agree with the law and see no reason why they should obey the law. White-collar crimes, vice operations, and organized crime offenses are hardly likely to be committed by amateurs, and whenever a violator of one of these types of crimes is questioned, the best results will probably be obtained by telling the individual what he is being questioned for, presenting him with the facts, and then soliciting from him any statements he wishes to make. Although I doubt that there is any individual who is totally without emotional feelings, except perhaps the sociopath, the people who respond to the logical approach seem to be those whose crimes involve intelligence or cunning, rather than emotional involvement as in the crimes of passion and sex offense.

Techniques for the logical approach generally consist of keeping the interrogation simple and to the point. State why the subject is being questioned and give him sufficient information to show him that you have reasonable cause for the arrest, while avoiding giving him more information than you hope to receive. You may give him some of the details of the case, then simply state that you believe he has a "side" to tell and that you want to hear it to determine the true facts of the case. Occasionally, this technique proves so effective that the suspect cooperates fully, and when he does give his "side" of the story, it becomes apparent that there has been no crime. If his story consists of lies and discrepancies, point them out to him and ask for an explanation. While using this technique, never assume that the suspect is lying and that the victim or witnesses are entirely correct. Many times the suspect will speak the truth, and the truth may bear no resemblance to the account of the crime as presented by the accusers.

Operational Suggestions

If in doubt as to which approach to use, try the sympathetic technique first, then direct questioning. Once the suspect indicates that the interrogation is over, it is. Beware of the confession that is too easy to obtain. As long as the suspect is willing to speak about his crime freely, have him prove his points by describing all the elements of the crime, plus whatever additional information may be necessary to prove his actual guilt. There will be fewer suspects to interview than witnesses and victims. You will have more flexibility in questioning witnesses than suspects because of the constitutional restrictions involved in questioning your suspects. Never underestimate the subject of your questioning; he or she may be quite deceptive and difficult, or uncooperative. Another piece of advice is: Never overestimate your own abilities. No one "bats 1000," not even the multimillion-dollar baseball player.

INTERVIEWING THE SUSPECT OF A CRIME

Constitutional Guidelines

Before you may begin a custodial police interrogation in which you intend to question anyone about their involvement—or suspected involvement—in any criminal act, you must advise them as follows:

> *You have the absolute right to remain silent. Anything you say can, and will, be used against you in court. You have the right to consult with an attorney, to be represented by an attorney, and to have one present before I ask you any questions. If you*

cannot afford an attorney, one will be appointed to represent you (free of charge) before you are questioned, if you desire.

Most prosecuting attorneys will recommend that you carry this warning on a printed card and that you read it to the suspect so that you will remember every word of the admonishment, and also so that you may present it in court when describing how you discussed the admonishment with the suspect.

The suspects must understand and communicate to you their understanding of the wording of the admonishment and its significance as it relates to them in their present predicament. If they do not understand any of the words, or their meanings, they must be explained. Once you have an agreement that they understand the words and their meanings, the Supreme Court has ruled: "the defendant may waive effectuation of these rights, provided the waiver is made voluntarily, knowingly, and intelligently." You may proceed with the questions only if the suspect understands the admonishment and you gain an affirmative response to this question:

With these rights in mind, are you ready to talk with me about the charges against you?

The suspect must give an oral waiver and consent to continue with the interview. A mere lack of response in the form of silence does not constitute a waiver. Once the suspect exercises the right to remain silent and indicates that there is no desire to answer any of your questions, you must discontinue the questioning because they will not be admissible in court. Do not persuade the suspect to change his mind or engage him in any "games" in an effort to trick him into changing his mind or giving you information inadvertently.

On June 13, 1966, the U.S. Supreme Court, in its *Miranda* rule,[2] delivered a decision dealing with the "admissibility of statements obtained from an individual who is subject to *custodial police interrogation* [italics added] and the necessity for procedures which assure that the individual is accorded his privilege under the Fifth Amendment to the Constitution not be compelled to incriminate himself."

A "custodial interrogation" is one that is conducted under circumstances when the subject of the questioning process is "significantly deprived of his freedom" in the words of the court, and under circumstances when the investigation is forced on the subject at an accusatory stage of the investigation. The crime may be a felony or misdemeanor.

To qualify as a "custody" situation, the suspect must (1) have, in fact, been deprived of his or her freedom in a significant way (cannot leave), and (2) must be personally aware of his or her lack of freedom or reasonably believe that it exists. Consider the situation and the location: Was it

---

[2]384 U.S. 436.

taking place in a police car or at the station, or was it in the suspect's home or car? Was it late at night, or during the day? Was more than one officer present, or did the questioning take place in the presence of the suspect's friends and family? How long did it last? How accusatory did you get during the questioning?

Victims and witnesses are not in custody and not in an accusatory stage, meaning that they are not suspected of a crime. There are many occasions on which you may question people in field interviews to ascertain their identities and the nature of their business in a particular location at an unusual time or under suspicious circumstances or to determine ownership of certain unexplained property in their possession. In most of these cases, the questions are asked and satisfactory answers received without incident and the interviewer never reaches an *accusatory* stage when you would focus on the subject as a suspect in a specific crime. Under most of these investigatory situations, it would be a personal affront to the subject of the questioning to advise him of his constitutional right to remain silent and to have an attorney with him, because to do so would be insinuating that he is suspected of having committed some sort of criminal act. In some situations, of course, the field interviews do lead to accusatory circumstances, and at those times it is necessary to lead into the *Miranda* admonition, as described earlier.

Once advised of these rights, the subject may exercise them, say nothing, and request the presence of an attorney. He may waive the rights by stating that he does fully understand them but that he still wishes to talk and answer your questions. Once he waives the rights he may reconsider at any time. In the words of the *Miranda* decision:

> *If, however, he indicates in any manner and at any state of the process that he wishes to consult with an attorney before speaking, there can be no questioning. Likewise, if the individual is alone and indicates in any manner that he does not wish to be interrogated, the police may not question him. The mere fact that he may have answered some questions or volunteered some statements on his own does not deprive him of the right to refrain from answering any further inquiries until he has consulted with an attorney and thereafter consents to be questioned.*

If a person is not actually the subject of a custodial interrogation, as when you are on the scene conducting the preliminary investigation (including most field interviews), and he makes any spontaneous declarations of any type—including what may amount to admissions or a confession—his statements are admissible in court regardless of whether you advised him of his rights to remain silent and to an attorney. There is no way of predicting circumstances under which a person will make such spontaneous declarations, and there can be no insinuation that you obtained statements of this nature under "custodial conditions."[3]

If a person is arrested and there is to be no questioning, there is no need to admonish him regarding his constitutional rights at the time. In some situations it is the wiser course of action to wait until after the heat of the situation has cooled down to the point where it is possible to rely on a rational discussion. Consider the following as an example of a time when it would hardly seem suitable to perform the advisement rites:

> *You are parked on a side street near one of the city's main boulevards when you hear from a radio broadcast that a green, two-door sedan containing two occupants has just left the scene of an armed robbery. The victim attempted to thwart the robbery by shooting at one of the suspects, but the victim was disarmed and beaten. You are alone and about three blocks from the scene of the crime, and suddenly a car matching the description of the wanted one appears. You negotiate a turn onto the street in medium traffic and are about five cars behind the suspect car. You radio in for a cover unit and decide to follow the suspects until they are out of the way of other cars and your follow-up unit is near to cover you. Suddenly, the driver spots you and begins a high-speed attempt to escape. You radio in this new information, then turn on the red light and siren, and take up the chase.*

> *The chase involves high speeds through medium to heavy traffic, including going against several signals and signs, barely avoiding some serious accidents. Finally, after about two miles of pursuit, you edge the suspect car to the curb. The driver stops, and you jump out and approach the suspect car to get to the suspects before they gather their wits and use any weapons that they might have.*

> *You know that this is not the academy-recommended procedure, but you believe it is better under the circumstances because there are so many other cars and pedestrians around that you believe you can avoid gunfire. You grab the door handle, open the door, and tell the suspects to get out. Shocked by your fast action, the suspects get out of their car with no struggle. As you quickly search the suspects for weapons, one of them tries to attack you. You subdue the one suspect and you are met by some resistance from the other. You regain control of the suspects just as the follow-up unit arrives. You take both suspects back to the other car, thoroughly search them this time, and place them in the back seat of the car.*

---

[3]See *Maxey*, 172 Cal. App. 3d 11 (1985).

At that particular moment when the action has calmed down at the scene, would you advise the suspects of their right to remain silent and to have an attorney present when they are being questioned? Are you prepared to begin an interrogation at that time and under those conditions? It is not difficult to imagine what the response would be from the suspects at that moment if you were to ask them, "Do you want to talk with me?" If you believe that an on-the-scene interrogation is essential to clear up some vital facts of the case or that it would be tactically wise to question the suspects at the time, then it is imperative that you proceed with the *Miranda* admonishment.

If you have sufficient evidence to lead to an arrest based on reasonable cause, and the tactical decision is to wait before any questioning, then do not advise the subject of those rights at that moment. When you make an arrest solely on a warrant, make the following determinations prior to admonishing the subject or questioning him: Are the officers who investigated the case and who should conduct the interrogation available? If so, contact them and follow their instructions. If the warrant is from another jurisdiction, do not admonish the arrestees or attempt to conduct any interrogation, as you have no information to prepare you for an intelligent interview.

Consider this interesting 1977 case, in which the subject—not a suspect at the time—was *invited* to go to the station for questioning.[4] Mathiason, a parolee, was named by the victim of a burglary as a possible suspect, but there was no hard evidence. The officer went to Mathiason's apartment and left a card and a note stating that he (the officer) would like to discuss something with him. Mathiason later called the officer and accepted the invitation to come to the office and talk. Mathiason arrived and the officer went into an office and closed the door.

The officer told Mathiason that he was not under arrest but that he had been called in to talk about a burglary. The officer then said that if Mathiason told the truth, it would help him with the district attorney or the judge. The police officer then told Mathiason that he believed Mathiason was involved in the burglary and that his fingerprints had been found at the scene of the crime (actually they had not been found).

Mathiason remained silent for about five minutes and then admitted to the burglary. At that point the officer advised Mathiason of his *Miranda* rights and took Mathiason's confession, which required about five minutes. The officer told Mathiason that he would not be arrested at that time and then released him. Mathiason went home. The case was referred to the district attorney. Mathiason was tried and convicted for the burglary. On appeal, the Oregon Supreme Court overturned the conviction and ruled the confession inadmissible, saying that the "environment was coercive."

The state of Oregon appealed the reversal to the U.S. Supreme Court, which reversed the ruling and reinstated the conviction. By a 6-

[4]*Oregaon v. Mathiasom*, 97 S. Ct. 711 (1977).

to-3 vote, the Court said that *Miranda applies to a custodial interrogation in which a person has been taken into custody or deprived of his or her freedom "in any significant way."* The Supreme Court noted:

> *Any interview of one suspected of a crime by a police officer will have coercive aspects to it, simply by virtue of the fact that the police officer is part of a law enforcement system which may ultimately cause the suspect to be charged with a crime. But police officers are not required to administer* Miranda *warnings to everyone. Nor is the requirement of warnings to be imposed simply because the questioning takes place in the station house or because the questioned person is one whom the police suspect.* Miranda *warnings are required only when there has been such a restriction on a person's freedom as to render him "in custody." It was that sort of coercive environment to which* Miranda *by its terms was made applicable, and to which it is limited.*

The warning regarding the individual's constitutional rights and his or her exercise of those rights, or waiver of such rights, only affects the admissibility of the subject's statements when later used against him or her in court. One exception to this provision is that in some states laws have been enacted that require that any minor who is arrested to be admonished regarding certain rights, including those to an attorney and against self-incrimination, whether the subject is to be questioned or not. A child may waive those rights in the same manner as an adult, but when the child does, the question arises as to whether he or she could actually comprehend the true meaning of the admonishment to make a value judgment and, then, whether he or she could make an intelligent waiver with that limited knowledge. This is a matter for the interviewing officer to decide at the time and the courts to rule on later.

When a police officer stops a car and asks the driver for identification and a vehicle registration slip, and upon receiving unsatisfactory answers, further asks the driver's destination and business, no "in-custody" interrogation, as discussed in *Miranda* takes place, according to a 1969 case.[5] In subsequent cases, it has been affirmed that traffic stops in which the officer routinely asks for a driver's license and registration were specifically excluded from the *Miranda* rule.

Miranda warnings need not be given in cases when the suspect is required by "implied consent" laws involving driving a vehicle while under influence of alcohol to submit to a blood or breath or urine analysis for the purpose of determining blood-alcohol percentage. The suspect need not be admonished prior to giving handwriting exemplars, before having his fingerprints or photograph taken for identification purposes, or before standing in a lineup. An individual may require his attorney to be present for the purpose of observing the lineup to assure his client that it is being handled correctly, but he need not be advised of his rights as provided in the

---

[5]*Lowe v. United States,* 407 F.2d 1394, 9th Cir. (1969).

Miranda rule for that purpose. He may be asked to speak during a lineup for identification purposes, and that is not a violation of the court's rule. The *Miranda* rule applies strictly to the admissibility of an individual's statements in court when used against him in his trial, and those statements that were elicited from the individual during a custodial interrogation.

Independent of the *Miranda* considerations, the test of "voluntariness" applies. Any threat or promise of any kind will nullify the admissibility of any statements or admissions made by a suspect. Threats or promises may be real or implied. The actual test is whether the court perceives an officer's conduct as meeting those criteria.

In certain cases when a person has exercised his rights against self-incrimination, he later indicates of his own volition that he wishes to resume the interview and that he wishes to voluntarily make statements or a confession. Under these circumstances such statements will be held admissible. The subject must initiate the action, however, and there can be no attempt on the part of the officer to take the initiative to gain the statements under conditions when it would appear that the subject was coerced or enticed to subsequently waive those rights.

Confessions and Admissions Made to a Private Person

The basic question is whether the person doing the questioning is doing so as a private person or acting as an agent of the police. If it is as a person acting on direction by, or as an agent of, a police officer, the *Miranda* rule would apply. The individual would then become a person *in authority* as the *Miranda* rule specifically stated: "When an individual is taken into custody or otherwise deprived of his freedom *by the authorities* [emphasis added] in any significant way and is subjected to questioning...."[6] However, in some situations, certain statements were excluded in the "person in authority" premise, such as (1) questioning by a pier gateman employed by a private detective agency,[7] (2) questioning by a person making a private person arrest,[8] or (3) questioning by a supervisor of a gambling casino.[9]

The courts do not seem to have spoken to the question as to whether the Constitution excludes an involuntary confession secured by a private person in any general rule regarding *Miranda*, but all the other rules regarding voluntariness would apply in such areas as threats, promises, and intimidation. As a police officer, be sure to follow the rules carefully, but also be sure to advise other people who are in the private security and retail business particularly that any means they might use to gain statements might negatively affect the admissibility.

[6]384 U.S. 436, 478 (1966).

[7]*United States* v. *Antonelli*, 434 F.2d 335, 2d Cir. (1970).

[8]*State* v. *LaRose*, 286 Minn. 517, 174 N.W.2d 247 S. Ct. (1970).

[9]*Shoumberg* v. *State*, 83 Nev. 372, 432 P.2d 500 S. Ct. (1967).

— SECTION 2 —
FIELD INTERVIEWS

INTRODUCTION

One of your basic responsibilities is to do whatever is within the scope of your duty and authority to maintain your assigned district as free from crime and disorder as possible. In fact, one of the principal factors considered in evaluating your efficiency and effectiveness is the *absence* of crime in your district. The well-trained officer knows that field interviews are among the most useful "tools of the trade," because it is largely through their use that the officer prevents and represses criminal activity. You are most productive in activities such as arrests and crime clearances when you aggressively make personal contact with the people you observe during the course of your patrol activities, particularly those who arouse your suspicions, and when you conduct thorough field interviews with those people.

You should know the character and nature of business of as many people in your district as possible. You should also know the identity and character of those who are occasional and frequent visitors to your district. In many instances, it is your responsibility to know what you can about certain "first-time" or "one-time-only" visitors to the district you patrol. The only effective means whereby such identification and character determination can be accomplished is by *observation* and *interrogation*. One of the most immediate ways to get an answer to your question, "I wonder who he is and what he is up to?" is by making contact with that person and asking him. Although this is the most obvious method, *too few* officers choose to use it as a matter of routine, which it should be.

OBJECTIVES OF FIELD INTERVIEWS

There are three principal objectives of having a department-wide, organized field interview program. These objectives are (1) identification, (2) prevention and repression of crime, and (3) centralized records of field contacts. Let's cover each of those three separately.

Identification. As we mentioned earlier in the chapter, you are responsible for knowing the people who live, work, and pass through or seek recreation in your district. You should know the identity and places of residence of people with criminal records and criminal tendencies as demonstrated by their past actions, which are a matter of record. You should likewise know the identities and any unusual hours or habits of the residents, such as the milkman who leaves home at 3:00 A.M., the person who works in the post office until 2:00 A.M., or doctors or other professionals whose work takes them out of the house at all hours of the day and night. You should know the businesses in your area and be aware of their irregularities in business practices and hours, such as overnight inventories, restocking the shelves between 2:00 A.M. and 10:00 A.M., or deliveries made at night to avoid parking problems. By having made previous personal contact with literally hundreds of people on your beat, you know who has the criminal records, who are the burglars, or thieves, and who is peddling narcotics. Armed with such information, you are better prepared to take appropriate action, such as a cursory search, surveillance, utilization of an undercover officer, or immediate arrest whenever the circumstances call for police response.

Prevention and Repression of Crime. An active and alert police patrol with an objective field interview program creates a continuous awareness of the omnipresence of the police. Law-abiding citizens have the feeling of security in knowing that their safety is assured, and criminals know that they have a greater chance of getting caught at their illicit activities or when they are in possession of contraband. The criminals who know that the police know them and their records, their addresses, their methods of transportation, their crime specialties, and the names and addresses of their associates are less likely to commit their crimes under circumstances when they also know that you are aware of their presence in the immediate or general vicinity.

Records. Every field interview or field contact (which may include mere observation of known criminals under circumstances that merit a record of time and place but no necessity—or opportunity—for a conversation) should be made the subject of a permanent or semipermanent record entry in the department files. A printed card the same size as the standard 3" x 5" cards used for a master alphabetical file is ideal, because it can be placed directly in that file along with other cards pertaining to the same individual. If your department feeds "FI" data into the computers, it is a good idea to build in a time limit for retention of the data, because people change appearance, residence, vehicles, and associates often.

The field interview cards provide a ready source of information about physical description, times and locations of contact, vehicle description, associates, employer or school, and circumstances surrounding such contacts (see Figure 6–1). The cards showing records of field interviews are most helpful in locating possible suspects and witnesses. Lovers in the park may later develop into victim and suspect in a rape case. The employee moving inventory from one store to another at 2:00 A.M. may turn out to be someone who was fired for theft two weeks previously who is stealing a former employer's inventory. There are many examples we can use from personal experience, such as the "student" with the stolen portable typewriter, a car thief driving a "borrowed" car, a "witness" to a hit-and-run accident later identified as the suspect, and known burglars observed in the area at about the same time a burglary was reported. Quite often a field interview card in the police file is more current than is a telephone directory published ten months earlier. The advantages of maintaining a permanent record of field interview records far outweigh

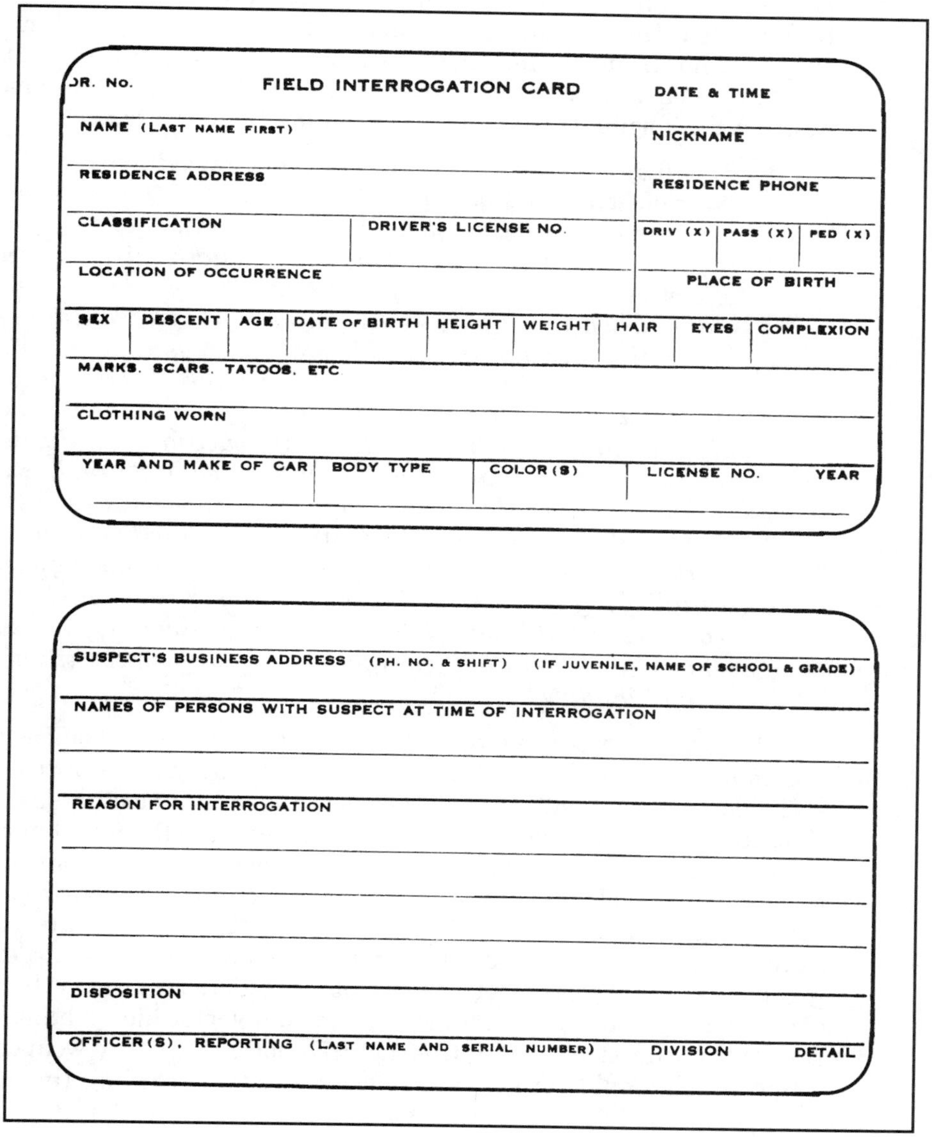

DR. NO. FIELD INTERROGATION CARD DATE & TIME

NAME (LAST NAME FIRST) | NICKNAME

RESIDENCE ADDRESS | RESIDENCE PHONE

CLASSIFICATION | DRIVER'S LICENSE NO. | DRIV (X) | PASS (X) | PED (X)

LOCATION OF OCCURRENCE | PLACE OF BIRTH

SEX | DESCENT | AGE | DATE OF BIRTH | HEIGHT | WEIGHT | HAIR | EYES | COMPLEXION

MARKS, SCARS, TATOOS, ETC

CLOTHING WORN

YEAR AND MAKE OF CAR | BODY TYPE | COLOR (S) | LICENSE NO. YEAR

SUSPECT'S BUSINESS ADDRESS (PH. NO. & SHIFT) (IF JUVENILE, NAME OF SCHOOL & GRADE)

NAMES OF PERSONS WITH SUSPECT AT TIME OF INTERROGATION

REASON FOR INTERROGATION

DISPOSITION

OFFICER(S), REPORTING (LAST NAME AND SERIAL NUMBER) DIVISION DETAIL

Figure 6-1 Field interrogation card.

the disadvantages. For the individuals who are interviewed rather frequently, it would probably be advisable to maintain only those cards related to the most recent two or three years.

LEGALITY OF THE FIELD INTERVIEW

For many years, the courts throughout the United States have held that police officers have the duty to protect themselves and the people who live in, and visit, their jurisdictions, and that they may stop and question any subject who arouses the officer's suspicion if the conditions at the time warrant such inquiry (see Figure 6–2). In one of the two early leading cases in California, the California Supreme Court stated

> *The duty of every good citizen is, when called upon, to give all information in his power to the proper officers of the law as to persons connected with crime; and this should be held to require that all proper information should be given on request of a personal nature, as affecting the one of whom inquiry is made, when the circumstances are such to warrant an officer in making an inquiry. A police officer has a right to make inquiry in the proper manner of everyone upon the public streets at a late hour as to his identity and to the occasion of his presence, if the surroundings are such as to indicate to a reasonable man that the public safety demands such identification. The fact that crimes had recently been committed in that neighborhood; that the plaintiff at a late hour was found in the locality; that he refused to answer proper questions establishing his identity, were circumstances which should lead a reasonable officer to require his presence at the station, where the sergeant in charge might make more minute and careful inquiry.*[10]

Recognizing the need for legal justification of the field officer's participation in a program of conducting field interviews in circumstances warranting such inquiry, many states have followed a trend of enacting laws requiring that certain people cooperate with the inquiring officers whenever public safety demands both the inquiry and the cooperation. Some of the laws, such as those in New Hampshire, Delaware, and New York, authorize the police to stop and question persons who they "reasonably suspect" are committing, have committed, or are about to commit a felony or serious misdemeanor. In many of these cases, the detention is not considered an arrest, but if the officers reasonably believe that they are in "danger of life or limb," they may search the subject to ensure that he does not possess any weapons or other items which would imperil the officers' safety. Providing that reasonable

---

[10]Miller v. Fano, *134 Cal. 106 (1906).*

Figure 6-2 Whether it is Hilo or your own city, the field interview is an integral part of police patrol. (Courtesy of the Police Department, Hilo, Hawaii.)

cause exists for the original stop and inquiry, some cases have indicated that this search may also extend to items under the immediate control of the persons searched, such as a woman's handbag or a man's attaché case. If the officers find weapons when conducting such a search, they may make an arrest for the violation and conduct a thorough search incidental to the arrest.

WHEN TO CONDUCT A FIELD INTERVIEW

A good police officer is suspicious by nature, always alert for anything that appears out of the ordinary. What is ordinary, of course, depends on where you are, the time of day, and the culture and habits of the people where you are. You notice people and events that are incongruous with the "norm." Some of the factors that should be taken into account when establishing reasonable cause for temporary detentions for field interview contacts are hours of darkness, a place where crimes of a particular nature are frequently and currently taking place, a neighborhood where there has been a recent rash of burglaries, particularly within the same shift or previous day or two, or when the individual observed at such a time and place has a record of criminal activity that has been occurring in that particular neighborhood where the contact is to be made. Other factors might be cases in which the subject is driving in an erratic manner, two persons are sitting in a parked car at a time and place that does not fit the circumstances, or individuals are overtly violating a traffic law or criminal code. A sharp robber may run away from the scene and then, when the officers begin arriving in response to the in-progress call, turn around and begin walking casually back toward the scene of the crime.

Going back to the laws, consider the individual who—because of circumstances—appears as if he is committing, did commit, or is about to commit a felony or misdemeanor. Consider the following factors as general grounds for a temporary detention for a field interview:

1. There must be a rational suspicion by the officer that some activity out of the ordinary is occurring, or has taken place.
2. Some indication must exist to connect the person under suspicion with the unusual activity.
3. There must be some suggestion that the activity is related to crime.

The circumstances must be sufficiently unique to justify your suspicions, and you should be prepared to explain the circumstances causing you to choose to conduct a field interview. You are an acknowledged specialist as an observer, and the court will expect you as that officer to call upon your expertise, your training, and past experiences with similar circumstances to "lay the foundation" justifying your cause for conducting the field interview.

There need not be sufficient cause to justify an arrest or a search, but there must be sufficient cause to indicate to you that your failure to make inquiry into the matter would amount to a dereliction of duty as a conscientious police officer.

Whenever there is sufficient cause to detain an individual temporarily for a field inquiry, there may be sufficient cause to perform a cursory "patdown" of the individual for any weapons with which he or she may attempt to inflict violent injury upon you or some other person. Although there are many occasions when a field interview situation may not call for a search for weapons, certain factors may indicate the need for a "pat-down." Consider these points when deciding your course of action:

1. The nature of the suspected criminal activity and whether a weapon would be used
2. Your situation: Are you alone or has assistance arrived?
3. The number of subjects and their emotional and physical state (angry, fighting, intoxicated)
4. Time of day and geographical surroundings
5. Prior knowledge of the subject's reputation and/or any police record he may have
6. The sex of the subject or subjects encountered
7. The behavior and apparent agility of the subjects
8. The circumstances as they present themselves to you at the time and as you evaluate them

FIELD INTERVIEW PROCEDURE

Use this procedure as a general guide for making field contacts, but always adjust your procedure to fit the person contacted and the circumstances involved.

Location to Choose for Field Interview

If you are in a well-lighted business area, or an industrial complex where there are many high fences and buildings with few open driveways, try to make the contact near a streetlight in the middle of the block. If you are in a residential area where there are many driveways and open areas, choose an intersection for the contact. The reason for selecting these contact locations is to make it easier for you to pursue the subject if he should *decide* to run. It is easier to chase a subject down a street than through backyards and alleys. Also, consider your own safety when selecting the spot for the contact.

The Approach on Foot [11]

If you are walking toward the subject and you meet him head on, let him walk past you, then turn toward the subject facing his right side. If you approach him from the rear, have him turn so that you are initially on his right side. As soon as you can determine whether the subject is right or left handed, take a position of advantage closest to the "dominant" hand.

---

[11]For the vehicle approach, see the section "Car Stops" in Chapter 11.

Depending on the circumstances leading to the field contact, you may order the subject to stop and place his hands on the back of his head or some place where you can see them. If you do not wish to alert him to your suspicions, you may simply state that you wish to speak with him. The person may be deaf or not understand your language, which may lead you to believe that he is not paying attention, while he is actually unable to do so. Avoid offensive terminology when directing the subject to submit to a field interview. Do not place your hands on the subject except to frisk, search, or control him. Be aware of every person's "personal space." When you get so close that the person pulls back, you will know the boundaries of that "space."

The Position of Interrogation

Stand slightly forward and to the right of the subject at slightly more than arm's length away. If he appears to be left-handed, stand to the side of his left hand. Look for the wristwatch, which most people would wear on the weaker hand. Stand at about a 90-degree angle from the subject. From this position, it is possible to grab the subject's arm and ward off a blow that he may intend to wield. Some weaponless defense instructors recommend that you assume a head-on position slightly out of range for the suspect's hands or feet to be used as offensive weapons against you. Your own training and experience will determine which stance you will assume.

If there is more than one subject, attempt to separate them as soon as practicable before questioning them to prevent them from preparing standardized answers to your questions. Keep them separated until you have completed questioning both of them. Until assistance arrives, stand in the position of interrogation next to the leading subject and have the others stand on the other side, all in plain view.

If there are two officers and one subject, the officer who will conduct the interview should stand at the position of interrogation while the second officer stands to the rear and the opposite side. If there are two officers and more than two subjects, use the same basic posture with the subjects between the officers. Once you have searched them, if necessary, separate them and question them separately.

Ask questions to satisfy your curiosity and your suspicions. Ask positive questions to secure positive responses, such as "Where is your car?" or "When was the last time a police officer questioned you?" Do not make the mistake of providing the subject's answers for him by asking questions such as "You don't have a car, do you?" or "You have never been questioned by the police before, have you?"

When you do not wish to alert the subject to the fact that you may suspect he is a wanted felon or that he matches the description of a person observed at a crime scene, it is advisable to use subterfuge while making the initial contact. The purpose of the deception is to avoid alerting him to your suspicions until you are in a position of advantage. It may

appear natural for you to ask the subject if he has seen a car you are looking for or if he is the person who called to report an abandoned car.

If the subject's answers and his behavior continue to pique your
curiosity and suspicions, you may change your line of questioning as soon
as you have a position of advantage.

*If the subject's answers, attitude, or other behavior indicate that there
is no further cause for action or detention, complete the form or notebook
entry required by your department and conclude the interview.* If the circumstances indicate the need for further inquiry, continue the interview.
Never lower your guard and "assume" that the subject presents no danger
to you. He probably does not, but you do not know that.

1. Check for identification. Be sure that the documents describe the
   subject. Indicate on your field interview card or notebook the types
   of documents you used for the ID, and list any numbers found on
   the documents. A card with a photograph, such as a driver's
   license, is far better than a social security card, which is virtually
   worthless as identification.
2. Ask the subject to repeat the nature of his business in the area.
   Does this actually make sense to you, under the circumstances?
3. Secure a statement as to where the subject is going and where he
   has been. Is this actually on the way? Ask the subject where he is
   now. The answer may surprise you. The subject may have no idea
   where he is.
4. Check out the story when possible. If two persons are providing
   different information, compare notes and get a reason for the differences.
5. Fill out a complete description on the subjects, including
   a. Visible scars, marks, tattoos. Draw a sketch, if practicable.
   b. Deformities, unusual characteristics. Describe carefully or
      sketch.
   c. Membership data as indicated by cards presented for identifi-
      cation, car club jackets, car plaques, business cards, gang
      insignia. Take photographs when practicable.
   d. Design of shoe and heel prints and shoe size, particularly
      those whose records indicate a history of burglary arrests.
   e. Subject's statement regarding past criminal record and/or
      prior contacts with the police. Check records and record the
      information.

The Interview

1. *Maintain a friendly, yet not overly familiar, attitude.* The attitude
   of the subject of the interview may be a reflection of that of the
   officer (see Figure 6–3).

Figure 6-3 Interrogation is an art. One of the most important factors is to establish rapport and maintain a friendly atmosphere. (Courtesy of the Police Department, Aberdeen, South Dakota.)

2. *Identify the subject.* One of the first questions to ask him is where he lives. He may be anticipating your asking him for a name and he may be prepared with a fabricated one, but he is less likely to have thought of a false address.

3. *Take out your field interview card or notebook only after you have identified the individual.* Some people tend to become uncooperative when confronted with something that indicates the imminence of a permanent written record.

4. *Determine the nature of the subject's business at the location where you contact him.*

5. *Ask the subject where he is going and where he has been.* The story should logically relate to his explanation for being where he is when you contact him.

6. *Determine how familiar the subject is with the neighborhood if he claims to be a frequent visitor.*

7. *Use the radio or a telephone—if available—to check records on the subject for a prior record and to ascertain if he is wanted.*

8. *Arrest or release the subject, depending on the circumstances as indicated by your investigation to this point.*

9. *Conduct a patdown or cursory search.* If circumstances warrant your field contact with the subject, the same conditions may justify the patdown for any offensive weapons with which the subject may attack you. The timing depends on the circumstances of the individual case, but the search should occur early unless a brief interview indicates to you that you do not wish to further restrict the subject's movement. If you do pat down the subject, do it early to avoid later regrets.

10. *Complete filling out the field interview card or the notebook entry.* When writing your reason for the field interview, indicate *what it was about the subject and/or the circumstances that caused you to first decide to proceed with the field interview.* Be specific, as this justification should be considered reasonable cause for the interview, the detention, and any other action you should take. Without this information, it is conceivable that you might lose an otherwise good case.

11. *Conclude the field interview promptly.*

    a. To the "legitimate" subject, a word of caution about recent crimes in the area, a brief explanation of the field interview program and its necessity, and a "thank you" for his cooperation.

    b. To the "suspicious" subject, a word of advice pertaining to the process of the field interview and its possible significance to him, depending on the circumstances of the contact and the character of the subject.

    c. If the interview and accompanying circumstances lead to the need for more intensive investigation and discussion of the matter at hand with the subject, you may have "focused" on him as a suspect in a specific offense and a custodial interrogation may follow.

Several years ago, a team of officers from several departments spent several weeks interviewing a burglar whose arrest cleared more than 800 burglaries. The purpose of the interviews was to understand better how a burglar thinks and operates to help the field officer prevent the crime more effectively and to apprehend the burglar. Whenever you question an individual whom you find to be responsible for certain types of crimes, listen to the answers that you get about method of entry, object of the crime, and other factors. Then add your findings to this list, which includes some of the observations made by the burglar of several years ago, plus additional comments by other burglars.

1. *Clothing worn by burglar*: Whatever fit the neighborhood being worked.

2. *Tools*: Seldom anything that resembles "burglar tools"; more often has a three-bladed pocket knife, plastic card, and penlight.

3. *Vehicle*: Stolen cars that had been stolen some time ago and were replaced on the hot sheet by more recent vehicles stolen. Plates were removed and replaced with those stolen from stored vehicles, usually from another state.

4. *License plates*: Same age and state of repair as the cars, such as new plates for new cars, beat-up plates for beat-up vehicles.

5. *Selection of victims*: Comfortable middle class observed in restau-

rants and bars during "happy hours" who used cash rather than credit cards.

6. *Casing the victim*: Try ringing the door bell. If no answer, try the phone in the garage. Dial the ring-back number and if no one is home, go into the house. Avoid barking dogs, but if dogs continue sleeping, they are no threat. Snoring sleepers no problem.

7. *Casing the police*: To find out how many officers and units on the air, go to the station at shift-change time and count the officers as they depart for patrol, listening on radio for their unit numbers. Watch officers on patrol and figure out their patterns. Usually one pass per shift is all they would make in any neighborhood. Look for discarded hot sheets and other valuable information in trash cans outside and behind police station.

8. *Field shakedowns*: Act natural and give all correct information from the stolen driver's license used (date of birth, etc.) and registration information about the car; know contents of trunk and glove box. If the burglar received a citation using another person's car and license, he would pay it to avoid it "going to warrant." Suspect always had a ready answer why stolen merchandise was in car, such as moving to another apartment. Acted "cool" because officers are suspicious of people who are nervous and "appear to be hiding something."

9. *Logical reasoning*: Most officers follow fixed patterns of patrol; they are creatures of habit. An officer may be taken off guard and not be able to react suddenly when there is an unusual event, such as the traffic violator waiting for the officer to get out of the car and approach, then the violator suddenly "digs out." "Officers seldom look up when looking for suspects and other items."

10. *The crime*: Best object of attack are glass patio doors, which can be lifted out of their tracks, whether locked or not, even with broomstick handles in the track while door is left ajar. Lots of people leave doors and windows open and unlocked. Burglars who find one fruitful house in the neighborhood will often return to the same house and to the same neighborhood. Burglars take stolen "loot" to bushes along the curb, attack another house and others, and then get their cars and go along the street and pick up all the loot.

11. *Flight*: When the police started closing in, subject sometimes approaches the officers and asks what is going on and offers to help; sometimes burglars climb trees, or crawl into attic crawl hole in resident hall. Burglars may flee over fences and bushes knowing that some officers don't want to get their uniforms dirty. Officers do most of their searching without getting out of their vehicles.

12. *Searches*: It appeared that officers search as though they do not expect to find anyone.

SUMMARY

Implementation of an active and objective field interview program is essential to the successful and effective operation of the modern law enforcement agency. The program not only gives you an opportunity to prevent and repress crime by meeting and counseling the actual or potential criminal law violators, but also provides you an additional vehicle for contacts with the law-abiding people in his district.

Indiscriminate field interviews and accompanying searches for weapons are not warranted. They must be based on reasonable cause factors and you must be able to articulate them. You must check into any individuals or circumstances that appear at the time to be deleterious to the good order and the peace of the community. Your diplomacy may ease the strain in situations that appear to you at first to be quite suspicious but after the contact turns out to be strictly legitimate and aboveboard. If you handle it correctly, the field interview will result in a favorable contact with someone who will appreciate your diligence and efficiency in looking after their safety by making such field inquiries, particularly at times and places where suspicious circumstances warrant it. The law-abiding person will appreciate you for your interest in keeping the streets free of undesirables and criminals, and the people who are intent on breaking the law may choose somewhere else to ply their trade.

When interviewing or interrogating anyone, be it the suspect, the victim, the witness, or some disinterested bystander, bear in mind your responsibility to seek the truth, whatever that is. Through perseverance, tenacity, and a great deal of skill and native ability, you will find that your success as a police officer will be greatly enhanced if you can interview and interrogate effectively.

EXERCISES AND STUDY QUESTIONS

1. Define *interrogation*.
2. Define *interview*.
3. Describe the difference, if any, between an interview and an interrogation.
4. What is Reik's theory regarding confession?
5. Why does the author refer to the process of interviewing as an art?
6. List and discuss the five basic objectives of interviewing and interrogating.
7. If you had a choice, where would you choose to interrogate a suspected child molester?
8. How would you go about opening an interview to establish rapport?

9. Give an example of the logical approach in interviewing.

10. Give an example of the sympathetic approach.

11. Explain the *Miranda* rule, and recite verbatim the admonishment.

12. How must the suspect respond for you to testify that you received an intelligent waiver?

13. Describe a custodial interrogation.

14. What do you do when a suspect has waived *Miranda* rights and talks freely about the crime and then suddenly has a change of heart and stops talking?

15. Describe what happened in the *Mathiason* case that caused the Supreme Court to rule as it did.

16. When you stop to cite a traffic violator, must you warn the offender of his or her *Miranda* rights before asking for the reason for not stopping at the intersection for the crossing pedestrian?

17. Are private security officers bound by the *Miranda* rule the same as city police officers? What makes the difference, if any?

18. What gives the peace officer the right to conduct a field interview?

19. What are the objectives of a field interview program?

20. Describe the legal basis for a field interview in your jurisdiction.

21. Design a field interview card that would be an improvement over the one depicted in this chapter.

22. List at least 10 different situations that you believe would justify a field interview.

23. Describe the correct procedure for approaching a person who is on foot, in an automobile, on a motorcycle.

24. What does the author say about stopping a suspect vehicle by pulling alongside and pointing a revolver at the driver, ordering him or her to stop?

25. Describe the method of approach of a vehicle by a solo officer, two officers.

REFERENCES

COLEMAN, JAMES C. *Abnormal Psychology and Modern Life*, 5th ed. Glenview, Ill.; Scott, Foresman, 1976, Chap. 4.

FREUD, SIGMUND. *Psychopathology of Everyday Life*. New York: Mentor, 1951, pp. 102–108.

GILBERT, JAMES N. *Criminal Investigation*. Columbus, Ohio: Charles E. Merrill, 1980, Chap. 6.

INBAU, FRED E., and JOHN E. REID. *Criminal Interrogation and Confessions*. Baltimore: Williams & Wilkins, 1962.

REIK, THEODOR. *The Compulsion to Confess: On the Analysis of Crime and Punishment*. New York: Farrar, Straus & Giroux, 1959.

SCOTT, JAMES D. *Investigative Methods*. Reston, Va.: Reston, 1978.

STOKKE, ALLAN H., and ROBERT W. FERGUSON. *Legal Aspects of Evidence*. New York: Harcourt Brace Jovanovich, 1978, Chap. 8.

WADDINGTON, LAWRENCE C. *Criminal Evidence*. Encino, Calif.: Glencoe, 1978, Chap. 11.

WESTON, PAUL B., and KENNETH M. WELLS. *Criminal Evidence for Police*, 2nd ed. Englewood Cliffs, N.J.: Prentice Hall, 1976, Chap. 13.

_____. *Criminal Investigation, Basic Perspectives*, 3rd ed. Englewood Cliffs, N.J.: Prentice Hall, 1980, Chaps. 9, 11.

7

THE "ROUTINE" ASSIGNMENT

INTRODUCTION

Under ideal conditions, the field officer, particularly the one who is just beginning a long and eventful career, will have an operational plan for just about every type of anticipated activity. A set of guidelines for every conceivable contingency would provide a broad base of information derived from the experiences of others and from recommended departmental policies. From there you could work out your own techniques in handling assignments that confront you. In the academy, the staff attempts to provide that broad base. In this and other chapters, we want to do the same thing. It is our intention to cover as wide an assortment of assignments as possible with methods for handling them. This chapter is devoted to assignments that do not fall in the category of "unusual" occurrences, or "crimes in progress"; we shall group them together here under the category of "routine," but you should never consider any assignment routine.

This chapter is devoted to the following subjects: (1) the lost child, (2) missing persons (considered separately from the missing child, whose cases are decidedly different in many instances), (3) intoxication cases, (4) civil and domestic disputes, (5) alcoholic beverage control and enforcement, (6) abandoned vehicle abatement, (7) nuisances (attractive and otherwise), (8) parades and special events, (9) fire scenes, (10) rescue and first aid, (11) courtesy services, (12) public utility assistance, and (13) handling animal calls. As you can see, this chapter is a variety act, and we cover some of the basic techniques in each category.

LOST CHILD

This is one of the most important of all police activities and should involve maximum personnel assignment at the earliest opportunity after the parent reports the child as missing (see Figure 7–1). There has usually been some lapse of time prior to the parent's report. Therefore, time is of the essence because of the distances the child may have traveled or the length of time the child may have been exposed to the many hazards he or she might encounter and possibly not be able to cope with.

Some children may have been taught to fear the police uniform and may hide from the searching officers without realizing that the police are trying to reunite them with their parents. Some children who are the object of a search may hide and play games with their searchers.

Secure any information you can regarding any earlier case in which the child ran away. The parents can sometimes provide valuable information, although they may be somewhat reluctant to do so because of embarrassment. If the child has run away or wandered off before, ascertain where he was discovered on the earlier occasion.

Consider the age of the child. Where would you go if you were that age? What type of entertainment or adventure would you pursue if you

Figure 7-1 Searching for a lost child is one of a police department's most responsible functions. Dogs are excellent aids in this type of activity. (Courtesy of the Police Department, Santa Ana, California.)

were on your own away from the sometimes prohibitive control of parents who may disagree with a five-year-old boy's concept of fun and excitement?

When you begin the search, start as though there had been no previous search by anyone. *Do not take anyone's word that a certain place has already been searched.* Search the immediate premises, including any containers that might conceivably contain the child and also smaller containers. Children, both alive and dead, have been found in suitcases, freezers, dresser drawers, clothes hampers, and the most unlikely of places. The child may have gone into hiding to avoid some form of punishment, yet he might not want to stray too far from the security of home. The child may have left the home and the premises earlier, but may have returned and may now be hiding under a bed, in a closet, or somewhere else in or near the house. Is one of the child's vehicles missing, such as a skateboard or bicycle? Look for the child at a favorite place to play or one that is a curiosity to a child, an attractive nuisance, or school grounds, or a park where older children play.

Establish the exact time and location at which the child was last seen. Set up a grid pattern on the jurisdiction map, and divide the search area into well-defined areas with specific assignments to assure complete coverage. Consider the maximum distance the child may have traversed during that period of time, then add more distance for additional coverage. Each assigned officer should then start at the outermost point and search the assigned area in a zigzag or cloverleaf manner, working in toward the center, or the location where the child was last seen, then working back out to the perimeter.

Use the loudspeaker on a police unit and consider having the parents, a relative, or a close friend of the child broadcast the appeal to the child to come out of hiding. Their voices may have a greater value than that of the searching officer. Also consider the use of plainclothes officers and civilian volunteers for extra help because the child may be hiding from the police uniforms, which the child may perceive as a threat.

Never overlook the possibility of kidnapping, and begin an early search for any evidence of such an event. Question parents and other adult family members about the possibility of a custody problem. A common form of child stealing is by a noncustody or limited-custody parent who chooses to defy a court order and establish his or her own custody rights. Sometimes you will encounter a childless woman who will steal a child to adopt unlawfully as her own; and there are people who steal children to sell in adoption businesses. An earlier contact with someone who paid particular attention to the child may be recounted by the parent; such a person may be a good suspect.

Check the files for any known or suspected child molester or registered sex offender who may live or be suspected of performing crimes in the area. Locate and question him or her, if available. Rather than harassment, this procedure is actually an assurance to him. It gives him an opportunity to exonerate himself early in the investigation. Continue a relentless search until you find the child.

Do not overlook the possibility that the child may have run away from an abusive situation that he or she is afraid to tell anyone about. After the chils is found, discreetly look for any signs of trauma, physical or emotional, and report any suspicions to your department's juvenile specialist. Listen to what the child has to say that might give a clue about any cause for his or her disappearance. But do not make the mistake of suggesting to the child anything that may inspire the child's imagination and lead to a witch hunt.

MISSING PERSONS

Many times friends and family members report someone missing. In most cases, that person has isolated himself for a purpose. Relatively few of the reported missing persons are actually the victims of amnesia or have become confused and lost. They are missing by choice. If the missing person is a juvenile, the matter will be handled as a juvenile case, with the child referred to his parents and possibly—in serious cases—to the juvenile court. In the case of missing adults, there is a somewhat different procedure.

Whenever a person is reported missing within a few hours beyond the time when he should have arrived home from work, or is overdue on some sort of trip, it is good practice to take whatever information the reporting party wishes to provide and to advise the person how to go about checking with hospitals where unidentified injured persons may have been taken. In addition, it is advisable to attempt to reassure the reporting party with what information you have about the lack of serious freeway accidents or aircraft crashes or with the information that your department has no unidentified victims of any crimes of violence reported during the time that the person has been missing. Beyond that first phase of taking the report and assisting the reporting party, the next step is to use the resources you have to locate the person and to put the case to rest as soon as possible, hopefully with the location and/or return of the missing person. We must keep in mind the mature adult's right to be missing by choice, and it is the police responsibility to respect that right, provided that such a case does not involve an attempt to evade legal responsibilities.

If there is some evidence or strong reason to believe that the missing person has met with some type of forced absence or violence, an immediate investigation should begin. You should not automatically assume that the person is missing by choice, although that is the case in a large percentage of missing adult situations. In other missing person cases, after a reasonable time has elapsed and the party has not yet returned to his expected destination, a concerted effort should be made to locate him. Once the person is located, if he or she is an adult and indicates a desire not to have his whereabouts made known, your own department policy may require that you notify the reporting party that you found the missing person in good health and that he does not wish his whereabouts made known. In the event of a missing husband, consider the possibility of an impending nonsupport situation with the husband absenting himself. If this is the case, the matter will be a criminal one. Every missing person case should be given adequate attention, but it must be carefully handled within the framework of department policy and law.

INTOXICATION CASES

Traditional police responsibility for arresting and incarcerating the drunks, alcoholics, and other persons whose actions in public indicate their apparent lack of ability to care for their own welfare, rests with the patrol officer. The primary reason for taking such persons into custody are to protect them from themselves and from the dangers of the elements, from traffic, and from any other hazards that they may be exposed to while in an intoxicated state.

Intoxication is relative, and the officer's discretionary powers are great in this area. The laws vary, but those concerning intoxication in public cover persons who are intoxicated to the degree that they are unable to care for their own welfare and are in that state as a result of overindulgence in alcohol, drugs, or other intoxicating or stupefying substances. One of your first considerations is to determine if the subject's condition is caused by some type of illness, poisoning, injury, or other condition, brought about by some situation other than voluntary ingestion by the subject, knowing that the substance used had intoxicating or stupefying affects. A smell of alcohol on the breath may not be alcohol at all. Look for the identification bracelet that many diabetics wear to warn anyone finding the victim of diabetic shock that the subject needs immediate medical attention and look for other signs of injury or illness that may or may not be accompanying the presence of alcohol. Question and examine the subject very carefully.

Since alcoholism is considered to be a disease as well as a criminal offense, many jurisdictions will take the person into custody for a specified period of time (four or five hours), then release him or her, and retroactively classify the arrest as a detention. In many jurisdictions that have the resources the drunk is taken to a detoxification center for "drying out" and treatment. This makes more sense, especially when the jails are so badly overcrowded with more serious criminal violators.

How to handle the common drunk or the intoxicated person in public depends on your own department's philosophy about the disease or the condition and enforcement policies. For coverage of the tactics and techniques involving the person who operates a motor vehicle while under the influence of alcohol or other drug, see Chapter 11.

CIVIL AND DOMESTIC DISPUTES

Other than prisoner transportation and arrest situations, probably the most dangerous police activity that you will be called upon to perform is the disturbance call involving neighborhood or family problems, or problems between landlords and tenants, and the dismissed or disciplined employee. You are usually called to the scene by one of the participants, or by a witness to the event, and you are usually called after the problem has accelerated to the crisis stage. Negotiation and conciliation have failed, and emotions are at their highest peak by the time you arrive.

Some of the participants or interested bystanders expect you to work miracles when all other efforts have failed. Once you arrive on the scene, your primary responsibility is to the safety of the participants. The next responsibility is to prevent any ongoing assault from taking place and to arrest the criminal offenders. Once you have determined that all urgent action has been performed, your role changes to that of invited arbiter and you must de-fuse the volatile event. You are going to be asked for advice, and what counsel you do give must be strictly within the scope of your authority. Be careful not to give spiritual or psychological advice, or legal advice, because you are neither licensed nor qualified for the role.

Diplomacy and tact are put into play almost constantly during these "referee" sessions. Occasionally you will be reminded by the calling party that it was he who called and that yhou should enforce his side of the argument, regardless of all other considerations. You are not—nor should you be—the "big bad officer" who is "going to get someone who is naughty," or the "cop who is going to take the bad child into the dark room and beat him up with a big stick," or any other type of demon described by some adults to get their children to behave.

You will often find yourself in what appears to be a "no-win" situation when you are dealing with family or other disputes when love and respect have turned sour. You will have people demanding that you punish the offender—"slap him around" like some of the motion-picture stereotype "tough cops" they envision. They will become angry with you when you refuse. Your role is to rise above the bickering and not be "sucked into" a partisan argument. It is necessary to maintain a professional aloofness.

The telephone operator or dispatcher who receives the original call for police presence at the scene of a civil dispute sets the tone for your initial response. From the details of the situation provided by the calling party, and from the tone of voice and sense of urgency transmitted through the telephone to the dispatcher, the dispatcher determines how many units will be assigned the call, and with what speed they must respond. They should be trained to screen calls, such as "the lady reports they have guns," because some zealous "safety consultant" may have told people that if you want the police to respond to your call and not take their time getting there, the thing to say is that firearms are involved. Irresponsible calls such as that have caused negative results. For example, my younger son and his girlfriend were sitting in his car for what a neighbor believed to be too long for "lawful" persons and called in that there were two suspicious people with guns in a car in front of her house. She got the response she wanted, because within a short time my son and his girlfriend were confronted by three police officers with guns drawn, one of them cocked and stuck in my son's ear. When I called the Watch Commander for an explanation of such behavior, he explained that the calling party set the tone for the officers' response.

The dispatcher may refer the call to another agency, such as a mental health unit that may be better qualified to handle the problem at hand. The dispatcher may advise the people to come into the police station the next working day and discuss the problem with a juvenile officer or some other specialist. These are some guidelines for the dispatcher to follow when taking the call and deciding the appropriate response [this may be at the same time unit(s) are on the way]:

1. Find out exactly what is happening, or as nearly as possible. Listen to the background noises as well as to the voice of the calling party.

2. Determine if someone has been injured and is in need of immediate medical attention.

3. Determine if there is an immediate and imminent danger confronting someone who is on the scene.

4. If there is such a danger, who or what is it?

5. If someone is armed with some sort of weapon, find out what type of weapon, the present whereabouts of the armed subject, and the individual's state of emotionalism and/or sobriety. Is the person using the weapon for self-defense or to assault another person?

6. Find out from the calling party—if possible—and by checking the records files if this is a recurrence of some similar activity that has occurred in the past. What happened that time? (Check records if time permits.)

7. Keep the caller on the telephone as long as necessary.

8. As any new developments arise while you are still talking with the calling party and the assigned officers have been dispatched, keep the officers updated on any information that will assist them in responding to the call.

9. Dispatch only those officers who are necessary to handle the situation effectively.

10. If the situation calls for response from another police agency, such as in a contiguous jurisdiction, or from an organization or agency that is specifically geared for this particular problem, advise the calling party that another agency should handle the matter. What

they may actually need instead of—or in addition to—the police might be paramedics or the fire department. Instead of instructing emotionally involved callers to dial another telephone number, either help them transfer the call or take what information you need, then instruct them that you will call the other agency and handle the matter. Do not add to the caller's frustration and/or anger by stating: "Sorry, ma'am, that's not our jurisdiction. Try the sheriff's office... No. I don't know what their number is, but I'm sure they are in the book."

11. Send backup cars, if necessary. Consider the specific location of the call, the individuals involved, experience with the nature of the call and the principals, the neighborhood characteristics—which may be hostility toward the police in general—and the information you receive by telephone.

12. Call off the units that are no longer needed if there is a change in the circumstances at the scene as reported by the first officer to arrive and other officers.

As the officer assigned to handle the call, your responsibility is to handle the case as well as possible under the circumstances. Any advice that you give should be kept to a minimum. Your role is to restore order, to protect the combatants from themselves and each other, to arrest for violations of the law when necessary, and to give instructions or take whatever action the circumstances dictate to settle the matter during your first visit. Whatever advice you give should be presented in such a manner that they will accept it and act upon it. Any warning you give concerning future arrests should the situation recur must be soundly covered by the law, because if it does continue and you do return, you are committed to make the arrest you promised. It is virtually impossible to make everyone at the scene happy, but they must be placated sufficiently to heed your advice and discontinue the disturbance. Following are some of the more commonly encountered civil dispute situations and a few basic guidelines to use when taking effective police action.

Domestic Quarrels

Arguments and fights among family members have probably been going on for some time and have been building in intensity prior to anyone's call for police intervention. There may be deep-seated emotional problems and irreconcilable differences with the outward manifestations in the form of verbal or physical violence serving only as symptoms of the problem. Under these circumstances, all you can hope to do is to address the symptoms.

Avoid as much as possible what might appear to be prying into other people's personal affairs. Do not give legal advice. Instead, suggest that the people contact a lawyer they trust and in whom they have confidence. They should then seek such legal advice and agree to follow whatever advice the attorney provides. There are qualified, licensed marriage counselors available for family advice. Once you temporarily take care of the symptoms, the people should consult experts to work on the real underlying problems. Do not take sides or become embroiled in the argument that may be taking place. This is the time to protect life and property against injury or destruction, not a time for gallantry to defend the unknown degree of honor of a woman whom you do not know over an issue that is none of your personal concern. Separate the protagonists and speak with them separately and privately, preferably out of sight and hearing distance from each other. Be careful not to make any movement or say anything that might later be used against you in a claim of sexual harassment or physical abuse should that person later complain about your behavior in any way. (This is where a small tape recorder would come in handy.)

In a domestic dispute situation, you may find that you will become the object of attack. Love and hate are strong emotions and they do not seem to be entirely unrelated. One spouse may be verbally and physically abusing the other spouse until a third party comes along and attempts to defend the person under attack. Suddenly the third party—in this case a police officer—becomes a mutual threat, and both spouses join together to overcome that threat. This is a phenomenon that occurs with alarming regularity.

Children may develop antipolice attitudes out of some domestic quarrel in which you as a police officer become involved because you have been called upon for help. This antagonism probably occurs through a transference process. The father may come home drunk and beat the mother. The children become emotionally involved because their security is threatened, or their father may find some reason to punish them in an unusually cruel manner. Eventually the mother calls the police because she cannot defend herself or the children.

You arrive and assess the situation. The mother consents to the arrest of the father, may even demand it under these conditions, because she fears for the safety of the children and herself. The man goes to jail, sometimes after a violent struggle with the arresting officers. Unfortunately, this often occurs in the presence of the children. Through this twist of fate, the police officers—not the father—become the hate objects of the children, because the officers further threatened their security by taking their father out of the home. The financial difficulties relative to posting bail or losing salary for the time in jail—possibly the loss of a job—are sometimes also blamed on the police officers.

Whenever possible during family fight situations, attempt to have the children removed from the scene. Whatever action that ensues is then less likely to involve them so emotionally. A violent arrest scene is not savored by anyone and perhaps it can be avoided altogether. During your assessment of the situation on your arrival, you may determine that a crime such as felonious spousal or child beating had taken place or was occurring during your arrival. Or you may observe that the environment is detrimental to the health and safety of the children, which may call for the arrest of one or both parents for maintaining an unfit home, for being intoxicated, or for performing lewd acts in the children's presence. In many situations, arrests will not be made, but many times such action is imperative.

In an emotion-paced domestic quarrel, it is not unusual for one or both of the principals to demand the immediate arrest and incarceration of the other party. At this point, your discretionary powers come into play. Analyze the situation. What is the present physical and emotional state of the participants? What signs are there of physical injury? What evidence is there that the purported action took place? What do the witnesses—if any—say? What is likely to happen after you leave? Is a crime being committed in your presence? Do you have reasonable cause to arrest for a felony that did not occur in your presence? If you believe that an arrest is warranted and can be effected in a legal and ethical manner, then by all means make the arrest. If you believe that the arrest is not the answer to the problem, you may refuse to accept an arrest by a private person if you do not believe there is legal justification for the arrest.

The age-old problem of convincing an abused wife or child to actually go through with the arrest of the abuser is still very real, although victim-witness and abused persons support groups have met with some success in advertisements stating that "wife beating is now against the law," and "if you really love him, have him arrested so that he can get help." You are on the horns of a dilemma when you witnessed nothing but you are sure that you are going to make a return trip if you do not settle the matter on your first visit. You and your fellow officers should confer with your local prosecuting attorney for advice on how to proceed in this type of a situation. You may be preventing a more serious crime, even a homicide.

Another frequently used alternative is to advise the parties to come into the office of the police department or the prosecuting attorney (depending on your own department practices) during the next business day and to discuss the matter at that time. Then, if it is determined that an arrest should be made, steps will be taken to secure a warrant and effect the arrest. This procedure gives the principals some time to reflect on the matter and to make a rational decision that will have long-lasting effects. If you use this alternative and so advise the principals, you may still need to warn them that if you have to return, you will be compelled to reassess and will have to make some arrests after all. Remember, though, do not make a promise that you cannot keep. Once you have made such a statement, you may be committed to take action or lose your effectiveness. Idle threats are more devastating than is taking no action at all.

Landlord–Tenant Disputes

You are not a bill collector. You do not have the authority to evict tenants from other persons' homes or apartments unless you are the civil division deputy from the sheriff's department or marshal's office who does so by court order. You act as an agent of the jurisdiction for which you serve in your official capacity, not as a personal representative of any landlord or tenant. As with any other incident requiring your attendance, your role is that of police officer to preserve the peace.

When responding to a dispute involving property rights and eviction notices or similar disturbances, approach both adversaries and advise them that your presence is to keep the peace and to prevent the commission of a crime. If they ask for legal advice other than an explanation of the criminal laws they may be contemplating violating, refer them to an attorney of their choice. Legal services are generally available to indigent persons at nominal costs, and small claims court actions for lawsuits involving amounts of money that would probably include the cost of rent may be instituted at a cost of just a few dollars.

There are certain times when a landlord may lock a tenant out of a room or apartment and hold certain luggage and other property to enforce payment of rent. Sometimes one of the people involved—either landlord or tenant—may be guilty of trespass, depending on the rental or lease agreement and other considerations. Keep the peace and advise the disputants to contact their respective attorneys. Even though you may know the correct answers to their various questions about the law, you are not an attorney and cannot give legal advice.

In some disputes in which tempers flare and the participants appear to be at an impasse, it may be necessary to order an end to the argument to avoid more serious problems that would inevitably lead to an arrest of one or both of them. The landlord may seek assistance through the courts, with eviction proceedings, and secure the services of the sheriff or marshal. Either party may seek legal advice. Both must be advised to discontinue their argument.

Mechanics' and Innkeepers' Liens

An auto mechanic or service station operator may retain custody of an automobile until the costs of repairs are either paid for or some arrangement agreeable to mechanic and owner is worked out for payment. Operators of hotels and rooming houses may hold certain belongings of the tenants to enforce collection of rent. All merchants, business owners, and others who provide goods and services are entitled to just payment for those goods and services. Many times you will find that the business operators have had similar problems more than once and that they have had sound legal advice, but occasionally you will encounter the business person who will take every opportunity to fleece unsuspecting victims under the guise of legitimate business.

When you are called to the scene at which the matter appears to involve nonpayment of charges for merchandise or repairs, or some other type of service, question all participants and witnesses carefully. Although you may not act as a bill collector in a civil matter, many nonpayment situations are nothing more than flagrant acts of theft or "defrauding an innkeeper" violations. If there is some dispute regarding charges, they may involve an amount that the party refusing to pay claims is too high. Whatever their statements, advise them that certain property may be held to enforce payment of debts. Also advise them of the laws concerning theft. If the matter cannot be amicably settled by the participants in your presence, advise them to seek legal advice. In the meantime, they should usually pay the bill to gain possession of the property being held and to avoid a charge of theft. If the charges are too high, a judge or jury would have to decide that point. Remind them that small claims courts are available for deciding matters such as fairness of charges for facilities and services.

Repossession Disputes

Modern conditional sales contracts have been standardized and designed to meet most conditions that one comes across in a contractual sale. They have been modified and clarified so many times that many of them are quite standard and free of "loopholes" that might render them invalid. About the only method that can be used to nullify the average contract is to show that some type of fraud was involved to induce a person to enter the agreement.

The title of the property covered in most sales contracts rests with the seller until the total debt is paid. Any default in payment is generally covered in the contract, which provides for repossession. There are only three persons who may legally repossess: (1) the seller and his full-time employees, or (2) a successor in interest (buyer of the contract from the original seller) and his full-time employees, or (3) licensed repossessors acting in behalf of their clients who are either sellers or successors in interest.

If a repossession is made peaceably, but in violation of the conditions of a sales contract, there is civil recourse. If the person in possession of the property does not peaceably accede to the repossession, the repossessor must go to the courts for judicial direction. At that stage, any legal repossession will be made by the bailiff of the court. The bailiff may use whatever force is necessary to enforce the court order, as directed by the court and by guidelines for repossession. The repossession may be made prior to a court hearing if the possessor waives the right to a hearing. Otherwise, a hearing must be held with the judge making a decision as to repossession rights during the hearing and then issuing an order as to whether or not there will be a repossession.

The repossessor cannot enter private property to repossess and cannot use force (this does not refer to the bailiff, who acts by court order). Usually, a repossession is made surreptitiously. If the repossessor is able lawfully and peaceably to gain possession of the property (dominion and control), the repossession is complete, and any effort to retake the property would not be lawful. The buyer who is in possession of the property to be repossessed has a right to object to the repossession at the time it is taking place either orally or physically. If the objection is made before the repossession is accomplished, then the repossessor must discontinue the act of taking the property in dispute. The repossessor should also report the action to the police department as soon as possible to avoid the risk of being charged with theft.

Other property, which is not subject to repossession, but happens to be inside a repossessed vehicle, for example, is the property of its owner and must be returned to that owner on demand. If a third person is in possession of property to be repossessed at the time the repossession is attempted, that person has the same rights as the buyer. If the property is in storage, or in a commercial parking lot, the person in charge may not give permission and cannot allow the repossession.

ALCOHOLIC BEVERAGE CONTROL INVESTIGATION AND ENFORCEMENT

Among the states there is considerable variety in the laws and their application. Laws generally prescribe the conditions under which alcoholic beverages are dispensed and distributed, the people who may serve and be served the beverages, and numerous license regulations. Licensed premises must abide by certain rules of decorum to assure against their becoming "disorderly houses," and the hours of sale are also regulated.

Rather than address the specific laws, which might not apply in the same manner from one state to another, or from one jurisdiction to another, this section deals with the general investigative techniques of alcoholic beverage control violations. The format and information contained in this section is based on an enforcement manual of the California Department of Alcoholic Beverage Control first published in 1968.[1]

Liquor Violations: General Investigative Techniques

Identification, Preservation, and Examination of Evidence. Adequate evidence must be collected to prove a violation and sustain a conviction.

1. Seize and book into evidence the alcoholic beverage (in the original container when possible).
2. Mark for evidence the same as any other item of evidence.
3. Seal the bottle in the presence of the person from whom seized, if possible, or in the presence of a witness.
4. Present a receipt for the evidence seized.

---

[1]State of California, Department of Alcoholic Beverage Control, *Enforcement Manual* (Sacramento, Calif.: State Printing Office, 1968), pp. 11, 12.

5. If the drink is a mixed one, immediately remove ice, pour the drink into an evidence bottle, and seal.

6. If necessary to establish alcoholic content, such as if you did not observe the bartender pour from a labeled bottle, taste and smell the beverage. Use a small straw and beware of the danger of germs or other harmful matter.

7. As soon as practicable, have the laboratory analyze the beverage to establish alcoholic content.

Establishing Age and/or Identity. For a licensee or employee:

1. Obtain name, age, address, telephone number, length of time with this establishment, and length of time in the liquor business.

2. Obtain the hours of duty for the person identified.

3. Observe and record the physical condition of the licensee or the server (or both), including vision, hearing, and state of sobriety.

4. Observe and record the condition of other individuals served by this employee or licensee, such as for a violation of serving to an obviously intoxicated person or an underaged person.

For minors:

1. Determine what documents were shown for identification, and examine them.
   a. Check carefully for alterations.
   b. Seize all false identification documents.
   c. Look for additional identification documents. Many minors will use a false ID for alcohol purchases, but will use authentic documents for all other occasions.

2. Question the minor on his or her age and determine if the server checked for identification prior to service.

3. If possible, verify the subject's age with a relative (by phone, if necessary, but by follow-up investigation prior to the court date).

4. A birth certificate may be used to establish age only; supplemental documents are necessary for establishing identity.

5. Carefully scrutinize all documents for validity, and ask the subject such questions as middle name, home address, and date of birth, and compare photographs with the subject.

6. Marriage status does not affect minimum legal age, and statements by other persons present do not legally verify age. Documents are required.

7. A person who refuses to present proof of age will be assumed by the server to be underaged. The establishment is authorized to demand documentary evidence.

8. Note the appearance and clothing of the minor.

9. Thoroughly search for other identifying documents.
10. Secure and record names and addresses of witnesses and prepare a complete report.

Essential Facts for Your Report

1. Condition of the premises: lighting, size of crowd, size of the bar, and general demeanor of the crowd.
2. Number of employees present.
3. Appearance and demeanor of the buyer/patron in violation.
4. The order as written (secure the actual check, if one is used).
5. Identify the type of beverage or name the cocktail, including the ingredients.
6. How was the beverage served: In a bottle? In a glass? Packaged?
7. Indicate the time the order was served.
8. Where did the beverage come from (back bar, speed rack, shelf, or refrigerator)?
9. Cost of the merchandise. Secure the receipt, if there is one.
   a. Amount requested by the seller.
   b. Type and amount of money presented by the buyer.
   c. Amount of change, if any.
10. If the license covers sale but not consumption on premises, wait and observe consumption on the premises.
11. Citation of arrest of the subject(s).
12. Search the premises thoroughly.
13. Secure signed statements when possible (remember *Miranda*).
14. Inspect and verify liquor license (type, number, and expiration date).
15. Note the correct time.
   a. Compare this with the clock on the premises.
   b. What time does the watch of the server indicate?
16. Note whether the licensee was on the premises and whether he or she took part in the violation.
17. Establish whether the licensee was in a position where he or she should have observed the violation. Was the person exercising correct management control, or is there criminal responsibility?

ABANDONED VEHICLE ABATEMENT

Trash should be removed from the streets, and from both public and private property, even if it carries a license plate. The idea of this type of activity is to keep vehicles off the street and out of public view when it is apparent that the owners have abandoned them or when it is apparent that there is no intent to make them operable again. Other purposes of vehicle abatement are to reclaim salvageable metals, dispose of neighborhood eyesores and attractive nuisances for children, reduce rodent and insect infestations, and reduce health hazards.

Certain legal proceedings are required, which usually consist of notification of the owner, waiting out specific periods of time to show noncompliance, having the property towed to government-subsidized locations, and holding public auctions the proceeds of which go to the general fund. Your primary consideration should be public safety and the general welfare of the community.

NUISANCES

There are two general types of nuisances that require the attention of the police department: the public nuisance and the attractive nuisance. Both may involve criminal code violations—and they often do—but they also involve civil, non-police matters.

The public nuisance often involves misdemeanor crime violations such as disturbance of the peace, boisterous conduct, loud and unusual noises during prohibited hours, drunkenness, assaults, delinquency of minors, vagrancy, and vice violations. It encompasses a multitude of encroachments on the peace and dignity of the community at large as well as the many individuals who are disturbed.

General public nuisances involve law violations such as offensive advertising signs that are too large or placed in locations where ordinances prohibit them, disagreeable odors caused by abandoned refuse in a vacant lot, automobiles that are either abandoned or placed on blocks in the street for repairs that never seem to get done, and the maintenance of an excessive number of animals for the size of the house or lot. An abandoned building that becomes the residence of drunkards and vagrants may soon present itself as a public nuisance.

One type of public nuisance that presents a special problem is the "party house." It is usually occupied by two or more people who legitimately pay the rent and then have parties involving more people than the place can accommodate. These often become too raucous and noisy. The place might become a gathering place for people to violate liquor laws ostensibly under the guise of "private property asylum" or a place for numerous narcotics and dangerous drug law violations. In some jurisdictions, it is possible to cause the owners and occupants of the homes or apartments involved to discontinue the nuisance or to vacate the premises. This action is possible if it can be shown to the court that the "party house" threatens and generally disturbs the "public" in the persons of the surrounding residents and others who are disturbed.

An attractive nuisance is usually given that designation because it is a condition or place that attracts children and poses an imminent threat to their health and safety (see Figure 7–2). The nuisance may in itself be entirely legal or innocent, but by its own nature it attracts young people who cannot understand the significance of the threatened danger. A legal definition of "attractive nuisance" has been presented as "an unnatural condition that attracts infants who do not understand the danger, and injury results because of the condition." Here is a list of what might be considered attractive nuisances under certain conditions:

1. Building under construction
2. Abandoned or unoccupied buildings that have not been adequately secured to prevent entry
3. Swimming pools without adequate fencing, gate locks, and reasonable means of prohibiting swimming without responsible persons in attendance
4. Accumulations of water of unknown, or excessive, depth
5. Piles of dirt, sand, or gravel
6. Excavations
7. Ladders and scaffolding
8. Dead trees and accumulations of dead foliage
9. Telephone and power poles with cleats close to the ground, making it possible for easy climbing.
10. Unattended construction machinery or farm implements that can be started without an ignition key

Some attractive nuisances are prohibited by specific criminal laws, such

Figure 7-2 Officers frequently inspect this canal, which runs through Billings, where several children have drowned. (Courtesy of the Police Department, Billings, Montana.)

as an abandoned refrigerator with the locking mechanism left intact, or an unattended motor vehicle with the motor running. They should be diligently investigated and the laws enforced. Most of this conduct is prosecutable under civil law, in tort actions. There are three types of conduct that may be considered cause for action: (1) intentional, (2) negligence, and (3) acts of peril. The third type involves certain situations when the defendant may be considered liable without fault, or culpability. Nevertheless, the loss of the lawsuit means two things: someone—probably a child—suffered the loss of life or some form of injury, and the defendant suffers the loss of money.

Your role in this matter is twofold. You should attempt to protect children by frequently checking the locations of such attractive nuisances, and you should remind the owners or other persons in charge of the nuisances of their existence and the possibility that they may suffer losses in tort actions. Whenever children or other persons are found at those locations, they should be told to leave, and the parents of the children should be notified of your action so that they may attempt to exercise appropriate controls to prevent tragedies from occurring. When notifying the owners or other responsible persons of the existence of nuisance conditions, prepare reports to permanently record the fact that you fulfilled your responsibility at that point. If the hazardous condition continues to exist, more formal action may be taken in the form of registered letters directed to the offenders or, possibly, civil action filed by the city attorney on behalf of the people to protect the lives and limbs of their children. Of course, private individuals will probably also take action on their own in aggravated situations.

PARADES AND SPECIAL EVENTS

The primary police responsibility at any special event, such as a parade, festival, or other occasion involving a greater than usual number of people, is to expedite vehicular and pedestrian traffic, and to keep the traffic lanes open for emergency vehicles. Spectator safety is paramount, particularly the safety of young children who may not be capable of looking after their own safety. Direct your full attention on the people, utilizing crowd and traffic control procedures.

FIRE SCENES

A fire scene is the responsibility of the fire department commanders and their personnel. They handle the rescue operations and extinguish the blaze. The police responsibility is the same as at any other location where crowds of people congregate: vehicle and pedestrian traffic and crowd control.

Upon your arrival at the scene, contact the fire commander, who will be in charge of the overall operations. Divert traffic away from the scene to prevent any further damage or injuries that might have already occurred. Keep the streets open to allow for the ingress and egress of fire vehicles, ambulances, and any other vehicles and equipment required by the fire department. Above all, protect the water hoses against tampering and do not allow any vehicles to run over them. Look out for, and interview, suspicious persons who might have started the fire, if it later turns out to be a case of arson. Instruct passersby and casual spectators to leave the immediate area of the fire to prevent any major disaster. Once you have handled the matters required of you in your police officer capacity, contact the ranking fire department officer and determine if there is any need for your assistance in rescue operations or any security matters involving the fire equipment or valuable property at the scene. If the situation warrants it, you may find it necessary to declare the area of the fire a disaster area and then to enforce the area control diligently as long as the emergency exists.

RESCUE AND FIRST AID

A police officer is authorized and—in some states—legally required to administer first aid and to perform rescue operations whenever the need arises. One of the prime considerations to bear in mind relative to that statement is that first aid does not mean to practice medicine or in any way to exceed the limitations of "first aid" treatment. Once you assume such treatment, you are liable for exercising reasonable care, which has clearly been defined and described in your training. Any rescue operations are subject to the same requirements.

Some people carry identification bracelets or necklaces or cards in their wallets that indicate a special problem that rescue personnel should be aware of (see Figure 7–3). Problems might be allergies to bee stings or certain medications, such as penicillin, sulfa, or antihistamines. The indi-

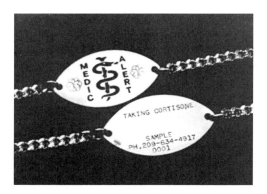

Figure 7-3   Medical identification bracelet.

vidual may be suffering from hemophilia, a heart condition, diabetes, or epilepsy; be wearing contact lenses or taking anticoagulants, or be breathing through a hole in his or her throat. Several organizations provide such bracelets and other devices and maintain a 24-hour call service for special notifications. One of the more widely known of those services is Medic-Alert. Whenever you encounter anyone who appears to be in need of medical attention, look for the special identification.

COURTESY SERVICES

It is a physical impossibility for the police department to provide all the services that would be requested once the service is started. Policy decisions should be made by your department as to which services will be provided; this listing should be communicated to all members of the department. Then those services should be uniformly provided by all officers. Personalized service for certain individuals merely opens the door for a long series of "modifications" in policy and procedure for certain individuals on a favoritism basis.

Merely having police officers on duty and on constant patrol throughout the various parts of the city encourages some people to believe that the officers are there to serve their whims. Such people do not consider any of the myriad other responsibilities with which they are charged. "They are on duty already, so why not have them do it?" may be asked by a councilman who has no idea of the full extent of the burden already carried by the police department. A simple reply to that question is: "Why not, indeed?" Using that oversimplified logic, why not assign certain of those services to the fire department, recreation leaders, license and building inspectors, or anyone else who is "on duty already"? The duties of the police department are defined, and they must be limited if the department is to be held responsible for the safety of the people in the community and their property. Escort service, messenger service, and a wide variety of other services are regularly provided by private enterprise for profit—or loss. Taxicabs are in the business of transporting persons for hire. Is it equitable for the police department to compete with private enterprise by providing free services to some people, while most others utilize the facilities of private businesses? Many of these services are not police responsibilities, and their perpetuation should not be tolerated. Tradition may be a safe answer to the question "Why are these services performed?" However, tradition does not necessarily offer the correct answer. Consider the advisability of performing these courtesy services; then respond to them in accordance with the policies of your own department.

Many courtesy services are performed by the patrol officer as a matter of routine, most of them because it has "always been done." Whichever of these services your department performs should be executed with tact, diplomacy, and courtesy. They are free services, and there should be no expectation of anything in return.

1. Check a house to see if the vacationer, who is calling from about a hundred miles away, did remember to turn off the gas furnace and lock all the doors.

2. Deliver a message to someone who has no telephone but who is needed in the office because of a company emergency that cannot wait.

3. Deliver a death message to the wife of a laborer who had been buried alive in a landslide. In such situations, consider stopping along the way to pick up the family minister, rabbi, or priest for spiritual guidance to the survivors. Neighbors may lessen the strain. Sometimes it may be wise to notify the fire department rescue team that you are going to deliver a message in the event that that unit is needed for an emergency in case of a cardiac arrest or other side effect from the shock. If the person to receive the message is known to be gravely ill, it may be advisable to call the family doctor to accompany you when you deliver the message or have him or her make the delivery.

4. Help a bedridden invalid who needs immediate assistance in securing an emergency delivery of medicine, or in being lifted back into bed after falling out. One serious problem that could result from giving such assistance is the creation of a dependence by the invalid on the service provided on a few occasions by the district police officer. If such a dependence becomes a habit and is allowed by the department, the invalid might someday call for emergency service that the department cannot provide because all the officers are busy, and because of such failure to respond, the invalid's condition may worsen or he or she may die. The question may be asked in court: "Why was the police department negligent in not responding to that individual's call for help?"

5. Escort a frightened or cautious woman or child down a darkened alley to her apartment in a high-crime area when a sex killer is at large.

6. Give directions or provide other informational services for guests or tourists in town. In many cases, the police officer on the street represents the entire community to the inquirer, and that officer's attitude is interpreted as the attitude of the entire community.

7. Help someone who has locked himself out of his home or automobile to break in. Some burglars and thieves have actually been assisted by unsuspecting police officers who have been entirely innocent of any criminal involvement. Some persons have sought the assistance of the police in gaining entry, then complained about the method used by the officer who assisted them. This type

of service should be strictly on an emergency basis. Occasions when there is clearly an indicated need for your assistance would be when a person's life may be endangered, which might be the case when a child is locked inside a car with the motor running, or when a person who has locked himself inside a house has indicated his intention to commit suicide.

Whenever you assist a person in gaining entry in a routine problem situation, be sure to get satisfactory proof of identification and ownership of the property, and limit your participation to advice except in unusual cases, as with elderly persons or invalids. When you actually assist in such matters, consider the advisability of having the persons assisted sign a waiver relieving you from liability. This procedure may help to avoid a later complaint.

ASSISTING PUBLIC UTILITIES AND SERVICE AGENCIES

Following are guidelines for responding to utility or other public service problems:

1. *Street lights out or damaged.* The lighting is to provide people with sufficient illumination to assure them of safety on the streets. The lights should be replaced as quickly as possible. Look for malicious damage, which may indicate some purpose to use the darkness as a cover for illicit activities.

2. *Electricity out and electric wires down.* The line that is out may be providing electricity for a kidney machine or an emergency surgery, as well as for hundreds of homes and apartments. Locate the wire that is down or the place where the cable has been cut and notify the power company immediately. While waiting for the arrival of the repair crews, keep curious onlookers at least ten feet away (the farther the safer), and take whatever precautions that are necessary to protect the area. Electric power is energy in motion, as are moving automobiles or flying bullets. It travels like water through a hose, but it is deadly power, sometimes fatal.

Have the dispatcher contact the power company and ask for instructions on what they would prefer that you do to keep the wires under control and to prevent serious injury to yourself as well as to others. While waiting for the crew to arrive, (a) keep the area lighted if during the hours of darkness, (b) keep yourself and others clear of metal or water, and (c) avoid being between any two wires or between a wire and the ground.

3. *Damaged water mains or fire hydrants.* When water mains or fire hydrants are broken, there are two dangerous effects that should be overcome as soon as possible. One is an almost sudden drop in water pressure in that area; the second is extensive soil erosion, particularly on a hillside. Either could be disastrous if not handled as an emergency situation.

It may be wise to evacuate homes on hillsides below the broken main because of possible earth movement problems.

4. *Telephone lines down*. Telephone repair crews should be notified as soon as the broken line or cable is discovered. Many emergency services depend on the telephone as their only means of communication and cannot function effectively without it. Watch for electric wires that might also be present.

5. *Broken gas pipes*. Domestic natural gas has odor-producing gas added and it is easy to detect if present in any quantity. The natural gas itself is odorless and may not be detected as easily, but lines extending within populated areas usually have the easily detected odor. If possible, locate the source and extent of the leak. Immediately notify the gas company and ask for any special instructions it may wish to give you pending the arrival of repair crews. Immediately evacuate persons from the vicinity of the broken line. Instruct the people to turn off all fires or flames, to refrain from smoking, and to avoid doing anything that might cause a spark, including turning electric switches off or on. If the gas leak seems to be inside a building or confined space, do whatever you can to allow maximum ventilation.

6. Defective streets and sidewalks. Holes and broken places in cement or asphalt may not be readily visible to the pedestrians who use the sidewalk or the drivers who use the street. Any defects in either of these surfaces should be reported as quickly as possible to the street department so that they may be repaired. If they are allowed to go unrepaired or with no warning barricades or lights of some type, the city might be held civilly liable in the event a lawsuit is initiated.

7. *Traffic signs, signals, other controls*. There is obviously a purpose for these various traffic control implements. Allowing any one to go for any length of time in a state of disrepair, or to be missing altogether, could result in traffic congestion or a serious traffic accident. Some signs lose their painted surface or their reflective quality, or they become illegible because of overhanging tree branches or shrubbery. If there is a need for them where they are, the traffic control devices should be functioning fully as intended.

HANDLING ANIMAL CALLS

How to handle stray animals, if this is a police department function in your jurisdiction at all, varies with local laws and policies. Animals that are suspected of having rabies require special handling and quarantine for a required period of time. If it is necessary to dispose of an animal suspected of having rabies, the head should not be destroyed, since the brain is used for analysis. If you must dispose of an animal, never do it in the presence of children.

EXERCISES AND STUDY QUESTIONS

1. How would you search for a child who may be hiding from the police?
2. When searching for a child who is missing from his or her home, where should you begin the search?
3. Where would you go if you were a child and had decided to run away from home?
4. Look around your own home and list all those places a small child might hide in each room.
5. What is the purpose for questioning people with records as child molesters who happen to live near a missing child's home?
6. What is the routine procedure for handling a missing adult in your department? Under what conditions would you delay the search, and for how long would you delay?
7. How does your department deal with nonbelligerent drunks?
8. From what other ailments might a person be suffering who appears to be intoxicated?
9. List at least five additional indicators that might lead to a drinking driver arrest but are not listed in the text.
10. What is your principal responsibility at the scene of a domestic dispute?
11. What type of information should the telephone operator/dispatcher attempt to learn before dispatching a unit to the scene of a domestic dispute?
12. To what extent, if any, may a police officer give marital or legal advice?
13. If you must arrest someone at the scene of a violent domestic dispute, what should you do about the children?
14. What property may a landlord hold to enforce payment of rent?
15. What is a mechanic's lien, and how is it enforced?
16. What must the repossessor of an automobile do if the buyer who is home at the time refuses to allow the repossessor into the garage where the auto is parked?
17. Who may use force to accomplish a repossession?
18. How do you check for the authenticity of an identification card of a driver's license issued in your state?
19. How would you preserve the evidence if you were to arrest an underage person in possession of a rum and cola drink?
20. What type of document would you accept as valid proof of age?
21. If you arrest an underage person in a bar, may you also arrest or cite the person who served the drink?
22. What is the purpose for abandoned vehicle abatement?

23. What is the definition of attractive nuisance? List ten places or conditions in your neighborhood that would fit that category.

24. What is your role as a police officer at a fire scene?

25. List 25 legitimate public courtesy services that your department should provide.

REFERENCES

LOS ANGELES POLICE DEPARTMENT. *Daily Training Bulletins*, Vols. I and II. Springfield, Ill.: Charles C Thomas, 1954, 1958.

STATE OF CALIFORNIA, Department of Alcoholic Beverage Control. *Enforcement Manual*. Sacramento, Calif.: State Printing Office, 1967.

8

CRIMES IN PROGRESS

INTRODUCTION

There are few calls for police service that more directly involve the field police officer than the "crime in progress" call. The response must be immediate and with the precision of fine machinery. Time is precious. Response time is often the determinant of whether the victim will suffer death or serious injury. The element of time also determines whether the culprit will be apprehended at the scene or elsewhere, if at all.

When possible, there should be some preparation and planning for the inevitable crime in progress to assure a fine degree of precision in handling the call and apprehending the suspect. During the planning process, locate those places within the city or county area of your jurisdiction that are potential crime hazards, such as banks and liquor stores for robberies, drugstores and restaurants for burglaries, and as many other places likely to fall prey to the criminal as can be anticipated. All of this preplanning can be done on computers for instant access when officers are dispatched to virtually any type of call.

Map out the surrounding areas, such as streets, alleys, dead-end streets, and cul-de-sacs. List and indicate the locations and numbers of entrances into the buildings. What are the most logical places where a burglar might enter? exit? Are there any low-hanging obstructions that will either provide the culprit an additional means of escape by access to the roof, or that an officer may run into in the dark? Who are the informants in the neighborhood, and how will they act under stress? Ask yourself virtually every question about the crime that may occur at each location, the suspected criminals you may encounter, and the victims and what their reactions may be under various in-progress crime situations. In every way possible, work out the police coverage of the crime that may someday occur, although it may be only once. If not this location, there is little doubt that it will be another place with similar characteristics. Consider all possibilities of escape, including time of day and various related traffic factors. Planning should be a regular part of your routine while you are on patrol and there are momentary lags in the demands on your time and energy.

In this chapter we cover some of the most frequently assigned "in-progress" types of crimes. In many cases, there is great similarity or commonality in responding to any type of incident that is in progress because of the urgency involved in responding to apprehend the culprit while still in the act, the safety of the victims and witnesses, and the immediate implementation of search and surveillance tactics. We also discuss communications procedures, field unit response, and specific types of crimes, such as crimes against person and crimes against property. Because the response required of the police is similar to in-progress calls, there is a discussion of gang activity. The chapter concludes with methods of coverage and search for suspects.

"IN-PROGRESS" COMMUNICATIONS PROCEDURE

When receiving the call that a crime is in progress, the dispatcher should immediately alert the various units and divisions that will be involved in the action, preferably by use of a "hot line," as described in Chapter 4. Impress upon the caller the importance of staying on the telephone, or at least keeping the line open, if it is at all practicable. When you begin the conversation with the calling party, state "Don't hang up. Stay on the telephone!" Ascertain as quickly as possible the exact nature of the crime, whether it is a robbery, a burglary, or a theft that occurred three days ago. To some people, every crime is a robbery, and their emotions may be so involved that it is a "right now" situation even though the just-discovered crime may have occurred several days earlier.

Secure the precise address and location within the building or place where the crime is occurring. Get as much descriptive data as possible about the suspect(s), including the number of suspects, distinctive clothing, the description of any hostages who might be taken away, any weapons, and the vehicle used, if any. Determine the location of the calling party and whether he is in any danger of being observed by the suspect or in danger of sustaining injuries if he should remain at the place. Broadcast the information and handle the essential preliminary assignments while keeping the caller on the open phone line; then go back to the telephone and secure any additional information that the caller may have to give about the initial event or any continuing sequence of events.

When first receiving the call concerning an "in-progress" situation, alert all units in the area of the nature of the event. Once the alert is broadcast, the units in the immediate vicinity should acknowledge receipt of the call and give their respective locations. The unit closest to the scene should be assigned to handle the call. This may not be the unit assigned to that particular district, but the urgency of the situation may call for a deviation from normal procedure. If there is a department policy that requires the district unit to be assigned the call, a reassignment may be made after the initial response has been taken care of. At this moment the most important need is to have a police officer at the crime scene as quickly as possible. After assigning the unit that will handle the call, designate follow-up units, and direct all other units to proceed to key locations around the crime scene. These locations should not be so close to the scene of the crime that their effectiveness will be reduced. Although the call is "in progress," there is a strong possibility that the suspects will soon be leaving—or may have been gone for some time—and too many units in the immediate vicinity will be a waste of time and effort for the officers responding.

FIELD UNIT RESPONSE

If it is possible that the suspect is still at the crime scene and that he is unaware that the police have been alerted, the objective is to get there as quickly as possible without signaling your arrival. Use red light and siren only if the dispatcher instructs you to do so. The factors that should be taken into consideration for a "code three" assignment are the urgency of the situation, the safety of any victim who may be under attack, the time of day, and traffic conditions for the responding units. Get to the scene of the crime as quickly as possible, but do not sacrifice your own safety or that of other people on the way. Know your streets and as much about your district as possible. There is usually some uniformity, some system in numbering the lots, all even numbers on one side, odd numbers on the other. The lapse between numbers may be in multiples of two, four, or ten, but whatever the configuration, it is probably uniform throughout the city. The naming and numbering system may also be according to some master plan. It is your area—you should know this.

En route to the scene of the crime, be on the alert for virtually anything or anybody that appears to be in the area. It is possible that certain individuals may not fit the given descriptions of the suspects; there is a strong possibility that the descriptions were not accurate. Most of the people whom you will encounter will have perfectly legitimate reasons for being where they are, and some of those persons may have information concerning minor items surrounding the crime that may help you further identify the suspect and his automobile and possibly lead to other valuable evidence. Call for a follow-up unit to check these people out and take down their names, addresses, and telephone numbers and any other information about them that you may refer to later should you have reason to question them further. The field interview card is an appropriate device to use for this purpose. Your role as the responding unit is to go directly to the scene.

En route, if possible, you should jot down or dictate into your personal recorder the license plate numbers and descriptions of vehicles leaving the scene of the crime or merely driving around in the area. One of these vehicles may later turn out to be the suspect vehicle, or it may contain key witnesses to the event of surrounding circumstances. Also, consider the possibility that the suspect may have fled from the scene for a couple of blocks, then turned around and headed back toward the scene, believing that the police would never suspect someone going *toward* the scene of the crime.

Except when you wish to announce your arrival at the scene as a strategic move to distract the perpetrator of the crime in an effort to prevent serious injury to his victim, make your arrival as quiet as practicable. Use of the siren while approaching may be unwise, because it may alert a perpetrator, who might panic and hurt someone, or take hostages. Make your approach to the location by way of parallel streets to avoid letting any lookout who may be in the area see your unit until about the moment you arrive. Avoid squealing tires and the sudden braking sounds of your unit sliding into "home plate." The arrival of your unit should sound and appear the same as any other vehicle approaching and stopping in the neighborhood. Do not park directly in front of the location in question, or pull into the driveway, unless traffic is heavy and no other place is available either on the street or near the location of the crime. If time is on your side, park a few doors down and walk.

At this point you have some important decisions to make. For example, if there are victims and suspects inside, your arrival might cause the suspects to panic and take hostages. A jewelry store being robbed in Beverly Hills was built like a fortress. The officers could not see inside and upon arrival found the steel security gate and front door closed. The suspect held the hostages inside and the officers had no way to get in. The only way they could communicate with the suspect was by telephone. While inside he killed one hostage, and while attempting to escape with other hostages a police sniper shot and killed another, mistaking him for the suspect. It is impossible to go back and try another approach, but what would you have done differently? Would it have been better to wait outside silently until the robber had completed his act and then attempt to capture him as he left the building? But what would bystanders and the media have thought if the police officers had waited, and while they were doing nothing the robber had shot and killed his robbery victims anyhow? We have been criticized for acting both ways, when the result turns out as though the officers "should have" done it some other way. Monday morning quarterbacking is sure to happen, but your decision must be made *now*, and you must act *now*.

Once you are in position and can observe the exact location where the crime is believed to be taking place, determine whether it is in fact occurring. Upon your arrival, radio in your "arrived on the scene" transmission, and any other information that is of immediate significance. If it is evident that there is no need for the follow-up units that are on the way, advise communications to call them off. If you are immediately made aware of needed assistance, such as an ambulance or rescue equipment, broadcast that information as well.

Keep communications informed as to what is going on at the scene. The 10- to 15-minute delay that sometimes occurs between the original "there now" call and the next transmission from any of the units at the scene of the "crime in progress" call may seem an eternity to the concerned patrol commanders and the dispatcher personnel, not to mention the many other units on the same radio frequency who are following the events with considerable anxiety.

If the circumstances at the scene permit, attempt as soon as possible to establish a telephone connection with the communications center. Perhaps the dispatcher or desk officer who received the original phone call was successful in getting across to the calling party that the line should be kept open so that the caller would continue to feed information concerning the ongoing crime—if possible—and to hand the telephone instrument to the first officer to arrive on the scene.

Once you are on the scene and establish telephone or radio contact with the headquarters personnel, report on the current status and progress on the case. Continue passing on your instructions for follow-up units, and request whatever assistance you need from other police units and other emergency services. While you are questioning the victim and/or witnesses about the crime, relay by telephone such pertinent information as descriptions of suspects, the suspect vehicle, direction of travel, and any other information that will aid in the location and capture of the suspect if he has left the scene by the time you arrived at that location. While this is all going on, the dispatcher personnel will continue broadcasting the necessary information.

If you are the first follow-up unit, proceed directly to the scene. Determine whether your presence is required at that location. You will assist in the initial response to ascertain if the crime is still in progress and to take whatever immediate action is warranted. You will then assist in locating and interviewing the victims and witnesses, searching for the suspect and taking him into custody, and generally work as the partner to the officer originally assigned the call. Remain at the crime scene until you are no longer needed, and then take part in the area search for the suspect.

TACTICS BY TYPES OF CRIMES

Crimes against Person

First determine the nature of the crime and whether it is still in progress. A robbery involves the taking of another person's property from that person or from his presence by means of force or fear. If the crime is still in progress upon your arrival, make an immediate assessment and determine your course of action. Take a position out of the line of fire and as much as possible out of the suspect's line of sight as well. Use the police unit or part of the building as a shield against any impending attack by the suspect. Determine if there is any immediate danger to the victim, such as an ongoing attack, or obvious immediate need for medical aid.

If the circumstances require your immediate confrontation with the suspect, approach him with extreme caution. It is at this point that many officers lose their lives either through carelessness or indecisiveness. Consider the possibility that your immediate approach may startle the suspect and lead him to take a hostage or to abuse his victim physically more than he may have already done. Under these circumstances, he may also attempt to kill or injure you as well as his other victim. If you must enter, do so quickly, moving to your left to make yourself a less conspicuous target and to compensate for any flinching the suspect may do if he fires a weapon at you. You are guessing, of course, that the suspect is right-handed. If the weapon is in the suspect's left hand, the flinching or jerking motion will probably be to the suspect's right, your left. In that case, your defensive movement should be to your right. Attempt to keep the suspect in sight and make every effort to gain physical control as soon as possible.

If you ascertain upon your arrival that there is no immediate additional danger to the victim, and if the suspect is not yet aware of your presence, remain outside at a vantage point and wait for help to arrive. There is no need to be foolhardy, and actions that are too hasty may cause serious injury or death to both yourself as well as the victim. If possible, wait for the subject to come outside so that the advantage will be yours.

There are several excellent reasons for waiting for the suspect to come outside. If the suspect is not aware of your presence, he may see no need to take a hostage. There may be less provocation to cause the suspect to inflict further injuries on his victim if the suspect's efforts to escape from the crime scene do not seem to him to be frustrated. While you are waiting for the suspect to come outside, your follow-up units may have additional time to arrive. They, too, should arrive as quietly as possible so as not to cause panic. When the suspect does come out, you have the advantage of cover provided by your vehicle, trees and shrubbery, walls of the building, and various other hiding places.

If the suspect has taken a hostage, be extremely careful to do everything possible to preserve the life of the hostage, but not at your own personal peril. While the robber is holding a hostage, if he were to demand that you give up your weapon, then he would have two hostages and you would have accomplished absolutely nothing to enhance the safety of the hostage or yourself. You will have increased the odds in favor of the robber. You are going to have a difficult decision to make under extremely stressful conditions, but your courage is not making a deal with a robber holding a hostage, and in not foolishly giving up your weapon so that you both may be killed, will probably save the hostage's life as well as your own. Survival is foremost on everyone's mind, and that includes the suspect, who must weigh the chances of living through the event.

Hostage negotiation takes a special talent and skill, and such a negotiator should be called into action if available. The negotiator is usually a father or brother or sister figure who can establish rapport with the hostage taker and form some sort of bond with the person to the extent that he or she will listen to reasonable arguments and yield to the logical approach that killing a hostage or prolonging the siege will be disadvantageous, or futile. The objective is to save the life of the hostage and to prevent bloodshed. Containment of the scene and talking and waiting out the situation may lead to an end to the problem. The hostage may escape or be released, and the desired result is that the hostage taker gives up without a firefight.

If you know that the suspect is gone when you arrive, immediately determine as best you can the condition of the victim. If there is no apparent urgency for rendering first aid, stop for just a moment and plan your action, trying under the circumstances not to destroy certain items of evidence that might be instrumental in securing a prosecution. Think of where the suspect might have walked and his possible point and method of entry, and then do what you can under the circumstances to preserve the evidence.

Proceed with as much deliberation and calmness as possible. The people you contact during the investigation of a robbery are inclined to be under severe emotional stress. Your leadership and display of courage and self-control encourage the victim and the various witnesses to remain calm. Consequently, they are likely to be far more effective in aiding the investigation.

Crimes against Property

A burglar alarm is activated, an open door is found, or someone may actually be observed inside a building. Any one of these situations may prove to be a burglary in progress. Or they may not turn out to be any more than a faulty alarm system, a door left open by a careless employee, or the owner of the store taking an all-night inventory. Each must be handled by the patrol officer as if it were a possible burglary in progress.

The statutes defining burglary vary somewhat among the various states. In some jurisdictions, burglary may be the term used to define the crime of breaking into a building for the purpose of committing theft. In other states, including California, the crime of burglary involves any entry (whether a breaking into the building occurs or not) with the specific intent at the time of the entry to commit the act of theft or some other felony.

Burglars are felons. They must be apprehended and prosecuted. Every means possible should be utilized to take the burglar into custody with the least amount of force or destruction. When it is apparent, or when all appearances lead you to believe that a burglary is in progress, you should anticipate that at least one burglar is inside and immediately plan your strategy to block escape and prevent your capture.

Arrange for adequate assistance before entering a building that may be occupied by a burglar. Unless there is someone inside who may be in danger of attack from the culprit, you are at a tactical advantage by remaining on the outside with the suspect inside. Time is on your side. If a silent alarm system is utilized by the establishment, there is a possibility that the suspect inside is not yet aware of your presence. If possible, do not enter until your backup officers are in position and you have the entire building covered.

Do not overlook the possibility of calling for assistance from an adjoining jurisdiction to cover the building and to attempt capturing the suspect should he attempt to exit from the building. It is better to have too much help, if available, than too little.

While you are waiting for backup officers, place yourself in a position of advantage from which you may observe as much of the building as possible near the area where the suspect is most likely to exit. Look up at the roof, which is a popular hiding place for some burglars who believe that police officers do not look up. When the assisting officers arrive, place the first two officers at opposite corners of the building. In the event that the building is oddly shaped and difficult to cover from the opposite corners, consider placing the officers at opposite corners of the block. From these positions, they may not be in a position to apprehend the suspect, but they will see anyone who enters or leaves the area under their surveillance, which is important in this type of operation. Place additional officers at the places through which the suspect may exit. Be careful to prevent danger from cross fire in the event that shooting occurs.

Check for anyone in the vicinity who is on foot or in a vehicle. It is not likely that a lookout will linger for long after your arrival, but some people serving in that capacity have remained throughout the entire series of events. They were successful in not being detected because of the plausibility of their "cover" role and explanations for being where they were located. Lookouts may pose as a deliveryperson, construction worker, utility meter inspector, stranded motorist working on his automobile, a pair of "lovers" sitting in an automobile, or someone walking a dog in the neighborhood. Do not overlook the most obvious, the person who appears as if he is trying to get out of the area without your detection of his presence.

Another technique of some burglars is to approach the investigating officer, ask what is happening, and then blend in with the other onlookers.

If there are no readily visible signs of entry at any of the doors or windows, consider the roof. Many roofs are accessible by climbing on boxes, adjacent utility poles, drain pipes, fences, or other nearby roofs. Some merchants lock their ground floors and windows securely, but leave upstairs windows or skylights unlocked because of their apparent inaccessibility. There are many other methods of entry, such as a tunnel from another side of a fence and up through the floor or a hole broken through the wall from an adjoining suite in the same building.

Approach the place where you intend to enter very carefully and deliberately. It is preferable to have the burglar come out rather than to go in after him. Keeping this in mind, pause and give him the opportunity to come out at your invitation. If the suspect comes out with the merchandise he has stolen, it is easier to prove his intention to steal those items he is carrying, which is one advantage of waiting for the suspect to come out. The most important advantage in waiting is that there is less likelihood that someone will be injured in the ensuing action when you begin to make your entry into the building.

Determine in advance exactly who is going to enter the building. Never have officers at opposite sides of the building enter at the same time. They may meet inside in the darkness and each believe that the other is the suspect. The officers who enter should do so as a single team, and they should work close together while constantly keeping an eye on each other. Either work back to back or side to side, or alternately take the lead with one officer behind the other in a leapfrog pattern. The purpose of this method of coverage is to assure the officers that they know exactly who and where each other is in the darkened and deserted interior of the building. Without such a system it is possible that one officer could walk into the pointed barrel of another officer's revolver.

If the point of entry is a door, look at the ground or floor at the entrance for footprints or any other evidence the culprit may have left while entering. Consider the possibility that he may have left fingerprints on the door or doorknobs. It may be necessary to give first priority to apprehending the culprit, while obliterating some of the evidence you might have otherwise been able to collect. Preservation of life and property includes your own as well as that of the other people you serve and protect.

When you use a flashlight, hold it away from your body, preferably with your weak hand. Most inexperienced shooters have a tendency to flinch to their left while shooting directly at the light source. When entering the building try to avoid making a silhouette of yourself by standing in the center of the doorway and, at the moment you enter, consider turning off your flashlight. When you open the door, stand to one side out of the line of fire if the suspect should choose to attack you. Open the door by slamming it against the stop to make sure no one is hiding behind the door. Step in quickly and immediately to the side out of the doorway. Wait until your partner follows suit. Then stand and listen for a few moments to get accustomed to the new lighting conditions and the sounds inside the building. There are some noises characteristic to the building that can be quite disquieting if you are not accustomed to them. Refrigerators, freezers, electronics equipment, animals left inside for security, clocks, heaters, and air conditioning devices all sound differently in a strange building.

Consider the use of building lighting. If you go from a lighted room into a dark room, each time you move to a new location, you will be blind for the several seconds it takes your eyes to readjust to the new lighting condition. For that reason, I suggest that once you prepare to leave a lighted area and move into a room or other area that is dark, turn on all the lights that you can before entering. As you continue moving about the premises, leave all the lights on. If anyone is hiding in the darkness, that person will be blind while his or her eyes are adjusting to the light. This will give you a few seconds with the advantage of seeing the suspect first. The time varies, depending on degree of darkness, but in total darkness, the time it takes for the eyes to adjust from darkness to light is from approximately 5 to 50 seconds. (This is not the same as checking for pupillary reaction to light of a person suspected of being under the influence of an opiate.)

If you use flashlights or other means of illumination in locations where there is no other source of lighting, make liberal use of whatever light that you have. Always maintain the advantage. Each time you enter another room, slam the door to the stopper or the wall to make sure there is no one standing behind the door.

Make a thorough and methodical check of the entire building to determine whether a crime has been committed and whether the suspect may still be inside. When people are hiding, they discover that they can literally shrink into spaces they never realized they would fit into. Look up! Burglars sometimes hide on closet shelves or in attics above closets where they may go undetected. Attics, large drawers, incinerators, storage cabinets, behind doors, under desks, and practically any place in the building is a potential hiding place. Once you have searched a particular room, or portion of the building, "clear" that searched area by closing the door and placing articles of furniture in strategic locations so that they would have to be moved for someone to pass through that area. If sufficient officers are available and if the area to be checked is large, an officer placed at a strategic location can guard closed and cleared areas.

As you proceed in the building search, make spot rechecks to compensate for the possibility that you may have a clever burglar who escaped detection or who sneaked past the searching officers. One morning, a team of officers who were checking out a building apparently overlooked one obvious place. After the officers had left the building, the burglar broke out and activated the alarm again. They were eventually able to catch the burglar in a nearby orange grove. When he was questioned about his ability to avoid detection, he stated that he had hidden under a desk in the office in the light manufacturing building. One officer had searched that room, discovered the phone, called the police station and conversed with the telephone operator for a few minutes, then had left the office and resumed the search with his fellow officers. The suspect stated that he had had a great temptation to untie the officer's shoelaces but decided not to.

If you find the suspect inside the building, search him or her immediately and use appropriate restraining devices. Never assume that he is working alone. Look for an accomplice either inside the building or nearby outside. This is one type of police activity for which the use of trained dogs is exceptionally valuable.

If it is determined that a crime was committed, proceed with the initial crime scene search and the preliminary investigation. If it turns out that the building had not been burglarized, but just left open, secure the building. In any event, contact the owner and advise him of your presence while requesting that he make an appearance. You may do this by phoning him direct from the office in his building if you can ascertain who he is, or you may have your communications personnel contact him. One method for determining the name of the owner is to check through records for a recent crime, such as a check case in which that business was listed as the victim. The report should reflect the names, addresses, and phone numbers of key company personnel. Business license files will reveal the same information. Perhaps your department has access to the computer containing that data. If it does, take advantage of it when necessary.

Questioning the Suspect

If you are going to question the suspect at that time and expect to use his statements in court at his trial, be sure to admonish him of his right against self-incrimination and of his right to counsel and to have counsel with him when he is questioned. However, consider the fact that the burglar may be making statements during the actual commission of the crime prior to your admonishment that will be admissible under most circumstances because they are part of the *res gestae*. The *res gestae* encompasses the crime and the surrounding circumstances that all constitute the crime. Spontaneous declarations made by the suspect may also be totally admissible without the *Miranda* warning requirement.

What to Do with the Weapon

What should you do with your gun while inspecting the interior of a building searching for the suspect? As yourself, "Where would be the best place to carry the gun so that it would serve its purpose most efficiently?" In the holster. By keeping your gun in its holster, you have it in a very accessible location, and your gun hand is free to handle doorknobs, to push aside obstacles that are in the way, to push the doors back to their stops, and to perform a variety of tasks while the other hand is holding the flashlight. If you practice regularly, you have no doubt found that it takes virtually no more time to draw your weapon from your holster and fire it than it does to fire a gun that is already in your hand. The time factor involves your reaction to the incident calling for your response. Your degree of alertness will determine how quickly you will react.

There is some disagreement with this philosophy among fellow officers. Some officers will tell you that they would never enter a building without a drawn gun. Of course, you will never see a television show or movie when an officer enters a building without his weapon in a two-handed grip looking as though he were searching an enemy village during wartime.

If you hold a gun in your hand, there is also a tendency to cock it unconsciously. On one occasion an officer did just that: he cocked his revolver while checking out a burglary scene, then replaced the revolver in his holster. He had not been aware that he had cocked the revolver and did not check it when he replaced it. Several hours later, that same officer was working a traffic control problem when he placed his hand on his gun in a resting position. He pushed the hammer when he placed his hand on the gun and shot himself in the foot.

A shotgun is impractical to use for checking out a building, except when there is a known felon inside, in which case one officer takes care of the door-opening and searching procedure, while the officer with the heavy armament stands back and "covers" the searching officer.

Prowlers

If you are familiar with the neighborhood where a prowler is reported, you have a tremendous advantage when responding to the prowler call. With such knowledge, it is possible to stop one or two houses short of the exact location of the prowler and approach silently on foot without warning the suspect of your arrival. It is also to your advantage to know how the numbers on parallel streets appear, so that you or the follow-up officer may park and wait on the next block in case the suspect chooses to hurdle fences, or to run down alleys. There is usually a plan for street numbering, and you should know what it is so that you will know an address without even looking.

Approach the prowler's location quietly, driving the police car in the same manner as any local resident would drive home when returning from an evening out. Although your approach should not be too secretive, which in itself would arouse the suspect's suspicions, it should not be as though the occupation army had arrived. It may be to your advantage to stop some distance down the street, turn off the lights, then drive along the curb with the lights out for the last few hundred feet of your approach. Use the emergency brake to avoid activating the brake lights, which would broadcast your arrival. Locate the calling party's address by shining a light on the curb or some other place across the street from the calling party's address. Of course, if you know your district as you should, you will already know that the house is third from the north end of the block on the west side of the street.

While approaching the scene, observe all the people who are in the area, whether or not they are making furtive movements, or signaling by suspicious conduct that they are involved in some sort of criminal activity. Someone who is running or sneaking around a place where a prowler had been spotted will automatically be suspect, but do not overlook the possibility that the "cool" individual walking normally along the street may be the real culprit. At the initial stage of the investigation of a "prowler there now" call, question everyone you encounter for possible leads as to the identity and location of the suspect.

Once you have arrived silently without your presence being detected and have made the initial attempt to locate the prowler, it will be apparent to him that you are there. Use plenty of light and conduct a very thorough and systematic search for the prowler. Look for wires, chuckholes, booby traps, duck ponds, and other hazards, particularly when going through backyards. Avoid disturbing the residents in the area. Keep your radio on low volume, close the doors quietly, and keep the noise level of your activity down. While searching, do not assume that any place is too small to hide. Stealth is the key to a prowler's success. It will take persistence on your part to outthink the prowler and catch him or her in the act.

Once you have searched a particular area, post someone at that location to assure yourself that the suspect will not move to a place already searched to avoid apprehension. When using the flashlight, use it in the same manner as when you are checking out a building: out and away from your body. When you shine the light on a suspect, keep the light trained on his face to keep him at a disadvantage if he has intentions to attack you. Watch his hands for any movement that may signal anticipated actions by the suspect, such as an attempt to escape.

When you are searching for a prowler, you are looking for a misdemeanant. Use of a firearm is not justified unless the suspect would attempt to commit some felony or unless it were necessary under the "reasonable force" decision that you would make when meeting with his resistance to arrest. Keep your revolver in its holster and keep the shotgun in the car. Although there are exceptions, most prowlers are not dangerous.

When working in a team with other officers, be sure to use a rehearsed technique so that all officers will understand what their parts in the search for the prowler will be and will have an idea as to the location and activities of the other officers. Discuss and rehearse your tactics and the various signals that you will use. Move in the shadows when you and your partner are aware of each other's whereabouts. Otherwise, stay out in the open to avoid meeting another officer in the dark who does not know or recognize you, even though you both may be wearing the same uniform. I learned my lesson by rounding the corner of a house while checking out a prowler and I found myself looking down the barrel of a cocked hair-trigger Smith and Wesson 6-inch revolver in the hands of a follow-up officer who did not anticipate my presence.

Interview the occupants of the homes on whose property the prowler was observed and ascertain whether the prowler might be a person who has any permission or lawful business on the property. Look for any evidence that the suspect may have left at the scene, such as footprints or semen on the ground beneath a window into which he may have been looking, articles that may have fallen from his pocket when reaching for an object in his pocket, or any other evidence that may have been left there. Look into nearby vehicles in an effort to determine the presence of anyone important to the case who may be hiding. Stand or park for a few minutes at various places while conducting the search to listen for any sounds and watch for any movements that are foreign to the surroundings and may indicate the presence of the prowler. Sometimes the culprit may gain confidence and believe that he may leave his place of hiding without detection and apprehension, and it is then that you may effect the arrest.

The calling party may have decided to have a friend or husband search the neighborhood for the prowler, and the searcher may have armed himself with a shotgun or a souvenir rifle. If at all possible, the telephone operator or dispatcher who receives the original call for police service should ascertain whether anyone is already involved in a search and if anyone is armed. If someone is armed, advise the calling party to invite the armed searcher back inside the house. When the officers search the premises and the general neighborhood, they will be less likely to encounter an armed individual, who may appear to be an armed suspect rather than a searcher. These "do-it-yourselfers" are sometimes far more dangerous than the prowlers or burglars you are looking for. Under stress conditions, it is sometimes impossible to tell the prowlers from the searchers, and someone could be seriously injured when people carry deadly weapons.

Some prowler calls involve nothing more than outside noises that may frighten the lone occupant of a house or apartment. Look for animals or shrubbery scratching the screens or rubbing against the buildings. Once you find the source of the sound, point it out to the calling party and recommend steps to eliminate the sound, for example, trimming or removing a bush or tree with long branches. Some "jungles" look pretty but are excellent hiding places for prowlers and burglars.

The prowler may be a burglar looking for a place to enter for the purpose of stealing. He may be a jealous husband or boy friend who is intent upon doing some spying on his wife or girl friend, or he may be a sex psychopath seeking out another unsuspecting victim so that he may satisfy his prurient desires. In most cases the prowler will be a curious adolescent or young adult with voyeuristic tendencies, seeking to expand his or her sexual awareness by peeking in on the private lives of others.

The average prowler is not dangerous, but he is a potential hazard.

There is no way to determine in advance whether he is one of those "harmless" persons who wants only to look into other people's bedrooms or a burglar who intends to commit his crime in spite of any obstacles he may encounter.

Usually when a person inside a house being "visited" by a prowler discovers the presence of that prowler his or her actions alert the prowler that he or she has been discovered. By the time the calling party goes to the telephone and notifies the police that the prowler is in the area, chances of apprehending him are slight. If a young lady were to become aware of the admiring eyes of a prowler looking in from some point of vantage, there would be a greater probability that he would be arrested if the object of his attentions would continue with whatever she was doing, then casually go to the telephone and notify the police department, and resume the same activity until the arrival of the officers.

The prowler might continue to watch the young lady practicing her exercises or combing her hair while the police officers proceed to the scene and attempt to catch the suspect in the act of peeking into the window. If they are successful in making their arrival quickly and silently, they may succeed as well in effecting the arrest. Asking a woman caller to cooperate this way to apprehend a prowler is "beyond the call of duty," but if she insists on helping, this is one method by which we have met with some success in apprehending prowlers.

Whenever there is a chronic situation with a voyeur who continually visits the same places to watch what is going on inside, there should be some preparation for surveillance of those places. Planning to apprehend the prowler should be no less elaborate than planning for any other major crime. Some people use transparent curtains or draperies or window coverings that are so sheer that everything in a room is visible from the outside when the room is illuminated. Some people are so proud of their furniture and interior decor that they leave their windows undraped so that people can look in; others leave the view clear so that they can see the ocean or the mountains. All these households are potential prowler victims. From your own observation while patrolling your district, you will see these people as needing a little extra patrol attention.

Gang Activity

The open hostilities exhibited by youth street gangs—such as fights between opposing gangs in a neutral area or on the "turf" of one of the opposing gangs or the more frightening activity of "cruising," which consists of a carload of gang members cruising another gang's territory and firing several rounds of shotgun or rifle bullets indiscriminately into a randomly selected home—is at epidemic proportions in some cities.

No longer are we plagued by the small bands of street urchins who fight with each other over territory as the only gangs we have to worry about. While we still have those types of gangs, we now have organized and well-trained—and well-armed—terrorists who kill rival gang members for franchise rights to deal in cocaine or "crack" (a type of cocaine), marijuana, and other drugs in a multibillion-dollar operation throughout the world. These organizations make the Mafia look like campfire girls by comparison, and their methods include killing pedestrians and strangers at random, and firing automatic weapons into homes of innocent people totally uninvolved in their drug business or turf rivalry. This is a civil war with gangs that have greater financial resources than the police to carry on their warfare, and far more sophisticated weaponry.

Walter Miller reported that "in most cities, youth gangs today typically consist of small loosely organized groups of about a dozen teenage males..."[1] Not only do they protect their turf, or area in which they live and claim as their place to operate, but many of these gangs have terrorized entire neighborhoods, they have formed marauding teams of robbers, they operate "protection" rackets, and they have taken over entire schools and recreational facilities.

"Taggers" may or may not be affiliated with other gangs and gang activity. A recent phenomenon has been the emergence of graffiti "tagging" by individuals and groups of young men and boys who compete for space on freeway signs and overpasses, traffic signs, fences, and buildings throughout entire areas. Some of these "taggers" claim that it is an addiction with them to express themselves this way. When apprehended, they and their parents are fined and the offenders are required to do "community service" by painting over and chemically removing their own graffiti. Many of these gangs have violent confrontations and should not be considered as innocent kids "just expressing themselves."

Gangs are not new. Originally the Sicilian underground who preyed upon the hated French soldiers who occupied Sicily for so many years and retaliated in kind whenever any of their people were victimized by the French, the Mafia began preying on their own countrymen in Sicily and elsewhere in the world, branching out into all categories of organized crime. With the fall of Communist rule in the former Soviet Union, those countries are experiencing their own gangster activities.

In Rio de Janeiro and São Paulo, the favelas (shanty towns) spawn thousands of homeless children known as *meninos da rua*, who have formed gangs such as Comando Vermelho (Red Commandos) that rule the favelas in the hills of the cities and make their living by extortion and kidnapping. In southern California a group of high school self-styled "lovers" formed a gang they called a "posse." and their objective was to score points in competition to have sexual encounters with as many different girls as they could. There are many different ethnic street gangs that started out in the larger cities and have spread out throughout the country, for a variety of objectives, but they are all gangs.

The gangs that give the police the most trouble are not the small

---

[1]Walter Miller, "The Rumble This Time," *Psychology Today*, May 1977, p. 52.

groups of neighborhood youths who put their graffiti on walls and fences and fight rival gangs; rather, they are the gangs that have objectives such as drug dealerships, robberies, muggings, shakedowns of merchants, and burglaries. The weapons they use are no longer "Saturday night specials," but are high-priced semiautomatic machine guns and pistols made by the world's best manufacturers.

Your responsibility as a field officer is to observe the people you contact on the street very closely. Look for signs of gang membership by hand signs or other signals they interchange, logos and insignia on their clothing and their vehicles, tattoos, and the graffiti they spray paint onto every blank space they can find. Try to determine their associates and their hangouts, their vehicles, their places of residence, their girl friends and relatives, and their organizational structure. Freely exchange this information with the specialists in your department who may be working a gang detail and also the investigators who are working the street crimes. In the field, be particularly wary whenever you see two or more gang members together who seem to have a purpose for being where they are or going wherever they are going.

GENERAL COORDINATION AND SEARCH

At the initial stage of an "in-progress" call, there is a tendency on the part of many officers to follow other police units in a "caravan" and to proceed directly to the scene, probably because of the intense desire to apprehend the culprit and to be on hand to "cover" a fellow officer. Both procedures must be avoided. The radio dispatcher should be responsible for assigning the units to proceed directly to the scene and coordinating all the other units by directing them to locations other than the immediate vicinity of the crime scene to take part in the search, if a search is necessary.

The assigned officer is in charge of the response, the investigation, and the search and continues to be in charge until the arrival of a supervisor, who will assume supervisory control. The supervisor will probably establish a command post at or near the crime scene and will coordinate the field activities from that location. At the time the field command post is established, the dispatcher at the communications center will discontinue the coordination activities and will provide subsidiary service to the field command post. If you are not assigned the call, remain in your district unless assigned elsewhere, but move in the direction of the crime scene or to a point of vantage so that you can observe and be in a position to take up pursuit in the event that the suspect flees past the point where you are positioned. If you are on the outer fringe of the perimeter of the search, cover the logical avenues of escape from the scene, but also consider the illogical ones as well.

Be sure that if you are maintaining surveillance over a particular street or freeway that you have access to that route yourself, or that you are spotting for another unit that does have such access. Ask yourself, "If I were attempting to flee, where would I go and what would I do?" Consider the possibility that the suspect may run or drive very quickly away from the crime scene for a short distance, discard his distinctive clothing or other items he may have worn to confuse the witnesses, and abandon the vehicle. It is not uncommon for professional robbery suspects to have two or three alternate vehicles parked within a few blocks of the location of their crime, and switch to whichever of those vehicles they are able to escape to during the first few minutes before the arrival of the first police units. Once they switch vehicles and discard the incriminating clothing, they find little need to hurry from the scene. They may also have a confederate pose as the fleeing bandit to draw the attention of the police while the culprit with the loot gets away. When you stop the confederate, he will check out okay because descriptions of the suspect and the one you have stopped will not match.

Some robbers have been brazen enough to drive past the scene of the crime, then park and walk up to mingle with the small crowd of onlookers, and inquire of the officers the nature of the trouble and whether they have had any success in locating the robber. For that reason, you should not overlook the possibility that the robber may still be in the immediate vicinity and that he may not be running or speeding away from the scene.

METHODS OF COVER AND SEARCH

There are several methods of searching for suspects who may be at the crime scene or its proximity or who may have fled the scene and be some considerable distance away. The methods that we will discuss here are the foot, spot, leapfrog, and quadrant methods.

Foot Search

Park your unit some distance—possibly a block or two—from the crime scene or the place where you intend to search. Walk in, using natural cover provided by buildings, trees and shrubbery, or any other objects that will conceal your approach and protect you against missiles that might be aimed in your direction. Stop frequently to look and listen quietly for anyone who may arouse your suspicions. Once you have established the fact that the suspect is not immediately observable, begin contacting anyone whom you see, and secure from them as much information as you can as to what or whom they may have seen. Perhaps a lookout was loitering on the street corner for some time prior to the crime. One of the residents or workers in the neighborhood may be able to point out a car that is strange to the neighborhood and this may be one that the robber "planted" as a possible alternate escape vehicle. Perhaps a witness has seen the transfer from one car to another.

The foot search is very effective when searching for witnesses as well as evidence in the vicinity of the crime, and sometimes it pays off in the search for the suspect. The robber is usually busy looking for police vehicles and may be caught off guard if you carefully and methodically cover the area on foot.

Spot Cover

This is usually a fixed post, generally at an intersection or some other vantage point overlooking one or more possible avenues of escape. When you are assigned to this type of detail, place your unit in a location that allows constant communications with the dispatcher and with other units and access to the means by which you will pursue the suspect.

Leapfrog

The term "leapfrog" describes the method of search, just as other terms do: "zigzag," "cloverleaf," or "criss-cross." In the leapfrog method, you and your partner alternately take the lead in the search and cover each other as you progressively move on. You may find many variations of this type of search very effective.

Quadrant

Using the scene of the crime as the center of the quadrant grid, divide the area to be searched into four equal "pie-shaped" quarters generating from the center. Assign at least one unit to each quadrant. Each unit begins the search of its assigned quadrant at the outer perimeter, then moves in toward the center—the crime scene—in a zigzag pattern. The units should overlap each other's quadrant areas and work back outward to the perimeters of their assigned areas again. They continue this until the culprit is located or the search is abandoned.

PLAINCLOTHES ASSISTANCE

Whenever "plainclothes" officers assist in a police incident such as a crime in progress, a pursuit, or a similar incident involving high levels of emotional involvement, they must work in a capacity in which they may be immediately identified as police officers. They should affix their badges to the outside of their chests to aid in the identification. Some agencies now provide their officers with "jump suits" that they may put on over their street clothing, and which have the word *police* and the name of the agency inscribed in large letters across the back.

If someone is required to operate as a communicator or coordinator at a command post, a nonuniformed officer should be assigned to the task. Plainclothes officers may also be assigned to work in a team with uniformed officers or to assign them as drivers of police vehicles. An exceptionally good way to utilize plainclothes officers is to put them on the streets as decoys. When there have been unusual numbers of street crimes, such as rapes and muggings, placement of officers, in disguise, it is hoped, will draw the suspects away from helpless, unsuspecting vulnerable victims. When the mugger or rapist selects one of the decoys as a victim, the officers move in and make the arrest. There is no entrapment because the criminal intent is wholly in the minds of the criminal.

One example of how a plainclothes officer may be mistaken for a suspect occurred some time ago, but it could occur again unless the proper precautions are taken for its prevention. One afternoon an armed robbery occurred, and the chase began. As the chase progressed, several police units took part and it soon developed into a caravan. As the suspect vehicle approached each city in succession, a police unit or two from that city would move into place in the caravan and assume the lead in the chase. In this case, as the robbers entered the fourth or fifth city, a plainclothes officer in his unmarked unit fell in behind the suspect vehicle. The other police vehicles had fallen some distance behind. The detective unit was successful in making the stop, and the lone officer in that unit approached the suspect with his revolver in his hand. He opened the suspect vehicle door on the driver's side and, with his left hand, grabbed hold of the suspect's arm. The officer was turned in such a way, with his gun in his right hand, and with the left hand holding the suspect, that when the first "uniformed" car from another city arrived, it appeared to him as if the suspect were armed and getting out of the car. However, the officer in that first "uniformed" unit to arrive had seen the plainclothes officer pull into the caravan and recognized the armed man as an officer.

A second, third, and fourth car from various agencies rolled up to the scene, and several of the officers in those care were not aware of the armed man's role in the action. To one of them, it must have appeared as if he were one of the suspects. As the plainclothes officer made a sudden move, a shot rang out. The bullet missed the officer, but it struck a wind wing on the car and shattered the glass. It was fortunate that the shot was not fatal. Unfortunately, however, the officer sustained a permanent eye injury from the flying glass particles and retired early from police service.

SUMMARY

In this chapter we covered the "in-progress" crime, including the crime against person and the crime against property. Critical to success in response to crimes that are in progress or believed to be while the officer is en route is effective and accurate communications. Responding officers should be kept totally aware of exactly what is happening with other responding officers and should be constantly updated on what is going on at the crime scene. If the officer who receives the call is able to keep the line open with the victim or witness, then the first officer on the scene gets to the telephone as soon as it is practicable and continues communicating. Once en route to the scene, be sure to be alert to people who are approaching or staying at the crime scene as well as those who might be hurrying away, because the suspect may not flee the scene as you might expect. If we were to wrap up this chapter with one phrase that would best describe possible success in apprehension of suspects at the scene of a crime, it would be "team work." You will be more aware of the value of good cooperative working relationships between officers when it is most important.

EXERCISES AND STUDY QUESTIONS

1. When a person calls in to report a crime in progress, what do you say to the person to keep him or her on the telephone?
2. What is the purpose for keeping the telephone line open?
3. What is the value of making a silent approach to the scene of a crime in progress?
4. Is there a standardized street numbering system in your town? What is it?
5. What should you be looking for while en route to the scene of a crime reported to be in progress?
6. Is it better to go into a building after a burglar or to wait for the burglar to come out?
7. What would you do if a robber who had taken a hostage asks you to trade yourself for the hostage or to surrender your weapons?
8. Explain how you and your partner officer would cover a building containing what you believe to be at least one burglar until your backup unit arrives.
9. Describe how you would assign two officers to search the interior of a building that showed signs of having been recently broken into.
10. In your opinion, where is the best place to carry your gun while checking out the interior of a building at nighttime and you expect to find a burglar?
11. How would you respond to a prowler call?
12. What is the extent, if any, of gang activity in the jurisdiction where you live?
13. List the names of the gangs in your own jurisdiction and describe their purposes (tagging, drugs, play), if known.
14. Is the ethnic composition of the gangs in your community mixed or single heritage?
15. Where would you set up a command post in proximity to a bank that had just been robbed?

16. Describe the quadrant method of search.

17. Describe at least five situations in which you would employ plain-clothes officers as decoys.

REFERENCES

The material for this chapter was devised for academy lectures in patrol procedures. Sources were numerous training bulletins and unpublished information memos from more than 20 different police departments, including Los Angeles, Santa Ana, Glendale, Riverside, and Oakland, California.

9 PRELIMINARY INVESTIGATIONS

INTRODUCTION

As a patrol officer, you perform many types of investigations, ranging from "investigate the woman screaming" to complicated multiple homicides and series of daylight residence burglaries. In some departments, particularly the larger metropolitan agencies, it has been customary for the field officer assigned to the district where the crime occurs to respond to every call and then to call in specialists for all but the "routine" nontraffic and noncriminal activities. Limits were set on the officer's responsibilities primarily because of the tremendous amount of time required just to keep up with responding to the calls. Once at the scene, the patrol officer would determine the nature of the problem, stand by to protect the scene, administer aid and comfort to the victims, arrest the culprit, and wait until the specialists arrived. In the large department, this procedure continues to exist, but it is not practicable in the small or medium-sized department. Even in the large departments, the problem of overspecialization will have a tendency to render a department ineffective unless the specialization is kept to a minimum.

Whenever a crime occurs, or its earlier commission is discovered and reported to the police department, the first officer to arrive on the scene is usually the patrol officer in whose district the incident has occurred. Because of your proximity to the scene, your high mobility, and the fact that you are first on the scene, it is most logical that you should be charged with the responsibility for the initial phases of the crime investigation (see Figure 9–1). This chapter covers some of the guidelines for

Figure 9-1   The preliminary investigation frequently involves a careful search for latent prints. (Courtesy of the Police Department, Aberdeen, South Dakota.)

this *preliminary investigation* process, which is normally handled by the field patrol officer. Investigations beyond that point will appropriately be covered in a good investigation techniques text.

PRELUDE TO THE INVESTIGATION

Investigations usually begin with personal interviews of people who are either witnesses or victims of the criminal acts of others. Sometimes the suspect is still on the scene, as is common in assault cases, and it is difficult to distinguish the respective roles of the participants in the action in an emotion-packed situation. In one case, two officers responded to the scene of what appeared to be a fight between some braceros. When the officers arrived, they discovered that no one at the scene could speak English and the officers knew no Spanish.

The officers immediately assessed the situation and found that two of the combatants were seriously wounded, one with slash wounds on his hand and the other with a cut throat that was bleeding profusely. The officers had to act fast. There was no ambulance immediately available, but the hospital was only six blocks away. Knowing that the two victims needed immediate medical attention, the officers placed them in the back seat of their unit, one officer driving and the other holding compress bandages on the wounded men.

Thanks to the quick thinking of the officers, both victims received emergency surgery and were on the road to recovery. It was only then that the officers discovered—with the aid of a Spanish-speaking doctor—that they had actually transported the combatants together, each having cut the other in the fight. The man with the slashed throat had averted a second blow, causing the second man to cut himself with his own knife.

This is an example of what could happen when an officer does not have all the facts at the beginning of an investigation. In an area where other languages are spoken, a valuable asset is to have officers who can communicate fluently in those languages. If none of your officers are so prepared, consider having a file in the office of people who have knowledge of many different languages. Your local college or university is an excellent resource.

One of the first and most important items on the agenda of the investigation is to assess the situation quickly and attempt to determine exactly what happened. Many questions must be answered. Determine what crime, if any, occurred, and respond accordingly. While making that determination, identify the principals. Who is the victim? Who and where is the suspect? If there is an immediate and imminent threat to the life of anyone at the scene, take steps to apprehend the suspect and reduce or eliminate the threat.

The victim of any type of personal attack should be the first object of concern. Is there any danger of further attack? What is the victim's condition? Is there someone present who can call for medical aid? If first aid is necessary, look after that need, and instruct anyone who is present to assist you. Even at the risk of destroying valuable evidence, the life of the victim has top priority. If the victim is dying, seek a declaration from the victim that will aid in identification and prosecution of the killer.

Quick apprehension of the suspect is high on the list of priorities, particularly if the crime is a personal attack and there is a likelihood that the suspect will repeat the attack unless taken into custody. Exactly which order of action you will follow will be determined by the precise facts as they present themselves to you. Regardless of the nature of the situation, use as much care as possible to preserve the evidence that will serve to establish the elements of the crime and the guilt of the accused (see Figure 9–2). Sometimes the destruction of evidence is inevitable when you are administering first aid or performing rescue services, or when taking the suspect into custody. If that is the case, do not overlook the possibility that some of the evidence may be salvaged even though partially destroyed.

Try to make mental notes of the scene and various related factors during these initial stages, although you may have other important responsibilities for the moment. Try to remember if any articles of furniture were moved, doors opened or unlocked, lights turned on or off, or any footprints or traces of evidence visible. Some evidence is very short-lived and will disappear unless it is quickly collected or recorded.

As soon as possible, attempt to process the short-lived evidence. It will possibly consist of a footprint outside a building in the rain, which may be saved by covering it with a box or a piece of some type of weatherproof

Figure 9-2 Searching for the point of origin in a suspected arson fire is challenging. (Courtesy of the Pennsylvania State Police.)

material. Sometimes during the night or early morning hours when the grass is wet, the suspect may leave wet impressions on a dry linoleum floor. This wet impression should be sketched and photographed as early in the investigation as practicable, because it will be forever lost once it dries.

Once you have looked after the welfare of the victim, ascertained whether the suspect was present and accomplished the arrest if he was present, and taken the necessary steps to preserve and protect the short-lived evidence, the next step is to protect the entire scene against any further contamination. Define the perimeter and close it to the entry of anyone but those people who are actually essential to the investigation. Highly visible ribbon will probably work better than rope because the ribbon is easier to store and to attach to almost any surface. Several manufacturers produce the ribbon, and some have the words POLICE—DO NOT ENTER emblazoned across the surface of the tape every couple of feet. To put up the ribbon, tack or tape it to existing surfaces or use small sign sticks and staples. Call for whatever special assistance you may have available to you, which may include recruiting curious bystanders or the witness who discovered the crime; then proceed with the investigation.

In the very early stages of the investigation, you are going to be extremely busy looking after the health and safety of the victims and per-haps several witnesses that you will want to interview once the dust has settled. Put the uninjured victims and the witnesses to work, assigning each one to a different task of guarding a piece of evidence—especially short-lived evidence that will soon disappear—or keeping other people away from the scene. This will keep them separated from each other so that they cannot form composite, or "jury," descriptions of suspects or of the events. What you want is each person's account of what occurred and a personal description of the suspect(s). If you have nothing else for them to do, hand them a pen and a sheet of paper and ask them to write down everything they can remember of the event.

You may have problems keeping two categories of curious onlookers away from the crime scene: fellow officers and the press. Neither has a license to contaminate the scene. Put them to work. Sometimes a posed picture or two, such as dusting a doorknob for prints, will appease a reporter for a while until your investigation is completed.

DEDUCTIVE AND INDUCTIVE REASONING

Inductive and deductive reasoning must be exercised in the investigative process. Taking specific facts and information, one employs inductive reasoning to attempt to arrive at general conclusions about what happened, causing one to take what is known and then attempt to reach a theory on what is unknown. Deductive reasoning involves the taking of general information and boiling it down to specific hypotheses. You take two or more premises and draw a conclusion from them as to what actually happened at the crime scene.[1]

THE INVESTIGATION

After all the immediate demands of the situation have been met, interview the people who are most likely to give you a preliminary description of the suspect and any contraband that the suspect may have with him. Broadcast the information by radio or telephone for immediate general rebroadcast. If a telephone is available, use it for greater reception and less interference, *and* greater secrecy. Some professional criminals carry scanners so that they can hear what the police broadcasts are saying about them and the crime they just committed. Pause momentarily and briefly plan your course of action. Consider the type of case. Ask yourself what most likely happened. Where did the suspect go? What did the suspect do with the evidence? What was left by the suspect at the crime scene? What did the suspect take away from the crime scene? Generally attempt to reconstruct the crime scene. Make mental—or written—notes of your impressions and physical

---

[1]For a more detailed explanation of inductive and deductive reasoning, see Lynn Quitman Troyka's *Concise Handbook*, instructor's edition (Englewood Cliffs, N.J.: Prentice Hall, 1992), pp. 100–103.

observations. This pause may give you time to look at the case more objectively. Proceed according to some logical plan that you have formulated during this pause.

Interview Witnesses

Separate the victims and witnesses. Interview them one at a time to secure as many individual viewpoints as possible. Sometimes a group interview will produce a *jury* description, one that is a composite resulting from a series of compromises between witnesses and one that will probably be incorrect. Remember that eyewitnesses are not always reliable, but they may be all that you have. Ask questions that compel the witnesses to give you their own information rather than a feedback of what you believe happened and their agreement that you are right, or nearly so.

Note First Impressions

Right from the start, you should be making written notes of information and evidence as the case develops. In these notes, include information on items that may be of incidental importance as well as of direct evidential value. List items such as your observation that the lights were on although the crime supposedly occurred in the daytime, a cigarette or cigar is still smoldering in an ashtray, a glass window appears to have been broken from the inside when it should have been broken from the outside. Note odors that may be foreign to the place, such as pipe or cigar smoke in a woman's apartment or the pungent smell of a particular aftershave lotion that you can identify. List your observations about any contradictions of witnesses or victims and various items of evidence or information that you collect. For example, the victim's statement that a shelf was full of merchandise may be refuted by the obvious presence of undisturbed dust on the shelf, indicating that nothing had been on that shelf that could have been removed. The loss may be an exaggeration or an outright lie for insurance purposes.

Collection and Preservation of Evidence

An officer cannot collect too much evidence. In your initial investigation, consider the possibility that virtually everything you encounter is potential evidence. Touch only those items that you must touch and touch them very carefully. Systematically collect every item that is—or might be—evidence. Sometimes the most seemingly inconsequential items turn out to be the most significant pieces of evidence when the case goes to trial. Consider what some investigators call the *theory of transfer*. In nearly every criminal case, the culprit leaves sometimes of himself at the scene and takes something from the scene. There are exceptions, but never discount the possibility of this occurring.

According to the transfer theory, the suspect may leave behind his fingerprints, footprints, semen, blood, saliva, perspiration, hair, fibers, lipstick, stains, odors, sounds, or his physical description. He may take with him such items as dust or dirt; broken glass in his clothing; the victim's hair, blood, body fluids, tissue; stolen merchandise; contraband; or the victim himself.

During the entire investigation process, record accurate notes and field sketches, preserve and transport the evidence in accordance with recommended procedures, and take every precaution to substantiate your allegation that a crime was committed by proving the elements of the corpus delicti of each offense. Have sufficient evidence to establish the guilt of the suspect. If a camera is available, make it a general rule to always photograph prints, traces, or any other item of evidence before attempting to collect or otherwise process it.

Whenever taking clothing from the suspect that you intend to search for items of evidence, such as narcotics or broken glass embedded in the material, pack each item in a separate container. The laboratory expert may then testify as to which article of clothing yielded which item of evidence. Whenever taking items of evidence from the custody or presence of anyone, it is a good practice to prepare an itemized list of the articles taken and to leave a receipt with whoever is in charge of the premises.

Consider the following as a recommended policy regarding property and evidence:

> *All property, regardless of value, the character or condition of the person from whom it is taken, or the circumstances under which it is acquired by the evidence section of the department, must be labeled and appropriately recorded. In all cases a receipt must be made for property taken or received. Whenever possible, this receipt should be made in duplicate, the original processed along with the evidence or property and the copy given to the person from whom the property is received. No member of the department shall assume a personal interest in, or possession of, any property that comes to him in his official capacity as a police officer.*

TYPES OF EVIDENCE

When conducting the search for evidence, an appreciation of the various types of evidence and knowledge of the methods for collecting the evidence is necessary. This phase of the investigation may be conducted by the officer assigned the initial investigation or by a specially trained patrol officer designated "crime scene investigator." Regardless of whether you are the officer assigned to collect and preserve the evidence, consider the following information concerning the techniques involved in the process.

Fingerprints

Three types of fingerprints may be found at the crime scene: latent prints, visible prints, and plastic, or molded, prints. The plastic prints are those usually found in soft, pliable substances, such as putty, wax, soap, butter, or grease. Visible prints are those that need no development to be completely visible to the viewer. They may be found in items such as dust, blood, or any smooth and flat surface the suspect may have touched with the ridged parts of his hands or feet when they contained ink or some other substance that might serve as a "printing" medium when coming in contact with the surface. Latents are invisible impressions that must be developed by dusting with a special fingerprint dusting powder, by chemical treatment, by "fuming" with the fumes from burning iodine crystals, or by any other means of drawing out the prints and making them visible for collection by photographing or by transfer to a transparent tape or similar substance.

Fingerprints that have the greatest value in a criminal investigation are those found in places where only authorized persons are allowed, such as in a cash box, the interior of a cash drawer, or inside some other container. Prints found on counters or desk tops, on the outside of a vending machine, or on an object that anyone could have handled during the normal hours of business may be of some value if the suspect claims that he was never inside or near the place where the prints appear. To help in locating these, turn off any glaring overhead lights and use a flashlight at an oblique angle. Consider items the culprit may have touched during the commission of his crime, then dust with fingerprint powder. Searching for latent prints on materials other than smooth surfaces, such as paper, or porous wood, should be left to the expertise of the fingerprint specialist.

Before dusting the surface where you anticipate finding latents, attempt to determine the direction that the ridges are most likely to run. Using a moderate amount of powder, brush with the grain or the lines of the pattern. Use powder that contrasts to the surface. Once you have developed the latent, or have discovered one of the other types of prints— plastic and visible—take photographs before attempting to transfer the prints to a tape or other lifting material, or before removing them in any manner for preservation. Consider also collecting samples of bare footprints, if there are any available. Some agencies, including the FBI, have done some work on classification of prints on toes and balls of the feet. It is worth a try.

Fingerprint Identification Systems

Computerized fingerprint identification systems now in use in many parts of the country and eventually throughout the United States have proven successful far beyond the expectations of their proponents. In California, the system, known as CAL-ID (see Figure 9–3), has already been utilized

Figure 9-3 Fingerprints are one of the most positive means of identification.

in locating and identifying several suspects in serious crimes, including multiple murderers. Taking a partial smudge or single print from the crime scene, the computer can search the files and make a tentative identification that is verified by personal examination of a specialist (see Figure 9–4). Some estimates have included the claim that one fingerprint examiner would take about 100 years to do what this new system's computer can do in 20 minutes.

Following is one method for lifting latents with fingerprint tape. Select tape that is free of bubbles; then pull a length of the tape free from the roll in one continuous movement to avoid creating a ridge at any point in the strip. Fold the tape back about ¼ inch on the end that is free of the roll. Place that end of the tape on the surface about 1 inch from the print that you intend to lift. Slowly press the tape down and move toward the print, keeping the free tape from touching the surface until you press it down. Continue pushing the tape smoothly until it is about 1 inch beyond the print. Cut the tape from the roll and rub across the entire surface to assure adhesion. Lift the tape slowly and place it smoothly on a card of contrasting color or on a piece of transparent plastic. There are many excellent materials available for this process.

Figure 9-4 Specialist Robert S. Johnson at the Fingerprint Input Monitor (FIM), Department of Justice. The FIM is used to correct the core point, the skeletal pattern of the print, and to key in classification and other data for print identification. (Courtesy of Attorney General, Sacramento, California.)

DNA, or Genetic Fingerprinting

The scientist who discovered this system of identification said that—except for identical twins, who have the same genetic code—the chance of two people having the same DNA is about 1 in 12 billion. For a world with only about 4 billion inhabitants, those are unusually good odds.

Discovered by Dr. Alec Jeffreys, a young geneticist at Leicester University in the town of Leicester in Leicestershire County, England in 1986, genetic "fingerprinting" was developed and employed in a celebrated murder case involving two victims three years apart, and an innocent man who had confessed to one of the murders was released as a result of the test. DNA, or deoxyribonucleic acid, is the most accurate means of identification in existence today.

A person's genetic "fingerprint" may be obtained from a blood cell, a piece of skin, hair, semen, or any other cell of the body. Blood is drawn from a suspect and is processed to ascertain the DNA code, or "print." A comparison is made with cells or tissue found at the crime scene and/or the body of the victim.

Referred to as a "Star Wars product" by Sheriff Brad Gates of Orange County, California (*L.A. Times*, April 20, 1989), this laboratory investigation also involves establishment of a genetic code library file of known offenders similar to the massive fingerprint files maintained throughout the world to provide the data base.

Shoeprints and Tireprints

In dust, dirt, mud, or plastic materials, you may find identifiable impressions of shoes or tire treads. They are often as distinctive as fingerprints, and the law of averages may be applied to show that the impression found at the scene of the crime was probably made by the shoes found in the possession of the suspect, or by the suspect's automobile. In one case, at the scene of a safe burglary, there were prints from two diffeent shoes that indicated that they belonged to the people who removed the safe from the premises. Some distance from the scene of the crime, two men were questioned in a field interview, and the officer had the presence of mind to look at the bottom of their shoes. The comparisons proved that the shoes worn by those two men matched the impressions left at the crime scene, and the additional factor of the combination of shoe designs narrowed down the averages in favor of the prosecution. The combination of designs at the scene of the crime as well as at the field interview, when the two men were interviewed together, was attributed to more than mere coincidence. These types of impressions are first photographed; then plaster of paris casts made of the entire circumference of the tire or as many of the shoe impressions as possible.

Tool Marks

Simple scratches, striations, and impressions are the most commonly encountered marks found at the scene of a crime, usually at the point of a forced entry. Simple scratches with no identifiable characteristics may occur on the inside of locks that have been picked with the aid of lock-picking devices. Striations and impressions are made by a variety of tools, and it is sometimes possible to match the marks and the tools. Whenever a tool is manufactured, it carries with it certain imperfections that are characteristic to only that tool. The tool-making tools are imperfect themselves and transfer their own imperfections to each new tool. Each time a tool is used, it undergoes an almost imperceptible change, but its distinctive markings can be identified by microscopic examination. It is impossible to classify and file in any organized manner tools and tool marks, but if the laboratory specialist has the tool and the mark it made, he may succeed in "making" the case on the basis of a single item of evidence.

Impressions are indentations made on a surface that is softer than the tool used to make them. They are usually found at the point of entry or at the hiding place of some object of theft. The most commonly used burglar tool is the screwdriver; some sort of pry tool is in second place. Hammers or any tool used to strike a surface will make impressions. Measure the impressions and allow for stretching of the material, which will actually make the impressions larger than the tools that made them. Take photographs and casts with material especially designed for this use, and take the actual impression whenever possible. This may necessitate taking out part of a door frame or window sill for a courtroom presentation, but it is worth the trouble and expense if you are to prosecute the case successfully.

Keep the tool and the impression separate and make the comparisons by measuring the tool and the impression rather than by contaminating the evidence by placing the tool in the impression possibly made by that tool. The laboratory specialist will make comparisons by making casts of the impressions and the suspected tool and matching them by microscopic examination and the comparison of photographs.

Striations are parallel scratch marks cut into the surface of some material that is softer than the tool or device that makes them. Any imperfections on the scratching surface of the tool making the mark, such as a slight nick or a blunted portion, will be transferred to the object scratched. Striations are made by a scraping, cutting, or glancing blow across the surface. Tools that may make striations are hammers, pry bars or screwdrivers used in a scratching motion, a chisel driven into metal, a bolt cutter cutting a padlock, a wire cutter, or a brace and bit.

Another common type of striation in criminal investigation is that made by the rifling and interior of a revolver, or other rifled firearm, on the bullet that travels through the barrel. Each time it is fired, the firearm changes, and it is imperative that the bullet and suspected gun be compared before it has been fired many times. Otherwise, the comparison will be worthless because of the change that has taken place.

The procedure for handling striations and the tools that are suspected of having made them is the same as that for handling impressions. They are usually compared by photograph and by microscopic examinations.

Soil as Evidence

Soil taken from the crime scene and that which is removed from the clothing or other effects of the suspect may be shown to have similarities that indicate that the suspect was probably at the scene. Different soils come from different source areas and include such distinctive items as seeds, fertilizer, building materials, insecticides, stones, minerals, and different types of soil. To collect soil, scrape the material onto a clean sheet of paper and fold it into a "bindle" or put into a clean plastic bag or bottle that locks or can be sealed on top. To collect it from the scene, such as where a footprint was made, take three or four samples from the immediate area and package in the same type of bag. Other types of containers may be a pill box or plastic tube with screw-top cap; .35 mm film containers, especially plastic ones, are excellent for evidence collection.

Biological Fluids

Stains such as those made by blood or seminal fluid may be classified by blood type and be subjected to other types of laboratory analysis if collected and handled correctly (see Figure 9–5). They may assume many colors by reacting to chemicals that may be on the surface where they are found, and often blood is found that does not resemble the reddish-brown color that one usually associates with dried blood. Seminal stains are usually found on articles of clothing in sex offenses. Collect this type of stain by handling the clothing as little as possible. If wet, allow the stain to dry without folding the clothing or covering it with any other article. Blood is found in various places and should be stored wet in a closed container if possible or be allowed to dry on clothing in the same manner as semen. Bloodstains may be found in the cracks of a freshly washed knife, in cracks in wood or tile floors, in carpeting, in towels or washcloths, in a clothes hamper or wastebasket, or in the drains of sinks or tubs.

When collecting bloodstains, photograph and sketch them first, showing their shapes and size, and the direction of the splash. Also indi-

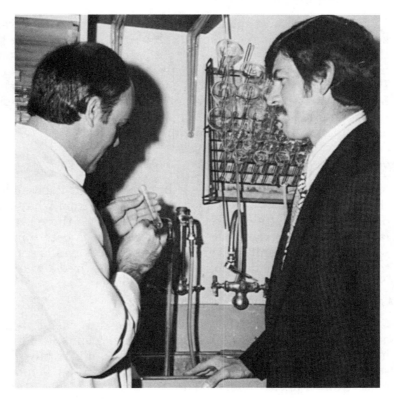

Figure 9-5   Laboratory analysis of evidence is extremely critical in all crimes, but more so in cases where the evidence is the only witness. (Courtesy of the Police Department, Santa Ana, California.)

cate on the sketch whether they are dry, moist, or wet. Collect wet stains by placing the substance in a sealed container with a mild saline solution of 2 teaspoons of salt to 1 quart of water. About 10 cubic centimeters of blood is a desired minimum if it is possible to collect that much. If the blood is in soil, remove any insects before storing. Wet stains may be collected by use of a blotter, which is allowed to dry and is stored in the dry state. Collect dry stains by scraping them onto a piece of clean white paper and folding up the paper securely or by scraping them into a small glass or plastic container designed for the collection of evidence.

Blood groupings are the basic O, A, B, and AB, but may be further classified into M, N, or MN according to the M-N system or another system known as the Rhesus, or Rh, system, How well the classification can be done depends on age and condition of the blood or other body fluid. Approximately 80 percent of the population are secretors, which means that blood is secreted into other body fluids and blood type can be determined by examining those other fluids.

Odontology as an Investigative Tool

Teeth are used as weapons of attack in such crimes as physical assault or sexual abuse. Burglars sometimes bite into food and leave the remains at the crime scene. By examination of the tooth marks, it is sometimes possible to identify the individuals' bite marks by comparing with their teeth. If you encounter any item that appears as though it might contain bite marks, or any wound on a victim's body, it should be carefully examined to determine if it has tooth impressions. Photographs and laboratory examinations might yield some interesting results.

Gunpowder and Shot Pattern Tests

From tattooing on the victim's skin or clothing it is possible to determine the direction from which a shot was fired and from what distance. This is determined by a study of the powder tattooing, if there is any present. The laboratory will do comparison testing when it is determined what type of weapon and ammunition were used. A suspect's hands and clothing will be tested for residue to determine if he or she has fired a weapon lately.

Fabrics as Evidence

Cotton and wool and other natural fabrics are easier to work with than are the synthetics, such as nylon and orlon. A sample of the victim's clothing compared with a piece of material that might have been left at the scene of a crime may be matched mechanically, as would be done with a piece from a jigsaw puzzle. The manner in which material is woven is characteristic of different mills, and it is also possible to determine the exact cloth content of the material. Dyes and other methods of coloring material may be determined by the laboratory.

Safe Insulation

Whenever a safe has been tampered with and the insulation has been taken out or has fallen out of the inner spaces of the walls, there is a chance you might find some of it in the clothing of the burglar. It is possible to determine that it is, in fact, safe insulation and from which safe manufacturer.

Wood Identification

Mechanical matches may be made if you have a broken piece of the wood and the object from which it supposedly came from. If a cutting instrument was used, matching striations may aid in more positive identification. It is also possible to determine the type of wood you have and also the various sealers, varnishes, and paints.

Paint Identification

All paints are different, but all contain (1) vehicles, which are used for drying, oils for mixing, and other substances that bind the pigments together; (2) pigments, which give paint a distinctive color and may include extenders; (3) driers, such as lead or cobalt; and (4) solvents and thinners, which adjust the consistency of paint.

Examination of dried paint may include a mechanical match of a chip compared with the automobile fender it was suspected to have come from. Layering will show the succession of colors that a surface has been painted, which aids in identification. How many 1968 Chevrolets, for example, have come from the factory with a metallic cherry red color, then were painted with a gray primer and a powder blue, followed by white, and finally a metallic black with gold glitter mixed in the paint? Make, model, and year of an automobile's production may be determined by examination of the original paint. Laboratory examination of paint will include spectrophotometry, X-ray, diffraction, and gas chromatography, which are covered in more detail in forensic texts.

Other Physical Evidence

At the crime scene, virtually any item may be evidence. Collect and itemize every article that in any way indicates that it may be used to aid the success of the investigation. Bullets or other projectiles are common to crimes against persons. Account for every shot fired and locate every projectile. If a bullet is lodged in a piece of wood or plaster surface, dig out the material surrounding the bullet and let the bullet fall out. Do not alter the markings made by the gun by prying directly on the bullet when trying to collect it for evidence.

Glass particles left at the scene of the crime may match those found on the suspect's clothing as a result of a search with a vacuum cleaner with a special filter. A button found at the scene may have been torn off the shirt of the suspect, and by matching thread or torn material, it may be possible to make an identification of the culprit. Tools and weapons are occasionally left behind. They may be examined for fingerprints as well as impressions or striations that they may have made. Sometimes the suspect will leave behind personal items without knowing it. At one armed robbery of a liquor store at night, two suspects walked in and selected some beer under the pretense of preparing to buy it. The clerk asked the men for their identification because of their youthful appearance. One of the suspects handed the clerk his driver's license, then took out a gun and told the clerk to give him all of the money in the cash drawer. The suspects fled, the one forgetting to take back his driver's license. Imagine his dismay when he remembered. At about the same time, the clerk was on the telephone telling the police that he had just been robbed by the person named and described on the license. Needless to say, he probably will never make that mistake again after he finishes "serving his time."

MARKING EVIDENCE

Mark, or in some other way identify, every item of evidence at the time you collect it. Make the mark distinctive enough so that you will later be able to examine the item and positively state on the witness stand that you made that exact mark and, therefore, that is the same item that you collected at the time of the investigation. Some items are of such a nature that it is impossible to mark the items themselves. In those cases, seal the items inside a container and place your mark on the outside of the container. If you use a sealing material, it will be possible for you to testify that you sealed the container and that it does not appear to have been broken.

Items that have serial numbers may not need marking because you may record the number. If in doubt whether to mark, do it. Make the marks very distinguishable, but small and in places where they will not destroy the value of the item you mark. Clothing may be marked with no damage to the material if you make the marks in places such as inside the waistband of trousers, on the manufacturer's label, or on the tail of a shirt. If you have several pieces of glass, sketch the outlines of the various pieces on a sheet of paper, and designate a number to each piece.

CHAIN OF EVIDENCE CUSTODY

When introducing an item of evidence at a trial, you must describe the location where you collected it and the manner in which you collected it. It is then necessary for you and the other people in your department to show the precise route of travel of that item of evidence, to assure the court that it has not undergone any change or other contamination between the time it was collected and the time it was presented in court. To be able to guarantee the most careful handling of evidence and its chain of custody, follow these guidelines when processing evidence.

1. Limit the number of individuals who handle the evidence from the time it is found to the time it is presented to the court.
2. Each time you handle the evidence, check its condition to assure yourself that it has not been damaged or altered.
3. If the evidence leaves your possession,
   a. Record the name of the person to whom it is given.
   b. Log the date and time the transfer of custody is made.
   c. Log the reason for the transfer of evidence, such as "to evidence man for analysis" or "for lab analysis."
   d. Log when and by whom it is returned, if at all.
4. Each person who handles an item of evidence should affix his identifying mark to the article so that he, too, may testify to the fact that it is the same item he handled earlier.
5. Obtain a signed receipt from the person accepting the evidence, or have some procedure for recording the transfer each time it is made.
6. When evidence is returned to your custody, assure yourself that it is the same evidence.

The handling and storage of evidence is one of the more vulnerable points in the chain of custody. It is critical to the evidentiary value of any items you send or take to the laboratory or to the evidence locker that everyone who handles the items does so with strict observance of the rules concerning chain of custody. Employees should be carefully screened to avoid such isolated incidents as the storage clerk selling 3 pounds of cocaine back to the suspect who was booked for its possession or the clerk who had his own auction of seized bicycles and firearms. Although such incidents are rare, and certainly are not representative of the thousands of honest workers for police departments, this news becomes a topic for debate in court when the chain of evidence custody is presented.

In addition to the need for tight security, attention should be given to the life expectancy of some evidence, which may be perishable. Correct marking and handling should make it possible to refrigerate and freeze those items that need it and to seal other materials. Perishables also include items that might not perish from time but whose value will, such as fashion clothing. Recovered fashion designer clothing that is held for months in an evidence locker will bankrupt the store owners. Consider photographing and otherwise documenting the lot; then hold a representative sample for evidence and present it and the photograph at the time of the trial. This will be matter for the prosecuting attorney to decide.

Whenever you send or take evidence to the laboratory for analysis, give the lab personnel as much help as you can by indicating what it is that you believe they should look for during the examination. You may not be correct, but it will at least give them a starting point.

PHOTOGRAPHS

The purpose of photographs is to provide visual aids to the case for the investigators, the prosecuting attorney, and, above all, the judge and the jury. A photograph must be an accurate representation of the scene as it appeared to someone who was present at the time the photograph was taken. If possible, photographs should be taken before anything at all is disturbed. This will make it easier to explain the scene because if anything has been moved, it will be necessary to explain why. If you must move evidence prior to the photograph, mark the location where it was located so that the photograph will show the mark where something had been removed. For example, in a homicide case, the victim may have been removed to the hospital because it may have appeared that he was still living. The body's location should be marked with a high-contrast material, such as a yellow marking crayon.

For closeup photographs, use a ruler or other marker of known size. When the print is made, it will be possible for the darkroom technician to use a ruler and reproduce the exact size of the item in the enlargement. When photographing flat surfaces, be sure to have the film exactly parallel with the surface. Any enlargement will be free of distortion that occurs when the photograph is taken from an angle. With each enlargement, the distortion is exaggerated if the film and the object are not parallel.

Take background, or condition, photographs to show general conditions at the scene. Orientation may include photographs of the exterior of the building, the hallway leading to the exact location where the crime occurred, and the exact location. These pictures take the viewer on a pictorial journey to the place of the crime. Consider the use of Polaroid pictures for immediate review and evaluation, and other pictures if the earlier ones do not come out. The Polaroid camera is designed for snapshot quality, and it should not be used exclusively.

Color transparency slides are excellent investigative and evidential devices. They may be projected in a fully lighted room on a rear projection screen, or they may be projected in extremely large magnifications on a screen in a darkened room. The possibilities for using slides are several, particularly in the examination of minute bits of evidence.

For courtroom admissibility of photographs, the photographs must represent the scene as observed by the person who testifies to that fact. They must be material or relevant to the case, and they must be free of distortion. Photographs also cannot be of such a nature that would prejudice the jury against the defendant. Each photograph used should be one that adds to, rather than detracts from, the case. There must be some meaning to the picture, and it must depict what the accompanying testimony purports that it will depict.

ACCIDENT AND CRIME SCENE SKETCHING

A rough sketch is the simplest and most effective method of showing the scene as it relates to the crime or accident and the corresponding photographs. The two very rough sketches in Figure 9–6 illustrate how simple the sketch may be. When measurements are necessary to the case, they may be either paced or measured. When you do put in the measurements, indicate in your legend that the measurements are or are not exact and that the sketch is or is not to scale. Obviously, the sketch that you put in your notebook is not to scale if it looks anything like those in Figure 9–6.

Before you move anything, make every attempt to take photographs and make a rough sketch so that you may reconstruct the scene with the aid of the sketch and photos, if necessary.

Police sketching falls into three types:

1. *Locality sketch:* view of the overall scene and its environs, including neighboring buildings, roads leading to the scene, and the location of the crime or accident in relationship to the surrounding geographical landmarks
2. *Grounds sketch:* scene of the crime or accident closer up, with its general surroundings

   Accident: point of impact, final resting place of vehicles, skid marks, and other evidence; nearby intersections, view obstructions, lighting devices, traffic controls, and related objects

   Crime: actual scene where the crime took place with its nearest surroundings, such as other rooms, house and lawn, garage, other floors in the building
3. *Detailed sketch:* immediate scene only, such as the room or place where the event occurred

Sketches are generally divided into two categories:

1. *Rough sketch:* made at the scene by the initial investigating officer. It need not be drawn to scale, but it should be in proportion, and the measurements indicated on the sketch or in the accompanying notes. Relative distances must be clearly indicated so that a finished drawing will show true perspectives.
2. *Finished drawing:* prepared primarily for court presentations by an experienced draftsperson (don't overlook your local public works department for an artist). This one is drawn to scale with exact measurements.

The materials you will need for sketching will be a pencil so that you

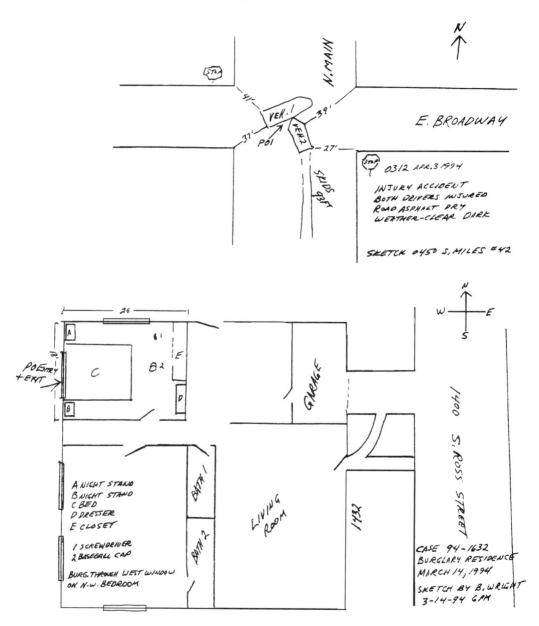

Figure 9-6 Rough sketches for notebook.

can make erasures; graph paper, which will make it simpler to show distances; clipboard or other hard surface for drawing; small ruler for straight lines; a compass for accurate directions and true north; a steel tape that does not expand or contract with the weather conditions; and marking chalk or crayon.

Basic Rules for Sketching

Measurements must be accurate, and measured by the person preparing the sketch. If someone else is nearby, have him or her measure again to assure accuracy. Take all measurements the same way, either paced or measured, and so indicate in the legend. Recommended scales for sketches:

Detail sketches: ½ inch = 1 foot

Large areas or rooms: ¼ inch = 1 foot

Larger areas and houses: ⅛ inch = 1 foot

Large buildings: ½ inch = 10 feet

Open areas, such as locality sketch: ½ inch = 10 feet

Your sketch must show essential items. Keep the sketch simple and uncluttered, free from unnecessary detail but including all objects related to the investigation.

Essential Elements for Crime Scene Sketch

1. If in an open area, perimeter of crime scene, showing relationships to landmarks and permanent objects, such as trees and buildings
2. If the crime occurred inside, outline of the room, including doors, windows, and permanent objects
3. Point of entry and exit by the perpetrator, if known or indicated by evidence or witnesses
4. If it is a crime against person, location and position of the victim
5. Weapons and/or tools used in the perpetration of the crime
6. Stains, marks, and other traces related to the crime, including fingerprints and shoe and tire impressions
7. Furniture and fixtures relevant to the investigation
8. Objects attacked or damaged, such as desk, safe, dressers, or articles of clothing

Essential Elements for Accident Scene Sketch

1. Point of impact by at least two measurements. For example, 8 feet north of south curb of Broadway, 68 feet west of east curbline of Main. This is determined by statements of witnesses and drivers, skid marks with abrupt change of direction, or gouge marks or debris in the street resulting from sudden jolt of the vehicle.
2. Location where the vehicles came to rest by three measurements. For example, distance from point of impact to a specific part of the vehicle, such as the center of the wheel; distance from one wheel to the curb; and distance from another wheel on the same side of the vehicle to the curb. When no curbs or edges of the road are present, use the polar coordinate method of measurement.
3. Location of the injured or deceased, if out of the vehicle. Measure from a specific part of the body to the point of impact (POI).

4. Identification and labeling of the vehicles (V1, V2).
5. Direction of travel of vehicles and pedestrians and which lane of traffic they were in.
6. Names of streets, their widths, and number of lanes.
7. Type and condition of road surface.
8. Indication of weather and lighting conditions.
9. Locations of traffic signs and signals.
10. Vision obstructions.
11. Skid marks.

Essential Elements for All Sketches

1. Compass directions: at least a north arrow.
2. Use a scale or draw in relative proportions.
3. Legend. Explain all symbols used in the sketch. Number or letter objects, with an itemized list, such as all numbered items are evidence and all lettered items are furniture.
4. Title block. List case number, date and time the incident occurred, date and time the sketch is prepared, description of the type of incident, the location, and name of the person preparing the sketch.

Measuring Methods

1. *Coordinate method* (Figure 9–7a). The simplest way to locate objects in a sketch is by giving distances from two mutually perpendicular lines, such as two walls of a room.
2. *Polar coordinates* (Figure 9–7b).
3. *Triangulation* (Figure 9–7c). If the distance between two objects is known, a third object can be located and distance determined even though it cannot be reached (such as a point across a ravine or river).

INVESTIGATION OF SPECIFIC CRIMES

The next few pages are devoted to just a few of the dozens of different types of crimes that you will be required to investigate during the course of your career as a field patrol officer. Consider the pointers as a guide to your investigation.

Arson

A serious problem with arson is that most evidence is destroyed in the fire. It may be significant information, although not evidence, to know that three days before the fire, the owner took out an insurance policy that more than adequately covered the building and all its contents. It

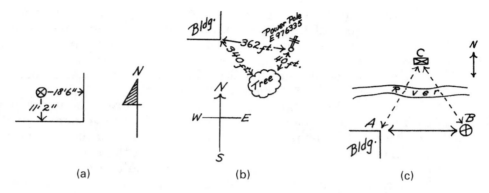

Figure 9-7   Measuring methods: (a) coordinates; (b) polar coordinates; (c) triangulation.

would also help the investigation, and this would be evidence, if you were to find out from nearby residents that the day before the fire, the owner of the building had several moving vans come in and had all the expensive furniture removed and replaced with junk from thrift shops. The actual investigation of the fire will be the responsibility of the fire department. When you are assisting, look for items that could have been used to start a fire, such as a discarded gasoline can half a block down the street, and help locate the point where the fire began. This is usually where the greatest amount of charring appears.

Many arson fires are started with a match and paper or other combustible material, and there is little likelihood of finding any evidence. Occasionally, an arsonist will use lighter fluid, gasoline, or alcohol. Some will use a wax candle set in a bundle of oily rags. Other arsonists use timed ignition devices, for example, an alarm clock wired to a pipe bomb. Whenever any substance turns up that even remotely looks as though it may have been used to start the fire, it should be considered as evidence.

Auto Theft

Special locking devices and alarms have slowed down amateur theft of automobiles, according to Bernard Edelman in "Auto Theft: for Police the Joyride Is Over": "The man geared to steal a car can steal one in minutes, no matter what safety or locking devices you put on."[2] The article points out that "chop shops," or professional car theft and stripping operations, are able to provide car parts at one-third the price that legitimate auto parts stores charge and can cut labor charges by 50 percent by selling pre-assembled units.[3]

Another type of auto theft is the insurance fraud perpetrated by the

---

[2]*Police Magazine*, Vol. 3, No. 5, September 1980, p. 17.

[3]Ibid.

owners themselves, who contract with professional theft rings to steal their cars so that they may collect insurance. Some owners have more than one policy, so when a car is stolen, the owner is paid by each of the two or more insurance companies; a $5,000 stolen car can yield $15,000 in returns. Some insurance industry sources estimate that 25 percent of all reported thefts of automobiles are fraudulent.[4]

When taking the auto theft report, inquire about the payments that might have been missed; the car may have been repossessed. Sometimes the owner loaned the car to a friend or relative and now wants it back and will report it stolen so that the police will make a dramatic recovery. Such a false report may result in the loss of someone's life, possibly yours, in attempting to apprehend a car thief who knows that no theft is involved and will violently resist or might make a game out of the chase.

Whenever you stop a person who might be driving a stolen automobile, ask the person who claims to be the owner or the borrower who cannot find the registration slip a few questions that the person familiar with the car should know, such as mileage, contents of the glove box, contents of the trunk, brand of battery or tires, recent repairs or new wiring, or when the car was last serviced and where. Car thieves seldom take the time to check those things out, and they are likely to reveal themselves as thieves. There are also those car owners who don't know the answers to any of those questions either, but they are in the minority. Look for the "dummy key" in the ignition or the driver who is unfamiliar with the car or how the parts work, and remember that even car thieves remain calm while being questioned by the police.

Burglary

Burglary is entry of a building or any of a number of different types of structures, or a vehicle or a vessel with the intent to commit a theft or any felony, according to California Law. The type of structure varies, but usually includes any type of place that has a top and sides and is enclosed and has a door or flap or cover that—when closed—is intended to protect the contents against the elements or people from entry: a tent, a mine shaft with an entry door, a telephone booth that Clark Kent would change clothes in, or even a showcase. In some cases a partially enclosed carport may be classified as a "building" if it is attached to a house. A vehicle usually has to be locked. However, breaking into the locked trunk of an otherwise unlocked vehicle, or pushing open the broken wind wing of an otherwise locked vehicle will be a burglary. No force is necessary to constitute burglary of a building, but some sort of force is necessary for an auto burglary. For example, merely unsnapping the canvas top of a jeep would not be burglary.

[4]Ibid., p. 18.

There are essentially three types of burglars: the opportunist, the juvenile, and the career criminal. Of the three, the career burglar is the most likely to have an explanation for being in the area or for having the property that he has in his possession. The opportunist will take advantage of the open window or unlocked door and will take almost anything that suits his fancy. The juvenile will probably be someone who lives in the neighborhood. Although none of the three neatly falls into any category, you should be alert to all three who might be operating in your district. The opportunist may be a delivery person who takes advantage of the open door while making the normal rounds of his job, such as selling spring water or ice cream bars, or the transient magazine subscription salesperson working your city before moving on to another city next week.

You will usually receive notification of a burglary through citizen complaints or by burglar alarm, either silent or audible. Neighbors watching out for each other's property are probably the best protection against burglaries, and neighborhood watch programs should be encouraged. If you frequently check out unoccupied buildings for security, you will find the places that the owners make vulnerable and will require more diligent patrol. If you actively and aggressively interview all people in your district who arouse your suspicions, you will get to know the burglars who have criminal records and the other individuals who seem to have nothing better to do than to roam the streets at unusual hours.

Whenever responding to a burglary call, assume that the burglar is still inside until you establish otherwise. Do not enter any building alone or before assistance has arrived when you suspect burglary. You have the advantage from the outside; the burglar has the advantage when you go in. Look for point of entry and point of exit. Attempt to reconstruct the crime from statements of witnesses and from your own observations. You may find that the "victim" has made a false report if you listen and observe carefully. An entry or exit may be physically impossible when you try to duplicate the event, being careful not to disturb any evidence.

Dead Body Calls—Homicide

Whenever responding to a dead body call, approach it from the standpoint that it is a possible criminal homicide. Your investigation might establish that the death was accidental, or natural, or a suicide, or caused by some other noncriminal means, but if you start out with the view that the victim died as a result of a criminal act, you are less likely to overlook valuable evidence.

Your first responsibility is to determine if death has, in fact, occurred. If there is any possibility whatever that there may be life in the victim, take immediate steps to attempt to preserve the life. This is unquestionably your first responsibility. Some bodies indicate by their appearance that death has unquestionably occurred, and you may proceed accordingly. Look for the presumptive and positive signs of death when examining the body, and note the observations you make.

The presumptive signs, which indicate that death has possibly occurred, but not conclusively, involve body temperature, heart beat, and respiration. To determine if the person is breathing, look for any movement in the area of the lower border of the rib cage. Absence of any respiration indicates death or a condition that may be produced in drowning, electrocution, or narcotic overdose cases in which the respiratory process is arrested. For the heart beat, feel for a pulse at the carotid artery on the right side of the throat, or at the heart itself. Body temperature decreases at a steady rate that varies with the individual. When death occurs, there may be a perceptible change in temperature. When examining the body for temperature, note any diffeences in temperature at the various parts of the body. If death has occurred not too many hours before your arrival, the differences in body temperature may help the medical examiner to determine the approximate time of death.

There are three positive signs of death: (1) absence of muscle tone in the eyelids, (2) rigor mortis, and (3) postmortem lividity. Bear in mind, however, that even though the person has obviously died and there is no question about it, you as a police officer have no authority to declare that death has occurred. Leave that task to the doctors, the coroners and their deputies, and other people who are authorized to make such a responsible determination.

Postmortem lividity appears on portions of the body that are closer to the surface on which it rests. It is a discoloration and appears something like a light-purple bruise with no obvious outer bruise on the skin surface. Lividity is actually a settling of all the body fluids by the pull of gravity to the lower parts of the body, and it begins about ½ hour to 3 hours after death. If it appears at some part of the body other than where it would be normally as a result of gravity flow, it may indicate that the body has been moved after death. Because of its resemblance to a bruise, do not overlook the possibility that it is actually a bruise.

Rigor mortis is a hardening, or calcifying, condition of the muscles throughout the body, usually beginning with smaller muscles and progressively developing in the larger muscles. For this reason, it appears to start at the face and head and work down to the feet. Actually, it is working in all parts of the body at the same time. Depending on the physical condition of the victim at the time of death, rigor mortis usually begins about 3 to 5 hours after death, is complete in 8 to 12 hours, then begins to disappear after about 48 hours. Sometimes a condition occurs that resembles rigor mortis and is misleading to the observer. This condition is known as a cadaveric spasm, which is an immediate rigidity of the entire body caused by an intense emotional situation that occurs at the moment of death. It is known to happen in crimes when the death occurs in a violent struggle or at an emotional peak. When examining the body, check various parts of the body to ascertain the presence of the rigor, but to not attempt to disturb the condition. Once the condition is "broken" by movement, it does not return.

The third positive sign of death is the total absence of muscle tone in the pupils of the eyes, the eye muscles, and the eyelids. This is also one of the first places that the decaying process in the human body begins. When checking for muscle tone, also look for a film that forms over the eyes, caused by the drying of the fluids that once were produced by the tear ducts.

Only a doctor or a coroner may legally declare death,[5] and until the arrival of such a person, it is your responsibility to make every effort to sustain what life may exist, except when there are such conditions as to positively establish the existence of death. The coroner takes charge of the remains and his possessions, and in cooperation with the office of the coroner, the police department investigates deaths as to their cause to determine what criminal law violations were committed, if any.

If there is a possibility that the death is anything other than "natural," by disease, or by accidental means, the investigation continues immediately. Except in departments that assign homicide investigators to take over the investigation immediately, your role as patrol officer is to assume the responsibility for the initial investigation. Specialists should be called in as early in the investigation as possible to handle laboratory and identification work, and the follow-up investigator may begin the follow-up at the same time you are conducting the initial investigation. Following is a list of guidelines that should be followed for the investigation of any suspected death:

1. *Examine the victim.* Look for signs of life, or death. Make mental notes (write them later as soon as practicable) about the differences in body temperature, state of rigor mortis, and other presumptive and positive signs of death that you observe. Consider the possibility of securing a dying declaration from the victim if he is still alive and coherent.

2. *Identify the victim.* Identification may be made during the victim's dying declaration, if there is one, and by examining the victim's personal effects. The property of the deceased is the responsibility of the coroner, but an officer may examine certain property to make an identification and to pursue the investigation. Sometimes the identity of the deceased will lead to the person who caused his present condition or to friends or relatives who should be notified of the death and may be of possible assistance in the investigation.

3. *Determine the cause of death.* The cause may be obvious, but do not overlook the not so obvious. For example, a known heart patient was found dead under what appeared to be "natural" conditions. The officer handled the case as he would handle any other heart patient until the ambulance had taken the victim to the morgue, and it was discovered that two puncture wounds were in the victim's chest. There was very little bleeding. Had there been, it would have given the officers a clue as

[5]Laws vary, of course, but such a serious determination should be made only by the specialists.

to the cause and nature of the wound. It was not until during the autopsy that the cause of death was determined to be two bullet wounds. The bullets were still inside the victim's chest. Sometimes the coroner or medical examiner has to investigate extensively to ascertain the cause of death.

4. *Protect the scene.* The scene includes the place of the death and the immediate surrounding area. Every death that occurs under unusual circumstances must be considered a possible homicide until the investigation establishes that it is not.

5. *Question witnesses.* Separate the witnesses and question them about the identity of the victim and any other matters that seem pertinent to the investigation. Ask about anyone who might have had a reason for killing the victim, such as a dismissed employee or an estranged spouse or some other relative. More than half of all homicide victims knew their killers, according to statistics compiled over the last several decades. The seemingly respectable or shy person should not be overlooked any more than the sinister or suspicious looking person should. The innocent-looking witness may be the killer.

6. *Draw sketches and take photographs to memorialize the scene before you remove any of the evidence or the body.*

7. *Remove the body.* Prior to the body's removal, arrange to have photographs taken, and prepare a field sketch. Specific parts of the body in relationship with fixed objects at the scene will aid in the preparation of the sketch. Note the exact location of the body, its position, and any relevant information. If there was an immediate removal of the body because of a belief that life may have existed, make notes of your recollections of the scene at your arrival.

8. *Search.* Search the immediate and general area for any evidence that may lead to the eventual solution of any crime that may have occurred or that may aid the investigation in any appreciable manner.

9. Reconstruct the occurrence. By organizing the statements, the facts, evidence, and whatever else is available, attempt to determine the cause of death and the circumstances surrounding it. Establish a motive for the homicide, if one is apparent. The motive is not necessary to prove guilt of the accused, but it often leads to the identification of the guilty party.

Laws in your state will specify which deaths must be reported to the coroner. Once the coroner or a deputy arrives, that person is responsible for custody of the deceased and all personal belongings. When evidence is involved, the coroner will not keep those items from you. California Government Code Section 27491 designates the following as cases for the coroner:

1. No physician in attendance

2. Wherein deceased has not been attended by a physician in the 20 days prior to death
3. Physician unable to state the cause of death
4. Known or suspected homicide
5. Known or suspected suicide
6. Involving any criminal action or suspicion of a criminal act
7. Related to or following known or suspected self-induced or criminal abortion
8. Associated with a known or alleged rape or crime against nature
9. Following an accident or injury (primary or contributory, occurring immediately or at some remote time)
10. Drowning, fire, hanging, gunshot, stabbing, cutting, starvation, exposure, alcoholism, drug addiction, strangulation, or aspiration
11. Accidental poisoning (food, chemical, drug, therapeutic agents)
12. Occupational diseases or occupational hazards
13. Known or suspected contagious disease, constituting a public hazard
14. All deaths in operating rooms
15. All deaths where a patient has not fully recovered from an anesthetic, whether in surgery, recovery room, or elsewhere
16. All deaths in which the patient is comatose throughout the period of physician's attendance, whether in home or hospital
17. In prison or while under sentence
18. Solitary deaths (unattended by physician or other persons in period preceding death)
19. All deaths of unidentified persons
20. All deaths of persons who are charges of the state (Fairview or Lanterman patients)
21. Fetal deaths where the attending physician cannot state an underlying cause of death

Forgery and Suspect Documents

Whenever searching the suspect and his or her property, look for anything that the person may have written under regular everyday conditions. Next, get sample writings while in your presence so that you will later be in a position to testify that you observed the suspect actually doing the writing or printing. These are a few guidelines:

1. If a handwritten document is in question, get the suspect's handwriting and attempt to get approximately the same type of writing. For example, if the suspected document is a check, have the suspect write out a check.
2. If all was done in capital letter printing, get capital letter printing.

3. If written in pencil or if written with ballpoint pen, use a similar instrument.

4. If written on lined paper or unlined paper, use a similar type of paper.

Dictate the wording if you are attempting to approximate the original document, but do not spell the words for the suspect, as the misspelling might be a clue. For the same reason, do not allow the suspect to copy another document.

Gambling

Undercover investigation is usually required to succeed in gambling cases. There is a brotherhood among gamblers and their bookies and other participants, a "we're in this together" conspiracy. Unless there is some cheating involved, it is difficult to find a complaining witness. Although a certain gambling operation might have the appearance of being a small-time operation among friends, it is hard for any gambling operator to survive without underworld connections or protection—any successful operator, that is.

Look for inconsistent situations, such as people coming out of a shoeshine parlor with shoes that have not been shined, or a barber shop without haircuts, or a butcher shop without meat. There may be an unusual number of people involved that could not be handled by the number of service personnel present, such as one barber who could not possibly trim 27 heads of hair in a half hour.

When approaching a suspected gambling operator, such as a bookie, look for water-soluble paper inserted in the mouth or a cigarette glowing next to flashpaper, which instantly melts and burns on contact with a flame. Once the suspect is in custody, and if the bookie had been near a telephone, you might find that by answering the phone for the next several minutes you will collect evidence that will establish the business nature of the calls, which may be used as evidence to establish that the suspect is a bookie.

Receiving Stolen Property

Mere possession of property that your record check reveals is stolen is not sufficient for an arrest of the person in possession of that property. You need to develop more substantial indicators that the person knows that it is stolen. The possession must be accompanied by what the courts will recognize as "suspicious circumstances." The following behaviors might indicate a guilty mind under the right circumstances:

1. Attempt by the person to flee when you approach him or her and you wish to interview

2. False statements offered by the subject as to how the property came into his or her possession

3. Use of a false name and inability to establish the existence of the person(s) from whom the property was supposed to have been received.
4. Sale of the property under a false name and at an inappropriate price (i.e., far too low)
5. Sale of the property with identification marks removed
6. An attempt to throw away or hide the property

Robbery

Consider your personal safety above that of all others, including hostages. A dead police officer will be of no assistance to any victim, regardless of age or sex. If you are able to negotiate with a robber, do so by telephone or through some remote means so that you are not exposed to possible gunfire. Determine as quickly as possible if the situation is actually a robbery and if the suspect is still on the premises at the time of your arrival. If the suspect has left, consider what you might do if you were the robber. Look in the logical places, but also look in those places where you think it would be most unlikely to find the suspect.

When having the victim and witnesses describe the suspect, have them write down their impressions and keep them separate. Rather than ask for the hair and eyes and height and weight, you might first have them tell you what it was about them or their appearance, mannerisms, voice, or the way they moved that was distinctive. What you are looking for is something that will set the suspect apart from all others. Did the suspect take anything away from the scene, such as a cola drink or a particular brand of beer? Whom does the suspect resemble that the witness knows? a brother? a fellow employee? Any idea at all will give you something more to work with.

Sexual Assault

In many kinds of sexual assault, you will find victims extremely defensive, sometimes because of strong moral-religious feelings that make them feel guilty and dirty at the same time. Victims might even show open hostility to you as an authority figure. Whatever your approach, you must be empathetic and nonjudgmental. Avoid at all costs making any statement or inference that would even indirectly imply that you are doubtful of the facts. At this moment of extreme emotional stress, it is possible for the victim not to remember details or for the entire situation to be exaggerated in the victim's mind. But there is no falsehood there. Be patient and understanding. What the victim needs at this time is someone who will offer reassurance and comfort.

Record your time of arrival and the condition of the victim. Have the victim do nothing to change the evidence, such as washing or changing clothes. If the crime is a rape, immediately have the victim examined by a doctor who is familiar with rules of evidence in rape cases and who has a rape kit. Your department may supply hospitals and clinics with the kits. All suspected body fluids, hairs, fibers, and inconsequential-appearing items of evidence might be the factor that will convict the accused.

In child molestations, be extremely careful not to suggest to the child the answers that you want. Ask the child to tell you in his or her own words exactly what happened. If a parent is present during the questioning, be sure that the parent understands that there is to be absolutely no interference and no leading questions. Children are very suggestible, particularly at a time of great emotional trauma, and should not be encouraged to say things that others want to hear. Question a child away from the parents, and have a witness present. You are dealing with a very sensitive situation, and hysteria is not unlikely.

Suicides and Attempted Suicides

You are responsible for protecting people against attempting suicide. You must take whatever steps you can to protect the life of a person who may want to end it himself or herself. Sometimes people with suicidal tendencies may attempt to bait you into a situation in which they hope you will shoot and kill them. Such people may cause the officer to fulfill their wishes.

When responding to an attempted suicide call, make every effort to preserve the individual's life. Although the person may not be "mentally ill" by definition, but experiencing a severe emotional crisis, he should be handled as a possible mental illness case and be subjected to an examination by a psychiatrist. Some jurisdictions provide for temporary civil commitment of people who attempt suicide until such time as they may be examined by a medical and psychiatric team and a determination made as to which treatment is best to prevent a recurrence.

Many fallacies exist concerning suicide, and some of these fallacies have been attacked by a Suicide Prevention Center at the University of California at Los Angeles Medical Center. Consider these views when responding to an attempted suicide call or when taking information concerning an individual's threat to commit suicide either immediately or some time in the future. One fallacy that has prevailed for some time is that a person who threatens suicide will usually not go through with it. It has been generally believed that such threats are bids for sympathy or attention, which they are. But it has also been shown through extensive study that the individual will commit suicide if he or she does not solve in some meaningful way whatever problem is the cause of the anguish.

Another fallacy about people who attempt suicide is the belief that they are so intent on killing themselves that they cannot be convinced to change their minds. This has been proven to be an invalid argument. Many people have been talked out of self-destruction, and, given proper treatment, they may permanently change their minds. They do not necessarily have to be suicidal for life. If they do not receive some counseling or other type of intervention, they may try again, and possibly succeed.

All people who attempt self-destruction are not necessarily mentally ill. The condition may be the result of complete despair or severe emotional problems caused by failure or unhappiness. Other causes of suicide may be a terminal illness, despair over losing a loved one, an extreme personal embarrassment, humiliation, depression, or loss of self-esteem. Once the crisis is past, the individual may realize how meaningful life may be, and he may never repeat his attempt to commit suicide.

Some university medical centers and medical associations have established "crisis centers" or similar services that provide psychiatric and psychological counseling by telephone for anyone who experiences an intense emotional or personal problem that he or she cannot cope with and who feels that there is no one else to turn to. There is no doubt that such centers have saved countless hundreds of lives.

TRAFFIC COLLISION INVESTIGATION

Your responsibility to investigate traffic collisions, sometimes erroneously referred to as "accidents," is to determine their causes, to identify traffic law violators and to prosecute them, to compile data for civil litigation, to accumulate statistics for the Three E's (education, engineering, enforcement), and to justify your department's selective enforcement policies and procedures. Following are the basic steps in traffic collision investigation:

1. Go to the scene as quickly and safely as possible. Plan ahead so that you will know the best routes to travel during peak traffic times. Sometimes red light and siren will hinder your travel and cause you delays.

2. Park correctly to avoid further collisions and to facilitate traffic flow.

3. Assess the situation and call for whatever assistance is necessary.

4. Care for the injured and protect their personal property.

5. Protect the scene against additional collisions. Sometimes moving a vehicle out of the roadway will be better than keeping it in the middle of the street and creating a hazard while waiting to take photographs and draw sketches. Laying out flare patterns may cause a circus effect and be more dangerous than moving the cars off the road and drawing as little attention as possible from passersby.

6. Locate drivers and establish their identities. While approaching the scene, be alert to hit-run suspects who might be fleeing the scene. If one of the drivers has left, get out a description of the suspect and vehicle as soon as possible.

7. Interview drivers, participants, and witnesses.

8. Note and record physical conditions at the scene, locations of vehicles, and evidence.

9. Take photographs when possible.
10. Test and inspect the vehicles when applicable.
11. Arrest or cite violators when applicable.
12. Have the scene cleared up. If tow trucks have been called, the tow company may clean the debris; otherwise, have public works department do it.
13. Follow-up at the hospital, if necessary, to determine the nature of any injuries sustained.
14. Notify relatives and survivors.
15. Prepare reports.

SUMMARY

This chapter covered a variety of activities that we categorized as "preliminary investigations." As with your field notes, you will find that the preliminary investigation will usually determine the success or failure of the supplementary investigations and prosecution that follow. The field officer is the first to arrive on the scene of an accident or a crime and it is critical that he or she immediately assess the situation, locate and preserve evidence that may later disappear or be overlooked, and protect the scene for the more complete investigation that follows.

The first officer on the scene not only protects the scene, but will also look after the safety of victims, seek out and question victims and witnesses, look for the culprit if there is any chance that he or she is still in the vicinity, and also the field officer will call for the expert assistance of specialists who will continue with the investigation following the initial phase.

In this chapter, we covered a few of the basic rules of how to locate, identify, and preserve various types of evidence and how the laboratory might aid in the investigation. The last part of the chapter covered some of the basic procedures in handling the initial phase of various types of crime and accident situations requiring investigation.

EXERCISES AND STUDY QUESTIONS

1. To what extent does the field officer in your department carry the initial investigation of property crimes? crimes against persons?
2. What is the advantage of having the district officer handle the preliminary phases of an investigation?
3. When you are making notes of your first impressions at the scene of a crime, what are some of the items you would list?
4. Describe the theory of transfer.
5. What is the purpose of photographing evidence before collecting it?

6. Name the three types of fingerprints that you may find at the scene of a crime.

7. Using the correct equipment, develop and lift a complete set of latent prints from two hands that someone has placed on a smooth surface.

8. Describe the procedures for collecting samples of wet blood from the scene of a crime.

9. How do you store for evidence certain items of clothing that contain wet bloodstains?

10. What is a striation? an impression?

11. How may tooth impressions be used as evidence?

12. Describe five types of evidence you might find at the scene of a burglary.

13. Describe five types of evidence (not listed in your answer to question 12) that you are likely to find at the scene of a rape,.

14. Describe the method for collecting each type of evidence listed in your answers to questions 12 and 13. Explain how each type may be marked for evidence.

15. Why is the chain of evidence so crucial?

16. What is the value of using color slides in court rather than 8- by 10-inch prints?

17. What should you do first when you arrive at the scene and discover someone who appears to be deceased?

18. Describe postmortem lividity.

19. How long does it take for rigor mortis to set in completely after death?

20. What are the positive signs of death?

21. What are the presumptive signs of death?

22. Define inductive and deductive reasoning, and explain the difference between the two.

23. List at least 10 circumstances of death that must be investigated by the coroner.

24. Draw a rough sketch of a hypothetical traffic collision.

25. Draw a rough sketch of a hypothetical crime scene.

26. What is a burglary?

27. Give three types of behavior that would lead you to believe that a person was possibly guilty of "receiving stolen property."

28. Describe the recommended procedure for reassuring a sex crime victim that you are serious about apprehending the attacker.

29. Name two characteristics about a butcher shop that might give you a clue that the shop is actually a cover for a bookmaking operation.

30. List at least two reasons not listed in this chapter why people commit suicide.

31. Describe the procedure for investigating a traffic collision.

REFERENCES

ECKERT, WILLIAM G., ed. *Introduction to Forensic Sciences*. St. Louis, Mo.: C. V. Mosby, 1980.

GODDARD, KENNETH W. *Crime Scene Investigation*. Reston, Va.: Reston, 1977.

HORMACHEA, CARROLL. *Sourcebook in Criminalistics*. Reston, Va.: Reston, 1974.

O'HARA, CHARLES E. *Fundamentals of Criminal Investigation*, 2nd ed. Springfield, Ill.: Charles C. Thomas, 1970.

SCHULTZ, DONALD O. *Crime Scene Investigation*. Englewood Cliffs, N.J.: Prentice Hall, 1977.

SCOTT, JAMES D. *Investigative Methods*, Reston, Va.: Reston, 1978.

WILSON, O. W. *Police Planning*, 2nd ed. Springfield, Ill.: Charles C. Thomas, 1958. Emphasis on reprinted article in the Appendix by Don J. Finney, laboratory technician for the Wichita, Kansas, Police Department, entitled "Police Duties at Crime Scenes," From *American Journal of Police Science*, Vol. 27, Nos. 2 and 3, 1936.

10

UNUSUAL OCCURRENCES

During your entire police career, you might never encounter a major transportation disaster, or a tidal wave, or an earthquake, or a hurricane, or a fire of holocaust proportions. Chances are, however, that you will be involved in many events of disastrous proportions. A real problem for the police when such natural or human-made disasters do occur is that the department has not prepared for such a problem. For that reason, it is extremely important to plan and rehearse so that you and your colleagues will be ready for any contingency that should arise.

Natural disasters, such as floods, hurricanes, tornadoes, earthquakes, or volcanic eruptions, are sometimes directly related to the weather and geological factors indigenous to that area. Other disasters, such as chemical or power plant explosions, or fires in fuel tank fields, or riots may erupt for any number of reasons. These types of disasters may take priority in your department's planning activities because they are known hazards. Some disasters, however, may not even seem remotely possible, such as a collision of two aircraft heavily loaded with fuel and/or explosives over a quiet residential neighborhood in the suburbs. For that reason, no police agency should consider itself insulated from disaster or disaster planning.

In this chapter we devote our discussion to planning and techniques in carrying out those plans in major areas: disaster response, aircraft crashes, bombing and bomb threats, crisis intervention, and mentally and emotionally disturbed persons, and riot control. The few times that you may be required to respond to these critical police problems will demand only the most precise performance from you because of the multiple problems facing you and the great numbers of human lives at stake.

Several aspects of disaster control directly involve the patrol officer. They include planning, training, and maintenance of a state of readiness. To some extent, the patrol officer is involved in logistics and public information when there is an impending problem about which advance information is available. Once the disaster occurs, the patrol officer is directly involved in all aspects of the disaster control activities. There is an immediate need for intelligence data to identify the nature and extent of the disaster, to notify persons to be warned and/or evacuated, and to contain the disaster area. Rescue operations, including medical aid for the injured, evacuation of survivors, and care for their property, are all tasks performed by the police in cooperation with the many other agencies similarly involved.

DISASTER RESPONSE

Rather than attempt to define and address each of several different types of natural and human-made disasters, in this section we cover the general problem of disaster response, which involves police planning and response whenever a disaster occurs. You should always anticipate the unexpected and be prepared for the inevitable.

In departments where participatory management is practiced, and in which you will have an opportunity to take part in disaster planning, you may participate in brainstorming, which is one of the more productive methods of gathering ideas during the preliminary stages of planning. During that time, everyone present is encouraged to contribute random thoughts, wild ideas, concrete proposals—anything that comes to mind—with no fear of being ridiculed or embarrassed because someone else thinks the idea is "stupid." Whatever the method for planning disaster response, it should involve you as the field officer.

Plan for the unexpected. Consider all the different things that could go wrong and develop alternative plans. Keep in mind the people who will be involved in certain parts of the activity, and capitalize on their individual strengths. It is usually impossible to predict who will be on duty at the exact moment any disastrous situation occurs. Therefore, plans should not be so complex that they will fail with the personnel on hand at the time of occurrence. Following the planning, or as a part of the planning, rehearsals and simulated problems should be worked out at training sessions. During some of those simulations, you may discover weaknesses in your plan that would hinder performance during the real event, but after more planning sessions and more rehearsals, you may refine your performance to more effective levels.

Disaster Control Procedures

1. *Identify the nature and extent of the problem.* Is it a single incident that has occurred, or is there a continuing hazardous condition that is going to repeat or extend over a long period of time? Determine if there is anything that may be done to prevent a recurrence of the situation. For example: An overturned and derailed train with many killed and others injured is the first disaster, but one of the overturned railroad cars contains highly explosive or flammable material that is likely to cause additional loss of lives unless something is done, such as evacuation. The fire company is reducing the hazard by neutralizing the volatility of the material. How much and what type of assistance do you believe you need immediately? What type of injuries have been sustained? Severe burn patients will need a different type of medical service than will victims of crushing, for example. If the disaster involves a public transportation vehicle, such as an airplane or bus, it will be necessary to notify the National Transportation Safety Board. If military vehicles or aircraft are involved, you will have to notify the nearest military base. You are going to need additional officers to control traffic, assist in evacuation of people in the hazard area, and help at the scene and elsewhere. At the time of your first assessment, it is better to overestimate the needs than to underestimate.

2. *Communicate your information by radio immediately.* If a telephone is immediately available, establish contact with the dispatcher and keep the line open. There will be more confidentiality by using the telephone, and there is less likelihood of curious onlookers who have the police radio scanners being attracted to the scene. If the radio frequency is busy, precede your transmission with the international distress signal by stating "Mayday." That should clear the air for you.

State the nature and extent of the damage and the problem. State the nature and probability of continued and additional hazards. If you know there are deaths and injuries, give the dispatcher some idea of how many people are involved so that sufficient ambulances or coroner personnel may be called. State the type of specialists who will be required, such as fire department, ambulances, rescue personnel, the "go team" of the National Transportation Safety Board, a geologist in the event of a landslide, or the bomb squad in case of an explosion or presence of explosive materials. Be sure to notify the dispatcher of any further hazard that exists and the location. If access of the scene is a problem, describe the best route for certain vehicles to travel.

While you are the only officer at the scene, it is usually better for you to remain at the location where you can maintain continuous communication with your headquarters to keep feeding new information and answering questions. An exception to this rule would be to save a human life when your presence will make the difference.

3. *Administer urgently needed first aid and other rescue activities.* At the initial stages of a disaster operation, your most critical duty requirement is to keep open the line of communication so that adequate help may arrive as quickly as possible. By leaving your radio or telephone post to start helping individuals, you will be far less effective than all the people you are summoning to the scene. For that reason, it may be more heroic of you to stay at the radio than it would be to rush in and single-handedly help a few individuals. If you were to lose your life or capability to communicate, you would become another victim and no longer of any value to the overall operation.

4. *Establish a command post.* If possible, this should be located at a place that has accessibility to a telephone so that you may open that line of communication as soon as possible. The post should be near enough to the disaster scene so that you may observe what his happening, but far enough away so that you are not in immediate danger. When additional officers arrive, you will probably continue to be in command until a higher-ranking officer notifies you that he or she is taking over. Depending on departmental policy, of course, the presence of a supervisor does not usually mean that the supervisor is assuming command. The supervisor may choose to observe and allow you to continue functioning as you are until it appears that higher rank is required. A more permanent command post may be set up if the disaster is of a continuing or more serious nature that is going to take more time than an hour or two to clean up. For the more permanent location, consider restroom facilities as well as a place to serve meals and a place of shelter for alternate teams of officers to rest between work periods. Temporary morgue and medical stations may be necessary. If there are many deaths and identification will be required, plans should be made to have refrigerated trucks or facilities available. The command post will have individuals assigned to coordinate such activities as personnel deployment, supplies and equipment, housing, meals and refreshment, weapons and ammunition, coordination of reserves and volunteers, issuance of identification cards or arm bands, perimeter control, spiritual assistance for both officers and victims, and public information.

5. *Contain the area.* Once you have identified the nature of the problem and its extent, established communications, and summoned aid, looked after the immediate first aid needs of the victims that you could assist, and set up the command post, you should set up the perimeters of the area if you have not already done so. Have officers assigned to the outer limts of the perimeter and instruct them to allow no one to enter but those engaged in the rescue operations.

There are several purposes for perimeter control. Chief among them is to keep the number of people exposed to any hazard to a minimum. Any disaster scene almost spontaneously draws crowds of curious people. They should be diverted away from the scene as soon as possible.

6. *Maintain open emergency lanes.* Certain streets should be kept open and free from congestion to provide for the free flow of emergency and other service vehicles into and out of the disaster area.

7. *Evacuate survivors and other persons in the area whose lives are in jeopardy.* People must not only be instructed to leave, but also be helped to leave in many instances. Seek the assistance of such organizations as the Salvation Army and the American Red Cross to assist in the movement of the people and their personal effects, and to provide temporary shelter.

8. *Provide public information services.* People who are directly involved should know of the incident. In addition to making personal contacts, local radio and television stations may broadcast warnings to the people to evacuate. Whatever information there is available should be released to keep residents who have evacuated informed as to the condition of their property.

9. *Provide for coordination with other agencies.* In your department's disaster plan, which should be constantly updated, arrangements will be provided for in advance of any need. Nearby military base and colleges are excellent for human resources, temporary emergency housing, rescue and communications assistance, and many other contingencies. Volunteer organizations, such as those with citizens band radios, are sometimes well organized and constantly available for both fixed-based radio and field units on frequencies not cluttered with police emergency traffic. Service people—such as plumbers, electricians, and taxi owners—all have their own personnel with radio-equipped vehicles that may be called into service. Many charitable organizations that salvage clothing and furniture for rehabilitation of workers and fund raising, such as Goodwill Industries, Salvation Army, Veterans of Foreign Wars, and others, have their own personnel with radio-equipped trucks that could be used for emergency operations.

Tow services and ambulance companies are in rescue and salvage businesses, and there should be preplanned major emergency mobilization programs for those companies to cooperate in disaster situations. Other emergency departments, such as fire departments, civil defense, neighboring departments of police and fire, the state national guard, and youth organizations, such as Boy and Girl Scouts and Campfire Girls, should all be part of the master plan for disaster mobilization.

Wholesale grocers and restaurant chains and gasoline and diesel fuel distributors may provide their products and services as needed, hospitals and clinics and their doctors and nurses will be available according to their mobilization plans, and utility repair crews will work overtime. Not to be overlooked are citizen volunteers with no special service to offer—it may seem—but clothing, food, and shelter to victims and rescuers and who may be trained for disaster response. Hotels and motels sometimes also offer accommodations at little or no cost to displaced persons, and religious organizations provide their many services.

10. *Arrange for access into the area by authorized people only.* Some agencies have prepared for such contingencies by printing color-coded identification cards that are issued at the command post or some central location and are collected after the need passes.

11. *Record the event.* If the event is of some magnitude and continues for a period of time, a scribe or stenographer may be assigned to transcribe all information provided by the various officers, supervisors, and field commanders or other persons. In other situations, the many officers who take part in the action may prepare a report covering individual participation. One officer is then assigned to coordinate all the reports and to prepare one "cover" report that ties all the information together and caps it off with a summation. The report provides a permanent chronological record of the event and the department's participation.

Logistics and Mobilization

As an emergency public safety agency, the police department should be equipped to meet the usual and unusual demands of various occurrences. The limitations on what a police department could keep on hand are defined only by the limitations of financial resources and the imagination of the officers who prepare the plans. Every contingency should be anticipated, although requests for supplies and equipment must remain realistic.

Local, state, and federal civil defense agencies and their personnel are similarly engaged in preparing for the many disasters that inevitably do occur. Any police department planning or training should definitely be in cooperation with those other agencies involved in civil defense or disaster planning.

Once a disastrous event takes place, there is little opportunity for advance planning. Most procedures should be fairly routine, at least during rehearsals, so that when an actual problem arises, mobilization for disaster control occurs almost automatically. Mutual aid plans and coordination with the various other agencies should be implemented immediately.

The first step to mobilization is to discontinue all nonessential police tasks, such as the routine patrolling and response to miscellaneous calls for service. Adequate personnel will have to be assigned to two locations at the beginning: the site of the event and the site of the complaint board. There will be a considerable increase in telephone and radio communications, and many of the nonessential calls will have to be postponed or "counseled out" by diplomatic desk officers. These officers must make it possible for all available field officers to respond only to emergencies in addition to the disturbance scene. On-duty personnel will probably also be extended an additional four hours, making it possible to assign the entire department to two 12-hour platoons that will alternate on duty as long as the need exists.

Off-duty officers and reserve forces should then be called to duty. To effect this process with the minimal interference with headquarters telephone operations, there should be some form of emergency call system with a pyramid-type procedure. Office personnel should be assigned to call up a few off-duty officers. The call system should then continue from strategic phone locations outside. This system will free both the department's lines and the people who would otherwise have ot be making the calls. When mobilizing off-duty officers, it may be wise to have the officers report in uniform to a staging area some distance away from the police headquarters building, possibly nearer to the location where the event is taking place and in a location where the officers' private vehicles will be safe. Using this staging area will keep the movement of the force of officers confidential, and it may add to the element of surprise when the officers arrive on the scene, especially a riot scene. If there were any organization to the agitation at the crowd scene, it would be possible for someone with a small two-way radio or telephone to watch police headquarters for personnel movement. In the absence of such organization, this remote staging process at least reduces confusion at the headquarters building.

Mutual Aid Agreement

In the years since World War II, many contiguous jurisdictions have had rather elaborate machinery for immediate coordination of combined forces under mutual aid compacts and agreements. In California, for example, the entire state is divided into mutual aid zones, and most of the cities in each county have mutual aid pacts. Whenever there is an alert of "limited peril," and the local police forces cannot adequately handle the problem, the alert is broadcast, and officers from the contiguous jurisdictions respond to assist. The jurisdiction having the problem maintains the authority for coordination and supervision. When the situation involves a larger area, such as two or more cities, coordination is assumed by a pre-designated administrator, such as the county sheriff. If the problem calls for more assistance than the county's police forces can provide, the authority and responsibility for coordination then goes to a zone commander, who is probably one of the sheriffs of the several counties in the zone. The chain of reinforcement continues to expand until the situation obviously calls for statewide coordination. At that point, the governor declares martial rule.

Martial Rule

Martial rule is a military state, and during its existence all constitutional provisions are suspended. There is no local control, and the objective of putting down the riot becomes a military objective for the National Guard, or state militia, under the control of the commander in chief, who is the governor, and his adjutant general. Because the condition of military rule is alien to a free society, the decision to impose martial rule is an extremely grave one, and the governor must use this power only when the local forces cannot handle the situation. Requests for the imposition of martial rule must come from the chief executive officer of the local government or from some other official source, such as the magistrate or the sheriff. The governor may also make the decision independently. The mechanics for the request and imposition of martial rule depend on the various state laws.

Once the local government officials see the need for additional assistance beyond the forces that they may utilize within their own jurisdiction, it is advisable to alert the governor's office and the National Guard so that they may plan for the contingency of martial rule. In the meantime, it is wise to activate the mutual aid plan and to proceed according to the needs dictated by the situation. When the governor authorizes the use of the National Guard, the first step in the military assistance is to place this force under the supervision of the local police administrator in an assisting capacity.

The governor imposes martial rule only when there is no alternative. During that time when martial rule is in existence, the military commander is in complete charge of the situation. The objective is to restore sufficient order to enable the local police to reassume control of the situation. The minute that objective is achieved, the governor orders the martial rule at an end. The National Guard then reverts to its "support" role until the governor and the local officials determine that it is no longer needed.

Federal Troops

If the situation gets out of hand and reaches such proportions that the local police must relinquish control of the state National Guard, state martial rule is not sufficient. The governor must then request assistance from the president of the United States. The president then goes through a process similar to that of the governor, and he may impose federal martial rule. The state National Guard becomes federalized, and federal military troops are sent into the jurisdiction. Once the president determines the need for federal martial rule, he makes the determination and proclaims it to be in effect. In the absence of presidential order, the military troops may be placed at the disposal of local law enforcement administrators when there is a grave need for such assistance. Actually, this determination of grave need may be made by local military commanders and the assistance rendered, but it must then be followed by satisfactory justification to the president through the appropriate levels of command.

The entire system of mutual aid and martial law is designed to provide for local control until all possibilities of quelling the disturbance have been attempted and have failed. Only then may the governor step in and impose martial rule, and he may keep it in effect only as long as the immediate need exists. The same procedure applies to the president of the United States. Local law enforcement has long been recognized as the primary law enforcement body in the country, and the laws have been passed with that concept in mind.

Assignment of Responsibility

If there is any advance warning about an impending disaster or civil disturbance of major proportions, and if planning may be accomplished in advance, such planning should include some serious consideration of which officers will be given the initial assignment to attempt to control the crowds and prevent riots and looting. The following factors should influence the administrators in selecting the officers for this duty. The officers should be in perfect physical condition and should maintain an immaculate appearance in uniform. In addition to being physically capable of doing an excellent job, the officers selected for a special problems detail should also "look the part." They should be cool and reflective, mature, and emotionally stable under stress conditions. They must have a certain degree of social sensitivity and be optimistic about their goal of restoring order through persuasion if possible, force only if and when absolutely necessary.

Intelligence Assignments

A staff officer should be assigned independently to define and measure the field problem in a detached manner, free of the emotional strain of making immediate decisions. This officer should report to the police chief and other command officers so that their decisions may be based upon the evaluation and the reports from the field commander. To assist in this information gathering operation, the intelligence officer may use a team of "scouts," who enter the field to observe and report on everything that comes to their attention from their points of vantage. When making intelligence assessments, the assigned officer will consult with various specialists to aid the staff in making judgment decisions about situations such as natural disasters, floods, earthquakes, hurricanes, or forest fires, that may accompany the civil disturbance.

Logistics

An officer should be assigned to plan in advance for the accumulation and proper dispensation of supplies and equipment and to handle distribution details during times of actual need. If a sudden need should arise to feed and provide rest areas for 2000 officers, for example, this officer should be ready to act at once to meet the emergency. A logistics officer must be ready for any contingency.

Public Information

An officer with sufficient rank to make judgments concerning information releases under various circumstances should be assigned to a post somewhere removed from the immediate scene of the event and also far enough away from the center of communications and headquarters operations to avoid interfering with those operations. The information officer should be the only one authorized to release information concerning the event. All units should be required to keep the information officer posted on changing events. The information officer will actually be the best informed of the noncritical operating personnel and can keep the news media informed on events as they happen. If such an officer is assigned, and the policy for "no news except through the information officer" is enforced, the press and other people who have a need to know about the situation wil go the information center to satisfy their needs and remain outside the critical operating areas.

Staging Area

The staging area may be at the headquarters building or, to reduce confusion and add to the elements of secrecy and surprise, at some high school or shopping center in the general vicinity of the event. Consider restroom facilities, which may not be adequate at a grammar school. Also, a large kitchen might come in handy in the event that the problem continues for an extended period of time.

Identification of Disaster Victims

The coroner or medical examiner is in charge of the deceased and their personal effects, but your responsibility will include assisting those individuals and their deputies in locating and identifying the victims. You will have the additional assistance of military personnel if military vehicles or aircraft are involved. Because of their expertise in such matters, as well as their scientific resources, agents of state and federal departments will be involved. If the vehicle is engaged in interstate transportation, or you are working with an airplane crash, federal agencies are required to investigate. These are a few basic procedures in identification of the victims:

All bodies should be fingerprinted (in some cases, as with infants, they will also be footprinted) regardless of any other means of identification.

The locations from which bodies were removed should be staked or located with another identifying device such as a traffic cone, and each location given a number. The body or body part will be given a corresponding number. These will be located on a master sketch and on finders' individual field sketches.

Prepare a field sketch, indicating all items found during the search. These should later be incorporated into a master sketch, and eventually a prepared chart, to aid investigators in reconstructing the disaster. (Parts of the vehicle or aircraft are handled similarly.)

Items of personal property should be placed with the body if they are still affixed to the body, such as in a pocket. Otherwise, found items will be itemized and filed separately, with their locations identified as are the bodies and body parts.

Photos taken by friends and relatives, including those taken at the time of departure, will help identify bodies by personal appearance as well as articles of clothing.

Pathologists will identify the bodies by the following: dental charts, body build and measurements, hair, and physical abnormalities. Scars, marks, and tattoos as well as surgical scars and body repair items, such as plates and screws in repaired body parts, will aid in the identification. The sex of the victim; physical condition, such as pregnancy; repaired fractures and missing body parts, such as a kidney or appendix; and vasectomies and hysterectomies will further aid in the identification process. Clothing and accessories will also help, including religious medals, jewelry, contact lenses, eyeglasses, cosmetics, and other grooming devices. No matter what the item may be, it should be collected and itemized, and its location of discovery charted so that the experts will eventually be able to complete as much as possible of this identifying task.

UNLAWFUL ASSEMBLY AND RIOT CONTROL

Operations

Once the mobilization of officers and the enactment of the plan for special action occurs, the senior patrol officer on duty must serve the dual purpose of attacking the problem and assuaging the people in the rest of the city by restoring some semblance of police patrol in those other areas as quickly as possible. In some departments, the patrol commander will turn authority and responsibility over to an operations officer, who will then coordinate the police control of the special problem. The patrol commander can then adjust to the situation and provide continuity in patrol coverage throughout the rest of the city as best as can be done with the resources remaining. The operations officer should be completely familiar with the overall planning and training for the problem and assign personnel in the strongest possible positions to implement the emergency operations. That officer must also have sufficient rank to command the immediate cooperation and compliance of all other involved personnel.

Civil unrest seems to be indigenous to civilization, although there are times when it is apparent only in isolated situations or among small numbers of people. Since the end of World War II, civil unrest in the United States has become increasingly widespread. Laborers, students, and minority groups have been most prominent and dramatic in their efforts to effect immediate changes in social practices and standards. They conduct demonstrations, sit-ins, teachings, and nonviolent civil disobedience, which usually begin as noncombative and nondestructive incidents but sometimes end in violence and bitter combat. Some movements include mass criminal conspiracies for the purpose of interfering with lawful processes. Others produce spontaneous riotous outbursts arising out of ostensibly peaceful assemblies.

The continually recurring conditions of civil unrest and lawlessness throughout the country make it apparent that it is possible for a major disturbance to occur any place and time there are enough people for a "quorum." Given the right combination of factors, any situation involving large numbers of people may evolve or explode into an unlawful assembly. Without immediate, decisive police action, the situation could quickly evolve into a full-scale riot.

Although reliable intelligence sources for your particular department may report to your command personnel that there is no impending large-scale unlawful assembly or similar confrontation with your forces, the same intelligence sources will report that the potential is almost always there. There are certain individuals and organizations that watch for potential situations with some "promise" for their own selfish motivation to gain sudden power and wealth under the guise of some seemingly self-less purpose. If the situation appears as though it will be newsworthy and the participants will gain sufficient publicity to serve their needs, there is little doubt that they will appear on the scene and make whatever capital they can out of an unfortunate situation.

Most unlawful assembly situations involve local problems. With quick action, they can be quelled and order can be restored with a minimum of property damage and injuries (see Figures 10–1 and 10–2).

Warning Signals

Sometimes it is possible to determine in advance the potentiality of a civil distrubance of major proportions. Although it may not be possible to predict exactly where or when such a situation may occur, some of the following warning signals should cause you to be more attentive to any event at which large groups of people gather for any purpose. The most volatile are those that are attended by groups of people with a common purpose in mind, such as a rally or advertised demonstration for some single cause.

1. An increase in the recurrence of the same rumor, or the sensationalism of rumors of similar design, such as alleged police abuse of people in certain neighborhoods, or of students, or other alleged defenseless persons.

2. An increase in threatening or insulting signs or pamphlets in commercial or other public places. There may be an attempt to make it socially acceptable to ridicule or display openly contempt for the field patrol officers, thereby reducing the general effectiveness.

3. An increase in the number of incidents of violence or threats of violence. In one incident, a self-appointed champion of a cause made frequent public statements that "if any policeman gets in my way, he should expect to suffer the consequences." One night, during a routine field interview situation, a lone police officer was killed by a single bullet. The next day the newspapers carried a story indicating that a suspect had been taken into cus-

Figure 10-1 At an induction center rally the Oakland police and numerous other agencies demonstrated their ability to cope effectively with a major problem as a team. (Courtesy of the Police Department, Oakland, California.)

Figure 10-2 Moving large numbers of people requires utilization of military formations and use of a reasonable amount of force. (Courtesy of the Police Department, Oakland, California.)

tody for the fatal shooting. It was the same individual who had made the threats.

4. Disturbances at various locations that appear to be of a similar nature as if designed to test the capabilities of the police department, or the decisiveness in the official in charge of an

institution, such as a school, as a prelude to more serious action later. This "testing" process may go on for weeks or months, sometimes for the purpose of stimulating interest and support. Minor confrontations planned for the purpose of causing an officer to become angry and take some injudicious action may be the object of such confrontations. The unjustified use of the police baton, or excessive force in an aggravated arrest situation, or use of a particular restraining technque, such as the carotid hold or neck arm bar, can be cited by any individual or organization that chooses to point to that incident as a visual aid to prove their claim that *the police* are brutal or abusive. Sometimes it is possible to gain the support of a great many well-meaning dupes in such a movement.

5. More than the usual number of disturbances at places of entertainment or sporting events. Again, the disturbances may be a form of "testing" and "baiting" to keep a cause growing. A "movement" must continually have something to stimulate its participants, or it dies of lack of interest.

6. Factional gang fighting or warfare or a series of raids on parties and places of peaceful congregation. These incidents create a dissipation of the police department's effective strength at a single location.

7. Threats and attacks on private property. Such attacks may be engineered to appear as a popular cause, and they may be used to draw the police into private affairs that are noncriminal in nature, placing the officers in an unpopular position. Sometimes the incidents are designed to appear politically oriented so that the police are condemned for acting as "political oppressors."

8. An increasing need for the use of force in effecting arrests, as though there were a planned effort to "bait" the police.

9. An accompanying increase in the number of complaints about abusive practices of the police, and continuing claims that such complaints are receiving no satisfactory action.

10. Public name-calling and a general attitude of contempt and disrespect for police officers.

11. Significant increase in the amount of graffiti observed throughout the jurisdiction, indicating an increase in intergang conflict.

12. Court cases involving police use of force, such as the police beating of Mr. Rodney King by the officers of the Los Angeles Police Department, and the subsequent state and federal trials that angered large segments of the population throughout the United States.

Police Purpose and Objectives

At the scene of a disturbance—major or minor—the police purpose is constant: to protect human lives and personal property and to restore order and peace in the community. The police officer is a *peace officer*, and it is your responsibility to maintain peace where it exists and to restore peace when there has been a breach. Restoration of the peace is accomplished by persuasion when possible and by force if necessary, but by that degree of force that is necessary, no more.

The objectives of the police department at the scene of an unlawful assembly are containment, dispersal, prevention of reentry arrest of violators, and operation according to some system of priorities.

1. *Containment.* Unlawful assembly and riot situations are as contagious as the bubonic plague unless they are quarantined from the unaffected areas of the community. Once the specific area is identified, it should be closed off and contained until the problem has passed.

2. *Dispersal.* Any large crowd that has formed that acquires the characteristics of an unlawful assembly must be dispersed. Although the original purpose of the gathering may have been lawful, the current nature of the assembly at the time of the officer's arrival may clearly distinguish it as being unlawful. Once that is determined, it is your sworn responsibility to command the people to disperse. Once you have given the order, allow them a realistic amount of time to leave and provide avenues by which they may leave.

3. *Prevention of reentry.* Once the people have been moved out of an area and dissipated into smaller groups, protect the area against their return.

4. *Arrest of violators.* Whenever practicable, one of the first acts of the first officers to arrive on the scene of a disturbance is to locate and isolate the individuals who are inciting the crowd to more positive action and those who are flagrantly violating the law. Once these individuals are removed, the problem is often solved. If you do arrest such violators, immediately remove them.

5. *Establishment of priorities.* Whenever you arrive on the scene of any sizable crowd disturbance, you will be outnumbered considerably. It is always necessary to establish a system of priorities depending upon the circumstances at the moment of the action, then to proceed according to those priorities.

Although you have given the order to disperse and must give the people time to leave the area, it may still be necessary to rescue people in the crowd who are under attack or have some other urgent need to be rescued. In that case, you may have to resort to a "flying wedge" formation on foot or by cars and/or motorcycles, backed up by horse patrol units to get into the crowd and back out as quickly and safely as possible with the person to be rescued. The use of officers on horseback works very well for crowd control. Avoid the use of police dogs in these situations, as they could become confused and not be able to distinguish the "good guys" from the "bad guys" with the large crowds of noisy and unruly people.

Psychological Influences

The agitator, or leader, who attempts to incite a riot, or who assumes control of a riot already in progress and directs it to serve his purposes, has several factors working for him in such a situation. He may use rumors and propaganda techniques that will give the lagging riot impetus by passing the word that someone has been killed by a police officer or that some reprehensible act has been committed by the opposing faction. In the mass confusion that is taking place, the "inciter" may actually create his own incidents; for example, he might bait an officer to use force upon him and then on to his injuries as "visual proof" of police brutality. Gaudy bandages or self-imposed head wounds, which are often superficial but which bleed profusely, are not unusual in some riotous situations.

The novelty of the situation works for the inciter, as the new an strange circumstances become a "fun thing" or a "happening" for the thrill-seeker. The anonymity works equally well for the agitator, or inciter, who remains in the background and directs others to carry out his orders in the "everyone is doing it" atmosphere. Under the guise of group behavior, the riot allows the individual to release inhibitions that he would contain under normal conditions. Consider the testimony of suspects in cases where brutal gang killings have occurred in mob actions. The suspects interviewed say such things as: "I hit him on the head too....Everyone else was doing it....Besides, he was probably dead already....If I didn't hit him, somebody would'a hit me."

There is always the feeling in a crowd disturbance situation that there is strength in numbers, and even the timid individual sometimes assumes the posture of the ferocious beast when backed up by several protectors. Suggestibility works to the advantage of the inciter in a crowd; the crowd is more likely to accept his ideas as their own and act on them than when its members are alone. Consider the situation in which a child molester is arrested after a chase and a tense neighborhood scene is created. The victimized child is screaming, the enraged parents are demanding action, the officer is attempting to talk to the suspect rationally and the suspect's obscene epithets are reaching the ears of the people in the crowd; suddenly, someone shouts, "Get that b——d!" This situation could quite easily evolve into a riot.

Stages in the Formation of a Mob

Many experts on mob psychology say that there are certain perceptible stages that manifest themselves during the formation of a riot. As a field police officer, I have felt or sensed these stages. They are more subtle than they appear on paper, but they can be recognized. To deal effectively with a crowd, it is imperative that you make an effort to ascertain what point of development the crowd has reached and determine whether it has yet reached mob proportions. A mob will have to be handled differently from a crowd, since there is little value in attempting to reason or debate with a mob. Only some sort of dramatic action will jolt the mob members back to the reality that they are individuals and that dramatic action should not assume the characteristic of an "overreaction" by the police officers.

Mob psychology experts have used various titles to identify the progressive stages in the development of a mob. For the purpose of this discussion, these stages are referred to as stage 1, stage 2, and stage 3.

Stage 1. At this stage, the crowd is still functioning as a conglomeration of individuals. There is some milling about, but any fighting or pushing taking place occurs in independent and unrelated events. The atmosphere is charged with some common feeling of impending activity that seems to act as a form of gravity that pulls the people together, but at this stage it is difficult to define the source of the feeling. It may be some widely spread rumor that a specific event, such as a gang fight, is about to take place.

At stage 1 it is possible to move spectators and disinterested bystanders away from the scene and to begin counteracting the problem by arresting individual law violators, removing them from the scene, and generally taking effective and decisive enforcement action. If you locate any anticipated agitators, divert them from the scene.

Stage 2. In the second stage, the crowd members lose their individuality and begin to function as a single unit. The agitators have assumed their positions and are beginning to see the results of their suggestions. Opportunists or confederates of the leaders may be circulating in the crowd, getting it moving and thinking as a single unit.

Stage 3. By now, the mob is functioning as a single unit and its leaders are in control. Any event is likely to precipitate violent action. Some officers have appropriately referred to stage 3 as the "riot just waiting to happen."

At this stage, the most effective action is decisive police movement in a show of force to move the people out of the area and to cause them to break down into small groups. Little reasoning, if any, is likely to be effective at stage 3. All three stages could probably be classified as unlawful assembly. Fortunately, it is possible to deal effectively with the majority of crowd control situations and thus prevent devastating riots.

Procedure for Handling an Unlawful Assembly

1. *Assess the situation.* Before you take any immediate action, except for a lifesaving rescue, see what you have. Determine how much assistance you are going to need, and where. If the crowd is large and getting larger, at least some of the officers should be assigned around the perimeter to "peel off" the crowd by diverting them away, and by closing the area and keeping additional vehicle and pedestrian traffic from coming in.

2. *Communicate.* As in the case of other types of major police problems, getting the information to your home base and other officers you are going to need to assist—opening up communications—is more important than attempting to tackle the problem yourself when it is obvious that additional help is needed. Keep this line of communication going, even if it means that you do nothing until help arrives. If you must leave to rescue someone from a brutal assault or to attempt an immediate arrest that cannot wait, make use of noninvolved bystanders to handle the radio while you are away from it. It is better than having no communication at all.

3. *Establish a command center and wait for help to arrive.* Try to position yourself and your unit close enough to the crowd so that you can see the activity and they can see and hear you when you give them the command to disperse.

4. *Take immediate rescue and rescue action once your help arrives.* Lives and property are always predominantly important. As for the persons you will arrest first, you should concentrate on the people who are causing the disturbance, if possible.

5. *Give the dispersal order and help the people leave the scene.* At this point your primary concern is to reduce the size of the crowd, hopefully to break it up completely, but at least reduce it to a core group of uncooperative participants whom you are going to arrest for failing to comply. The procedure should be similar to the following:

    a. Assign witnesses at strategic locations who can testify that they saw and heard you issue the command to disperse. Use reliable witnesses for this purpose, including news reporters, judges, and public officials. Television crews and news photographers are ideal for witnessing the event, and their assistance should be solicited.

    b. Order the crowd to disperse. Use amplification equipment, if available. The order should be in accordance with the laws of your state and should include a statement of your identity and the authority for the order. It is an order, not a threat. Give the crowd a realistic time limit within which to disperse.

    c. Order all assigned officers to stand ready, guarding the perimeter, but making it possible for the people to leave as directed. Officers who are carrying batons should hold them with both hands at port arms position, never in a menacing manner, such as in a waving position.

    d. Expedite the departure of the people who are commanded to disperse.

    e. Repeat the order at least three times so that as many people

as possible can hear you. Be sure that all the people understand you. Use interpreters, if necessary.

f. Wait until the expiration of the time limit. Do not use a "count-
down," or "baiting," technique with the people. Merely wait the
stated time.

g. At the end of the time limit, arrest the offenders. If the crowd
is complying but for some reason there is a slowdown in traffic,
it may be necessary to use a "long count" for the time limit, but
do not make a game of it.

Crowd Control Formations

Three crowd control formations are shown in Figure 10–3.

To Assemble the Squad. The command is: SQUAD, FALL IN. At the
command "FALL IN," the members of the squad form a line according to
height. The tallest officer, referred to as the "Point," stands at the right
end of the formation. As each officer falls in to the left in descending order
of height, each officer except the one at the left end extends the left arm

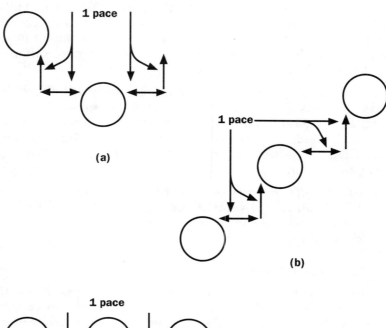

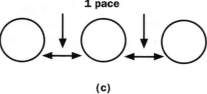

Figure 10-3 (a) Wedge, (b) diagonal, and (c) line formations.

laterally at shoulder height, palm down, fingers extended and together, touching the shoulder of the officer to the left.

The point officer looks forward, while all others in the line turn their heads and eyes to their right and adjusts position as necessary to make sure the right shoulder is touching the extended fingers of the officer to the right. As soon as the line is correct, all officers promptly drop their arms to the side and face forward.

To Align the Squad. The command is: DRESS RIGHT, DRESS. At the command, each officer except the one on the left repeats the procedure followed when they fell in. The squad leader steps to the end of the line and faces down the line to see that it is aligned. If necessary, the squad leader directs any officer to move who is not aligned. When the alignment is correct, the command is "FRONT." and all squad members drop the arms to the side and turn their heads to the front.

To Count Off. The command is: SQUAD, COUNT OFF. At the command "COUNT OFF," the squad leader, who is standing and moving to be in the best position outside the line, will call out "ONE." On command of "COUNT OFF," all officers except the point on the right will turn their heads to the right. Starting with the point officer, who calls out "TWO," each officer in line will call the next number in sequence and turn the head forward as the number is called. This counting-off procedure is necessary when the squad leader is going to designate different officers by number to different assignments.

The Squad. A police squad is approximately 12 officers, including the leader, but it is not mandatory. In a 12-officer squad, the leader is number 1 and the assistant is number 12 (see Figure 10–4). If special weapons or tear gas is used, the next-to-last, or number 11 officer carries the weapon. More than one officer may carry special weapons, which is optional with the squad leader.

Squad, Single File (Column or Line). The verbal command is: SQUAD, FALL IN, SINGLE FILE. The hand signal is: hand above the head with index finger extended vertically.

2 3 4 5 6 7 8 9 10 11 12
1
Line of movement

Squad, Column of Twos. The verbal command is: FALL IN, COLUMN OF TWOS. The hand signal is: two fingers extended vertically from the fist held above the head. (As a general rule, a single column is used to move the squad through a narrow passage, and the column of twos is the formation from which crowd formations evolve.)

2 4 6 8 10 12
3 5 7 9 11 odd numbers on left
1
Line of movement

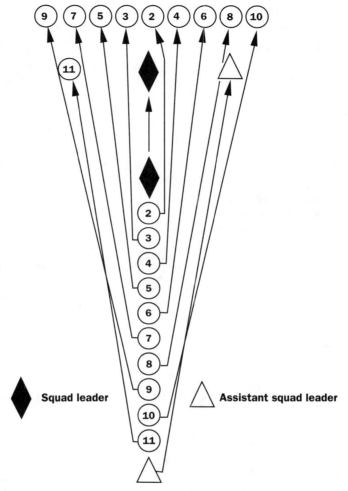

Figure 10-4   Squad line.

Squad Column Change: Single File to Column of Twos. Marching in a squad column, the squad leader now wants a column of twos in preparation to form other formations. The command is: Column of twos, march (two fingers). At the command, the even-numbered officers will "mark time," or march in place. The odd-numbered officers will take one step to the left and one step forward, then "mark time" while aligning themselves. All officers will continue marking time until the squad leader commands them to "HALT" or move into another formation.

Squad Column Change: Column of Twos to Single File. The command is: SQUAD COLUMN, MARCH (one finger). At the command, the squad will continue to move at the normal pace unless ordered to "DOUBLE TIME." The odd-numbered officers will find their respective places and move back into the single line and check to be sure they are in a straight line and continue to move until they receive another command.

Squad Diagonal. The verbal command is: SQUAD DIAGONAL, MARCH. The hand signal is: hand circled above head as one would use the "assemble" signal, then pointed in the direction the diagonal is to go. The number 2 officer moves to the location designated by the squad leader, and the other officers follow in the same direction, assuming a position one-half step to the rear and left (or right) of the officer immediately in front (see Figure 10–5).

Squad Wedge. The verbal command is: SQUAD WEDGE, MOVE. The hand signal is: hands above head with fingers meeting in an inverted V. The number 2 officer moves to the spot designated by the squad leader, with the even-numbered officers on the right and the odd-numbered officers to the left diagonally off the number 2 officer (see Figure 10–6).

Drawing Batons. Batons should be drawn prior to moving the squad into a crowd formation. The most effective position for batons in most

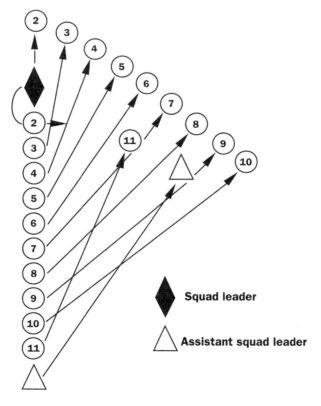

Figure 10-5 Squad diagonal.

crowd situations is the PORT position. The command is: PORT ARMS. The squad leader signals by drawing the baton and placing it in the port position, making sure that the thong is securely in place. The thongs are positioned on the command "PORT" and drawn on the command "ARMS."

Strike Duty

The key to effective police action at the scene of a labor–management conflict is to be completely fair and objective. It is not your role to assume that either side is right or wrong. The police responsibility is to establish contact with both the company being struck and the leader of the strikers

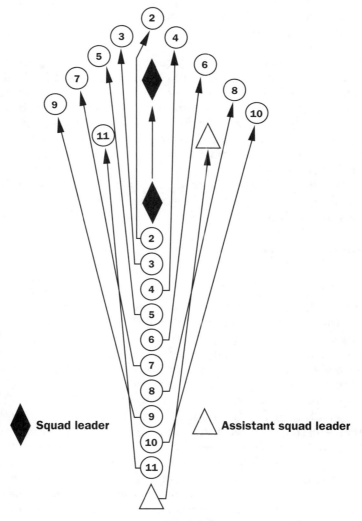

Figure 10-6   Squad wedge.

and to point out the police role to enforce the law and to protect life and property. Ask for the cooperation of all parties on both sides of the dispute. The police concern is compliance with the laws and protection of the people from personal injury or property damage.

When working at the scene of a strike, provide for the free flow of pedestrian and vehicle traffic on the streets, the driveways, and the sidewalks. Whatever you do, handle the matter in such a way that it does not indicate any alliance or sympathy with either side of the dispute. In one strike situation, officers erred by using the company parking lot for their personal vehicles. In another, some of the officers used the company cafeteria to eat their lunch, and in still another, one or two of the assigned officers took advantage of discount prices to buy hams. None of these actions can be condoned any more than can an officer be allowed to carry one of the picket signs for an elderly worker who may have stopped to rest his or her feet.

Injunctions are often obtained to keep the pickets to a minimum number. Enforcement of injunctions is handled by bailiffs of the court, such as the sheriff, marshal, or constable. The municipal police officer cannot generally enforce injunctions. Arrests should be made for flagrant violations, but any situations that have personal animosity involved as well should be referred to an office conference on the following day. Take all the necessary information and prepare a complete report. After a night of calm deliberation when the parties can discuss the matter away from the picket line, a more appropriate course of action can be worked out. Of course, this is limited to nonaggravated situations and should not include cases in which it is clearly obvious that an arrest is necessary.

AIRCRAFT CRASHES

An aircraft crash involves police response similar to that response that would follow any disaster of the same proportions.

Injuries and damage are usually of great magnitude because of the large number of passengers involved and the size of the airplane falling from great heights. Aviation is increasing in importance as a mode of commercial and personal travel as well as an integral part of our military defenses. Aircraft crashes—as with railroad and motor vehicle crashes—are going to happen. Certain procedures should be followed when they do occur.

Military aircraft accidents are the primary concern of the military service concerned. Aircraft accidents are the concern of the Federal Aviation Authority and the National Transportation Safety Board and are covered by the Federal Aviation Regulations for pilots. Methods for responding to an accident involving either type of aircraft—military or civilian—are the same as for medical aid and rescue operations, but there are other important differences. Once the immediate emergency needs are met, yet while they are still underway, certain critical factors must be borne in mind. Victims and debris may be dispersed over a wide area surrounding the accident scene, and the danger of fire may be great. Approach the scene with extreme caution. As quickly as you can, take immediate steps to close the area to everyone except those whose presence is absolutely essential.

When approaching military aircraft, stay clear of the front and rear of any tanks or pods that are carried externally on the wings or fuselage. They may contain missiles or rockets. Establish a *no smoking* rule to help reduce the possibility of fire. The following information has been taken from a Department of Defense booklet *What to Do and How to Report Military Aircraft Accidents.*[1]

HOW TO USE ACCESS HATCHES, RESCUE POINT, AND EXITS

Locations of escape hatches, doors, and exits from all military aircraft are indicated by orange-yellow markings on the outside of the aircraft. On jet aircraft a red rescue arrow will indicate the rescue points. Instructions are stenciled at this arrow for the jettisoning of canopies or hatches. Use care in jettisoning these cartridge-actuated devices as they are displaced violently. When operating jettisoning controls always position yourself well to the side.

(The booklet depicts an inverted triangle inscribed warning, which gives instructions for jet aircraft equipped with ejection seats. The marking is place don the side of the aircraft.)

1. *Push button to open door.*
2. *Pull "T" handle out (distance will be specified for various aircraft) to jettison canopy.*

Do not raise, move, or tamper with arm rests or crewmembers' seats, or any controls painted yellow and black as these activate the ejection seats and are extremely dangerous. Never move any handle, lever, or device inside the cockpit if you are not thoroughly familiar with the canopy jettison and seat ejection mechanism for that particular aircraft.

Before removing survivors, always unfasten the seat belt, shoulder and/or parachute harness, and oxygen mask as well as radio cords and oxygen lead.

---

[1]U.S. Department of Defense, *What to Do and How to Report Military Aircraft Accidents,* Joint Service Booklet 1 (Washington, D.C.: U.S. Department of the Navy, 1968). Available from U.S. Naval Aviation Center, Naval Air Station, Norfolk, Va.

CHECKLIST: HOW TO REPORT

Tell the operator (or radio dispatcher) that you wish to report a military aircraft crash, collect, to the nearest military installation.

When the call is answered, state that you are reporting an aircraft crash, and include at least the following basic information in your conversation:

1. *Give your name and location where calling from.*
2. *Report that a military aircraft crashed at (time) and that there (is) (is not) a fire.*
3. *Give accurate geographical location, road net, distances and/or compass directions on how to reach the crash site. (Prominent ground and air landmarks can be useful to both military ground vehicles and rescue and fire fighting helicopters.)*
4. *Crew parachuted (or landed with airplane).*
5. *Medical help needed.*
6. *Crew believed to be all dead (give number).*
7. *Report damage to private property or civilian injuries.*
8. *Report any of the followiong:*
   a. *Number on tail of aircraft*
   b. Type or model of aircraft
   c. *Where someone will meet the rescue team*
   d. *Nearest suitable helicopter landing area (flat open field, free of poles and wires)*
9. *Make sure the report is understood.*
10. *Any other information of possible immediate value.*
11. *Please wait for any questions before hanging up.*
12. *Leave number for possible callback, if possible.*

The press may be represented and such personnel may be collecting data for their media. The military team that will be dispatched to the scene will have a press relations officer who will handle all information releases. Except for injured persons, leave everything as you find it and wait for the military to assume control of the site. If there is some distance to the nearest military installation, certain rescue operations may continue, including the extinguishing of a fire or prevention of further damage, but nothing else should be disturbed for any reason.

In the event of a civilian aircraft crash, perform whatever rescue operations are necessary and evacuate the immediate vicinity as a precautionary measure. Notify the nearest office of the National Transportation

Safety Board: Anchorage, Alaska; Chicago, Illinois; Denver, Colorado; Fort Worth, Texas; Kansas City, Missouri; Los Angeles, California; Miami, Florida; New York, New York; Oakland, California; Seattle, Washington; and Washington, D.C. If the field office is some distance away, notify the nearest airport that has a control tower and request that the crash be reported to the Federal Aviation Administration. The actual reporting of any aircraft accident is the responsibility of the pilot of the involved aircraft, but notification should be prompt. If the pilot had filed a flight plan while flying under visual flight rules or was flying under instrument flight rules, his failure to report in within a prescribed period of time will cause a search for his whereabouts to be instituted by the agencies concerned.

When reporting a civilian aircraft accident, be sure to provide the airplane identification number and its exact location. As with the military aircraft, close the area to spectators and allow only authorized personnel. The National Transportation Safety Board or Federal Aviation Administration investigator will assume responsibility for any of the wreckage, cargo, records, or any other items they deem necessary for their investigation. They are the only persons who may release any of those items. According to Section 430.10(b) of the National Transportation Safety Board regulations, wreckage, mail, or cargo may be moved prior to the time the board or an authorized representative takes custody of such articles only to

1. Remove persons injured or trapped.
2. Protect the wreckage from further damage.
3. Protect the public from injury.

Whenever it is necessary to move any items, if possible arrange to have photographs taken of the scene, prepare a sketch, and make sufficient notes so that you may be able to reconstruct as accurately as possible the scene as you found it.

BOMBS AND BOMB THREATS

Anarchists have been known to use bombs quite effectively to destroy lives and property and to cause a demoralizing effect on people. Sometimes as devastating as the actual detonation of a bomb is a telephoned threat that there will be a bombing. Although you may be reasonably sure that a bomb will not go off as announced, you are probably in no position to decide to "call the bluff" by telling the caller to go ahead and blow up the building named in the threat. The call must be handled as though you expect to find a bomb, and your search must be so exhaustive that you are reasonably sure you have not overlooked a single possibility (see Figure 10–7).

There are two reasons why it is of tremendous importance to identify

Figure 10-7 Handling and disposing of bombs is a task for specialists. (Courtesy of the Police Department, New York, New York.)

the party who telephones someone to notify them that a bomb has been planted in a particular location. One is that the threatening call itself is a crime whether an actual bomb was planted or not. The second is that in the event that a bomb has been planted, the caller is a key person to locate and question. He may be the individual who planted it, or he may have participated in the crime, or he may have information concerning the crime and want to do what he can to preserve lives without having to identify himself. If possible, determine what type of bomb was planted. Sometimes the caller will tell what it is and where it is.

In the event that the telephone operator who receives the bomb threat call has a tape recorder attachment, now is the time to activate the recorder. It may be possible to match voices later when a suspect is located. This is an excellent reason why all police lines should have recording capabilities to tape incoming messages.

Upon arriving on the scene where the bomb is purported to be, contact the calling party—if he or she is at the scene—and locate the device reported to be a bomb, if its location is known. Immediately report to the dispatcher that you have arrived, and report also the progress of your investigation to date. If one is available, consider the use of a telephone for the call because you might have a radio-activated device in the vicinity. Keep in continuous communication with the dispatcher if possible so that any progress reports ay be made as the need arises. If the bomb has not been located, take immediate steps to begin a search and protect the people who may be injured from any blast.

Establish a perimeter within which you believe the bomb may be found. Request additional assistance to help keep the area closed, if any need exists. Decide whether to evacuate the premises or to conduct your search without the knowledge of the people who occupy the premises. If the bomb threat involves a school or some other building where infrequent and unannounced fire drills are held, consider having a fire drill to evacuate the building without fanfare. If you must evacuate, do so quickly but in an orderly manner. Evacuation should be to a distance of at least 300 feet (or half a city block).

Your own calm manner under situations such as this may be the deciding factor in whether or not other people at the scene will panic. Keep cool at all costs.

Search the premises for the device, with one officer in charge of the search. Be sure to search every available part of the premises, including those where you believe no bomb would be planted. When searching for a bomb or anything that is foreign to the place being searched, take along someone who is familiar with the place to be searched. If any item is unfamiliar to that person, then it should be considered suspect.

A bomb may be *any* size or shape, and it may be placed inside *any* kind of container. When you find any object that looks as though it may be what you are looking for, evacuate that portion of the building and isolate the device. Allow no one to enter the area or to handle the object. At this point you should have someone contact the nearest military installation or one of the larger neighboring police departments—unless your department is that one—and request the services of an explosive ordinance disposal team. If such a team is at your service, protect the area and wait for their arrival; then continue according to their instructions.

If no bomb disposal team is available and the task of removing the suspected bomb from the premises falls to you proceed carefully with the operation yourself. Have gas and electric utilities shut off if possible. Set up a *no smoking* policy immediately. Remove any flammable or explosive substances from the vicinity of the suspected object to avoid a more serious problem than would occur if only a suspected bomb would go off. Do not attempt to open any container or twist any mechanism. If you must remove the device from the premises, do so with extreme caution. Some explosives may detonate quite readily, while others require another explosive to cause a chain series that results in the final explosion of the more powerful material. Move the device to an open area and place it under guard; then contact bomb experts by radio or telephone and follow their instructions.

CRISIS INTERVENTION

A crisis as seen by the patrol officer is any event that involves individuals—usually two or more in conflict—who have reached such a debilitating mental state that they seem to have lost the ability to cope with a situation through what one would consider normal methods, such as discussion or negotiation. The event that precipitates such a crisis may be a problem that the individual cannot cope with, such as loss of a loved one, dismissal from a job, an unwanted or unexpected pregnancy, notification of divorce, or marital unfaithfulness. Other situations that may lead to a crisis situation include interpersonal relationship breakdowns, notification that someone has a fatal or incurable disease, a sudden loss of position, or situation that will cause irreparable damage to one's reputation. Excessive use of alcohol or drugs may cause the person to lose ability to reason things out. The crisis occurs when the individual reaches that point when there seems to be no way out of the problem, whether the event occurs instantaneously or whether it has been building up over a period of time.

As a field officer, you will usually be dealing with the symptoms and the crisis itself rather than the causes. Your role will be into intervene and defuse the situation and then attempt to arrange for some sort of immediate assistance with referral for professional assistance. If your department has a crisis intervention team, or a staff psychologist who is specifically trained and assigned to crisis intervention, you will have support available to you. In some jurisdictions a mental health unit may be available for field follow-up to crisis situations. In other jurisdictions, it will be you alone, with a possible follow-up by the family minister or rabbi or family doctor.

Since this book is not intended to prepare you to be a crisis intervention specialist, but is merely a guide in how to proceed with the initial stages and what to do until the specialist arrives, here are a few basic guidelines.

1. *Assess the situation.* Immediately upon your arrival, attempt to identify the cause of the crisis and what you may do to defuse the hostilities or high emotionalism. Is there a crime being committed that will require immediate enforcement action? Is there a severe medical problem, such as wounds or injuries that must be treated? Are adversaries still in confrontation who must be separated? Is there someone present who appears to be making the problem worse by continuing to harass or agitate the disturbed individual?

2. *Take immediate corrective action* Separate the combatants and isolate them sufficiently that they cannot see or hear each other. If arrest is warranted, do so and immediately have the offender removed from the vicinity. If medical help is needed, see that appropriate help is provided. If the crisis is an impending suicide, attempt to defuse any contributory factors, such as distraught friends or relatives whose presence and actions are making matters worse. Get those people out of the area. Taking a minimum of risk for your own safety, attempt to disarm or neutralize any individual who is intending immediate violence to self or another.

3. *Listen and observe.* In a crisis situation, one of your most effective techniques is to make a deliberate effort to see exactly what is happening. At this point, attempt to be totally nonjudgmental, and devote your full attention to what the principal actors in this crisis are saying and doing. You may be confronting a self-blaming victim of a sex crime who believes that the only way to preserve his honor is to kill himself. A person may have been disgraced by discovery of fraud by the auditors at the person's bank. If the crisis stems from a situation that has been exaggerated in the person's mind, you may be able to discuss the matter and bring it back into a more rational perspective.

4. *Employ crisis diffusion techniques.* When you are attempting to diffuse a crisis situation, there are a few suggestions for you to consider:

a. Keep your voice at a low volume and speak slowly. With an agitated adversary, your own attempts to outshout or dominate the conversation are not likely to work. Calmly repeating words of comfort or assurance or understanding may have a soothing effect on the agitated individual. If the individual wants to argue with you, it will be necessary for that person to quiet down to listen to what you have to say.

b. Nonverbal communications should indicate openness and willingness to listen. A posture of folded arms in a dominant position will not get the same positive results that you are likely to get by keeping your arms open and your gestures indicating that you are willing to negotiate. Consider your earlier exposure in this book to body language.

c. Make eye contact with the person you are addressing. This tends to underline your sincerity and willingness to listen. It also indicates to the subject that she or he has your full attention.

    d. Touching the person you are talking with may help to keep the lines of communication open. This one you are going to have to play by ear. Some people will interpret your touching them as overly dominant or sexually aggressive. With others, there seems to flow the energy of a positive contact, and the person you are touching on the arm will probably give you more attention because there is physical contact as well as visual contact.

    e. Attempt a compromise. If the person you are addressing feels that there is some dignity even to the situation of being taken into custody, you will probably have more success in keeping the person under physical control as well as emotional control.

    5. *Follow-up.* Even if you have diffused the crisis situation, you have probably not solved any problems. At best, you have more than likely only postponed a problem. At your earliest convenience, make follow-up reports and arrange for professionals in psychology or family counseling, or spiritual guidance, or whatever other need there appears to be, to pursue the matter so as to avoid any repeat performance of the crisis you have just addressed.

MENTALLY AND EMOTIONALLY DISTURBED INDIVIDUALS

Civil laws usually provide for temporary custody of individuals who appear to be in need of immediate emergency observation because of some emotional or mental breakdown. They are called to police attention usually through some erratic behavior or act of violence that the subject's friends or relatives cannot handle without assistance.

    In some states, the patrol officer is empowered to take people suspected of being in need of emergency care to a psychiatric clinic and have them held for observation by psychiatrists, if the officer believes such action is necessary to the health and safety of the subject or other persons. In some cases, it requires more formal action, such as court hearings similar to a trial, which will require testimony of witnesses as to aberrant behavior and other actions of the person alleged to be in need of psychiatric care.

    When responding to a call involving an individual who appears mentally or emotionally disturbed, be extremely careful to handle the person with understanding, diplomacy, and tact. Symptoms may include such things as dramatic and sudden changes in behavior, loss of memory, mistreatment of a loved one, a sudden, impulsive act of theft, extreme depression, or anxiety that is out of proportion to the circumstances that appear to be causing the anxiety. There may suddenly be a strong dependence on someone to make simple decisions, or an intense suspicion or distrust of theirs, or an intense feeling that someone is plotting against the individual. The individual may talk to himself or hear voices, or he may be displaying dangerous or belligerent behavior for no apparent reason. The mentally or emotionally disturbed individual may be in a very docile mood for a while and then become extremely violent without any apparent cause. For that reason, whenever you believe you have such a person in custody, use ample restraining equipment as a precautionary measure for his protection as well as your own. Be aware, also, that certain symptoms may be mistaken as indicators of mental or emotional disorders, for example, the sweating or twitching of a diabetic, the delirium that accompanies fever or severe infection, the irritability of the person suffering from meningitis, or the violence or confused state of an epileptic.

When arrested, some felons may feign mental illness in an attempt to avoid punishment for their crime, using the pretense of disorientation as a defense against the claim that they formed specific intent to commit their crimes. To place such a suspect in a psychiatric ward might provide the subject with his defense. He can, for example, show that you were obviously impressed with his lack of mental or emotional control because you placed him in a psychiatric ward for mental observation. If there are obvious manifestations of mental or emotional upset, you have no choice but to place him under mental observation. But if there is some doubt and the case is an extremely important one, it might be sounder to place him in an isolated cell and immediately consult with the prosecuting attorney. The attorney may decide to have a psychiatrist conduct an immediate examination and make his evaluation, to assure proper care and treatment for the suspect if he is truly in need of psychiatric care. Some jurisdictions have a standing procedure that requires an immediate psychiatric evaluation at any time a criminal homicide suspect is arrested. This policy allows the officer to obtain a determination as to the suspect's mental state as soon after the commission of the crime as possible. At the same time, the act of causing the psychiatric evaluation carries with it no reflection of any opinions the arresting officer may or may not have had.

As an aid in understanding the mentally and emotionally disturbed, the following descriptions and definitions are presented from a layperson's point of view. They are merely items of information, and in no way should they ever be used as a guide for making any type of diagnosis.

A *psychosis* is a gross and persistent falsification of conventional reality that leaves the person unable to manage conventional reality with any degree of effectiveness. The major components of psychosis are delusions and hallucinations. A *delusion* is a faulty belief that is motivated primarily by the individual's needs or wishes and has no basis in fact. An *hallucination*, conversely, is usually manifested in a visual image that is quite vivid and real to the individual who experiences it. The hallucination does not actually exist, but there is probably some correspondence between the hallucination and some actual sensory input, and the individual is willing to take some action based upon that perceptual experience. Many people have hallucinations when encountering unusual situations and are not necessarily suffering from psychosis, but the hallucinations do not recur once the situations have passed. Hallucinations include those visions that appear in the middle of a desert highway as puddles of water or an oasis in the middle of sand dunes. Another hallucination might be something that looks like a prowler, which is actually a hibiscus shrub brushing against the screen. Psychoses are mental illnesses.

Paranoia is a set of fixed delusional beliefs that are accompanied by clear and orderly thinking outside the delusion system. The true paranoid, or "classical paranoid," as some psychologists prefer, may be highly intelligent and so persuasive that he will successfully recruit other persons to help him in his war against his enemies. He may not be identified as easily as the individual with a *paranoid reaction*, who does not handle the problem with as much logic or intelligence as the true paranoid. Paranoia manifests itself in inferences and beliefs that the subject is "being talked about," "being made fun of," or "is the object of a hate campaign" or that someone is trying to get rid of him. The paranoid has been described as "vigilant, suspicious, distrustful, insecure, and chronically anxious." According to some theorists, the paranoid may justify his intense hatred of some object, such as Hitler's hatred of the Jews, by stating, "I hate you so intensely because you hate me and you are trying to get rid of me."

Schizophrenia is a thinking disorder. According to some experts, approximately 80 percent of the mentally ill population is schizophrenic. There are several subcategories of schizophrenia, such as the catatonic state, demonstrated by the patient's rigidly held position for sometimes interminable periods of time, and the hebephrenic state, in which the subject continually acts childlike and silly. Indications of the schizophrenic condition appear in three different ways: (1) The subject's language may be rambling or tangential; he may make up meaningless rhymes, or echo everything he hears. (2) The subject may show his split personality by an incongruence between his expressed ideas and his emotional responses, which indicate two thought processes operating simultaneously. (3) The subject may isolate or alienate himself from the rest of society and pull himself into his personal shell.

A person who is suffering from a *psychoneurotic condition*, or a *neurosis*, is most likely to be observed in a continuous state of anxiety. The erratic behavior would more than likely be displayed by reaction to the anxiety in the form of rationalization, projection, or displacement. The individual may be shaking uncontrollably. Another symptom of the neurosis is depression without explanation. Reaction to a police contact might be exaggerated by a psychoneurotic condition, and the person might react violently to an arrest, or a field interview, or some type of personal confrontation.

As a field officer, you will not be expected to diagnose the individual, nor are you expected to distinguish between the many variations of psychoses and neuroses. Your principal concern is for your own safety and then that of the individual, and making an effort to see that the person receives appropriate professional attention.

You are likely to encounter the mentally or emotionally disturbed individual under almost any type of circumstances. Many people are emotionally upset for the moment because of the nature of the situation, such as an intense family fight or a repossession confrontation, but they return to a state of relative normality fairly quickly. Whenever you encounter a person who appears to exhibit a mental or emotional problem more deep-seated than the immediate circumstance warrants, the following guidelines may assist you:

1. Approach the subject with extreme caution. Maintain a calm and casual manner.

2. Speak to the subject by name, if you know it. Your tone of voice should be soothing, but firm and businesslike.

3. Say or do nothing that might threaten or intimidate.

4. Avoid arguing or scolding the subject, and don't allow anyone else to do so.

5. Make use of friends or relatives who know how to talk to, and deal with, the subject, unless there is friction between them. The subject might have more trust and confidence in you if you appear to be getting along with the friends or relatives.

6. Whenever possible, try to stall until you have a follow-up officer on the scene. This type of situation might be more volatile than a routine arrest.

7. If the situation warrants it, and you take the subject into custody, do so carefully. Avoid pain-producing holds, if possible, and keep your gun and other weapons out of the subject's reach.

8. When you transfer custody to psychiatric personnel, give these people as much information about the symptoms you observed and all the details about their behavior. This will help in the diagnosis. Do the same when you prepare your reports.

SUMMARY

Unusual occurrences may require more planning and preparation than other types of situations that you encounter on a more regular basis. There is always the possibility of some type of disaster occurring in your jurisdiction, regardless of where you work. In this chapter, we have discussed some of the basic procedures to follow whenever you are confronted with a disaster, such as an airplane or train crash, a bombing or bomb threat, flood, or other natural disaster.

Although civil disturbances of any magnitude do not occur with the same frequency as in the 1960s, they still pose serious problem to the police, and we have covered some of the basic concepts of crowd control and riot prevention.

We then covered somewhat more routine types of situations as crisis intervention and handling the mentally and emotionally disturbed. You will be expected to handle those types of situations with the delicacy of an angel and the firmness of a warrior. Of primary importance is your own personal safety.

EXERCISES AND STUDY QUESTIONS

1. Describe the equipment that your department has at its disposal for disaster response.
2. What special types of training would you recommend for your department, keeping in mind the geography, topography, and other unique characteristics of the area?
3. What type of unexpected disaster could occur in the jurisdiction where you live?
4. List the locations and types of disasters that could occur in the jurisdiction where you live that might be anticipated as a once-in-a-century event or that might occur any year.
5. Describe in sequence how you would respond to the scene of an aircraft crash.
6. What is the purpose for using the term "Mayday" in a radio transmission?
7. If you are the first officer at the scene of a disaster, what is the advantage of your staying with your unit and radio rather than running in and immediately attempting to begin rescuing the survivors?
8. What other agencies or companies might you call upon for additional transportation and communications needs to aid in disaster response?
9. What personnel assignments would you make with the officers already on duty so that you might adequately cope with an unexpected disaster, such as a broken dam or a volcanic eruption?
10. What can the field officer do to address the problem of unfounded (you believe) rumors being circulated about police abuse?
11. List and discuss the five police objectives at the scene of an unlawful assembly.
12. Define *mob psychology*.
13. What kind of a gathering of people would lend itself to the possible formation of a mob?
14. What is the difference between a crowd and a mob?
15. Describe how a crowd may turn into a mob.
16. Describe the three stages in the development of a mob.
17. List and explain the several steps in handling an unlawful assembly.

If the police officers who respond to a "keep the peace" call at the scene of a labormanagement dispute happen to be members of a union related to that of the strikers, what must the officers do to assure fairness in their enforcement of the law?

18. Devise a disaster-riot mobilization plan for your department, and submit it to your field unit commanding officer.

19. What is the advantage of having a staging area away from police headquarters?

20. Describe martial rule and how it is put into effect in your state.

21. At what point do federal troops get involved in local martial rule?

22. Check with your local military air base and compare their recommended procedures regarding a military aircraft accident with the information outlined in this chapter.

23. Describe the procedure for responding to a bomb threat phone call when one of the building's occupants has found what appears to be a bomb.

24. Give an example of how you would talk with an arguing couple to diffuse the argument.

25. What is your primary role in crisis intervention?

26. What are the advantages of touching the person with whom you are talking during a crisis intervention situation? What are the disadvantages?

27. What is the difference between psychosis and neurosis?

REFERENCES

Abnormal Psychology, Current Perspectives. New York: Random House [Communications Research Machines, Inc. (CRM Books)] 1972.

AGUILERA, DONNA C., and JANICE M. MESSICK, *Crisis Intervention: Theory and Methodology*, 3rd ed. St. Louis, Mo.: C.V. Mosby, 1978.

COLEMAN, JAMES C. *Abnormal Psychology and Modern Life*, 5th ed. Glenview, Ill.: Scott, Foresman, 1976.

DAVISON, GERALD C., and JOHN M. NEALE, *Abnormal Psychology: An Experimental Clinical Approach.* New York: Wiley, 1974.

DIXON, SAMUEL L. *Working with People in Crisis: Theory and Practice.* St. Louis, Mo.: C. V. Mosby, 1979.

"Facts about Suicide and Some Warning Signs." *Today's Health,* June 1967, p. 33. *Federal Aviation Regulations,* 1988 (annual).

INTERNATIONAL CITY MANAGERS' ASSOCIATION. *Training and Equipping Police Crowd and Riot Control Officers and Units.* Chicago: International City Managers' Association, 1966.

Los Angeles County Sheriff's Department. *Crowd and Riot Control Instructional Guide*. Los Angeles: Sheriff's Department, 1963.

_____. *Supervisor's Role in Emergency Operations*. Los Angeles: Sheriff's Department, 1967.

Los Angeles District Attorney. *Civil Disturbance Manual for Law Enforcement*. Los Angeles: D. A. Evelle J. Younger's Office, 1967.

Los Angeles Police Department. *Daily Training Bulletins*, Vol. I. Springfield, Ill.: Charles C. Thomas, 1954, Chaps. 17 and 18.

Matthews, Robert A., and Lloyd W. Rowland. *How to Recognize and Handle Abnormal People: A Manual for the Police Officer*. New York: National Association for Mental Health, 1960.

U.S. Department of Defense. *What to Do and How to Report Military Aircraft Accidents*, Joint Service Booklet 1. Washington, D.C.: U.S. Department of the Navy, 1968.

11

PURSUIT DRIVING, CAR STOPS, & THE DUI

INTRODUCTION

This chapter deals with three of the more important facets of the field officer's work: the police pursuit, car stops, and the most dangerous killer of all—the DUI, or the person who operates a motor vehicle while under the influence of alcohol or other drug that impairs the judgment and ability to operate an automobile. Not only are the pursuit and the car stop extremely hazardous activities for the participants, but the officer is additionally threatened by the specter of liability charges that loom overhead. There are times when the victims in serious tragedies involving pursued vehicles will charge the pursuing police officers with the responsibility for the collision or the suspect vehicle careening off the road out of control into a group of innocent bystanders. The officer must not only operate the police car, but is also driving the pursued vehicle as well in many situations.

Stopping a vehicle loaded with suspects in a robbery is certainly hazardous, but what about the lone traffic violator who does not seem to be a threat at all? You don't know it at the time, but the driver who just "busted" the stop sign may have just murdered three members of his family 15 minutes ago, or may be wanted in another state as a prison escapee. Not only is the actual stop hazardous, making sure that no other vehicles are involved in a collision when the suspect vehicle is pulling over to the side of the street, but addressing the driver and passengers, getting them out of their car, and making personal contact with them is a time when officers lose their lives or sustain serious injuries.

The "drunk driver" is no longer a funny character that people joke about by saying such stupid things as "I hope that guy's driving because he's in no condition to walk"; or the night club comedian ending the show by saying: "Remember, drinking and driving kills, so let's go out there and get 'em." Too many drinking drivers have done just that: gone out and killed people. Attorneys for drinking drivers have specialized in getting their clients' charges reduced to reckless driving, and many judges have gone along with it. It seemed as though no one really took the problem too seriously. Then along came some very angry mothers and others who had lost children and other family members to the drunk driver who said *"enough"* to their legislators. They have made an impression on legislators, judges, and the police to the extent that now everyone takes the matter seriously.

The laws and the procedures suggested in this chapter have been used with success by many leading agencies in the country, and are currently being taught in their basic and advanced academies. Although California code sections may be quoted, other states are quite similar because of recent efforts to standardize, following the lead of model codes developed by the bar associations. There may be some variance from your specific jurisdiction. The procedures, however, are reasonably standard throughout the country.

PURSUIT AND EMERGENCY DRIVING

Pursuit and emergency driving involve the same driving skills that the field officer should master for normal driving, with an extra emphasis on defensive driving techniques. For this type of driving, you must be at your peak efficiency and extremely alert, a condition that is actually enhanced by the increased activity of the nervous system and other body functions that are stimulated by the excitement of the situation. However, most police vehicle accidents occur during "normal" patrol driving, and it is imperative that you be equally alert at all times to avoid serious injury and property damage.

A prime consideration when making the decision to begin a high-speed "code three" run is the nature of the situation. The decision is made by the dispatcher in accordance with established policies when it is in response to a call for service or help, such as a "no detail" accident (injuries, if any, are unknown) or an armed robbery in progress. The situation in the field that arises in your presence requires your individual decision as to whether or not to pursue. You must immediately evaluate the situation and decide whether it is imperative that an apprehension be effected.

Relative locations of the police unit and the vehicle to be pursued play a significant role in the evaluative process. Can you get into position for the chase without causing an accident or jeopardizing the life of pedestrians? Think ahead. Where is the pursuit going to take you? Is there a school or playground down the street? a dead end? a cross street? What is the estimated speed of the violator, and how fast will the police car be required to go to overtake him or her? Is another police unit in a better position to apprehend the violator if they are notified by radio of the wanted vehicle approaching their location? These questions must be repeated throughout the pursuit in a continuing process of reevaluation. Also, what condition is our police unit in?

If it appears that the pursuit is not possible, it is better to use your time and efforts to alert another unit to the description, the direction of travel, and any other pertinent information that will enable the other unit to locate and apprehend the violators. By means of radio, it is possible to pursue actively the individual in coordination with other police units.

Once you make the decision to pursue, get into position as quickly and efficiently as possible. Notify the dispatcher of your pursuit, the nature of the situation, the direction of travel, your location, and a description of the pursued vehicle. The information that is most critical at the beginning of the pursuit is the direction of travel. Other units in the area may be in a position to assist in the pursuit, or they may clear traffic on side streets to reduce the possibility of traffic collisions involving the police car or the pursued vehicle. During the chase, make frequent broadcasts to keep headquarters and the other police units advised of your changing location and any additional need for assistance. Some departments tape all pursuits, and the dispatcher will periodically broadcast the time for later reference, if necessary.

If you use the red light and siren as warning devices, *use* them. Using a siren and turning on the lights only at intersections is unwise and generally illegal (there are exceptions, of course). An emergency vehicle is authorized to violate the rules of the road only when functioning in a "code three" situation, which requires red light and siren. Never assume that anyone will see the lights or hear the siren, particularly when you are approaching intersections, but use them nevertheless. When you turn on the siren, look for nearby motorists who will be startled by the sudden noise and who may do strange things, such as stop suddenly or swerve into your vehicle. At extremely high speeds and on roads where there are no side streets, such as a freeway or expressway, the siren may serve no useful purpose once the driver of the pursued vehicle clearly understands that it is he that you are chasing and it is apparent that he has no intention of stopping.

Depending on the type of siren equipment you have, be sure to utilize it to the maximum, using also the horn, and use the headlights, blinking the high and low beam alternately. Use your seat belts, safety helmets, shoulder harnesses, and any other safety devices provided by the automobile manufacturer and your department (see Figures 11–1 and 11–2).

Shooting any type of weapon at a fleeting vehicle is not advisable and should be limited to extreme cases when there is absolutely no other way to save a human life. In both of these situations, however, it is more logical to assume that the pursued vehicle will be caused to go out of control and someone may die or be seriously injured as a result.

Figure 11-1 The standard police pursuit vehicle is usually the basic patrol unit, such as this one. (Courtesy of the Florida State Highway Patrol.)

Figure 11-2 Some departments are fortunate enough to have special pursuit units, such as this one. (Courtesy of the California Highway Patrol.)

Drivers of other vehicles, pedestrians, or occupants of buildings in the area may become the innocent victims of an officer's poor judgment. Pursuing another vehicle is almost the same as if you were pushing it, even though you may be hundreds of feet behind the other vehicle.

Consider this liability problem. A police officer and his department were being sued for several million dollars and an "expert" was consulted by the attorneys for the defense. What do you believe to have been the result of this case?

It was late in the evening. The weather was cool and the sky was moonless. The officer had pulled into the parking lot of a business-industrial area and was slowly checking out the doors and windows for signs of burglaries. His headlights were off and he used the hand brake so that the flash of a brake light would not alert anyone to his presence. While he was cruising the lot, he heard the squeal of tires and looked around as a sedan took off from the intersection at a high rate of speed.

The officer decided to follow the car to see if the tire squealing was accidental or deliberate. As he pulled out into the street and proceeded in the same direction as the car in question, his headlights were still turned off. He followed the car, which kept speeding up. He began the pursuit, turned on his headlights, and by the time he turned on his red lights and siren the suspect vehicle was traveling at least 85 miles per hour on this residential street, which had a 35 mps speed limit. The suspect car continued at about the same speed for about 2 miles with the officer in hot pursuit, but as the suspect vehicle sped through two intersections that fortunately were not busy at the time, going against the red light in both instances, the officer had to slow down so that he could safely get through the intersection. He was about a half-mile behind the suspect vehicle when the car went through the second intersection. As the officer sped to catch up, the suspect suddenly turned north. The officer continued in the same direction through the intersection. He turned off his red lights and siren, turned around, then turned north to follow the suspect.

The officer was accelerating on this street, which had no traffic, and had not yet turned his lights and siren back on. By that time, the suspect vehicle approached a fairly busy intersection and did not slow down. He went against the red light and ran broadside into a small car containing two elderly women. The impact was so great that the violator totaled the car he struck plus his own. He was slightly injured, but both women were killed instantly.

The prosecution in this civil lawsuit contended that since this uninsured offender was being pursued by the police, he was actually being "pushed" into the accident, causing the fatal injuries. He stated that the officers should have abandoned the chase, and that if they had, the young man being pursued would have slowed down and the accident would not have happened. Do you believe that the officer was liable under the circumstances presented here?

The "expert" reviewed the reports, visited the scene of the chase and the accident, and mentally re-created the event. His opinion, presented in a deposition, was that the officer was not responsible, that he had actually discontinued the chase when he overshot the street where the suspect vehicle had turned, and that the officer had actually turned off the red light and siren. The "expert" added that even had the officer not overshot the street and had had the emergency equipment turned on, the officer would not have been at fault in this case. The police department did not lose the case. (The expert was a former police lieutenant who writes textbooks and teaches criminal justice classes.)

While driving under pursuit or emergency conditions, approach each intersection with extreme caution, slowing down to avoid an accident with someone who may not hear or heed the warning siren of the approaching police car. Never pass a vehicle on the right with your red light and siren on. You may encounter another individual who is completely oblivious to your proximity until you start passing, when the other driver suddenly sees or hears you and does what is required by law: to immediately drive to the right side of the road and stop to allow the emergency vehicle to pass.

Caravans of several pursuing vehicles should be avoided (see Figure 11–3). There is no need for more than two or three cars to be directly involved in the chase of even the most dangerous criminal. Consider the driver who pulls over to the side of the street to allow the police unit to pass, then immediately returns to the traffic lane and follows the police car to see where it is going. Such a driver normally returns to the traffic lane at about the same time that the second police car reaches the same spot. The second police car is probably not operating with red light and siren, thereby placing the officer in a civilly liable position, not to mention the hazards involved at the time.

Roadblocks may be utilized, but they should seldom, if ever, involve the placement of police vehicles directly in the traffic lane to present a physical, impassable barrier. Barricades, flares, and other objects may serve the purpose without assuming the risks of causing loss of life or destruction of property. Portable spike bars, similar to those used at the

Figure 11-3   The helicopter is an excellent backup unit to assist in pursuits. (Courtesy of the Pennsylvania State Police.)

exits of parking lots and apartment complexes where you are warned of severe tire damage if you back up, are effective as road blocks when they cause tires to deflate.

Always consider the possibility that the pursued vehicle will stop suddenly and without warning. The driver may not actually be aware of the chase or may be under the influence of alcohol or drugs. The subject may suddenly realize the futility of attempting to lose the police vehicle. Another possibility is that the driver of the pursued vehicle may make a sudden stop to gain strategic advantage by stopping earlier than the police vehicle, placing the officer in front. The subject could then either attack the officer from this position of advantage, or escape by making a quick U-turn, or by alighting from the vehicle, get away on foot. Keep some distance between your vehicle and that of the subject you are pursuing to avoid the possibility of collision when the subject stops suddenly and to avoid placing yourself at a position of disadvantage in front of him.

When you are pursuing another vehicle, you will probably find that you will have a tendency to stay too close. Back off enough to leave a "cushion of space" between the vehicles in case the other driver crashes or stops suddenly or does something that jeopardizes your safety. Consider also the possibility of a blowout, a crash from the front or rear, a fire, or being forced off the road. In case of a blowout, take your foot off the accelerator and slow without braking, steer firmly and in a straight line until you are almost stopped; then pull off to the side of the road. In the case of an imminent crash from the rear, take your foot off the brake and lie across the seat to avoid whiplash; then apply the brakes immediately following impact. A head-on collision is likely to be fatal, so try to run off the road or strike another vehicle going the same way. In case of a fire, pull over and stop as quickly as possible, use sand or dirt if you have no extinguisher, and get away from the vehicle if the fire is out of control.

Whenever pursuing another vehicle, there may be a time when it is strategically sound judgment to abandon the pursuit. During a high-speed chase when it appears futile to assume that the pursued vehicle will stop for any of a number of reasons, there is always the danger that the chase will become a matter of personal pride to the officer driving the pursuing vehicle. It may be a matter of competition in driving skill, and the officer may become so intent on winning that the objective of the chase is no longer clear. Under conditions that develop during such a contest, any subsequent actions during the chase and eventual capture of the suspect may be quite injudicious. Intelligent and professional police officers cannot lose control of their faculties to the extent that they lose their objectivity.

Protection of life and property, which applies to the high-speed chase, includes the lives and property of the individual being pursued, the officer, and any innocent people who might become involved in a traffic collision as a direct result of the chase. At some time during the chase, it may be necessary to abandon the chase to uphold this police responsibility. The decision to abandon the chase involves factors such as the seriousness of the situation precipitating the chase in the first place, the possibility of identifying the driver and the vehicle for a later arrest with a warrant, and the road conditions at the time of the chase. What is the weather condition? Are there other vehicles, pedestrians, or children nearby that might be injured if the chase continues? Consider also the likelihood that the driver of the pursued vehicle will slow down to a normal speed once he makes good his escape. Or will he continue jeopardizing the lives and property of everyone who gets in his way until he collides with something, runs out of gas, or is apprehended? There are many times when circumstances may dictate the abandonment of the chase.

Ramming Vehicles

Ramming is done only in extreme cases and only when the calculated risk indicates that lives of innocent persons would be saved by such action and that danger to the officer driving the ramming vehicle is not imminent. Running into another vehicle from behind or from the side, or in any other way attempting to push the vehicle off the road, is extremely dangerous with unpredictable results, sometimes even suicidal. There are very few times when such action is worth the risk of your life or that of another person, particularly innocent third parties who have the misfortune to be nearby at the time.

A very skillful driver may succeed in pulling alongside another vehicle, locking the two together, then edging the other vehicle to the side of the road. Or the skillful driver may actually brake both vehicles to a stop, taking advantage of the other driver's hesitancy to accelerate and his willingness to allow himself to be stopped in this manner. Ramming has about the same value as shooting at a car in the hope of puncturing a tire or rupturing the gas tank. The chance of ricochet is greater than either of these two hoped-for effects.

Code Three

In an urban community of any size, there may often be more than one emergency vehicle traveling along the streets in response to different and unrelated emergencies. The possibility of their colliding always exists, particularly when the emergency vehicles belong to different agencies that have no idea of what the other is doing. At best, the situation is complicated and hazardous, but the danger can be compounded if more than one vehicle is responding to a single emergency. In this case, the vehicles' convergence is imminent. Several agencies may be involved in a single incident, or only one. For example, a routine injury accident involving gas spillage will require code three response by a police unit, at least one fire unit, and an ambulance. Each is a separate and distinct agency and usually on a different radio frequency.

Considering the hazards involved in code three, the following guidelines should be established and followed:

1. Only one police unit will use the red light and siren on any one emergency call.

2. The unit responding to the assignment, or initiating a pursuit, will identify the unit and broadcast by radio the location at which you begin the pursuit.

3. The dispatcher should repeat the acknowledgment and broadcast to other units the location and direction of travel, if known.

4. The assigned unit will broadcast an "arrived on scene" (10-97) transmission to indicate the conclusion of the trip.

Escorts

In traffic of any type at any time of the day or night, driving a police vehicle with red light and siren is extremely hazardous. To drive a police vehicle with red light and siren for the purpose of clearing the way for a following vehicle is generally unwise and places too many lives in jeopardy. The officer driving the police vehicle is actually driving both of them, and you are assuming responsibility for the skill and judgment of the other driver as well. You will be specifically liable if there is a collision.

The driver of the escorted vehicle may be emotionally upset or physically incapable of performing under these conditions. It may be that the driver should not be driven even under normal conditions. He or she may not be skilled enough to maintain a safe distance behind the police vehicle and may either get lost or follow too closely. Since the escorted vehicle would not be equipped as an emergency vehicle, it would appear to others as just any other car that might be following a police car on an emergency call.

Consider the possibility of the police vehicle clearing the way for itself and the car following. The drivers of other vehicles must yield to the emergency vehicle, pull over to the side of the road, and wait until the police car passes. They then immediately pull back into the street and resume driving with the normal stream of traffic. The escorted vehicle speeding along behind the police vehicle may be forced to stop because of congestion that is caused by the resumption of the traffic flow or because of a traffic control sign or signal.

What of the legal consideration? Under no circumstances does the escorted vehicle become an emergency vehicle. The driver does not become exempt from the traffic laws, and he cannot be exempted from any civil liability in an accident that may occur during the escort operation. In most jurisdictions, state law prohibits any type of escort with the use of red light and siren. Any justification for a breach of the law allowed by a police officer would have to concern an extremely grave situation. The exception would have to be justifiable not only in your own eyes at that moment, but also in the eyes of your superiors, the courts, and the other private persons who enjoy no such immunity and who would expect the escorted vehicle's driver to be held to answer for breaking the law in the same way as they would be held to answer.

In view of these considerations, it would seem that the best method of operation is to decline the request to serve as an escort and to either call an ambulance or transport an injured person in the police vehicle, which is an emergency vehicle when operating with red light and siren. Another option, of course, is for one officer to drive the victim in his or her own car with the other officer following behind—or in front—as an escort. What you have here is actually an Oliver North situation: If everything turns out okay, you will be a hero, but if something goes wrong and you get into an accident, you are in deep trouble.

Transporting Injured Persons in Police Cars

A police vehicle is *not* an ambulance. There are times, however, when there is no other feasible means of transportation available under certain emergency conditions. In such cases, use of the police vehicle for this purpose is not improper. Consider these hypothetical situations, and you be the judge as to what course of action you as the officer should follow.

- While parked near an intersection, you see a two-door late-model sedan speed through an intersection while the traffic signal for his direction of travel is red. The car narrowly misses another car, which had just started with the green light. You pursue the violator and chase him for about two blocks before you get him to stop. As you alight from the patrol car, citation book in hand, you meet an extremely agitated middle-aged man. The man literally shouts at you that he must get to a hospital because he has been stung by a bee, and he will suffer serious consequences because his is allergic to bee stings. He hopes to reach the hospital before he loses consciousness, and he asks you to please get out of his way so that he can resume his fateful journey. What would you do?

- A young man and woman drive up to you where you are parked alongside the street, bringing your activity log up to date. The man says: "My wife is having a baby. Will you escort us to the hospital?" Will you perform the requested service?

- In response to a call for service in an "unknown trouble, see the woman," call, you meet a woman with a small child in her arms. The child is unconscious and seems to be losing its normal color. The woman hysterically screams that the child had lost consciousness while eating a piece of beef, and she cannot revive him. You begin cardiopulmonary resuscitation and determine that there is a possibility that life still exists in the child but that he will probably die without immediate medical attention. No ambulance is available because of a major traffic accident on the highway in which several people were killed and others injured. The child is dying and needs attention. What is your decision?

If your department has not already done so, you should formulate a set of standards so that you make value judgments. Ask yourself the following questions before making your decision: Would transporting the individual increase the severity of the injury? Is the service in direct competition with another agency's service that is available and actually better prepared to handle the matter? Is the need really an emergency? Is it wise to allow a person to drive a vehicle when it is possible that the person may lose consciousness at any moment? Is another emergency service available? Is the individual under arrest? What are the alternatives? The decision you make each time a situation arises is actually based upon consideration of the alternatives, and selection of the right one.

Legal Aspects of Emergency Driving

Basic laws in virtually every jurisdiction provide for the emergency operation of appropriately equipped and authorized vehicles, including police vehicles. For your consideration, five examples of such laws follow:

1. Whenever an emergency vehicle approaches while displaying legally authorized red lights and sounding a siren, the drivers of other vehicles shall yield the right-of-way and wait for the passage of that vehicle. Although most laws are quite specific about *both* red light *and* siren operating, some case law has been generated because of the impracticability of operating a siren on a freeway at extremely high speeds, and under certain conditions it may be permissible to use red light only. These are exceptional cases, however, and the need rarely manifests itself.

2. Emergency vehicles are exempt from most regulations, such as speeding, right-of-way, stop signs and signals, and other rules of the road when responding to an emergency, engaged in rescue operations, in actual pursuit of a violator, or when responding to a fire *if* the driver is sounding the siren and displaying the red light.

3. Emergency vehicles are generally exempt from civil liability when operating in accordance with the emergency provisions and when properly using the legally required red light and siren clearly indicating "emergency vehicle" character.

4. The driver of an emergency vehicle under any conditions, including emergency conditions, is not relieved from the duty to drive with due regard for the safety of all persons using the streets and highways. Moreover, the law does not protect the driver-officer from the consequences of an arbitrary and unnecessary exercise of the privileges granted in the exempting sections. The officer is thus limited to real emergency needs and is prohibited from using

the red light and siren to avoid a traffic signal because of impatience rather than actual necessity.

5. Emergency vehicles are forbidden to use the siren or to drive at an illegal speed when serving as an escort *except* for the preservation of life or when escorting supplies and personnel for the armed forces during a national emergency.

CAR STOPS

The Approach by Automobile

Prior to making the stop, communicate by radio your location, the place where the stop will occur, the license number of the vehicle, and any other pertinent information that you have time for. Other information should include the number of occupants, clothing descriptions of occupants if you believe a pursuit is about to take place when the occupants alight, and a statement to the effect that you have reason to believe they are armed. Also, if you anticipate the need for follow-up units, request them. A follow-up should be automatically assigned, but the dispatcher may be compelled by a personnel shortage to assign units on a priority basis. Yours would be at the top of the list.

When approaching the suspect car, be on the alert for any sudden movements by the people in the car. There may be a sudden panic stop by a timid individual who suddenly realizes that it is he whom you wish to stop. The subject may attempt to ram the police car, or try some evasive action to avoid the contact. If the subject appears to be armed and it looks as though he may shoot at you, back off and follow at a safer distance until follow-up units arrive and you can make the stop with the aid of several additional units. At this time, also watch for any objects that the vehicle's occupants may throw out the window. Narcotics, dangerous weapons, and other contraband are often disposed of in this manner.

Making the Auto Stop

Pick your location where there is adequate lighting and where you will not be at too great a disadvantage should the subject or any of his passengers choose to attack you. You should try to see the people at all times. Signal the driver to pull over to the side of the street, and point to the location where you wish him to go. Use the red light and horn—or siren—to attract the driver's attention and to signal other vehicles to make room for you and the vehicle you are stopping. The object of the maneuver is to stop the other car as quickly as possible, then issue the citation or conduct the field interview while attracting the last amount of attention from other people.

Once you have the vehicle stopped and the cars are not parked in a hazardous location, turn off the overhead red lights to avoid setting up a distraction for passers-by. If necessary to divert traffic away from your vehicle and the one that you have stopped, or to alert other police units to your exact whereabouts, do not hesitate to use the lights. Sometimes the blinking lights cause the curious to slow down and drive without paying any attention to anything but the blinking lights and collision scene, which creates an additional hazard.

In some cases when you have information or reason to believe that the subjects in the vehicle you are attempting to stop may have committed a felony, you may choose to draw your revolver, pull alongside the other vehicle, and order the driver to stop while pointing your revolver at them. This is extremely dangerous. Many officers have been killed or seriously wounded attempting to hasten a stop in this manner.

If time and circumstances permit, it is wise to refrain from attempting to make contact until a follow-up unit arrives on the scene to cover you while making the stop.

When stopping felony criminals, consider the following points. Some felons actually believe they are being stopped for a minor traffic violation, and they will "play it cool" to receive their citation and avoid the arrest for the felony they had committed, hoping to avoid the detection of the officer. Other felons may consider the gun a challenge that must be met with violence, and they may begin firing at you. Let the circumstances indicate your course of action, but first try the red light and siren or the horn and hand signal. If the suspect shoots at you, attempt to back off and avoid a gun battle while you are operating your vehicle. Shooting firearms at a moving vehicle while operating a vehicle yourself is highly inadvisable and not likely to yield very accurate results. The hazards would probably be greater than any advantages.

The final stopped position for maximum safety to both occupants of the suspect vehicle as well as yourself is with the suspect vehicle pulled to the curb as far as possible and your vehicle directly behind and/or slightly to the right. Of course, if the suspect vehicle is against the curb, you have no ᶜhoice but to park likewise, unless you can drive safely up on the curb or on the shoulder to the right. When there is little or no traffic, and when the stop is in the daytime and/or it is clear to you that the hazard does not seem to be present, you may offset your vehicle to the left and provide for yourself a safety lane along the left side of the vehicle you are stopping if you choose to address the driver from that side of his or her vehicle (see Figure 11–4). When there is heavy traffic, or you think that the driver may present a problem, approach the vehicle from the right, or passenger side. This is better strategy, as a suspect is more likely to expect an officer's approach from the left. With the police unit offset to the left, there is the problem not only of possible collision by partially blocking off one lane of traffic but also of the vehicles suddenly changing lanes to the left, which may cause a collision while all the motorists are straining to see what the police are up to this time.

Leave about 15 feet to a full car length between the vehicles, and set your emergency brakes to avoid an out-of-control vehicle. If you cannot

Figure 11-4 The police car should be parked about 3 feet farther from the curb to provide a "walking line" for the officer. This is for the solo officer routine vehicle stop. (Courtesy of the Police Department, Scottsdale, Arizona.)

slide across the seat of your vehicle because of computers and consoles and other paraphernalia, you will have to alight from the driver's side. When you get out, stand there with your door as a shield until a follow-up units arrives or, if you are going to handle the matter alone, make your move cautiously to the suspect vehicle. If you are dealing with a dangerous fugitive and you are not yet aware of it, you must take care lest the suspect attempts to avoid the police contact and assault (see Figure 11–5).

The space between vehicles is out of bounds for standing. There is a danger of another motorist slamming into your vehicle. Therefore, if you must cross that spot, cross it quickly. At nighttime, leave your headlights on unless you are going to cross in front of them, making yourself a silhouette target. Aim your spotlight into the rear window and point at the rear view mirror inside the car.

The Approach

Two Officers. This procedure may be used for a two-officer unit or the lone officer working one unit with a solo follow-up (see Figure 11–6). Hopefully you will have a two-officer team to handle all but the most routine car stops. While the driver officer of the first unit remains standing at the unit just outside using the door as a shield, the second officer approaches the suspect vehicle from the right. The reason for staying with the unit if you are that first officer is to remain close to your radio for emergency communications and to take immediate pursuit should the

Figure 11-5   When you first make contact and you are not sure of your subject, protect yourself against possible attack. People stopped by the police often jump out and approach the officer, either because they wonder why they were stopped, or because there is something in the car they do not want the officer to see. (Courtesy of the California Highway Patrol.)

Figure 11-6   A solo officer may choose the approach from the driver's side in a routine stop for a traffic citation, or as the second officer in a two-officer stop. Note the space provided for the officer's protection against passing cars by parking the unit outside to the left.

suspect suddenly decide to flee. If you are the officer approaching from the right, take a position at the right rear of the suspect vehicle and look inside to ascertain if there is any hazard. Tap a part of the vehicle (be careful not to damage a thousand-dollar paint job), or make some sort of a noise to let the occupants of the vehicle know of your presence. Once the officer on the right sees that there appears to be no immediate danger, the first officer may approach the vehicle and issue the citation or handle the field interview.

One Officer. Alight from your vehicle and pause to determine that the driver has completely stopped and has turned off the engine. Approach the car from the right side, and at the same time direct the driver to lean across and open the window on the right side. This will keep the driver off guard and permit you to observe any movements inside the vehicle. You will also be able to see more of the interior of the car, including the glove box if it is opened. If the driver gets out of the car while you are issuing a citation, or if you intend to question him or her outside the vehicle, instruct the driver and other occupants, if any, to get out on the right side, thereby avoiding getting struck by passing vehicles (see Figure 11–7).

Whatever method you use for the routine vehicle stop for a citation or warning for some type of violation, or for a field interview, keep your suspects in plain view at all times and watch them continuously. Most of the hundreds or thousands of people you encounter in this manner will be cooperative and absolutely no danger to you, but you will never know until it actually happens if, and when, one of them proves to be a danger.

Figure 11-7 Position for interrogation. (Courtesy of the Police Department, Scottsdale, Arizona.)

Approach, Suspects in Vehicle

Assuming that all persons in the vehicle could well be felons, use extreme caution when approaching such persons in any situation in which you anticipate making arrests. Whenever possible, whether you are solo or with a partner, call for a back-up unit and wait for their arrival before taking any action beyond the car stop. If you are working alone this is particularly critical. Solo patrol was never intended to be carried into the potential arrest situation.

The driver officer alights from the left side of the unit and stands there, using the door as a shield and keeping the microphone immediately available in case of the need for further communication by radio with other units or headquarters. The passenger officer—or follow-up officer, if the first unit on the scene is a solo unit—stands behind the passenger door of the same police unit. If follow-up units are on the way, take as much time as possible to give the other units time to arrive. Sometimes this is not possible because the occupants of the car don't have a copy of the script and will not know what you intend for them to do without your telling them.

If you have a public address system in the unit, use the outside speaker and communicate with the occupants of the suspect vehicle so that they may hear you more clearly. If you have no PA, speak very loudly and clearly so that there will be a greater chance that everyone will hear what you have to say. Only one officer gives the commands. Usually, this will be the driver officer of the first unit on the scene. Although the script may vary, you must immediately notify the occupants of the suspect vehicle that you are in charge and that they are to do exactly what you tell them to do. Your command may be as follows:

> *Police officers. All of you, remain in the car. Driver, turn off the ignition. Move very slowly and you will not get hurt. All occupants, let me see all of your hands. Driver, take the ignition key and drop it outside the window so that I can see it. You, in the front seat, put both of your hands up against the windshield with your palms up against the glass. You, in the back seat, move very slowly and put your hands on the back of the seat in front of you with your palms up. Remain in that position until I tell you to move.*

Your objective is to keep all occupants of the vehicle under control. You want the vehicle stopped and the keys outside so that someone cannot suddenly drive it away, and you want to see the hands of all the occupants of the vehicle. You don't want them to be fumbling around under the seats or elsewhere in the vehicle and coming up with weapons they might have concealed. If these particular subjects have been through the routine before, they might be totally cooperative, or they might also have weapons conveniently stashed for defense in just this type of an event. Be careful! With occupants under your control in this type of situation, you should have your handguns and/or shotguns in your hands pointed at the suspects, but not in a cocked position.

At this point, wait for your follow-up units(s) if they have not already arrived. Once you are sufficiently covered, you will want to get the suspects out of the vehicle and immobilized so that you may search them and their vehicle with the least amount of danger to yourself, the other officers, and the suspects. Your next objective is to take them out of the car one at a time, and according to your instructions.

Removing the Occupants from the Vehicle

Both officers in the leading unit should maintain their position of advantage behind the door for maximum safety. While one officer is giving the commands to the vehicle's occupants, the other officer is covering the suspects with the shotgun or handgun in a two-handed position. The object is to get the occupants out of the vehicle, all from the right-hand side away from traffic. Tell each one—passenger on the right front, driver, passenger on the right rear, and others—to get out of the vehicle one at a time, and continue until they are all out. Direct each one to step outside the vehicle, then lock their hands above and behind the head, kick the door closed, and then to walk backward to a position where the passenger officer will instruct each suspect to stop, kneel in a cross-legged position, or lie prone. The passenger officer will handcuff each suspect and search him or her. This routine is continued until all occupants are out of the vehicle.

Now that all suspects are still handcuffed on their knees or are lying prone on the ground, the passenger officer should use one of the handcuffed suspects as a shield and advance to the vehicle to see that all occupants have left the vehicle. As a precaution to avoid having to resort to deadly force, shout to the vehicle and any possible occupant that you are coming up to the car and that you have one of their compatriots that they will be shooting if they are foolish enough to try. Using that person as a shield, check the trunk; then advance to look inside the vehicle. You should be satisfied that no one remains in the vehicle and that you have all the suspects in custody. As you bring them back from their vehicle, bring them all the way behind the first police unit, using the assistance of your backup officers (if any). At this location, you will then be able to complete the activity most appropriately for the circumstances.

Traffic Citations

When, where, and how to stop the traffic violator sometimes takes the talent of a choreographer in maneuvering through traffic and getting the violator to stop when and where you direct that he or she should. Consider the violation. If there are two or more violations at the same time, your decision should be to go for the violation that shows in your department's collision statistics as the more serious offense. But there may be a problem in getting to the more serious violator, as when you may not get to the violator without causing a collision yourself or when access is not possible. Then your selection of which violator to stop will be the second one on the list. If possible, stop them both.

You should make your decision to cite or warn the violator when you observe the violation. If you wait until you contact the violator to hear what explanation he or she has for the violation, and decide at that time whether or not to warn or cite, you are opening yourself up to a charge that you issued the citation for some prejudicial reason other than for the actual violation. Of course, there may be exceptions, such as the doctor who is rushing to the hospital to perform surgery or the driver who is transporting the expectant mother whose contractions are 30 seconds apart. But those should be the exception rather than the rule.

When making the violator stop, do so with consideration for the flow and condition of traffic. The stop should be as soon as possible after the violation so that the violator will remember where it was and what it was that caused the stop. Stopping a violator in a stream of traffic that causes an entire lane to divert during a rush hour does not make as much sense as directing the violator to turn the corner off the busy street. Watch for sudden stops and erratic behavior once the violator is aware of your presence. Sometimes the reaction is dramatic. Also, be careful to avoid attracting too many gawkers who might cause more collisions. As soon as possible, when you are sure of your safety and that of the violator, turn off your flashing lights that attract the curious like moths to a candle.

Your salutation to the violator should be polite and professional and free of any familiarity or condescension. Have the violator remove the operator license from whatever container it is in and hand it to you. Tell the offender that you are going to issue the citation, and for what charge. Explain the offense, if necessary, but do not argue or lecture. Above all, do not quote the amount of bail unless it is the policy of your department. One of the problems caused by quoting bail is that the judges might have changed their bail schedule since the last time you saw it. Then, when the violator goes to court, posts bail, and finds it to be different from what you quoted, you are going to be subjected to some very uncomplimentary verbiage.

While issuing a traffic citation, do not lean on, or support any part of your body on, the violator's vehicle. It might be interpreted as "adding insult to injury." Not all violators are going to thank you for giving them the citation you believe they deserve. Whenever you issue a citation, it is acceptable to use a "cheat sheet" or card listing in abbreviated form all the most commonly used violations. It is acceptable, that is, if you know the violations. For example, a California Vehicle Code section prohibits allowing an unlicensed minor to drive a car, but for the person to be guilty of that specific section, the person who allows the unlicensed minor to use the car must be a parent, guardian, or employer of that minor. A minor detail, perhaps, but sufficient to cause a judge to dismiss the charges.

Car Stops—Legal Considerations

A temporary detention or vehicle stop is an act of authority by a police officer that is something less than an arrest but more substantial than a simple contact or consensual encounter. The detention occurs the moment you turn on your red light or otherwise stop a vehicle to investigate a possible crime or to issue a traffic citation. Once you start writing the citation, it is an arrest until the subject signs the promise to appear and is on his or her way. As you know, if the subject refuses to sign the promise to appear, the officer is empowered to book the person for the traffic violation. Signing the citation is a form of posting bail (own recognizance) with a promise to appear in court at a later date to answer the charges.

To make your car stop, you must have a reasonable suspicion that (1) something relating to crime has just happened, is happening, or is about to happen; and (2) the vehicle or person in the vehicle you are about to detain is connected with that activity.

When deciding whether to order the detainee to get out of the vehicle, consider the circumstances. If it is strictly for a traffic citation, there is no need to. Otherwise, if you are going to investigate a possible DUI or other crime, you will get the person(s) out of the vehicle.

A thorough search is not warranted for the person or the vehicle. You can enter the vehicle to search for registration or to retrieve a driver's license. It is also reasonable to conduct a frisk, or pat-down, of a person for a weapon, or the car for a crime-related situation, as described in Chapter 10.

Federal rules allow a full body search, including any container, incident to any kind of custodial arrest, from murder to outstanding traffic warrants (*Rn*, 1973, 414 U.S. 218). Your jurisdiction may be more stringent. A car passenger compartment may be searched incident to an arrest, but not the trunk. However, you may have sufficient reasonable cause to search the entire car for specific evidence if you can show that you believe what you are looking for is inside those portions of the car to be searched.

A motor home is a vehicle when it is being operated on the highways or is capable of such use and is found stationary in a place that is not regularly used for residential purposes. If the motor home is hooked up in a campground or other residential park, particularly if the plumbing is connected, the vehicle is treated as a private home and a warrant is needed.

DRIVING UNDER THE INFLUENCE: THE DUI

According to the Bureau of Justice Statistics publication *Drunk Driving*, published by the U.S. Government Printing Office in 1992, the number of licensed drivers increased in this country from 1980 to 1989 by 14 percent, and during the same time the number of DUI arrests increased by approximately 22 percent. At least one bit of good news is that the arrests of persons aged 18 to 20 went down 21 percent during that time, and the rate of drivers between the ages of 21 and 24 decreased by 9.9 percent. This must be attributed partially to the fact that by the time of this publication, all states will have raised the minimum drinking age to 21.

Another interesting fact is that the same publication reported that overall consumption of 95 percent of alcoholic beverages in the United States is by about one-third of the people and that of those, approximately 5 percent of them drink about half of all the alcoholic beverages consumed. The average person over the age of 21 drinks about 34 gallons of beer, 3 gallons of wine, 2 gallons of hard liquor, 27 gallons of coffee, 26 gallons of milk, and 42 gallons of soft drinks.

For many years the National Highway Traffic Safety Administration and many other traffic control agencies have been saying that approximately one-half of all fatal traffic collisions involve alcohol and/or drugs; 50 percent of drivers killed have a blood-alcohol level of 0.10 or higher, which is considered presumptive evidence that the person is guilty of DUI, not necessarily intoxicated but sufficient to sustain a conviction for operating a motor vehicle while under the influence. Sixty to seventy-five percent of all drivers killed in single-car collisions have a BA (blood-alcohol content) of 0.10 or above.

Detection of the DUI may occur in several different ways. They include (1) direct observation by the officer of the person while operating a motor vehicle; (2) a call from a concerned witness such as another driver or a bartender who advised a person not to drive, even a friend or family member; (3) observation of a driver at the scene of a collision; or (4) while stopping, or after stopping a driver for some other type of violation. However the driver comes to your attention, be sure to include all observations and information on your report because you will be asked to justify your cause for the arrest.

While observing drivers in your district, keep these indicators in mind. They might alert you to the DUI:

1. Slow reactions to traffic signals when stopping or starting, sometimes suddenly "waking up" and making a quick move to compensate, such as slamming on the brakes at the last minute

2. Overcompensating or exaggerating a turn or lane change

3. Inability to maintain a consistent, or appropriate, speed

4. Apparent confusion in coping with traffic, the lights of oncoming cars, or passing cars

5. Indications of faulty judgment, or dumb moves in traffic

6. Weaving, drifting, or changing lanes without apparent reason

7. A fixed stare straight ahead with apparent disregard for peripheral sighting, or turning to look before turning or changing lanes

8. Jerking driving movements from side to side or slowing and speeding up

9. Cutting in or giving too much clearance after passing another vehicle

10. Overshooting or disregarding traffic signs or signals

11. Driving at night without lights, or delay in turning them on after starting from a parked position

12. Failure to dim lights or to turn them on after opposing drivers have signaled the problem

13. Unnecessary use of turn indicators

14. Straddling lane-divider lines or hugging the curb

15. Windshield wipers working when they are not needed

16. Driving with head sticking out the window

17. Unusual situation, such as open windows when it is cold or raining outside

18. Subtle movements after you stop the suspect violator, such as falling down when getting out of the car, or fumbling while looking for the driver's license in the wallet, or losing balance while turning around

Once you identify the problem, you should not allow the person to move the vehicle, not even to park it. If they cause physical injury or property damage because they are following your directions, you may be found liable.

Stopping the Suspected DUI

Use the car stop techniques covered earlier in this chapter, but with more caution because you are dealing with a person whose behavior may be unusually bizarre and totally without apparent reason, such as suddenly stopping in the middle of the street or running into your car when you pull alongside. Watch for the behavior of the suspected driver and the passengers during the stop, including some of the following behaviors:

1. Sudden stopping or slow response to your signals to stop, indicating slow reaction time

2. Attempt to evade by turning suddenly or by speeding up

3. Unusual behaviors that were described in the preceding list

4. Driver switching places with passenger, or some other movement within the vehicle as though to hide alcohol or drugs

Once you stop the suspected DUI, you are going to use all your senses to see if you can detect the reasons for the suspected driver's behavior. Ask questions to determine if there is an injury or illness involved, or some problem other than alcohol or drugs. You will be able to smell what might be alcohol, and you will see the person's bloodshot eyes and hear the slurred speech. By this time you have probably made a determination that the motor vehicle operation has been impaired by something the subject has ingested. Later you are going to give the subject the choice of a blood-alcohol test via blood, breath, or urine, but now you will perform the field sobriety test. It is useful as a guide to keep in mind information regarding the ascending effect of alcohol while performing the test and determining level of alcoholic influence.

The following information provides guidelines only; precise, scientifically accurate information is readily available elsewhere. Here, one beer is one 12-ounce bottle of 3½ percent alcohol content beer, a glass of wine is one 3-ounce glass (most bars will serve a 10- to 12-ounce glass which equals four), and one cocktail is 1 ounce of 0.86-proof "hard liquor" (many bars pour "heavy"—about 1½ to 2 ounces of alcohol per mixed drink and sometimes as much as 4 ounces at "happy hour"). The list applies to a person who weighs about 150 pounds, and the amount of alcohol is that remaining in the body. This is conditioned by physical condition, how much and when the person last had something to eat, and how often he or she is taking each of these drinks, plus other variables.

- *One drink: 0.02 BA.* Loss of restraint and awareness, overconfident, careless, underestimates road hazards.
- *Two drinks: 0.04 BA.* Loss of concentration, has tendency to drift into daydreams, inattentive to traffic around him, unpredictable and impulsive.
- *Three drinks: 0.06 BA.* Loss of judgment, unreasonable, argumentative, indecisive, may begin slurring speech. The person is beginning to get sensitive to light and sound. May complain that your flashlight in the face causes pain.
- *Four drinks: 0.08 BA.* Reduction of depth perception and peripheral vision, loss of some muscle coordination.
- *Five drinks: 0.10 BA.* Presumptively under the influence, but the law might be different in your state. Operation of a commercial ship or airplane calls for a much lower level of BA for a violation. By this point the person's driving is impaired to the extent that it is probably obvious to the observer, but may not be.
- *Six to ten drinks.* Driver gets progressively worse with obviously impaired driving and extreme hazard to others.
- *Fifteen drinks: 0.30 BA.* Stupor. If you do not have the subject off

the street at this point, and there is a collision, the person is a time bomb.

- *Twenty drinks: 0.40 BA.* Coma.
- *Twenty-five drinks: 0.50 BA.* Death.

Field Sobriety Tests

You will need a level surface for these tests. Be sure that the subject understands you (of course, if she or he is too intoxicated, you may have a problem here) and demonstrate all the physical tests. In your report you will describe how the subject performs each test.

1. *Finger to nose.* The subject stands erect with the feet together, eyes closed, and arms outstretched. Alternating right hand, then left hand, and by direction of the officer, the subject swings his arm, bending at the elbow and touching his nose with the tip of the index finger (see Figure 11–8). The purpose of this test is to determine ability to coordinate movements, follow directions, and retain balance.

2. *Modified position of attention.* The subject is instructed to stand at "attention" position, arms at side, heels and toes together, eyes closed, head tilted back slightly. The purpose of this test is to determine ability to retain balance.

3. *Heel-to-toe walking on straight line.* Direct the subject to walk in a straight line, placing one foot before the other in succession (see Figure 11–9). Then turn around and walk back to the starting point. The purpose of this test is for balance, ability to walk a straight line, and ability to retain balance while turning.

Figure 11-8   Finger-to-nose test. (Courtesy of the California Highway Patrol.)

Figure 11-9   Heel-to-toe test. (Courtesy of the California Highway Patrol.)

4. *Pronunciation.* Have the subject repeat the alphabet. Be sure that the subject has mental capacity and/or language skills, plus the absence of a serious speech impediment. The purpose of the test is to show that a normal, sober person should be able to recite the alphabet.

5. *Dexterity.* Have the subject count on his or her fingers, counting them one at a time, then reversing the order. Test is to determine if the subject can coordinate finger movements with thought process.

6. *Lateral gaze nystagmus test.* For this test an officer completes a short course on DART (Drug, Alcohol Recognition Training). The officer has the subject stand facing him or her (see Figure 11–10). The officer holds up a finger directly in front of and a few inches away from the subject's nose. Directing the subject to follow the officer's finger with his or her eyes without turning the head, the officer moves the finger to the right, then to the left. An officer with the training and expertise can determine that at about 40 degrees the eyeball begins to flutter, which means that about the time the finger has moved to a point even with the subject's ear, the fluttering moves. This indicates that the subject is either under the influence of alcohol or has some serious medical problem with the eyes. Experienced officers claim to be able to determine approxi-

Figure 11-10   Lateral gaze nystagmus test. (Courtesy of the California Highway Patrol.)

mately what the BA is by this test, although the courts will accept it only as indicative of alcoholic influence.

7. *Other tests will be used by various departments, which you will encounter while in the academy.*

Now that you have performed your field tests and have decided that you have a bona fide DUI, the next step is to take the subject into the station for a BA test, using the subject's choice of blood, breath, or urine. The blood specimen is taken by a licensed physician or technician and analyzed by a laboratory; the urine is taken in the presence of the arresting officer and is sent to the lab; and the breath test is made at headquarters or in the jail and is operated by a trained operator, usually a fellow officer. The results of the breath test are available immediately. These tests are covered in greater detail in a traffic text and course.

The DUI Report

Your department will have standardized forms to use for this arrest (see Figure 11–11), and at points of the interview with the subject, you will be required to admonish him or her about the implied consent to take blood-alcohol tests under these conditions as a condition of retaining an operator's license. You may repeat the field sobriety test to be sure that your test is fair and on level ground with professional witnesses, and your report should recount every observation that you make from the time of your first contact up to—and including—the

DRIVING UNDER THE INFLUENCE ARREST REPORT   DR No.

VISIBLE SCARS, MARKS, DEFORMITIES—EVID. OF NARCOTIC USE	ARRESTEE'S NAME (Last, First , Middle)	BOOKING NUMBER
RESIDENCE ADDRESS CITY	CHARGE (Section No., Code and Definition)	☐MISD. ☐FEL. ☐OTHER
EMPLOYED BY OCCUPATION	LOCATION OF ARREST	R.D. DIV. & DET. ARREST
NICKNAME, ALIAS SOC. SEC. NO.	DATE & TIME ARRESTED DATE & TIME BOOKED	DIV. BKG. EVIDENCE BOOKED YES ☐ NO
DRIVER'S LIC. NO. STATE BIRTH PLACE	SEX DESCENT AGE HEIGHT WEIGHT HAIR	EYES BIRHTDATE
COMPLAINTS OR EVID. OF ILL. OR INJ.—BY WHOM TREATED	LOCATION CRIME COMMITTED	PROB. INVEST. UNIT
LIST CONNECTING REPORTS BY TYPE & IDENT. NUMBERS	DISPOSITION OF ARRESTEE'S VEHICLE	HOLD FOR
VEHICLE USED (Year, Make, Body Style, Colors, Lic. No., Identifying Marks)	DRIVING VEHICLE (Direction and Name of Street)	
AT OR BETWEEN STREETS	CLOTHING WORN	

CODE: V–VICTIM   W–WITNESS   P or G–PARENT OR GUARDIAN

NAME	CODE	RES. / BUS.	CITY	PHONE	X
		RES. / BUS.			
		RES. / BUS.			
		RES. / BUS.			

JUV. ONLY:	PARENTS NOTIFIED BY	TIME	PLACE JUV. DET.	DIV. OF APPEAR. DATE/TIME	BKG. APPROV. BY	DETEN. APPROV. BY	PRINTED?
							PHOTOS

ADMONITION IF RIGHTS: The arrestee was "warned" that he had the right to remain silent, AND THAT if he gave up the right to remain silent, anything he said can and will be used against him in a court of law, AND that he had the right to speak with an attourney and to have the attourney present during questioning, AND THAT if he so desired and could not afford one, an attorney would be appointed for him without charge before questioning.

ADMONITION IF RIGHTS GIVEN BY:	FIELD SOBRIETY TEST GIVEN BY:	CHEMICAL TEST GIVEN BY:

FIELD SOBRIETY TEST ADM. ☐ YES ☐ NO	ATTITUDE	BREATH	COORDINATION	EYES	FACE	SPEECH

Walking Line Test: ◯ R. Foot △ L. Foot	BALANCE	PUPIL REACTION RIGHT EYE │ LEFT EYE	◯ Right Index △ Left Index
TURN	WALKING		
	TURNING	TIME TEST ADMIN.	

Are you sick or injured? ☐ Yes ☐ No	Are you under care of doctor or dentist? ☐ Yes ☐ No		
Are you diabetic or epileptic? ☐ Yes ☐ No	Are you taking any medicine or drugs? ☐ Yes ☐ No		
Do you take insulin? ☐ Yes ☐ No	Do you have any physical defect? ☐ Yes ☐ No		

If answer to any of the above is "Yes", explain completely on Continuation Sheet, Form 15.9.

WHAT HAVE YOU BEEN DRINKING?	HOW MUCH?	WITH WHOM?	WHERE?
NAME OF LAST DRINK	WHAT TIME IS IT NOW?	WHERE ARE YOU NOW?	WHERE ARE YOU GOING?
WHAT HAVE YOU EATEN TODAY?	WHERE?	WHEN?	WHEN DID YOU LAST SLEEP? HOW LONG?

Arrestee was requested to submit to a chemical test of his blood, breath, or urine, and was informed of his failure to submit to such chemical test of his choice would result in the suspension of his privilege to operate a motor vehicle for a period of six months.

CHEMICAL TEST ADMINISTERED ☐ BLOOD ☐ URINE ☐ BREATH ☐ ALL TESTS REFUSED	BREATHALYZER TEST NO. %	LOCATION	TIME ADMINISTERED	IF NOT BOOKED STATE REASON

In the opinion of the arresting officer(s), arrestee was intoxicated and unable to safely operate a motor vehicle.

Use a Continuation Sheet, Form 15.9, for circumstances of the arrest. Include statements of arrestee's understanding of his rights, manner of operating motor vehicle, unusual actions during field sobriety test, and any other information necessary in the completion of this report.

SUPERVISOR APPROVING SERIAL NO.	ARRESTING OFFICER(S)	SERIAL NUMBER DIVISION—DETAIL	VACATION DATES
DATE & TIME REPRODUCED DIVISION CLERK			

Figure 11-11   DUI report.

booking. The thoroughness of your report may lead the subject later to plead guilty, particularly if the blood-alcohol report comes back showing 0.10 or more, which is accepted as proof of "influence." Although it may be more difficult to get a conviction with a BA of less than 0.10, the driving and the field sobriety tests might have been so poorly done that you will still get a conviction.

EXERCISES AND STUDY QUESTIONS

1. Explain the types of situations when a police vehicle may violate the rules of the road as an emergency vehicle.
2. Under what conditions may the officer violate those rules of the road?
3. Write a general order for your department to use regarding escorting vehicles with nonpolice personnel driving.
4. Give one good reason for abandoning a police pursuit.
5. Is it acceptable police practice to abandon a pursuit?
6. For what reason might you decide *not* to pursue a traffic law violator?
7. How could an officer be held liable for pursuing a violator?
8. How many vehicles should use red light and siren when following a violator?
9. What does the author say about ramming a pursued vehicle?
10. Under what circumstances would you transport an injured person in your police vehicle?
11. When you stop a car for a citation, why would you park your vehicle behind and about 3 feet farther out into the street than the suspect vehicle?
12. Why would you park your vehicle parallel with, or to the right of, the suspect vehicle?
13. Describe what instructions you would use to get four suspects you believe to have been involved in an armed robbery out of their car.
14. When you stop a person for a routine traffic citation, are you justified to search him and his vehicle?
15. What is the BA level at which a person is presumed to be "under the influence"?
16. List and discuss five types of behavior that might alert you to the presence of a DUI.
17. Describe the field sobriety tests that are used in your jurisdiction.
18. Approximately how much alcohol must a person have in his or her system to have a BA of 0.10 according to the list in this chapter?
19. Which of the several field sobriety tests described is conclusive proof that the driver is "under the influence"?
20. Take the field sobriety test yourself and describe how well you did with absolutely no alcohol in your system.

REFERENCES

California Vehicle Code (annual).

FALES, E. D., JR. "New Facts about Skidding: They May Save Your Life." *Law Enforcement Bulletin*, May 1965, pp. 13–16.

Various training bulletins from Los Angeles Police Department, Santa Ana Police Department, California Highway Patrol, Golden West College, Orange County Sheriff's Department, academy training outlines, and various other sources were used for the compilation of this chapter.

12

ARREST, SEARCH, & CUSTODY

INTRODUCTION

Among the many critical discretionary decisions you make every day of your career as a police officer, the decision to arrest is one of the most significant for you as well as for the person you arrest. Although laws may read as though they are cut and dried and that you have little choice in deciding whether or not to arrest, you are the only person who can—and should—actually make that ultimate decision. At the moment you announce to the person that you are making the arrest, you are in great peril. At that point, you may meet violent resistance or an attempt to escape. In this chapter we cover some general laws of arrest, some of which perhaps vary from those of the jurisdiction in which you work; then we cover some procedures and guidelines in arrest, searching, transportation, and custody.

LAWS OF ARREST

The laws providing for arrest by peace officers may vary from one state to another, but for the purpose of discussion, we shall use California laws. Where there is a variance with the laws of your state, make the appropriate adjustments. Generally, a peace officer may arrest on authority of a warrant for either a felony or misdemeanor with the only restrictions on the arrest conditions differing on time of day when the arrest may be made. For example, most misdemeanors, unless the warrant indicates otherwise, are made during the daytime hours, while all felony warrant arrests may be made at any time of the day or night.

The amount of force that may be used depends on the amount of resistance that is offered by the person being arrested or other persons who might be attempting to help him evade arrest. When in immediate pursuit of the subject to be arrested, the officer is empowered to continue the pursuit until the subject is in custody, and this involves entering private property and breaking into—and back out of—places where the subject has fled and into other geographical jurisdictions. These laws are covered in more detail in the police academy and are directly related to state law and department policies.

Section 836 of the California Penal Code provides for three conditions when a peace officer may arrest without a warrant. They are

1. Whenever he has reasonable cause to believe that the person to be arrested has committed a public offense in his presence
2. When a person arrested has committed a felony, although not in his presence
3. Whenever he has reasonable cause to believe that the person to be arrested has committed a felony, whether or not a felony has in fact been committed

In the matter of misdemeanor arrests, the first factor in the "reasonable cause" consideration is that you should be reasonably familiar with the laws in the various codes that you enforce. Assuming that you have a better than adequate base of knowledge in that area, the next step is to determine whether or not you can deduce from your observations that an act—or failure to act—on the part of the person to be arrested is a violation of the law. Is the individual crossing that white line after the signal light has clearly turned to red? Is the man striking the woman with his fist? Are the words being shouted within earshot of that group of women actually obscene as defined by some earlier court decision, and are the women listening to those words and are they offended? What is your "presence," as far as the law is concerned? Let's look at some court decisions.

A federal court in 1924 noted that "presence" continues to be a requirement for a police officer to make a warrantless arrest "only if he had reasonable cause to believe it had been committed in his presence."[1] "In presence" means that which is directly perceived by any of the senses.[2] Of the senses by which law violations are perceived, eyesight is most common and the use of binoculars or a telescope is permitted.[3] Eyesight aided by a flashlight is acceptable.[4] Hearing without artificial

[1]*Garske* v. *United States*, 1 F.2d 620, 86h Cir. (1924).

[2]*Beck* v. *Ohio*, 379 U.S. 89 (1964).

[3]*People* v. *Steinberg*, 148 Cal. App. 2d 855, 307 P.2d 634 (1957).

[4]*Dorsey* v. *United States*, 372 F.2d 928, C.A.D.C. (1967).

aids was ruled as being in the officers' presence in *People* v. *Goldberg*.[5] Smell was similarly ruled in a 1922 case.[6]

The sense of touch is considered in shakedown or patdown searches when the officer detects an object through the clothing that feels like an automatic pistol, or a knife. Taste usually accompanies sight and smell, such as the person who might have the expertise to taste a suspected powder to determine if it is cocaine or heroin (although I do not recommend this taste test procedure because it could contain poison), or for the alcoholic nature of a beverage, such as beer or wine. Perception may also be accomplished through a team effort to qualify for the "presence" requirement, such as the 1968 case when one officer observed a burglary and described the fleeing suspects in a radio broadcast. Another officer heard the broadcast and stopped the suspects on the basis of the description.[7]

The second subsection of the arrest laws, which states "when a person arrested has committed a felony, although not in his presence," also presupposes that you are familiar with the felonies in your state and the elements of the corpus delicti necessary to prove for a conviction. This, too, would depend upon your perceptual abilities; your presence would not have been required, but you would be required to explain to the court how you knew the person had committed a felony. Perhaps you were informed by the detectives working burglary, or by radio broadcast, or by reading a bulletin listing wanted felons.

The third subsection is more complex, and is principally what distinguishes a private person arrest from an arrest made by a peace officer. By the very nature of your work, you are trained and are required to be more suspicious of questionable activities. You are charged with protection of life and property in your assigned district. You must be diligent and must constantly exercise an inquiring mind. Based on your observations, your interpretations of those observations, your reasonable cause to believe certain things that you presume to be true as related to other facts, and the requirement that you act as a police officer, whenever the situation calls for it, you may arrest on the basis of this portion of the law. Later, it is affirmed or disaffirmed that the person arrested did in fact (or did not) commit a felony as you suspected. Let's consider two examples.

- While cruising in your district, you are passing a restaurant when you observe a crowd gathering inside. Several of the people appear to be watching some sort of struggle inside a circle of onlookers. As you break through the crowd, you ask several people what is happening and receive no answer. They just point to a man lying on the floor and another man kneeling over him with a butcher knife in his hand. The person with the knife is cutting the other man's

[5]*People* v. *Goldberg*, 280 N.Y.S.2d 646, 19 N.Y.2d 460, 277 N.E.2d 575 (1967).

[6]*McBride* v. *United States*, 284 F.416, 5th Cir. (1922).

[7]*Robinson* v. *State*, 4 Md. App. 515, 243 A.2d 879 (1968).

throat. Acting on the belief that what you are observing appears to be an attempted murder, you immediately disarm the man with the knife and place him under arrest. You are then informed by several people in the crowd and the man with the knife that what you actually observed was a choking victim with a piece of meat lodged in his throat and a doctor who is performing a tracheotomy on the victim to save his life. After you release the doctor and allow him to continue the emergency surgery, you ask yourself "was I legally correct in what I did, based on the information I had to operate under?" The answer is "yes."

- Under circumstances that lead you to believe that a group of people in a car is cruising an area where there have been numerous burglaries at that particular time of night, you stop the car and conduct a field interview. The occupants of the car choose not to answer any of your questions designed to explain their presence in the area or any of their activities, and you observe several household items in the car, such as stereo speakers and components, a portable television set, and three small radios. You ask the occupants about the items, and your response is that it is none of your business. You check records on the occupants and discover that three of the four have extensive records for burglary. You sincerely believe that you have probable cause for an arrest. You arrest all four of the subjects for suspicion of being in possession of stolen property. You impound their car, book the suspects, put the property you believed to have been stolen in the evidence locker, and prepare your reports. The next day, detectives working burglary check out the property and the suspects and find out that none of the property was stolen and that their only crime was failing to cooperate with you. The detectives release the suspects and return their property to them. Did you commit a false arrest? No.

WHAT CONSTITUTES AN ARREST?

Actually, there are many different types of situations when an officer makes contact with a person which may appear to be an arrest but is not. According to the courts in various situations, the contact may be a "contact," a "consensual encounter," a "detention," or an "arrest."

In the "contact" situation, the person contacted remains totally free to leave or not to cooperate with you. In the encounter, you may not restrain the person or exert any authority over him or her. (*Roger*, 1983, 460 U.S. 491). You may continue to ask for the subject's cooperation, but do not demand it. If necessary, tell the person you are not detaining him and that he is free to leave, but you would like to ask a few questions. Once you start giving orders, the contact becomes a "detention."

A detention is something less than an arrest, but it is more than a "consensual encounter." In this situation a reasonable person would believe that he or she is not free to leave, and it is under conditions when an officer believes that the person is in some way involved in a criminal activity (*Terry* v. *Ohio*, 1968, 392 U.S. 1). You should have sufficient facts, coupled with your unique training and experience as a police officer, to be able to articulate to the court a reasonable suspicion that something related to crime has happened, is happening, or is about to happen and you believe the person to be connected with that activity.

Police actions in a detention situation would include:

1. You may question the person about his or her identity, conduct, and reason for being at this particular location at this time. You may ask for some type of documentary proof of identification, such as a driver's license. If he or she states that he or she has ID but is not going to produce it, you may conduct a limited search for it.

2. You may detain the subject while you contact other persons to confirm the information given by the subject, to verify the identification, or determine if further investigation or an arrest is warranted.

3. You may detain the subject while checking premises at or near the place of contact, or contact residents or businesses nearby to determine if a crime has been committed, or to check out suspicious items that might be stolen merchandise.

4. You may detain a subject for the purpose of bringing a victim or witness to that location for a field "showup."

Avoid using any type of physical restraints, such as handcuffs when detaining a person, because it then takes on the characteristics of an arrest. Survival is essential, however, and you may take whatever precautions are necessary to avoid injury to yourself or the subject. Move the subject under detention only when absolutely necessary, such as from a hostile crowd.

ARREST PROCEDURES

Use of Force

"Only that force which is necessary" or "no more than is reasonable" are two phrases describing how much force you may use in effecting an arrest. You may ask: "How much is necessary?" or "What is reasonable force?" Those questions are easier to ask than to answer. Since most of the decisions that you make about use of force in any police situation are dependent upon a unique situation that is unlike any other, and your action is a reaction to whatever the person to be arrested takes, it is impossible to develop a simple formula. Consider the Los Angeles officers charged with using too much force on parolee Mr. Rodney King, a young African-American on whom the officers testified they had to use so much force because they "feared for their lives" and that they believed that he was continuing to attack even though he was down on the ground and appeared to be going nowhere on the videotape that we all saw on television.

Although the criminal codes of your state cover the laws of arrest and define how much force you may use, do not take those words at face value. For example, consider the California Penal Code sections that cover the use of deadly force:

> **Sec. 834a. Resistance to arrest.** *If a person has knowledge, or by the exercise of reasonable care, should have knowledge, that he is being arrested by a peace officer, it is the duty of such person to refrain from using force or any weapon to resist such arrest.*

A problem with this section is that the person who resists arrest may plead that he had no idea that the badge the officer was wearing was real, or that he believed he was being pounced upon by a gang of cab drivers, or that he was so full of drugs or narcotics that he was out of his mind and did not know what he was doing.

> **Sec. 835. Method of making arrest; amount of restraint.** *An arrest is made by an actual restraint of the person, or by submission to the custody of an officer. The person arrested may be subjected to such restraint as is reasonable for his arrest and detention.*

What about the level of training and experience of the officer; the relative sizes of the officer and the suspect; the appearance of the person to be arrested (threatening, massive, extremely agitated, may be in possession of a weapon) and the individual officer's perception of danger from the subject? What is *reasonable*?

> **Sec. 835a. Use of force to effect arrest, prevent escape, or overcome resistance.** *A peace officer who makes an arrest need not retreat or desist from his efforts by reason of the resistance or threatened resistance of the person being arrested; nor shall such officer be deemed an aggressor or lose his right to self-defense by the use of reasonable force to effect the arrest or to prevent escape or to overcome resistance.*

Here we see the word "reasonable" again. What is "reasonable" depends on the independent judgment of the officer at the moment of decision. A lot depends on the skill of the officer and his or her own confidence in the use of that skill in a given situation. Unless the officer has been in contests with the arrestee before, the officer has no idea of the skill and experience, or intent of the arrestee.

> **Sec. 196. Justifiable homicide; public officers.** *Homicide*

*is justifiable when committed by public officers and those act-
ing by their command in their aid and assistance, either:*

1. *In obedience to any judgment of a competent Court; or*

2. *When necessarily committed in overcoming actual resistance to the execution of some legal process.*

3. *When necessarily committed in retaking felons who have
been rescued or have escaped, or when necessarily committed in arresting persons charged with felony, and
who are fleeing from justice or resisting such arrest.*

The first part applies to carrying out a legal execution, but the next
two parts ask the officer to decide what is "necessary."

None of these sections are self-defense situations. That problem is
addressed by the justifiable homicide sections that cover all persons,
including peace officers, and are based upon life-threatening situations—
the person's fears of imminent death or grievous bodily harm to himself or
another person. These justifiable homicide situations also depend on
whether such action was reasonable under the circumstances.
"Reasonable" is determined by the officer who responds to the call, or by
the supervisor in case the defender is a peace officer, by a prosecuting
attorney or a grand jury, and eventually by a judge or a jury.

In your own mind, and within the policies of your department, there
must be some guidelines for you to follow when it comes to the use of
force. As a general guideline, it seems to me that taking a person into custody is absolutely essential for the ends of justice to be met. That said,
now let's look at reality. We are dealing with human beings, who are entitled to be treated as humans. Depending on the actions of the person to be
arrested, your actions are reactions. When you tell a person that he or she
is under arrest, and the person willingly complies with your directions
and submits to custody, handcuffing and transporting would normally be
no problem. But we know that nothing is normal in police work. If the
subject gives token resistance or verbal indications that there is going to
be some resistance, then some degree of force is necessary to control the
arrestee. If there is forceful resistance or you have the sense that the
forcible resistance is imminent, you must use whatever force you believe
at that moment to be adequate to continue to maintain control over the
arrestee. As the forceful resistance escalates, so will be your degree of
force, with the arrestee actually calling the shots. If you anticipate deadly
resistance, your use of deadly force is justified.

As you can see, there are no "exacts" in the use of force, because it is
difficult—if not impossible—to predict precisely what the arrestee is
about to do. When it comes to making an arrest of someone who is not an
imminent threat to your life or that of another person, deadly force is
never justified. It is better to let the fleeing felon get away than to take
that person's life. If the felon is pulling a bloody knife out of the chest of

his victim or is stepping away from a dead or dying victim that he or she just shot with the smoking gun in hand, and you believe that his or her escape is going to lead to the death of another person the moment the suspect rounds the corner or gets over the fence and makes an escape, your use of deadly force may be reasonable and necessary. If there is no sense of imminent deadly consequence of the suspect getting away from your custody, better to let the person go and get him or her at a later time. This should be the same as your decision when to abandon any pursuit. It is not a contest and you will not be judged no longer champion if you let one get away.

Breaking into a Building to Arrest

You may break into a door or window to gain entry into any place where you know or believe that a person you have legal cause to arrest is sheltered. In most situations, you must first identify yourself as a police officer to establish your authority to enter and then demand admittance and state your reason for the demand. In general, you will need an arrest and a search warrant when you are entering a person's private residence. If there is no response, or the people inside refuse to admit you, you may then make the entry. An exception to this rule would be if such announcement and delay in gaining entry would further endanger someone's life, if critical evidence would probably be destroyed during the delay, or if it would otherwise frustrate the arrest. Once inside, and if, for some reason, you are trapped inside, you have the same authority to break out to free yourself.

Resistance to Arrest a Crime

When you are making an arrest, be sure to identify yourself so that there can be no question as to your authority; then make it clear to the person you intend to arrest what you are going to do and for what charge. If he knows that he is being arrested, according to law he must submit to the arrest without offering resistance. If he claims innocence of the crime, or positively knows that he had nothing to do with a criminal matter that would lead to his arrest, he should present his case at a more appropriate time. It is your responsibility to act on valid information and good faith, assuring yourself that the arrests you make are valid.

Warrant Arrests

A warrant is usually directed to any peace officer with jurisdiction in the state. One of the most important aspects of a warrant arrest is to make sure that the warrant is valid. There have been occasions when the arrest had already been made in the warrant, but for some reason, it was not removed from the files. If you are in doubt as to the validity of the warrant, it is usually wiser not to make the arrest.

The warrant must state the specific charge for which the person is to be arrested, such as "Criminal Code Section 123, Loitering." There must be a description of the person to be arrested. Generally, a person's name is considered his identification, but there is room for error when arresting by name only. You must be sure that you are arresting the individual for whom the warrant is intended. There are several principal "identifiers" useful for a warrant, including name, address, driver's license number, date of birth, place of birth, sex, color of hair and eyes, height and weight, race, nationality descent, and visible scars and marks.

The warrant must also bear the signature of the issuing judge or magistrate. If the warrant is for a felony, the arrest may be made at any time. In the case of misdemeanors, however, the warrant must specifically state that it is for nighttime service or that it can be used as a basis for arrest only during daytime.

The warrant requires that the person named be taken to the judge who issued the warrant or to the court of issue. In your own jurisdiction, it may be a standard procedure to take the arrestee directly to jail to go through the "booking" process. He then posts bail and receives a specific time to report to the court. In these cases, the arrestees are not generally taken directly to the judge unless they demand it. Once the subject named on the warrant has been arrested and processed according to its instructions, the officer signs that portion of the document known as the "notification (or certification) of service," and the document is returned to the court.

Arrests without a Warrant

Except when it is obvious that you are arresting the subject for a crime that he is committing at the time of arrest, or are arresting him immediately following a pursuit, it is mandatory that you identify yourself, that you announce your intention to arrest him, and that you state the crime for which you are arresting him. Review the facts that you have and make sure that your justification for the arrest is valid.

Prepare for the arrest by arranging for adequate support if time permits. Use common sense and distinguish between bravery and foolhardiness. A single-handed arrest accomplished by a brave officer looks good in the personnel jacket, but do not risk it at the expense of possibly losing the suspect or causing yourself to sustain an injury or death because of your failure to call for assistance. Charisma, or command presence, is essential. Make it clear to the suspect that you are arresting him or her by your actions, your appearance, and your command voice. Give clear and concise orders. Use only that force that is necessary. Maintain constant visual and physical control of the arrestee. If the situation is serious enough to call for an arrest, it should be standard procedure to consider the possibility that the suspect may try to attack you or attempt to escape. Never turn your back on the suspect; always "keep on your guard."

Diplomatic Immunity

The F.B.I *Law Enforcement Bulletin* of August 1973[8] presented an updated set of guidelines entitled "Procedures and Policies Relating to Diplomatic and Consular Officials." The guidelines that follow reflect the amended rules enacted at the Vienna Convention on Diplomatic Relations of December 13, 1972. The guidelines were explained by the Office of the Chief of Protocol, U.S. Department of State.

The Chief of Protocol defines "diplomatic immunity" as

> *the freedom from local jurisdiction accorded to duly accredited diplomatic officers, their families, and servants. Diplomatic officers should not be arrested or detained for any offense, and foreign career consular officers should not be arrested or detained except for the commission of a grave crime. Family members of diplomatic officers, their servants, and employees of a diplomatic mission are entitled to the same immunities under current U.S. law (22 U.S.C. 252), if they are not nationals of or permanently resident in the receiving state.*

> *Associated with this personal diplomatic immunity is the inviolability enjoyed by the premises of the mission of the sending state and the private residence of a diplomatic agent, his property papers, and correspondence.*

What this means, essentially, is that diplomatic officers and their families, official staff, and servants, who are not citizens of, or permanent residents of, the united States, are totally immune from arrest, detention, or prosecution for any civil or criminal offense. They are identified by credentials issued by the State Department, and although their offices are located in Washington, D.C., or New York City, they may be encountered almost anywhere.

Consular officials are accorded some limited immunities, but their families and other members of their household or other entourage are not covered by the immunity. As with all individuals you encounter in any given situation, they should be treated fairly and courteously. Credentials for consular officials are also issued by the State Department.

A foreign career officer may not be arrested or held pending trial for any criminal charge except a grave crime, defined by the State Department as a felony offense that would endanger the public safety and "pursuant to a decision by the competent judicial authority."[9] The guidelines further point out that this immunity to criminal prosecution involves only "acts performed in the exercise of consular functions and is

---

[8]Federal Bureau of Investigation, *Law Enforcement Bulletin*, August 1973.

[9]Ibid., p. 14.

subject to court determination."[10] From that statement, it would appear that consular officials other than those protected by diplomatic immunity would be subject to the same law enforcement as any other persons in your jurisdiction, although there might be some delicate international issue in balance. If in doubt, contact your local prosecutor or judge for guidance.

A consular office or building and official papers and documents of such a consulate post and in possession of consular officials are protected by diplomatic immunity. Entry of such official premises that are used exclusively for work may be done only with permission of the head of that post or the head of that diplomatic mission or without permission if there is an urgent need to put out a fire or provide some other protective service.[11]

Entrapment

Sooner or later, the entrapment issue will be raised when you make an arrest, particularly when the arrest involves some sort of undercover or decoy operation. Because you were not standing directly in front of the violator at the time in full uniform, you may be accused of entrapment. The issue was addressed in the *Sorrells* case in 1932, when the Supreme Court stated: "Society is at war with the criminal classes and courts have uniformly held that in waging this warfare, the forces of prevention and detection may use traps, decoys, and deception to obtain evidence of the commission of crime."[12] Although there has been some erosion by rules involving interrogation and lineups, that statement still carries considerable weight. Undercover activities may include placing an informer among criminal ranks to build a case and collect evidence, having officers pose as "hit men" to gather evidence against people who are looking for someone to kill a friend or relative for insurance purposes, having an officer pose as a prostitute or a "john" on the streets to arrest solicitors, or having a team of officers go out on the streets posing as derelicts and drunks so that they may draw the muggers to them as potential victims.

Undercover operations, plants, informants, and decoys are all used at one time or another in this "war with the criminal classes." And it's legal. The test as to whether entrapment occurred is "with whom did the idea to commit crime originate?" The narcotics dealer, or the mugger, or the prostitute are all plying their trades on the streets, and the officers working such clandestine assignments are not putting the ideas to commit crime in the offenders' minds. They are merely increasing the odds for protecting other people and in catching the offenders at their occupations.

---

[10]Ibid.

[11]Ibid.

[12]*Sorrells* v. *United States*, 287 U.S. 435 (1932).

Whenever you work such an assignment, the key to prosecution free of entrapment is to make yourself available for the criminal to operate in your presence and not to induce him or her in any way that could be interpreted to mean that the idea to commit crime was yours and not the offender's.

In a 1979 California case, the California Supreme Court in *Barraza* gave their definition of entrapment:[13]

> *Entrapment—which is a defense, not a crime—means inducing a person to commit a crime which was not contemplated by him, for the purpose of prosecuting him.*
>
> *The current judicial test for entrapment is whether your conduct was likely to induce a mythical, innocent, normally law-abiding person to commit the offense. If it was, then you have gone too far, and the defense is available.*
>
> *On the other hand, if you just provided the opportunity for the crime to be committed by someone who was already of a mind to commit it on his own, then there has been no entrapment.*

Investigative Detention

There are many occasions when you will temporarily detain a person in the field or possibly transport the person to the station for a short period of time to investigate the individual and circumstances that seem to warrant further inquiry. The field interview situation, or the field identification of all people who happen to be in the vicinity of a crime are just two examples of such temporary detention. In *United States* v. *West*[14] and *United States* v. *Allen*,[15] the courts stated "The local policeman...is also in a very real sense a guardian of the public peace, and he has a duty in the course of his work to be alert for suspicious circumstances and, provided that he acts within constitutional limits, to investigate whenever such circumstances indicate to him that he should do so."

In 1968 the U.S. Supreme Court ruled that

> *where a police officer observes unusual conduct which leads him reasonably to conclude in light of his experiences that criminal activity may be afoot and that the persons with whom he is dealing may be armed and presently dangerous, where in the course of investigating this behavior he identifies himself as a policeman and makes reasonable inquiries, and*

---

[13]23 Cal. 3d 675 (1979).

[14]460 F.2d 374, 5th Cir. (1972).

[15]472 F.2d 145, 5th Cir. (1973).

where nothing in the initial stages of the encounter serves to dispel his reasonable fear for his own or others' safety, he is entitled for the protection of himself and others in the area to conduct a carefully limited search of the outer clothing of such persons in an attempt to discover weapons which might be used to assault him. (Terry v. Ohio 392 U.S.1)

A temporary detention for additional investigation beyond the frisk may be necessary, according to the courts. The Fourth Amendment is not so restrictive that a police officer should allow a crime to occur or a criminal to escape apprehension just because the officer lacks the precise amount of information necessary to show probable cause for an arrest. For example, an officer may have probable cause to search a person, but at that moment not have enough cause for an arrest. Then, during the search, the officer finds a weapon or contraband and now has the probable cause for an arrest. With the continued validity of court decisions reinforcing age-old police procedures of stopping persons for investigation and searching for weapons and the constitutionality of temporary detention upon reasonable cause, officers may perform their jobs when they can show probable cause for their actions at each step along the way.

SEARCHING TECHNIQUES

Officers who sustain injuries while searching persons are apt to be those with several years of experience. They have probably made hundreds, or thousands, of arrests without incident and have grown confident that they are doing everything right. Actually there is a possibility that those officers are developing bad habits without realizing it. One way to counteract this development of bad habits is to approach each arrest and each search as an entirely new experience, and strictly according to an established procedure.

There are two essential aspects to search and seizure: law and procedure. The following section covers the procedure. It is extremely important that an armed and potentially dangerous suspect be disarmed as quickly and efficiently as possible.

Types and Methods of Search

The patrol officer conducts three basic types of searches: the frisk, the field search, and the strip search. Each has its own distinct procedure.

Frisk, or "Patdown." The frisk is the cursory search. It generally accompanies a field interview and is not considered an exploratory search. The only objects for which you can search during the frisk are weapons. However, if the frisk reveals other contraband and it can be truly shown that the discovery was incidental to the frisk, rather than the frisk being used as an excuse to look for some objects, the discovery of the contraband is sufficient cause to conduct the more thorough search. Start at the head and work the hands along the outside of the clothing wherever weapons may be found. Do not place your hands inside the clothing unless the outside patting process reveals something that feels like a weapon, in which case you may search inside to verify your suspicions. Then have the subject face you while you examine the mouth, nose and ears, and the female's bra area.

Field Search. This search may be conducted on reasonable cause to search without an arrest, or prior to an arrest, and it should be routine whenever you perform an arrest.

1. Keep the person off balance. This can be accomplished by three basic methods: the kneeling search position, standing search position, and prone search position.

For the standing position, have the subject stand with fingers locked together. Have the subject lean back while you maintain complete control. (See Figure 12–1).

Figure 12-1   The position for search is to have the suspect stand with hands locked behind the head. The officer holds the suspect off balance while searching. (Courtesy of the Police Department, Santa Ana, California.)

For the kneeling search position, have the subject kneel on both knees, and cross his legs behind him. As you search him from behind it is possible to exert a slight pressure on the top of the crossed legs to maintain control. Have the subject hold his hands above his head and lock his fingers behind his head.

For the prone search position, have the subject lie face down on the ground or floor surface with arms and legs outstretched. This position of disadvantage makes it very difficult for the subject to assume a combative position.

2. Handcuff each subject prior to conducting the search.

3. Maintain your own balance on your toes, and always keep your eyes on the subject. While your back-up officer assumes a cover position, the best place for the searching officer's weapon is securely fastened in a holster. It is not unusual for a suspect to attempt to attack an officer during the initial phases of an arrest and search.

4. Search with one hand. Use the other hand for defense and to place on the small of the suspect's back during the search. You can hold him off-balance with this hand.

5. Start at the head, running your hands through the hair, and watching for straight-edged razor blades that might have been planted for the purpose of injuring the searching officer. (Other places for planted razor blades are inside small trousers pockets and along the inside of the waistband.) While standing to the right rear of the subject, run your hands around the collar of his jacket or shirt, down the front of the shirt, and starting at the shoulders, down the inside of the sleeve up to the armpits. The armpit area of a bulky jacket or coat is a favorite hiding place for pistols or revolvers. Run your hand down the outside of the arm, feeling the sleeve, then around the waistband. At the waistband, feel for any string that may be hanging from the belt and be holding a gun or knife at the other end for easy access. Loosen the belt or remove it entirely, if necessary.

Search the legs, starting at the crotch area and working down from the outside and the inside. One popular hiding place for weapons is inside the shorts in the area of the genitals, because of the knowledge that there will be a natural reluctance to touch the private parts. If you want to live long enough to retire, you had better get over that squeamish attitude. Another popular place is on the inside of the calf of the leg, where a garter or elastic part of a sock may be used to hold a weapon. Feel inside the subject's shoes or boots. After completing one side, go to the other side and repeat the operation. Remove boots or shoes and socks and search thoroughly.

6. Make all your commands and instructions clear and brief.

7. When other officers are assisting you in the search, have them stand off to one side opposite the side you are working on. If there is more than one subject, search each one in turn, starting with the one on the left while your "cover officer" is standing at the opposite side of the line.

Search the first subject from the left; then move him and yourself to the right end of the line and search him from the right. Repeat this procedure with each subject. By using this method, it is possible to search as many people as there are in the line without ever placing yourself between two of the subjects you are searching. By having the "cover" officer move to the opposite side of the line whenever you move, you are assuring maximum coverage of the subjects during the entire searching process. If you have enough officers, each suspect may be searched by a different officer at the same time.

8. Never turn your back on a subject.

9. Do not be timid when searching an individual, but do not use abusive methods or abusive language.

10. Do not get too close to any subject before you have him at a position of disadvantage.

11. Your search is for weapons, tools or implements used to commit crime, evidence relevant to a crime, or the fruits of a crime.

Strip Search. This search is conducted in the privacy of headquarters and eventually in jail during the booking process. The most efficient means of searching an individual's person and clothing is to have the person remove all clothes and then perform a systematic and thorough search of the body and of each item of clothing. Carefully examine the individual's body from head to toe, looking for any item that may be attached to the body by means of tape, a bandage, chains, straps, or various types of jewelry. Favorite hiding places are the hair, bottom of the feet, in the mouth, near the genitalia, and in the body crevices. If necessary to search the interior of the body cavities, call upon the services of a physician to conduct the examination under clinical conditions. Be sure of your legal limitations in this type of search.

Search of Women. There is no legal distinction between searching a man and searching a woman, and searches may be conducted by police personnel of either sex. However, propriety should prevail unless the life of a person is endangered. When a search is essential for the protection of life, it must be conducted, but it must be justifiable in the eyes of many other persons at a later time. The most acceptable arrangement for a search of a woman is to have a woman conduct it. In the absence of a woman who may conduct the search, handcuff the female suspect with her hands behind her back, and place her pocketbook or purse where she cannot get her hands inside. You may roll the police baton across any suspected bulges, particularly in the breast, pelvic, and buttock areas.

To ascertain if bulges are caused by some hard object such as a weapon, a cursory search may be made by any woman in the immediate area if she is willing, but a thorough search must be made by a female employee of a law enforcement agency who has been adequately trained in the art of self-defense and in searching techniques.

As with the male suspect, search of body cavities should always be made by a medical doctor or other qualified person under dignified and sanitary clinical conditions.

Searches of Persons at Airports. Skyjacking is not new. Actually, the first commercial aircraft to hold the distinction of being taken over forcefully was a Peruvian airplane in 1930.[16] Since then, there have been several hundred similar crimes. As the crime became more frequent, the Federal Aviation Act of 1958 was amended to include a possible death penalty for the crime. In the years that followed, security at airports became more and more critical. Until February 6, 1972, airport security was voluntary. On that date, the Federal Aviation Administration made it mandatory that all airline passengers be screened by one or more screening devices, such as the electronics weapons detector, interview by airline personnel, interview by law enforcement personnel, or a patdown or frisk for weapons. Now it is a routine preboarding experience for all passengers to pass through a metal-detecting unit or to be searched with the aid of a portable metal-detecting unit and to have carry-on luggage and other items searched and/or x-rayed.

In addition to the routine gate procedures, airport personnel are trained to look for individuals who appear to match a "profile" of potential skyjackers and drug dealers. The exact nature of the profile is kept secret. Whenever suspicions are aroused by a person matching the profile, or by some other behavior, the search and personal attention is considerably more intense. Luggage that is being sent through may be searched as well as the carry-on luggage. Such a search is usually conducted by airline personnel and is then continued by law enforcement personnel if the initial search reveals material of significance.

Since January 5, 1973, every air carrier is required to inspect all carry-on baggage and to screen all passengers through a metal detector or, if no such detection device is available, to require a consent to search prior to boarding. According to those regulations, issued under Federal Regulations 25934-35 of December 6, 1972, the airline personnel actually do the screening, but law enforcement personnel will be present to assist when necessary. From that point on, probable, or reasonable, cause justification dictates how you may proceed with further searches.

Vehicle Searches. Not all occasions on which a police officer looks through a vehicle are necessarily considered searches. For example, when you must have someone's automobile stored because it was parked in a hazardous location, or was recovered stolen, or was being held for some other legitimate reason, it should be routine for someone to *inventory* the automobile. Because you will be held responsible for the vehicle and its contents, you should conduct a careful inventory of the condition of the

[16]David G. Hubbard, *The Skyjacker and His Flights of Fantasy* (New York: Macmillan, 1971). p. 258.

vehicle and itemize all contents while taking steps to provide for the safe-keeping of those contents. It is also possible that you might be looking through an abandoned vehicle and find something that will later prove to be of evidentiary value. Another occasion might be when you approach a vehicle and look inside to determine that there is no one hiding in the back seat who might be a threat to your safety. What is in plain sight, even when illuminated by flashlight, is not being searched.

The issue of whether you may search a vehicle has been addressed in many court decisions, and the usual guideline is that, whenever an officer has reasonable cause to conduct a search and whenever it appears that such a search is consistent with good police work, you may search a vehicle without a warrant, whether under suspicious circumstances or whether incidental to an arrest. Automobiles and other vehicles that are highly mobile could be moved so easily and quickly that evidence could be destroyed or taken completely away from its original location before you could get a warrant. As with any other searching procedure, these are merely guidelines and are subject to change by rapidly changing court decisions.

Whenever possible, you might consider trying for a consent search. By merely asking a question such as "You don't mind if I search your car, do you?" or "I would like to look in your trunk. You have the right to refuse. May I look?" you may receive blanket approval. Situations that may negate any consent include the use of restraint, a display of force or weapons while you are asking, the number of officers present, the issuance of threats or promises, or the use of trickery or deceit in gaining the consent. To show consent, you must prove the following:

1. The person was informed of or indicated a knowledge of the right to refuse admittance to the search.
2. The person consenting understood his or her rights and knowingly consented to the search.
3. The waiver was given in a clear and positive manner.
4. The waiving party was in a legal position to give consent.
5. The consent was free of duress or coercion.

Whenever you search a vehicle incidental to an arrest, conduct the search when it is contemporaneous with the arrest and when the subject is present. While searching, you may show the subject certain items and ask for a statement of ownership or other knowledge about their presence in the vehicle. Also, the subject will be witnessing the search and discoveries you make and will be less likely to claim that you planted evidence in the vehicle.

You may move the vehicle prior to searching under certain conditions, for example, poor lighting conditions at the scene, gathering hostile crowds, severely inclement weather, traffic congestion or road hazards, or lack of special searching equipment—vacuum, ultraviolet light—at the place you are conducting the search.

The method for searching vehicles should be as thorough and as imaginative as possible. The most effective means is to begin at the front and work systematically to the back on one side and then work back to the front of the vehicle on the opposite side. If two officers are working together, they should conduct the search independently of each other, with each officer conducting a complete search in succession. In this manner you are getting a "second opinion," so to speak.

This procedure is far more efficient than having each officer search a portion of the vehicle. There are so many hiding places that it is easy to overlook one, and two complete searches are better than one partial search.

Where to Search

This is a real challenge to the inquiring officer. Evidence and contraband have been found in virtually every place where anything may be concealed. Consider the places where objects have been found by other officers. Where would *you* hide something?

In the bumper and grill areas, certain items may be concealed by the use of masking tape or wire. Look for boxes, which may be welded in, that serve no functional purpose for the operation of the vehicle. The area under the hood provides many excellent hiding places, for example, inside the air cleaner, the vents, or the air conditioner. Certain accessories may be inoperable and the housing parts may be used to store items such as smuggled marijuana or other narcotics.

Under the dashboard, there are several places that may hold evidence, for example, the area above the glove compartment, the fuse box, or the underside of the dash. Use a flashlight and a mirror to search this area. Under the floorboard may be a good place for a built-in carrying case. In one smuggling case, an officer lifted the floor mat and found a trap door. Opening it, he found a large storage box welded to the underside of the car. The box was full of narcotics.

Look for torn places in the upholstery, in the headliner, and in the side panels; these may signal the presence of a hidden pocket for carrying a concealed weapon. The area inside the dome lights and similar empty places are accessible for hiding, and they should also be searched.

Move everything that is movable and look inside, behind, and under it. Ask yourself where you would hide a weapon, narcotics, or stolen merchandise, or whether you would hide it at all. One burglar carried his stolen merchandise right out on the seat of the car and was stopped for routine questioning on several occasions. When asked about the merchandise, he stated that it was his. When asked about his success, he explained that his secret was to remain calm and cool when questioned, because his natural manner did not arouse any of the officers' suspicions. He added that some officers erroneously believe that a thief or burglar will become very nervous in the presence of an officer, obviously for fear of being found out.

Generally, when searching an automobile for evidence, it is good practice to be familiar with the particular body designs and to look for modifications or deviations from those designs. Conduct a thorough search and use your imagination. Pickups with campers may have false walls, with the outside and inside appearing to correspond, while there may actually be a foot or two of space between the inside and outside walls. Vans and trucks may be similarly designed.

Search of the Premises

Except under conditions when you pursue someone into a house or apartment or other private place, or when contraband or other evidence is in plain sight while you are lawfully inside the place, or when you can show that you did not have time to get a warrant prior to the search because the delay would result in destruction of the evidence, your best option is to seek permission for the search from a person who has a legal right to give consent to search the place or person you wish to search.

Whenever there is time, particularly if you know when and where you are going to make the arrest, what evidence you intend to look for, and that you will probably find it, secure a warrant for the search before you go to the place you wish to search. Your search may then be much more methodical and complete.

According to the *Chimel* decision,[17] a search that is coincidental to an arrest requires that the arrest must have been based upon a warrant and upon reasonable cause (or probable cause, whichever term you prefer), and the search must be contemporaneous with the arrest. You may search only that portion of the premises where the subject is located at the time of the arrest (his sphere of influence or control) where the subject may have deposited or disposed of what you are searching for. Your search will be limited to only those areas that were within the sphere or the area where the subject may have placed or deposited evidence or other contraband along his route of travel or where he is located at the time. You may search only for weapons that were used in the crime in question or with which the subject might attack you, tools or instruments with which the subject might have used to commit the crime, fruits of the crime or evidence taken from the crime scene, or contraband that is unlawful to possess such as drugs or counterfeit money.

Notebook Entries Regarding Searches

Whenever you discover items of evidence during a search, record in your field notebook an accurate description of the item, and describe exactly where and under what conditions you found it. If the owner or driver of the vehicle is present, ask for a state of ownership for each item you find, and record his response. Handle the items as you would handle any other evidence.

[17]*Chimel* v. *Calif.* 395 U.S. 752 S. Ct. 2034 (1969).

Review of Legal Considerations

The rules of search and seizure are principally court-made rules developed over the past 200 years, with the major thrust having begun in the 1960s. The courts review cases brought before them on a case-by-case basis and determine which evidence should have been suppressed, or "excluded"—hence the "exclusionary rule." Reasonableness or unreasonableness of the search made by the police or their agents is determined in light of the provisions of the Constitution and the Bill of Rights, which restrict their activity.

A person's place of residence, personal property, and personal places within a person's place of business present an expectation of privacy. For example, a paying guest in a hotel room has a greater expectation of privacy than does one of his casual visitors to whom the room has not been rented, and the driver of a vehicle has a greater expectation of privacy than does his passenger, unless, of course, the passenger is the owner of the car. The private office of the manager of the insurance company has a greater expectation of privacy than do persons in the adjoining general office area. The general rule is that before an officer may search any place or person, a search warrant must be issued by a judge who has reviewed an affidavit signed by a witness alleging facts supporting the need for a search of a certain place or person, describing what the search is expected to turn up, and what it is expected to prove.

Searches conducted without warrants are based on "good faith" exceptions to the rule. According to the Court in a 1979 case (*Sanders*, 442 U.S. 753): Warrantless searches are presumed to be illegal and will be upheld only if the prosecution can prove that the police conduct came within one of the few "carefully circumscribed and jealously guarded" exceptions to the warrant requirements. Examples of such exceptions include (1) consent searches, (2) emergency searches permitted because of exigent circumstances, and (3) searches conducted incident to arrest. Loosely defined, an exigency is an emergency.

According to the ruling made in the *Chimel* case (1969, 395 U.S. 752), after a lawful arrest you may search the arrestee and the immediate area around him or her incidental to the arrest. A full search of the person is admissible, plus the immediate area, that within arm's reach and the space from which the suspect could reach for a weapon or to destroy or conceal evidence. The search may be for (1) instrumentalities used to commit the crime, the fruits of that crime, and other evidence thereof which will aid in the apprehension and conviction of the criminal; (2) articles whose possession is itself unlawful, such as contraband or goods known to be stolen; and (3) weapons that can be used to assault the arresting officer or to effect an escape.

It is unreasonable for a police officer to enter physically into an area where a person has a "reasonable expectation of privacy" in order to conduct a search or for the purpose of seizing something unless (a) you have a warrant, or (b) emergency circumstances exist, or (c) you have obtained a valid consent.

If you are already inside legally, there is no rule which says that you have to shut your eyes. If you are outside a house and see something inside, secure a warrant unless the criterion (b) or (c) is present. A driveway has no privacy, and a backyard deserves more privacy than does a front yard. It is permissible to look through an open window, but it will be ruled unreasonable if you peer through a hole in a blind or a drape.

Walls or fences pose different problems. If you can see across a fence without climbing on something to see, such as if you are in a next-door neighbor's second-floor room and you can plainly see into the yard, there is no intrusion. You may use binoculars or zoom lens on a camera to enhance your observation, as such an observation is in plain sight.

When flying overhead in a fixed-wing airplane or in a helicopter, what you observe below is generally admissible, unless your flight is for the purpose of looking into a specific enclosed residential yard which is not otherwise open to ground level view for suspected evidence of a crime within that yard. In the latter case, the observation may be inadmissible in your state. Because of the drug epidemic in the country, many of the courts are relaxing rules in this respect, and the rules change from day to day.

Who has authority to consent to a search varies from state to state, but these are general rules: Joint occupants may consent to search of that area which is jointly occupied. Husband-wife consents are generally admissible, except if the one spouse has a private space or room that is not available to the other spouse, such as a workshop or office in the house, or a private storage area. Children have limited authority to consent to a search, while parents have considerably more authority to consent to searching a child's room or space, unless the child pays rent and the parent does not regularly go into the room and clean. Also, the parent cannot consent to searching the personal effects of the child, such as a suitcase.

Searches with Search Warrants

Unless justified by an exception, such as consent, incident to an arrest, emergency and there is no time to get a warrant, vehicle search, and other exceptional cases, a search of private property may lawfully be conducted *only* if authorized by a search warrant. The rule also applies to commercial property, except where open to the public.

Searches made with a warrant are presumed to be lawful, principally because they have been subjected in some degree to judicial scrutiny. You have developed sufficient information and have either filled out an affidavit yourself based on your personal observations, or the affidavit is sworn to by a person with personal knowledge about what the warrant seeks to find as a result of the search. This puts you well ahead of the game in getting the fruits of the search introduced into evidence.

Even with a warrant, it is always a recommended practice to ask for consent before presenting a warrant. Then, if consent is given, you may then show the warrant and proceed with the search.

In the *Leon* case[18] it was ruled that under a "good faith" exception to the exclusionary rule, evidence obtained with an arrest or search warrant will be admitted even if the warrant is later found to be defective.

PRISONER CONTROL AND TRANSPORTATION

Specific techniques will be covered in your academy, but these are some of the general procedures for handcuffing and control of the prisoner and transportation of both male and female subjects.

Once you have the suspect in the hands-over-head position, this is the most logical time to handcuff the suspect, and it should be prior to the search. Place one cuff on the wrist of the subject, make it sufficiently tight so as to maintain control. Instruct the subject to keep the other hand in place until you tell him to move. With the cuffed hand under control, bring it down in an arc to a position behind his back with the palm out. Then, while holding onto the one hand tightly, instruct the subject to slowly move the other hand down to a similar position with the palm out. Attach the other cuff. If you have a control problem, quickly tighten the one cuff that you have already attached. You will usually discover that this is sufficient to regain control. A tight handcuff can be painful. Once you have both hands cuffed, you might want to adjust the pressure slightly if you had to tighten one or both of the cuffs while getting them on. Do not release; merely turn the key while quickly loosening the cuff one notch at a time and quickly turning the key back to the locked position. Use the double lock so as to prevent the subject from tightening the cuffs later, cutting off the circulation, and working on your sympathy to get you to loosen the cuffs, giving him an opportunity to get away.

Whether to handcuff or not, and under what conditions, depends on your own department's policy. Whatever the policy, there are good reasons for using the handcuffs. Don't hesitate to use them in arrest situations, keeping in mind that they are for the safety of the suspects as well as yourself.

Once you have the subject cuffed, make your search. As presented earlier, do not hesitate to make a thorough search. Each time a different officer assumes custody of a subject from another officer, it should be standard operating procedure to search the subject again. Never take another person's word that there is no need to search again.

Whenever you receive custody of a prisoner from another officer, conduct a thorough search for your own satisfaction. This should be a department requirement. It is not a surprise to hear that the second officer who searches a suspect comes up with some weapon that had been

[18]468 U.S. 897 (1984).

somehow overlooked on the previous searches. In one case a subject had been arrested for driving while under the influence of alcohol. He was a jovial fellow, but he was going to jail because he had violated the law. He did not resist, and he had all the appearances of a harmless drunk. He was first taken to a local police station to be held for transfer to the county jail. He was searched in the field by the arresting officer, searched by the booking officer at the jail, and searched again when another officer took him out of the cell and placed him inside a transportation unit to take him to the county jail.

While they were en route down the highway, the suspect pulled a small-caliber automatic pistol out of his undershorts and fatally shot the officer. When the officer died, he lost control of the vehicle and the car crashed into a retaining fence. The killer was still in the back seat after the accident, but his gun had been thrown from his hand and had slid under the front seat where he could not reach it. There was a steel mesh case between the front and rear seat. A passerby discovered the accident. The suspect pleaded to be let out, but the man observed the officer with the bullet wound and the gun on the front floorboard and presumed that the suspect had committed the murder. He used the police car's radio and called for assistance. Thanks to his presence of mind, the suspect did not get away and was held to answer for his crime. Three complete searches and the gun was not discovered! A terrible price to pay for a slipshod series of searches.

Maintain visual supervision of every subject in your custody until he has been thoroughly searched and securely held in jail or a holding room. Whenever you place a prisoner in a cell containing other prisoners, first instruct the others to step back away from the door. This will prevent any rushing movement by the prisoners inside when you place the new prisoner in the cell.

Female Prisoners

Female prisoners pose special problems. They may attempt to use their charm and femininity on the gullible male officer. They may use tears and attempt to elicit sympathy for their plight or speak of their importance in the social, political, or economic structure of the community. A woman may also become sullen and uncooperative. Some females may charge that a male officer has taken improper advantage of them and attempt to bargain to drop their charges of rape in exchange for the officers' dropping criminal charges against them.

Use courtesy and diplomacy with all prisoners. When making an arrest, it should be perfectly clear that any placing of the hands on the person is to accomplish the arrest. If you adopt a policy of handcuffing all arrestees, the female should be handcuffed. In addition to adding to the safety of the situation, the handcuffs will also serve to show other people that the woman is in custody of police officers and that her charges of "rape" are probably false, even though the officers are not in uniform.

Self-defense by the officer against a woman who violently resists arrest or who attacks the officer should consist of the same basic techniques that are used against attacks by male protagonists. "Necessary and reasonable force" is justifiable against an attack by either sex. Be extra cautious that nothing you do while defending yourself and maintaining control of the prisoner can be misinterpreted as an undue amount of liberty taken under the guise of self-defense. Avoid making any injudicious remarks that may later be taken out of context and quoted, or misquoted. Use no statements that have double meanings. A double entendre may sound quite funny at a party or in a barroom under social conditions, but in an arrest situation, it can sound insidious and evil.

Transportation of Prisoners

At the beginning of the tour of duty, when you assume control of your vehicle, you should search the entire vehicle, particularly that portion that is used for transporting prisoners. When making an arrest, each subject should be thoroughly searched prior to being placed in the vehicle. Additionally, it should become routine to search the vehicle again after each time a prisoner is transported, to be certain that the subject did not secrete something in the unit. Items such as revolvers and knives are occasionally found, but other items of value to an investigation may likewise be disposed of, such as narcotics, pawn slips, slips of paper containing names and addresses of accomplices, or stolen documents used for false identification.

If the transportation unit is equipped with a screen or shield separating the driving compartment from the rear of the vehicle, the prisoner should ride in that compartment alone or with other prisoners, with the officers in front. If the unit does not have this equipment, place the prisoner in the right portion of the rear seat and the second officer immediately behind the driver. If there is any indication that the prisoner will attempt to kick out the windows or kick at the transporting officers, remove his shoes. For additional safety to the prisoner during this trip, fasten his seat belt. With his hands cuffed behind his back and the seat belt fastened and looped around at least one arm, the prisoner's likelihood of escape is lessened. If the prisoner has any apparent injury, or makes any complaint of pain, be sure to see that he gets appropriate medical attention prior to booking at the jail.

If the situation occurs when there is one officer and one prisoner, and the police unit is not equipped with a screen between the front and rear compartments, consider placing the arrestee in the front seat with the seat belt securely fastened and his hands cuffed behind his back. Watch his feet; but if he is securely fastened, he will not be able to reach your feet or the car's foot pedals. If necessary, use restraining devices on the feet as well. A triangular bandage placed on a mouth might serve as adequate protection against those subjects who try to spit on you.

Transporting Female Prisoners

Two officers, one preferably a female, should be used to transport a female prisoner. If a female officer is not available, consider the use of a woman volunteer from the scene of the arrest, who will accompany the officer and the prisoner to jail or headquarters and then be returned to her home. Seating while transporting a female prisoner is the same as that when transporting a male prisoner.

At the beginning and completion of each trip involving custodial transportation, indicate in your field notebook the exact time, the mileage to the tenth of a mile, and the location. Radio in this information to the dispatcher at the same time. The dispatcher should use a time-stamp machine or some other means to indicate the time the trip begins and ends, and record the locations and the mileage readings that you call in. A convenient aid for this process would be a printed form that the dispatcher would fill out correctly, time stamp, and then forward to you at the time you file your report concerning the arrest. The "trip" card could be attached to the original of the report and become a permanent record. If your department continuously records all radio traffic, you will have this additional support, with the dispatcher periodically stating the time of day throughout the recording.

SUMMARY

Arrest, search, and custody are three very important topics in your training as a police officer. Personal safety for yourself, your fellow officers, and the subjects you are dealing with is paramount. It cannot be emphasized too strongly that there is no simple arrest situation. You are dealing with the personal lives of the individuals you are arresting, and how they may react at any moment is totally unpredictable. Be constantly aware that you must act judiciously, diplomatically, and with extreme caution.

Not only must you be aware of the proper mechanical procedures for arrest, search, and custody, but it is your responsibility to keep abreast of the changing laws and court decisions that affect those areas of your job. Never underestimate the suspect.

EXERCISES AND STUDY QUESTIONS

1. In your state, what is the basic difference between an arrest by a peace officer and an arrest by a private person?
2. Is there any difference in procedure for making an arrest for a felony in your department than there is for making a misdemeanor arrest?

If so, what is the difference?

3. Give at least one example of how a witness might be considered in the presence of an event when using each of the following senses: (a) sight, (b) hearing, (c) smell, (d) touch, (e) taste.

4. Describe a situation in which an officer may have cause to arrest for what appears to be a crime in progress, yet it is actually not a crime at all.

5. Give an example of a situation when an officer may have cause to arrest a person for a felony, although the crime was not committed in the officer's presence.

6. How much force may an officer use to make an arrest and/or to provide self-defense?

7. Give an example of a situation in which a peace officer may use deadly force.

8. In your jurisdiction, may a person forcibly resist arrest legally if that person knows that there is no probable cause for the arrest?

9. What difference, if any, is there between making an arrest with a warrant and without a warrant?

10. Describe the correct procedure for stopping a traffic violator on a busy street and how you would approach the vehicle to make your initial contact with the driver.

11. May an ambassador's spouse be protected under the diplomatic immunity laws?

12. Give an example of police entrapment. Give an example of a situation that a person with less knowledge of police procedures than you might misinterpret as entrapment.

13. Describe the correct procedure for taking four suspected felons out of a van.

14. List at least 20 places in a passenger car where you might expect to find hidden contraband.

15. Describe a searching technique that is used in your area but is not described in this text.

16. Draw a chart showing the escalation of use of force based on the actions and reactions of a person being arrested.

17. What is *reasonable use of force* ?

18. What are the laws in your state that correspond with those in California, and how do they compare?

REFERENCES

California Penal Code (Annual).

FRICKE, CHARLES W., and ARTHUR L. ALARCON. *California Criminal*

Law, 11th ed. Los Angeles: Legal Book Corp., 1977.

JONES, DAVID A. *The Law of Criminal Procedure: An Analysis and Critique*. Boston: Little, Brown, 1981.

KLEIN, IRVING J. *Constitutional Law for Criminal Justice Professionals*. North Scituate, Mass.: Duxbury, 1980.

LENN, PETER D., THOMAS F. MASER, and R. BRYCE YOUNG. *Arrest, Search, and Seizure*. San Francisco: American Analysis Corp., 1973.

RUTTER, WILLIAM A. *Criminal Procedure*. Gardena, Calif.: Gilbert Law Summaries, 1981.

WADDINGTON, LAWRENCE C. *Arrest, Search, and Seizure*. Beverly Hills, Calif.: Glencoe, 1974.

WELLS, KENNETH M., and PAUL B. WESTON. *Criminal Procedure and Trial Practice*. Englewood Cliffs, N.J.: Prentice Hall, 1977.

WESTON, PAUL B., and KENNETH M. WELLS. *Criminal Evidence for Police*, 2nd ed. Englewood Cliffs, N.J.: Prentice Hall, 1976.

See, also, numerous cases referred to in the footnotes.

13

OFFICER SURVIVAL

INTRODUCTION

In this chapter we consider the general area of survival under normal and abnormal police field work. Because there is so much variance in departmental policies, as there is in various methods of using the revolver, in weaponless defense, in the baton of traditional style and the modified (PR-24) form, and in the various martial arts, what we shall attempt here are some basic guidelines that will follow something of a "middle-of-the-road" posture. Depending on the agency that employs you, there will be considerable variations in rules and techniques of self-defense. Public and political pressures, as well as the attitudes and philosophies of your own administrators and supervisors will dictate policy in those areas. As a writer of textbooks and as a college professor, it seems to me that I would be somewhat presumptuous if I were to try to tell those professional colleagues of mine what their policies should be. It is they, and not I, who will be on the mat when the referee makes the count.

This chapter is divided into five parts: (1) stress, (2) officer survival, (3) rules of self-defense, (4) choice of weapons, and (5) use of firearms. In the section on stress we address the common everyday stresses as well as the unusual events and give a few suggestions on how you might address the stress problem that plagues all police officers. In the survival section we present a few guidelines on alertness and state of mind while you perform your field duties that might help you stay alive and healthy. The third section, rules of self-defense, deals with your rights and liabilities as a police officer and as a reasonable person in preserving your own life and that of others. Next, we discuss some of the more traditional weapons and give a few suggestions as to when to use them (*how* to use such weapons should be the academy's responsibility, and the subject is covered extensively in texts exclusively devoted to the subject). The fifth and final section of the chapter is devoted to firearms, some pointers about their use, and a suggested policy statement on the use of deadly force.

STRESS

As a police officer, you do not have a monopoly on stress. Many of your fellow officers, instructors, supervisors, and people outside police service will emphasize the amount of stress that a police officer must sustain. While this is so, it is important that we keep the subject of stress in its proper perspective and deal with it as we would any other job-related problem.

Some of the major causes of stress are that you are not suited for the position in which you find yourself, that you are not comfortable in the position, that you find the position frustrating, that you lack adequate training, and that the position is emotionally disturbing. Selection of police officers must include a complete psychological workup, including testing as well as a thorough background investigation. Some individuals cannot handle stress well, no matter what they do for a living. Although a person may display traits that appear desirable for a police candidate to have, such as aggressiveness, such an outward display of what appears to be good may actually simply be bravado that compensates for an inferiority complex that will fall to pieces when that person's true strength is called upon to manifest itself. The result is a police officer who is totally unqualified to perform with self-assurance and considerable restraint. The person who should not be on the job in the first place will continue to perform behind this facade, hoping that no one will find him or her out. The bravado continues, but so do the insecurities. The result may be hypertension or alcoholism, overreactions to stressful confrontations, or all three. The result is a sick officer who is prematurely retired from service because of stress.

The police officer is not the only person whose personal and professional life is stressful. Although it is true that not many other professions call upon a person to face a crazed gunman or a burglar inside a building, or an unknown situation when you don't know what or who is inside a darkened building with a broken window, those situations do not make up the police officer's total career. Police work has been described as "hours of sheer boredom interspersed with moments of stark terror." There are some risk takers, including police officers, who consider it a necessary part of their lives to jump out of airplanes, to race cars or boats, to climb mountain peaks, or to perform other death-defying feats. There are also some psychologists who will say that such peaks of emotion are essential to the healthy psyche.

For comparative stressful situations, consider the entertainer who waits in the wings to go on stage in front of an audience of 3,000; the student who just completed three years of law school who is taking the bar exam that only 40 percent will pass; the airline pilot whose plane has just lost part of its skin and nine of its passengers were sucked out, who now must safely land with the remaining 237 passengers aboard; the computer programmer with an insoluble problem that must be solved within minutes or the space shuttle crew will be lost in space forever. Perhaps you remember how much stress you felt before your first date, or the day of your marriage and the wedding night, or that important baseball game when your base hit would win the game. Those are all stressful situations that will have the same effect on your system as a "man with gun" call.

If you are well matched to your work, and if you like your work so much that you look forward to going to work every day, no matter what it is, chances are that the accompanying stresses will not seem half as bad nor will they have the same debilitating effects.

The stress confronting you as a field officer includes supervision, conflict, too much work, not enough work, inactivity, responsibility for others, crisis situations, real danger, imagined danger, frustrated anger, a feeling of helplessness, tragedy, inadequate equipment, lack of recognition by superiors, inadequate pay, disrespect from citizens, negative attitudes of fellow officers, unusual and long hours, having to testify in court, having to speak in public, and self-consciousness. Other types of stress that compound on-the-job stress include marital difficulties, family problems, family tragedy, negative image of police by friends and/or relatives, financial problems, alcoholism, pregnancy, sex problems, acquiring a new home, and outside employment.

In this text, we shall address just a few of the stresses of the job and suggest a few activities that might help you deal with stress.

Forms of Stress

Supervision. Keep in mind that supervisors and administrators may have greater pressures on them for your performance than you have. A technique used by some supervisors is fear, which is quite effective when used on a subordinate whose tenure depends on that supervisor. They might threaten and impose sanctions for virtually anything but perfect performance. The supervisors may fear for their own tenure or believe that they must outperform their competing supervisors to gain promotions. You can survive in this environment only by doing the best that you can. If the situation becomes unbearable, document the incidents of abuse by recording times, dates, people present, and the exact nature of the situation. It may be possible to go to the next higher supervisor, if there is an open-door policy in your department.

Conflict. Some people try to avoid conflict. You may be a person who finds any kind of conflict depressing. Look at yourself. Are you able to put these conflicts in their proper perspective as being the natural part of your job, or do you internalize them and take them as personal affronts? If there are conflicting personalities on the job, only a transfer or a resignation will likely resolve the problem. If you find that arguments and physical confrontations between yourself and other people cause you to have headaches and suffer from fits of depression, you are probably in the wrong profession.

Too Much Work. When the demands are for more than you can handle, and when such demands exceed what is customary for the position you fill, ask for an audience with your supervisor and discuss the problem. Do the best that you can and make it apparent to your supervisors. If it becomes apparent that you simply cannot keep up because of your own inadequacy, change assignments or professions.

Not Enough Work. Sometimes assignments do not demand enough of your time. In that case, discuss the situation with your supervisor and point out that you would like to have additional work. You may be assigned to conduct special surveys or compile statistics or maintain pin maps. Bring along with you to work study materials that are related to your assignment. Try to devise some way to make your job more of a game. For example, how many buildings have telephone poles next to walls that provide access to roof burglars? How many buildings have skylights? Which buildings and apartment houses in your district have names inscribed on their fronts? What are the names? Compile a directory of various types of information that will make your work easier and more interesting.

Inactivity. The best way to cope with this stressful situation is to make activity, but not meaningless "make-work" activities.

Responsibility for Others. This may take some attitude adjustment. It is true that you are responsible to do the best that you can to protect people and their property. You cannot prevent violent crimes that are committed by friends or members of the victim's family in the privacy of their homes, and you cannot stop a burglar from breaking into a house unless you are standing alongside him, and even then you might not be able to stop him. People are responsible for their own lives and must make their own decisions. Your way to cope with your feeling of responsibility is to devote your full attention to what you are doing while on duty and to make the best possible effort to make the right decisions and to be in the most appropriate places; then you must let happen whatever happens. The doctor in surgery does not save every life, but he or she does the best possible. If the patient dies, it is no fault of the doctor, who will perform many more surgeries when patients will not die. You will probably never live to see a crime-free society no matter how hard you try. Although many do not make it, the salmon still swim upstream every year. The big league baseball batter has more strike-outs than he has home runs, but he still plays the game and sets new records for the team.

Crisis Situations. Many of the crises you encounter do not involve you personally, and you are not expected to inject yourself into the situation. You should have empathy, or the ability to understand why a person cries, but you are not required to cry too. Professional detachment is essential. When you go to the accident scene and find three children with arms and legs severed and crushed, your effectiveness in getting those children the best care will be seriously decreased if you find yourself grief-stricken and unable to think and act clearly. Set those feelings aside and remember that you do not have the "luxury" of getting emotionally involved. This professional aloofness is not "callousness." Resiliency in being able to "bounce back" and put those unfortunate experiences into the past and keep them there is essential to your role.

Real and Imagined Danger. At the time you are approaching a house and you have been told of a sniper inside who threatened to kill the first police officer he sees, the danger is real. It only becomes imagined after you have secured the scene and have found that the person was inside sleeping off a drunken interlude and there was no gun after all. This is a hazard that goes with the job. You must understand the dangers when you are first hired and should not forget them throughout your career. Every officer copes differently. Whenever you sense that any of these situations is having a negative effect on you, arrange to see your department's psychological counselor, or one who is privately contracted, who has experience in dealing with police emotional crises.

Frustrated Anger. This will occur more frequently if you take it personally whenever someone calls you names or questions your legal status at birth. Two ways to cope with this problem are to counsel yourself and learn to ignore the name-calling and to get involved in some type of physically exerting activity. Racket ball or tennis may help you overcome the urge to strike out at someone. Other sports, such as running or swimming, may help you work out some of the built-up anxiety.

Feeling of Helplessness. This occurs when you watch someone whom you are attempting to rescue die or when you do not succeed in saving the life of a drowning victim. There are also feelings of helplessness when you arrest someone and later see that individual go free. The best way to cope with that stressful situation is to remember that you are not superhuman and that you have no control over the results of most of the things you do. This also applies to those tragedies you witness and later feel that there is something more that you should have done. You cannot "Should Of."

Inadequate Equipment and Insufficient Pay. These are matters for personnel negotiations. You should be fully aware of these conditions when you apply for the job. Although it is a real problem, the situation reminds me of the famous television personality who decided he could not afford to run for Congress because he could not afford the cut in pay. He is still in the entertainment business—never did run for office.

Lack of Recognition by Supervisors. This is a two-way situation. Perhaps a little work on complimenting your superiors and recognizing them for their good work will result in their reciprocating. Try it. The same suggestion applies to the complaint about lack of respect by the public. By showing respect, you might receive some in return. At least, you know that you are okay and that you are doing a good job. Don't expect to be complimented for doing a good job, as many people believe doing a good job is what you are getting paid for.

Speaking in Public. Having to speak in public or testify in court are fears known to everyone. Be prepared, gain competency and self-confidence in what you are doing, and you will find that these stressful problems will lessen with time. Some professional entertainers never overcome stage fright, and those individuals are among the first who will tell you that the anxiety makes them better performers.

Dealing with Stress

Involvement in outside interests, such as family matters, boys' and girls' organizations, church or community activities, sports, hobbies, or other avocations may be so distracting that they have the effect of putting the pressures of the job into a different perspective. For example, the anxiety of facing a flight test for a pilot's license during your day off next week, or the opening night of a play in which you have the leading role, or a showing of your paintings at a gallery in a major city will give your life more breadth, so that the "chewing out" you received last night for writing a "substandard" report does not seem so humiliating. Moreover, you will know that your next report will be up to par and that the world will not have stopped turning because you "screwed up."

Some of the activities suggested by psychologists and other stress specialists as diversions from pressures of the job include biofeedback, meditation, yoga, good nutrition, running, bicycling, contact and other competitive sports, exercise, music, acting, art, water sports, camping and other outdoor activities, high-intensity sports such as sky diving, hang gliding, mountain climbing, or automobile racing. Although there may be disagreement among specialists, some "workaholics" do not do better or more work than do some of those individuals who spend half the time in the same occupations. Worrying more about the job does not necessarily produce better results. For many of the individuals I have encountered, I have had to advise them to wait to see what happens, that their worrying about an outcome will have absolutely no effect on the success or failure of the project or the event. I have even offered my services to worry for them (for an hourly fee, of course).

OFFICER SURVIVAL

Throughout your tour of duty, you should always be alert for any activity that seems out of the ordinary and that arouses your suspicions. The most important life that you are charged to protect is your own, because without you and your fellow officers, there is no one to do the protecting. Paranoia will not help, but you should be wary of any situation that might lead to an open or ambush attack. Even normal-looking people might take advantage of the opportunity to assault a police officer. Common sites for attacks on police officers are lunch and refreshment stops, places where officers park their cars, places where officers gather at the scenes of disturbances or other calls where there are several officers, where an officer is called to an isolated area for nonexistent problem, and places of officer recreation. Usually, the attackers' success depends on the element of surprise. Your awareness of what is going on around you might be the factor that will save your life and cause the would-be assailant to choose another time, another place, and possibly another victim.

The routine traffic violator, hitchhiker, transient, lovers in a lovers' lane location are all potential hazards. You are also, no doubt, highly aware of the hazards involved in responding to family and neighborhood disputes, when tempers are always unpredictable. The arrest situation is also dangerous, no matter how docile the arrestee appears to be. Be wary of the individual who immediately alights from his vehicle and approaches you when you make a stop or when several people appear to be converging upon you from two or more directions at once.

Terrorists and other people who have to "get even" with the police for whatever their reasons use sniper or ambush tactics. Both types of assault require planning, tactical advantage, and surprise. If you were to commit one of those types of assault, where and how would you do it? Sniping requires a clear line of vision to the victim from some place of concealment: consider the phony call for help to get the officer to the scene, an attack from a place of concealment may be the approach, and then a hasty and safe escape.

Situations you might watch for and suggested countermeasures include the following:

1. You are approaching a location to which you have been summoned by a call for service, such as a neighborhood disturbance, but it appears that the call was false, and people appear to be leaving rapidly, as though some invisible person had told them all to leave. This may be a setup. Call for assistance and proceed only when the assistance has arrived.

2. You are pursuing someone who jumps out of a vehicle and runs into a building. It appears as though he is making it too easy for you to catch him, but you have to go into the building to appre-

hend him. Wait for a follow-up and cover possible avenues of escape; then invite the person to come out as you would with a crime in progress situation.

3. You are inside your car and someone throws a firebomb at your car. The device breaks and ignites on the top of your car. Immediately roll up all the windows, close the door, and leave the scene. If the fire is entirely outside the car, you will find that the temperature inside will not change appreciably and you will leave most of the fire behind you.

4. If the same situation in case 3 results in the fire bomb igniting inside, you will have about 1 second to get out of the car before it turns into a funeral pyre.

5. If objects are thrown at you, or if you are fired upon, immediately drive out of the street, such as up a driveway, toward the source of attack. As soon as you can, get out of the car and away from it. In a police car in the middle of the street, you are a target. If you have time, radio for help.

6. If under attack while not in a vehicle, start yelling and making as much noise as you can. Consider running toward the source of the attack because you have a better chance of seeing and counterattacking your assailant than if you are predictably running away and making an excellent target with your back and unable to return fire. Use ammunition wisely and fire only at a target.

7. If you are being held at gunpoint, you can guess that the person holding the gun had some reason for not having already shot at you. If you are immediately facing the suspect and are within reach of the weapon, consider grabbing the cylinder of a revolver, which cannot fire a second time if already cocked and cannot fire at all if not cocked yet. Some automatic pistols cannot be fired if the barrel is jammed back. These measures are extreme and should be tried only as a last resort or when there is no other alternative.

8. If a suspect demands that you give him your gun, there is no assurance that you will not be killed with that gun. You may have a better chance for survival if you decide to counterattack.

9. If fired upon, jump to your left. Most people are right-handed, and when a right-handed person fires a gun, there is usually a sharp pull to his or her left. If you see the gun in the person's left hand, jump to the right.

10. Any kind of a loud noise and sudden defensive movement may be all you need to gain an advantage because of the suspect's slow reaction to the surprise. Strike the subject with something if you can grab a handful of dirt or sand, a handful of coins, your baton, or spray of aerosol tear gas.

11. Try the old trick of shouting to the imaginary officers behind the suspect, an old trick that might buy you a second or two.

12. Immediately drop to the ground and roll toward the suspect; then attack him however possible. You have only one chance and you are probably fighting for your life.

13. If there is a chance while you are being led from one place to another, such as to a place around the corner where you know the suspect is going to kill you, run. He might miss, or the gun might misfire. Your only alternative is to be killed.

14. Maintain a positive attitude and a strong will to live.

15. If you are so inclined, prayer might help, but do it quickly.

RULES OF SELF-DEFENSE

When you add any weapon to your personal arsenal, you have the very serious and very real responsibility to know how and under what conditions you may use the weapon. You must develop considerable skill in its use as well and be ready and willing to use the weapon without hesitation when the times comes for you to use it. Above all, you are required to assume responsibility for the ultimate consequences that use of such a weapon may cause. I know of no officer who has a *desire* to kill, but you have no business carrying any type of firearm if you do not carry it with a *will* to kill. The baton, when applied to a suspect's head, may cause brain damage or death, and you have no business striking anyone on the head unless you are willing to accept responsibility for the consequences. Most of the weapons and techniques of restraint and self-defense that are provided you as a police officer can result in someone's death. That is a serious responsibility.

In this section of the chapter, we shall cover the basic rules of self-defense—that is, defense of yourself and others you have sworn to protect. Whenever you are using any amount of force to take a person into custody or to recapture someone who attempts to avoid arrest, or when you are restraining that person while holding or transporting him (or her), the force that you use should only be "that which is necessary," according to the rule and law books. If the individual resists or counterattacks, you are then in the position of defending yourself, and possibly others. It is not you who is the aggressor, but the suspect who chooses to force you to react. Therefore, the following rules generally apply when you use any degree of force, including deadly force.

1. The amount of force that you use may be in direct proportion to that force or degree of injury you believe is about to be used on you. As a police officer, you will be considered a *reasonable* person unless proven otherwise in court. As a reasonable person, it is also understood that you are charged with the responsibility of preserving lives and

arresting people and that the choice is not yours as to whether you should act as a police officer or run away to avoid a bad situation. There is no legal reason why you must retreat or first notify the attacker that you are going to defend yourself. It is at that moment when you—in your own mind and using your own logical thought process—*believe* that you are going to suffer attack unless you immediately defend yourself. This also applies to defense of another person. This belief that you have of impending attack may be used on actual fact, or it may be based on your assumption of what you believe to be fact. For example, a suspect alights from a car you have stopped for a routine traffic violation. As the suspect approaches you, he states in a very threatening manner, "____ing cop. I am going to kill you," while he reaches in the direction of his right waistband. He pulls something out of that location and you see the reflection of metal. At that instant you see a gun. You shoot the suspect to stop his attack. He falls to the ground and dies. As you approach the suspect you see that he actually has in his hands a handful of keys. You saw a gun, you acted on the belief that he was going to kill you because he said that he intended to, and you had no reason to believe that he was not telling the truth.

You have no legal or moral obligation to wait to see if the suspect has a gun, or if he really intends to use it, or if his aim is any good before you defend yourself. Self-defense has never been intended to be a contest, and you are supposed to survive. If you believe that the suspect is going to strike you with a fist or a stick and you have no reason to believe that the blow will be fatal, you will have no justification to kill the suspect. In that case, your defense will have to be another of your alternative choices. If there is mere pushing or shoving, you may use only enough force to stop the pushing or shoving. However, you are not expected to enter a pushing and shoving match; therefore, your defense may be one well-placed kick or blow to some part of the anatomy that will cause so much pain that the fight is ended.

2. Fear is a personal matter. To defend yourself, you have to be operating under the belief, or *fear*, that you are about to be attacked. This fear element does not mean that your heart rate or blood pressure has to change or that you have to be shaking or in a state of panic. Exactly what and when and how to *fear* is hardly something that one can learn. It is something that someone experiences. Fear may be influenced by previous similar experiences, such as a previous attack with a gun that had a certain result or simulated training experiences in the academy may stimulate certain responses. Your state of awareness of the event, or the amount of importance you place upon it, influence your actions. An event immediately preceding this one may magnify or dwarf the fears because you are comparing situations.

Because of the individuality in perception and interpretation, you as an individual must make a personal assessment of the situation and then act in whatever manner you believe appropriate at the moment. Later, your peers, your supervisors, and others who will be judging your actions must put themselves in your shoes and try to evaluate the uniqueness of the specific situation that caused you to interpret the event and to act as you did.

3. The danger must be imminent. There must be a clear and present danger of an immediate attack that calls for a decisive act of self-defense. If an attack has ended, there is no justification for a counterattack, because you would no longer be defending yourself. You would be "getting even." However, if the attack has paused momentarily and it is obvious that the assault on you or someone else is going to continue unless you do something to stop it, you are still acting in self-defense.

4. After the attack has been completed and the attacker is leaving the scene, any action you take is then dependent upon the legal and moral justification to restrain or arrest or prevent the attacker from leaving the scene when it is apparent in your mind that another attack is imminent. For example, if it is apparent that the attacker has committed his crime and is "done with it," you may not execute the suspect because you do not have the legal or moral right. However, if the attacker has just disemboweled someone with a knife and is leaving the scene with the bloody knife still in his hand and in such a manner as to indicate to you that another attack by the same suspect with the same knife is imminent, then you have an obligation as a police officer to save the next life even though you were not able to do so with the assault at hand.

5. You must pass the "reasonable person" test. Not only must your actions be justifiable in your own mind, but there may be witnesses whose assessment may differ from yours. Your supervisors, your peers in shooting boards and internal affairs investigations, coroners, prosecuting attorneys, and the administrators of your department must all agree that what you did was "reasonable." If, for any reason a decision is made that what you did was a prosecutable offense and not—in their opinion—self-defense, you may be subjected to criminal prosecution or disciplinary action. In that case, the judge or a jury will decide whether your actions were those of a "reasonable person" and whether you exercised good judgment in accordance with the professional "standard of care" required of you in your position as a police officer.

Consider the following scenarios and decide whether the officers passed the "reasonable person" test.

Scenario 1. It was a balmy afternoon on the bluffs overlooking the American River. There were several homes under various stages of construction, with some of the homes already occupied. Most of the occupants were away at work during the day, but there were workers from the various utilities and construction companies performing their respective jobs. While connecting the telephone at a neighboring house, the worker observed two young males crawl into a side window of one of the homes. It appeared as though the window had been left open, so it could have been an occupant who had lost his key crawling in so that he could open the front door from the inside, or it could have been two burglars. The witness called the sheriff's department and reported what he saw.

The deputy assigned to the area responded to the call. When he arrived he called in that he was on the scene, then approached the front door. Two young males, burst out the front door, almost knocking the deputy down. The deputy called to the two young men, who appeared to be in their middle or late teens. The deputy saw something in their hands, but could not describe whatever it was that they were carrying. The boys did not stop. The deputy chased them across several lawns, through backyards, and over a couple of six-foot backyard fences. He lost them. He returned to the house and verified that the place had, in fact, been broken into. The boys who ran were apparently running to avoid apprehension. The deputy called for backup, then resumed his search for the suspects.

As the deputy was continuing his search, the original witness described what he saw, and added that when he saw the boys run away from the site, one of them was carrying what looked like a "gun with a long barrel." The deputy inquired of several other witnesses along the route of his search, which led him to the edge of the granite cliffs, which rose about 100 feet above the American River. Two other witnesses, each questioned separately and out of earshot of each other, pointed out the direction of travel and said that one of the boys was carrying a weapon; one described a rifle and the other thought it was a shotgun.

The officer was met at the top of the cliff by fellow deputies. They saw the boys climb down the cliff, which had paths, considerable scrubs and weeds, and some shallow caves where someone could hide. At the top, the officer had a fellow deputy drive to the edge, where they tied a rope to the bumper. The deputy used the rope to rappel down the side of the cliff along the treacherous paths. He was down about halfway, or 50 feet from the water below, when he saw one of the boys. The other boy was out of sight. The boy he did see had something in his hand, and the officer believed that it was a rifle or shotgun, and it was pointed at him. Keep in mind the statements by three independent witnesses that one of the suspects was carrying a gun.

When the deputy saw the boy with the gun, he shouted at least three times. He shouted loud enough that some witnesses across the river heard him. He shouted that the boy should drop the gun or that he (the deputy) would shoot. Receiving no response but the boy continuing to point the gun at him, the deputy believed that the boy was going to shoot him. The deputy fired several shots, apparently striking the suspect. The boy and his companion, who must have been right there with him, both fell to the river below. At the same time the deputy lost his footing and he, too, fell into the river. He holstered his weapon and swam to the two boys. The boys were unable to swim, but the deputy was able to rescue both of them and hold them up against the cliff while still in the water. He held onto the boys until rescuers arrived with a boat and pulled the three of them into the boat. At that time they discovered that the one boy had been shot in the shoulder, with the bullet going down (into the heart, it was determined during the autopsy). By the time the ambulance arrived, the boy had died.

Question: Based on the preceding information, is it your opinion that the officer met the "reasonable person" requirement for self-defense, or was he wrong? (See the last page of this chapter for the answer determined by a federal court jury.)

Scenario 2. This is a city in northern California. The time was November in the early evening hours, and the weather was cold, dark, and drizzling. It was a miserable night for both human and beast. During the previous several weeks, a gang of young black youths was terrorizing the neighborhood beer bars where factory workers and day laborers cashed their checks on Friday night and spent half of their pay buying beer and wine before going home. These places were excellent targets because of the extra cash they carried to cash the paychecks. These youths had already robbed six or seven of the establishments and it appeared that they were going to hit every one at least twice. During each robbery, which were committed with the use of shotguns, shots were fired and several victims had been shot. The more serious ones included a bartender who moved too slowly and lost the use of his hand because of a shotgun wound; another victim was a pregnant woman in the ninth month who was sitting at the bar when one of the robbers made some vicious remark, then shot her, causing her to lose half of her right thigh. (Fortunately, the unborn baby did not get hurt.)

All the bar owners in the neighborhood were in a state of near hysteria, to say the least. They had set up a system whereby if anyone were to see what appeared to be the suspects at or near their establishment, they would immediately telephone a predesignated neighbor, say: "This is 23. They're here!" then hang up. The neighbor would then call the police and give the location of the suspects. The MO of this particular band of robbers was that they would usually shoot anyone who was on the telephone. On this particular evening, two sergeants of the city police department just happened to be within blocks of the location when the dispatcher stated: "Possible armed robbery suspects observed at… " What had actually happened, but was not known to witnesses or the police, was that two youths who had heard of the robberies and the hysteria that they had created decided that they would have some fun with those frightened people. They cut down a couple of broomstick handles to resemble shotgun barrels, then painted them black. These boys then went to one of the bars in the neighborhood where the robberies had occurred, stood outside the front window, and stood there displaying their weapons (actually not weapons at all) until they saw the woman inside look in their direction, then dash to the telephone. The boys ran to the alley, apparently feeling satisfied that they had done what they set out to do: scare someone. They meant no harm, one of them said later. They were just having some fun.

The two sergeants converged at the scene, each one at opposite ends of the alleyway they thought the boys had probably entered. Both officers were armed with shotguns. They had been advised that their suspects were similarly armed. The two suspects ran directly toward one of the officers with what looked like shotguns. The sergeant shouted to them to drop their guns or that he would kill them. They did not, but kept coming toward him. As he shot one of the suspects, the other one ran the opposite direction into the arms of the other waiting officer. When the sergeant approached the suspect that he had shot, he turned the boy over on his back, and it was then that he discovered two things: the boy was quite young (although about 5'-11", 150 pounds) and the weapon was nothing more than a stick painted black.

The second sergeant was able to disarm his suspect and bring him to where the other suspect was shot. By the time the paramedics had arrived, the one suspect had died.

Question: Did the officer who shot and killed the suspect in this case meet the "reasonable person" criteria? (See the last page of this chapter for the answer determined by a superior court judge.)

CHOICE OF WEAPONS

As a recently appointed "rookie," or as a future officer, whatever your current status, you will have little or nothing to say about what weapons your agency authorizes you to carry. You will have certain weapons specifically prescribed for you to carry, and there may be some "optional weapons." Our purpose is not to discuss which weapons should belong to either category. Rather, our purpose is to point out that whenever you have several weapons at your disposal, you must choose among them when you take someone into custody or defend yourself. Let's look at some of the weapons.

Automatic and Semiautomatic Rifles. Special weapons teams are armed with rifles because of the unusual nature of their assignments, such as dealing with barricaded felons with hostages. These types of weapons are not a part of your regular equipment. Some of your suspects may be thusly armed.

Shotguns. For short-range person-to-person assault, the 12-gauge shotgun with 00 buckshot is extremely effective and standard equipment in many departments. Not only does the weapon have a dramatic effect on a suspect, but it is extremely effective when used by an officer with no great marksmanship skills. There is also less danger to surrounding neighborhoods because of its limited range. It is to be used only for felony situations or when there is reasonable cause to believe that a suspect may attempt a fatal assault. For greater range and accuracy, the shotgun may be loaded with rifled slugs.

Handguns. Whether to carry a revolver or semi-automatic pistol is usually a matter of policy in your department. Each has its merits, and proponents for each will extoll those virtues. These are the traditional and most common of all police weapons and will be covered in more detail in the next section of this chapter.

Tasers. This is a relatively new weapon, consisting of a tube from which two small barbed darts are shot and penetrate the suspect's skin. Wires leading from the darts go back to the handle of the dart gun. When both darts are attached to the suspect, the officer pushes a button, which activates an electrical charge that arcs and gives the suspect an electrical jolt that temporarily immobilizes the suspect. The circuit has to be complete and both darts attached for the taser to work. The effect is similar to the cattle prod or the electrically charged baton that shocks the suspect to immobilize him or her. Two or more officers should be present to allow the officer using the weapon to get an accurate shot or to fire again until both darts penetrate the suspect's body.

Stun Guns. A stun gun looks like a flat flashlight but has a nine-volt rechargeable battery and two prongs extending from one end. By touching an assailant with the two probes and pushing a button on the side of the weapon, the operator is able to send a high voltage charge of electricity (but very low amperage) giving the recipient a terrific shock that causes muscle spasms and disorientation. The feeling is about the same as if you were to stick your finger in a light socket.

Chemical Fire Extinguisher. Sometimes this device is used as a weapon. I would suggest its use only as an emergency option and not as a preplanned weapon of self-defense. It is not designed as a weapon, nor is it considered one.

Hand-Saps. There are several variations of this weapon. A lead weight placed inside leather gloves on the palm side or the knuckle side will give the hand extra weight and striking power when used as a means of aiding the officer when it is necessary to use the fists for self-defense. The same principal applies to the sap, which is like the old blackjack used by motion picture criminals, contains a lead weight, and is used to slap the suspect on the arm, shin, or any place other than the face or head. Many officers consider these items useless, while others would not trade them for any other weapon. The disadvantage is that it requires the officer to be at close quarters with the suspect to use them effectively.

Baton. This is probably the most regularly used police weapon other than the gun. It has been used as a pry tool as well as a come-along device and as a striking weapon. A more recent modification has been the addition of a handle attached perpendicular to the baton itself, which gives the weapon greater variation in its use.

Tear Gas. Explosive canisters or projectiles that may be fired out of shot-gun attachments and that expel smoke and tear gas have been used by the police and the military services for well over half a century, and their effects have been excellent in many cases. In 1966, when other products such as hair spray and air freshener were being packaged in aerosol dispensers, several tear gas manufacturers introduced aerosol tear gas as a new police defensive weapon. When the liquids and vapors of this remarkable weapon contact the skin, particularly the softer tissues of the eyes, the nose, and the sinuses, the person feels extreme irritation and usually can direct his or her attention on nothing other than the pain and the blinding effects of the chemicals, which provides the officer some time in which to seek cover or to restrain the suspect. Tear gas includes CN, CS, and O.C.

USE OF FIREARMS

Carrying and using the firearm should never been taken lightly. A firearm is an instrument of death, and when you carry it as part of your uniform, you are doing so with the awesome realization that whenever you fire the gun, someone may die. For that reason, never fire the gun unless you sincerely believe that you have legal and moral justification to do so and you are willing to accept responsibility for someone's death. Contrary to the fictional image of the police officer using the firearm on a daily basis, you will actually have rare cause to use it, considering the many thousands of potentially dangerous situations you will be facing throughout your career.

The police mission is to preserve life, including that of the people you are required to arrest. Although your primary purpose is to preserve life, the time may come when it will be necessary for you to take the life of another in order to protect yourself or another victim of criminal assault. You must decide when you accept the position as a police officer and the gun that goes with it that you can and will kill, if necessary, for the purpose of preserving life (see Figure 13–1). That "will to kill" in *no way* should ever be interpreted as anything but acceptance of the responsibility that goes along with carrying the firearm. In most situations you will have to make a split-second decision to shoot in self-defense; that will not be the time to search your conscience to determine whether or not you are willing to take a human life.

"Why not shoot to disarm, or shoot the person in the leg?" Since criminal officers have easy access to firearms, and may have had extensive training in their use in or out of the military service, you may have only one chance to shoot to save your life or that of someone else. In the highly emotional situation, you will be lucky if you hit any part of your

Figure 13-1 Mastery of skill in using a weapon develops the officer's confidence that he or she will be prepared to use it when necessary. (Courtesy of the Missouri State Highway Patrol.)

target. Therefore, you have to aim for the biggest part of the target, or where the target is going to be when the bullet reaches it. No one is such a good shot that he or she can shoot a gun out of a hand under a sudden attack situation. Even when you strike the center of the target, bullets in the heart sometimes do not even stop an approaching attacker. A bullet in an arm or leg is certainly not going to stop that person. Your goal is to shoot to stop and expect that the attacker may die.

Here are a few basic rules to follow when handling firearms:

1. Never take another person's words that a gun is not loaded. Handle the gun as though it were loaded, and examine it yourself.

2. While examining a firearm, or cleaning or handling it for any purpose, keep the action or cylinder open, the muzzle pointed in a safe direction, and your finger off the trigger.

3. When carrying the gun in your hand outside of a holster, have the action or cylinder open and hands off the trigger.

4. Be careful where you store a firearm. If you have it stored for self-protection, it must be in an accessible place, but weight the hazards of children and the curious getting hold of the gun against the benefits of the gun as protection.

5. Whenever you fire a gun, know your target, consider ricochets, and be aware of the route the bullet will probably travel.

6. If you "dry fire" your gun for practice, be sure that the gun is not

loaded and point it only in a safe direction even though it is empty.

7. Keep the gun in a perfect state of repair and be sure the trigger pull is not so light that it could be considered "hair trigger."

8. *Think safety.*

When to Shoot

State laws and your own department's policies will dictate when you may use deadly force. Consider also the following as your personal policies.

As a police officer, you will never be exempt from the legal and moral responsibilities of using good judgment when resorting to the use of a firearm. Its use is usually irreversible. Never remove the weapon from its holster unless you believe that you have cause to use it. Never point it at anyone unless you believe that you will be legally and morally justified to use it if you have to, and never shoot anyone unless you are willing to accept responsibility for that person's death (see Figure 13–2).

Figure 13-2 Firing a gun is serious business.

If you intend to make loud noises, find some means other than shooting a firearm. Warning shots are a waste of ammunition. You should never point a gun at someone for the purpose of frightening the person. Your pointing should be so that you will be ready to fire if you have to.

Use of deadly force may be justified only when defending yourself or someone else from what you believe to be an attempt at deadly force. Although the law may provide for deadly force in taking a felon, or retaking a felon who has escaped, or someone who has committed a serious felony, your consideration will be whether it is morally justifiable. There are other means for arresting the felon or someone who has escaped. The firearm is the last resort, not the first. Your role is that of protector, not executioner. The general rule should be "self-defense" as discussed earlier in this chapter.

As a police officer you may use reasonable force to make an arrest. What is reasonable depends on the specific set of circumstances that present themselves to you, and you must consider the overall picture when making your decision as to how much force to use. A misdemeanor certainly does not justify deadly force. If you are making a felony arrest, no matter what the crime, and if you are meeting no resistance, then any force at all beyond merely restraining the subject is too much force. "As much force as necessary" depends on what the suspect does. Whether a felon or misdemeanant, if the suspect pulls a gun out of his or her pocket and starts shooting at you, you are now in a self-defense situation.

After any police shooting, immediately isolate the officer who did the shooting. The last words an officer wants to hear at that moment is any kind of praise, such as "that was great, you sure blew that guy away." Provide a time for the officer to be alone. If a department chaplain or psychological counselor is available, and the officer wants to talk to someone, let it be one of those individuals. Human life is so delicate and so precious, and probably no one appreciates that more than a police officer.

Additional Guidelines for Officers' Use of Firearms

Policies and procedures for officers' use of firearms, or any other statement of policy for that matter, are guidelines on standards of practice. They do not relieve the individual officer from making the ultimate decision and taking appropriate action that will be judged retroactively by others. It is the officer's discretionary prerogative to assess the situation personally and to act decisively.

The value of human life is paramount in any life-threatening situation, including the life of the suspect, no matter how heinous his or her crime. The officer's life—yours—should be right at the top of the list when it comes to the preservation of life. There is nothing in the regulations or code of ethics that requires an officer to have suicidal desires.

The threat of life that leads to the officer's defensive action must be evaluated carefully, taking into account the total picture, such as the danger of wild shots striking innocent bystanders, the age of the offender, and whether moving vehicles are involved. Statistically, the younger person with a gun is more likely to shoot than an older person who has lived long enough to respect life more. Shooting at or from a moving vehicle is extremely hazardous, actually foolhardy except under extraordinary circumstances.

Shots to destroy animals should be only for (1) self-defense, or (2) to prevent substantial harm to the officer or another, or (3) when an animal is injured so badly that humanity required its relief from suffering. The first consideration should be whether animal control personnel are available to handle the situation. If so, the decision is theirs. In any event, disposal of any animal should be made out of the presence of children when possible.

Warning shots are not justifiable except in a correctional situation when a violent assault takes place when the officer is too far from the assailant and the victim to intercede. The first shot may be into the ground, with the next shot in rapid succession into the body of the assailant in case the first shot did not stop the assault.

Secondary weapons carried on the officer's person, whether in uniform or plainclothes, makes sense to me, but depends on the policy of your department. If a secondary weapon is authorized, it must be of the caliber and type that is approved by the chief executive officer, and the officer must qualify with the weapon at the range.

Off-duty weapons may be optional, particularly for such activities as beach parties, out-of-town trips, participative sports events, but officers should be encouraged to carry firearms whenever there is a possibility that they may be called upon to use them.

Duty weapons should be standardized and officers required to qualify at least once a quarter. If ballistic samples of bullets fired by the weapon are kept on file by the department, new samples should be collected occasionally to update their validity. The barrel interior changes drastically when a large number of bullets have been fired through it.

Personnel Services Following an Officer-Involved Shooting

Immediately following a shooting, the officer should be required to be separated from all other department personnel until he or she has had an opportunity to go through a counseling session with a psychologist and/or spiritual counselor and consultation with an attorney of the officer's choosing. The attorney should be present when the officer is questioned by department and other agency personnel to assure protection of the officer's rights. An officer placed on administrative leave immediately following a shooting should not be considered prejudicial.

EXERCISES AND STUDY QUESTIONS

1. Describe the various types of stressful experiences encountered by such nonpolice practitioners as the following: (a) musicians, (b) students, (c) teachers, (d) attorneys, (e) operating room nurses, (f) ambulance drivers, (g) bartenders, (h) used car salespeople, (i) escrow officers, and (j) auto mechanics.

2. Expanding on the list of stressful situations confronting a peace officer, add at least ten types of stress that are jointly experienced by *both* peace officers and the people in those other walks of life.

3. List and discuss at least five different activities that you believe would help you with your personal stress problems, if you have any.

4. Look over each of the sources or causes of stress listed in the text, and list which ones directly involve you. Write a paragraph on what you intend to do to relieve the stresses of each one.

5. What has your department planned to handle terrorist activities, should terrorists strike with little or no advance warning?

6. List as many types of unexpected occurrences you can think of that are not given in the section on officer survival. Next, describe what you should do to lessen the danger to yourself and other officers.

7. List and explain the five basic rules of self-defense. Give an example of how each would be applied to real-life situations.

8. What is the greatest advantage of the shotgun as a police weapon?

9. What new weapons have been recently developed for the police arsenal? Describe how they work.

10. Write a policy statement on police use of firearms.

ANSWERS TO SCENARIOS

1. The jury found the officer not civilly liable for the shooting. It did not have a happy ending, however. The officer went to trial six years after the shooting, and the shooting must have weighed heavily on him for that time. Two weeks before the trial began, the officer was confronting an armed suspect and did not shoot when the situation called for it. The officer was shot and killed by the assailant.

2. The judge directed a verdict of *not guilty*, but did state in open court that whereas the officer was justified in taking what action he did, he was *not* justified in using the racist language that he used while firing his weapon. Since then, all personnel in that department receive very intensive instruction on the appropriate use of language in all racially sensitive situations.

14 THE COMMUNITY & THE POLICE

INTRODUCTION

The police department and its members cannot separate themselves from the community they serve, with the police on one side of an invisible barrier and the people on the other side, or an "Us versus Them" attitude. You are a part of the community you serve. You were probably selected from among the ranks of private persons who populate that community or one nearby. You probably live in the same community, or at least within commuting distance. You are an integral part of the community as it is part of you. You reflect its habits, cultures, social pressures, economic conditions, and prejudices as well as its outlook on law enforcement. You shop, seek recreation, raise children, attend school, go to church, visit with friends and neighbors, and function as a member of the community.

When you are on the job, you play the role of police officer, which is just one of the many roles that you play. You do not lose your identity as a police officer while you are playing all those other roles, and the way in which you play those other roles as well as that of police officer influences the attitudes of the people you encounter.

The police department is not generally looked upon as a single unit. It is many individuals who are viewed by other individuals in a variety of ways. To the mayor or the city manager, the *police department* is the chief, possibly also the captains or deputy chiefs. To the service club member, the *"police"* is the officer who also belongs to the same club. To the lodge fellows, the officer is just another one of their brothers or sisters. Each individual in the community perceives the police department through a different set of eyes, and the police department is no stronger or greater than the officer who is its weakest link. The *"police"* may be viewed as the married man with two teenage children, who sits in the backroom of the neighborhood tavern after closing hours and drinks beer while on duty, and makes passes at the divorcee who works in the doctor's office down the street. To the average person, the police department is the patrol officers who patrol the streets and perform the many hundreds of police services in their own quiet, efficient manner. The police department is what the people see it as being, and what the police officers are, not what the city charter says they are. The police department must be above reproach, which means that every one of its members should likewise be above reproach.

You must have impeccable manners, you must be unquestionably honest, your moral standards must be almost cherubic, your bravery must be undaunting, and you must have all those qualities that are described in your Code of Ethics and in the laws that relate to your job. More important than *having* all those attributes, you must have them *in the eyes of others*. In short, you are on display no matter what you are doing or where you are.

We shall approach police—community interaction from the viewpoint that you as a field officer are involved in this relationship constantly. In this chapter we shall also take a look at the various responsibilities and activities of the police department in its role as the most highly visible branch of the criminal justice system.

The second half of this final chapter is devoted to community-oriented policing in its many forms as practiced by many police and sheriff's agencies throughout the country. Although not a new concept, it is getting renewed attention by departments that have decided the best way to address growing community problems is to do them with everyone getting involved.

THE FIELD OFFICER AND THE COMMUNITY

Your real authority is actually little more than that of the average citizen, but your responsibilities are far greater. You are compelled by law, by court decisions, and by the department's policies to take decisive action whenever a criminal law violation comes to your attention. You are limited in that you may arrest for misdemeanors only when they are committed in your presence, and you may make suspicion arrests for felonies based upon reasonable cause, which is narrowly interpreted by the courts to assure the accused of their constitutional guarantees of the "due process" clauses. Every arrest or law enforcement action that you make must be justified in the eyes of your superiors, the prosecuting attorney, the courts, and eventually the U.S. Supreme Court.

You must develop considerable skill in using the correct choice of words at all times, according to the situation. Sometimes poorly—or accidentally—chosen words may cause unexpected conflict. Words are spoken by attitude and innuendo as well as by actual utterance. Choose them wisely. Any antagonism that arises during a citizen-officer contact should not be a reflection of your poor attitude. Virtually every ethnic and religious minority has at least one nickname that is considered insulting when it is directed by some non-member toward a member of that minority in a disdainful manner. These words are sometimes referred to as "trigger words." It is the responsibility of every police officer to learn what those words are, and then to make it a point not to use them even during friendly locker room kidding. Take them out of your vocabulary.

Overfamiliarity with the people in your district may result in difficulties caused by a lessening of their respect for you. You should be friendly in your field contacts with the people in your district, but not to the point where you lose your police "image" or objectivity. Consider the "good Joe" officer who was such a nice guy and wanted everyone to like him. He would drive through a certain neighborhood and smile and wave at the kids, and sometimes even stop awhile and "chew the fat" with them before going on about his patrolling. The young children loved him. So did the young delinquents and some of the young adults, who were in the habit of playing poker for money on the street corner, and who committed various types of minor crimes without having to worry about "good old Joe." When asked about how they were able to get away with such obvious law violations, several of the people questioned replied: "Oh, good old Joe? He wouldn't arrest us. We weren't hurting anyone, and Joe didn't mind as long as we were minding our business and not hurting anyone."

Your personal appearance and grooming must be acceptable to the majority of the population. Adopting current fads in facial and head hair, makeup, and jewelry is not advised; the people who live in your community want their police officers to represent "middle America." Your uniform must be immaculate and have a semimilitary appearance. Personal cleanliness must also be above average. You must be free of offensive body odors, which may include too much cologne or perfume. You cannot have foul breath or dirty fingernails, and you should use a handkerchief when you sneeze.

You should never limit your organization membership exclusively to police-oriented clubs. You are a part of the larger community and should not isolate yourself from that community. When someone finds out that you are a police officer, they may want help in "fixing" a ticket, or they may just want to "gripe" about the "bum tickets" they received the last four times they were stopped. Doctors are plagued with requests for free diagnoses or a tip; electricians are expected to provide free installation services. Unfortunately, the nature of the work and the strange hours that usually accompany employment as a police officer preclude an active participation in community organizations. But social interactions as an individual and as a family member are important.

Youth groups, parent organizations, religious clubs, lodges, and service organizations all have memberships from all segments of the population. Participation in these groups yields results, not only for the individual but also for the community. They allow you and the people you contact while on duty to interact as social equals and to gain an insight into each other that could not be gotten otherwise.

Your contact with the traffic violator should be pleasant and friendly, yet not overly familiar. Sometime following the experience of receiving the citation, the individual will see for himself the violation that he committed and will agree that he should have received the ticket, providing his contact with you was pleasant (see Figure 14–1). If there was an unpleasant scene, the same individual will relive the experience and build his own case for his innocence. In addition, he will find good cause for growing angry over your unprofessional attitude and conduct.

You may be a member of an ethnic minority, but once you become a police officer, you lose that individuality. You become a faceless badge and uniform. You must guard against developing strong prejudices and not allow any of your intense feelings *for* or *against* any individual or group of people to influence your decisions to act as an ethical police officer.

When dealing with your people in any type of police action, you should always avoid attempts at intimidation through your language or your attitude. The juvenile should be dealt with positively and with respect if you are to expect any respect in return. Kindness and understanding are sometimes received by some youngsters with contempt and you may find it extremely difficult to hold your temper. In such cases, a positive and firm approach in the manner of a benevolent but strict parent may be the better approach. Never resort to losing your temper or name-calling, thereby denigrating the objective status of the law enforcement officer.

Figure 14-1   Every contact with the police need not be a bad experience. (Courtesy of the Police Department, Santa Ana, California.)

You are gauged by many people on the type and quality of service you perform. You can perform a tremendously important crime prevention service for the merchants and business owners in your district by making an occasional inspection visit. You should drop in and ask the owner or manager if there is any objection to your making a few observations about his building security. You will probably find the front doors in good shape. However, the back doors, through which burglars would rather enter, are more likely to need improvement. You may suggest that the merchant put the safe in a location where the patrolling officer can see it from outside or that a silent burglar alarm system is installed. Dead bolt locks are excellent devices for slowing down burglars, providing that the doors and frames are well constructed.

While on patrol, you are in an excellent position to develop informants. Contrary to popular belief, your most frequent source of information is not the underworld "rat" or "snitch." Most of the people who give you information are those in whom you have developed a feeling of pride and respect by keeping their neighborhood crime-free. You will have also given them a feeling of confidence that any information they give you about known or suspected crime violations will not immediately get back to them as a source of the information. By your own courteous service, you create in the people you contact a feeling of obligation to help you continue to perform an exemplary job. While on patrol, never accept, or expect, any free or cut-rate refreshments, gasoline, or services.

One of the community interaction programs that many police departments have established on a more formal basis during recent years has been the "lunch bag," or "adopt-a-cop," or "officer-on-campus" program.

This is an assigned function, established in cooperation with various schools, colleges, or organizations, at which one or two officers meet with several people in an informal setting while having lunch or refreshments together. The meeting is generally an unstructured affair, with the officers attempting to "break the ice" with some of the people they may meet on the street under different conditions (see Figure 14–2). Many of the group's questions are answered in such a way that the rapport extends far beyond their informal meetings. It is not uncommon for officers to find that a great many of the questions asked of them are based on misinformation or complete lack of information about the police role in the community.

POLICE DEPARTMENT COMMUNITY RELATIONS ACTIVITIES

Every police department in the country is involved in community relations or police-community interaction. The police department is a service organization and its service involves a direct interaction with the community it serves. During recent years, the trend has been to formalize many

Figure 14-2   The Delaware State Police Officer is explaining the police role to an interested audience. (Courtesy of the Delaware State Police.)

of the functions that had previously been conducted on an informal basis (see Figures 14–3 and 14–4). Some departments have created special bureaus or divisions with staff responsibility and full-time, assigned personnel to coordinate the community relations activities of the department.

Figure 14-3   The police officer's community relations activities involve more than formal prepared speeches to large audiences. This officer and his friends are participating in a "Trooper Dan" program. (Courtesy of the Delaware State Police.)

Figure 14-4   These school safety patrol boys are visited by a friend-ly trooper. (Courtesy of the Delaware State Police.)

Others have added this function to the list of responsibilities of one or more of the staff officers, to be handled along with various other assignments. Often the various programs of interaction with the public that are not directly related to law enforcement or crime repression activities are cataloged, and an effort is made to measure their effectiveness in terms of public acceptance and changes in crime and accident trends. The following deals with some of the police department's community interaction programs and activities.

Community Relations Unit

Someone within the organization should be charged with the responsibility for the department's community relations activities. That person should possess commensurate authority to implement techniques and programs, both formal and informal, that will create and maintain a better community understanding of the police role and a better police understanding of the various peoples and their cultural backgrounds and respective roles in the community (see Figure 14–5). The program must have the complete endorsement of the police chief, because some of the activities break with years of tradition, and they may be rejected at the level of execution without such backing. This community relations unit may function as a rumor control center in times of turmoil. At all times it should operate as a communications vehicle between the people and their police department whenever and wherever there is a need for the communicating process.

Figure 14-5 Police officers make the community relations unit work by going into the community instead of waiting for it to come to them. (Courtesy of the Lexington-Fayette (Kentucky) Urban County Division of Police.)

Community Relations Policies

The police department must have a set of workable, and working, community relations policies. If your department does not have a human relations statement of philosophy, consider this one:

> *The mutual advantages of a friendly relationship between the people of a community and their police force should be widely understood and more fully appreciated. The success of a police department in the performance of its duties is largely measured by the degree of support and cooperation it receives from the people it serves. It is of paramount importance, therefore, to secure for this department the confidence, respect, and approbation of the public. The cultivation of such desirable attitudes on the part of the public is dependent upon reciprocal attitudes on the part of this department. These policies are designed to enhance good public relations and [we] anticipate active participation therein by every member of the department.*

This statement is based on three major premises.

1. The attitude of the people in the community is affected by the degree of efficiency demonstrated by their police officers in the performance of their duties.

2. There must be a mutual understanding between the people of all backgrounds and ethnic origins and the officers who comprise their police department.
3. There must be a continuous, free flow of information about the activities of the police department to the public through the news media. The information must be honest and frank.

COMMUNITY–POLICE PARTNERSHIP

One excellent method for developing a closer working relationship with the community is to assign officers on a permanent or semipermanent basis to designated districts. By breaking down the department into smaller units, sometimes in such a way that most police activities, including juvenile, detective, traffic, and patrol, are all handled by this "neighborhood police force," the people in each district have the feeling that they have their own police department. This concept, sometimes referred to as "team policing," is usually well received by the people, and their cooperative efforts with the police usually improve. The people are constantly reminded by their regular police officers that crime prevention and the apprehension of criminal offenders depends on citizen and police cooperation. Taking the concept a little farther, some departments organize neighborhood "watch" groups, sometimes naming the project "community-oriented policing."

Police-community partnership (CPP) depends on mutual trust and respect between the community and the police (see Figure 14–6). Continual dialogue is essential, and we must be honest and candid with

Figure 14-6 The children should get to know the police as their friends. (Courtesy of the Police Department, Lexington, Kentucky.)

each other during that dialogue. Neighborhood meetings are held to identify local problems, committees are formed, and each committee elects its own leader, or "block captain." The neighbors get to know each other and develop methods for watching the neighborhood for unusual events and for immediately notifying the police department. They know and feel that the partnership will enhance the police department's effectiveness and that they are participants.

Fair and Equal Treatment for All Persons

Selection of the men and women who comprise the ranks of the organization is significant in setting the tone for a department that operates free of bias or prejudices. Everyone has the constitutional right to be prejudiced, but police officers relinquish the right to let any prejudices be reflected in their official actions. If they are so colored by prejudice that they lose their objectivity in their personal contacts with people, they will not be effective as police officers. Police actin should be dictated by the circumstances, and the officers' discretion in taking police action must be without regard to the individual's ethnic, religious, or moral characteristics.

Understanding the People in the Community

Seminars and conferences may be specifically programmed to bring together in educational debates police offices and people from various minority groups or philosophical organizations, political or religious. The aim of such debates is to promote a free exchange of views on various community concerns. They allow the police officer to explain the purpose and intent of the laws and the philosophy of his particular department, thereby reducing the amount and degree of misunderstanding of the police role.

Community Leadership Participation

It has been said that a camel is a horse put together by a committee. I agree, particularly if the committee is formed to accomplish a specific job. However, committees do serve a purpose if their goal is to develop a broader base of understanding among the people in the community of the many problems confronting their police department. A committee could be established, for example, for the purpose of disseminating information about the juvenile laws of the state and the community, and the police department's enforcement attitude toward those laws. The committee could present their opinions and representative views as citizens of the community at a meeting with the police chief and juvenile officers, and the police department would establish its own policies using the committee's suggestions as guidelines rather than mandates. The police department would then disseminate to the general public, through the committee and the press, the department's policies and enforcement program. This procedure could be effective in dealing with various major problems confronting law enforcement and the community. Some jurisdictions use a more formal approach by creating citizens crime commissions, which have more authority in developing police policies.

Police Reserve Corps

There are many outstanding ladies and gentlemen who might have been excellent police officers or other police department employees, but who decided to enter other lifetime pursuits. By establishing a reserve program, it is possible to create in a segment of the population a greater sense of involvement in their police department's activities through actual participation. Under normal conditions, the reserves train and serve alongside the regular officers once or twice weekly. Then, in case of a sudden emergency calling for personnel far in excess of that which the department could provide, the full complement of the reserves could be called into action to handle the immediate problem. Men and women could be used for a variety of functions, including actual field duties, such as operating a patrol unit, protecting a crime scene, directing traffic at the scene of an accident, or handling an unruly crowd. There are many other functions that need equal attention during times of emergency, such as preparing meals for officers who cannot leave their posts, manning telephones and radio equipment, maintaining radio and automotive equipment, and sketching robbery suspects. These and myriad other functions could be performed by people from a variety of occupations and professions.

Public Information

There should be some means for keeping the public informed about new laws and procedures, enforcement policies, and crime statistics. It is no secret that the police department cannot survive as an effective instrument of the government without the cooperation and support of the people, as we have already stated, but the public's support should be based on knowledge gained from accurate information. The department should neither ask for, nor expect, blind faith. Through the medium of personal appearances before every organization that will listen, the police chief and his direct representatives must appear and discuss frankly the actions and intentions of the police department. It is essential that we overcome some of the apathy which is expressed by lack of intercourse with the people. The people and their police department should be discussing the important problems of today and the ways in which these problems can be solved through mutual cooperation.

Press Relations

Whenever anything in the field occurs that appears to be newsworthy, such as an accident or a human interest story, it should be standard operating procedure to call it to the attention of the press. The "exclusive" should be avoided by adopting a standard department procedure for news releases and sticking to the procedure. An information officer may be assigned on a permanent, full-time basis, or one should be assigned each time a newsworthy situation occurs. If the department utilizes this practice, it should then be a department policy for all members of the department to adhere to it by referring any inquiring reporters or press people to the single individual who is responsible for releasing the information. Such a procedure reduces the disparity between stories emanating from several officers about the same case, and avoids what might be a legitimate complaint of "reliability gap."

The department philosophy should be one of complete cooperation with the press. All information that will not directly hinder the ongoing progress of a case currently under investigation should be released. Withholding information concerning some cases is essential, but in most cases it is not. As a matter of fact, it may be wise to discuss even the confidential information with the press representatives, explaining to them why the release of such information is harmful to the case. They then will act as responsible people should and refrain from releasing the information. This candid approach may be wiser than withholding certain facts and running the risk of their discovering the information through other means and inadvertently releasing their "inside" or "exclusive" that may ruin the case. If the news reporters are truly serving the public as they claim, they will respect the request and withhold printing of certain details until given clearance from the department. As a result, both the police and the press will improve their efficiency.

COMMUNITY-ORIENTED POLICING

In a concerted effort to get the people of the community more directly involved in police problems and challenges, many police agencies have gone back to the drawing board and have come up with a myriad of ideas to get all the communities involved. They have developed police–community partnerships with the beat officers working in their neighborhoods with greater autonomy and incentives to work with people rather than taking the somewhat aloof approach some of us were using during the "professionalism" era of the 1950s and 1960s. Working apart from the community created chasms that led to problems and suspicion, sort of an "us versus them" philosophy, with the result that considerable alienation developed.

Lieutenant Christopher M. Robertson of the Cincinnati (Ohio) Police Department wrote in an unpublished paper in the spring of 1992:

> *Community-Oriented Policing (C.O.P.) is a nontraditional, proactive approach to crime control, order maintenance, crime prevention and basic service delivery. C.O.P. utilizes modern*

problem solving techniques to identify and correct conditions which contribute to an atmosphere conducive to criminality, thereby expanding the traditionally narrow definition of police responsibility.

Fundamental to the concept of C.O.P. is the formation of a cohesive, working partnership between the police and the community to address both crime problems and quality of life issues which may impact, indirectly, on the crime situation. C.O.P. aggressively solicits input from the citizenry regarding their perceptions of neighborhood problems, both individually, through one-on-one street contacts, and collectively through regular community council meetings, church groups, schools, recreation centers, etc. This connection is crucial, as the police tend to overlook the more subtle aspects of neighborhood life which may be of major significance to the community.

Chief of Police Phil Green of the twin cities of Corte Madera and Larkspur, California, in a personal letter dated March 23, 1992, wrote: "Community policing means different things to different people. Also, some people have put the name of Community Policing for what many of us have been doing for years."

Williams and Wagoner made this assessment: "Community policing requires a substantial change in both structure and form, including attitudinal, organizational, and subcultural change. It represents a "new" philosophy of policing whereby police officers and the community work together to solve community problems of crime and related social ills. This means giving citizens...a direct say in the solutions and activities that regulate crime."[1]

In the Fall/Winter 1988 publication *Footprints*, Robert C. Trojanowicz wrote:

Community relations and team policing are only two of the most obvious recent examples [of well-intentioned modern policing reforms that have faltered and died]....Community policing means freeing the officer from the isolation of the patrol car and putting the same officer into direct, face-to-face contact with the same community residents every day. It means allowing that officer the freedom to explore new ways the police and community residents can work together to solve the problems of crime, fear of crime, and physical and social disorder.[2]

[1]Frank P. Williams III and Carl P. Wagoner."*Making the Police Proactive: An Impossible Task for Improbable Reasons," Police Forum,* A.C.J.S. Police Section, Vol. 2, No. 2, June 1992.

[2]Robert C. Trojanowicz, *"Serious Threats to the Future of Policing" Footprints,* Community Policing Newsletter published by the National Neighborhood Foot Patrol Center, Michigan State University, Vol. 1, No. 3, and Vol. 2, No. 1, pp. 1–3.

Now that we have seen what the experts say about Community Policing, let's take a look at what the many police and sheriff agencies are doing about implementing some of their programs that fall into the category of community policing. They are not listed in any order of importance or priority, and what may be attributed to any one department does not in any way mean that their program is theirs exclusively or originally.

Neighborhood Watch (Santa Fe, New Mexico, Police Department). This is a program of neighbors watching each other's property while they are absent, such as during working hours, while on vacation, or other absence. The neighbor who sees someone or some event that does not seem appropriate at the neighbor's residence, such as strange vehicles or people who have never been seen before around the residence, calls the police to check it out.

Target Area Program (Jackson, Michigan, Police Department). An officer is permanently assigned to a specific area to work exclusively on foot or on a bicycle. The officer is equipped with a beeper and is available to the people as their personal police officer. The officer maintains a close working relationship with the residents (see Figure 14–7) as well as other city departments such as Community Development, Building Inspection Division, Fire Department, Parks and Recreation, and the Department of Public Works. The officer serves as a link between the public and whichever of their needs can be addressed by the police or other agencies.

Figure 14-7   Officer A. Hart and the Airlie Neighborhood Watch group following a street parade. (Courtesy of the Police Department, Charlotte, North Carolina.)

Citizen Volunteer Program (Merced County, California, Sheriff's Department). Citizens are recruited to work for no compensation to aid sheriff's deputies and other employees in their many nonconfrontational duties, such as warrants, records, greeting and directing people at the information desk, assisting officers in patrol, detective, identification divisions, dispatch, and patrolling in sheriff's cars, serving as extra sets of eyes and ears in a nonpolice capacity.

SAFE (SAFety for Everyone) Program (Minneapolis, Minnesota, Police Department). Citizen volunteers assist the police department in identifying and attempting to solve such problems as property crimes, undesirable housing conditions, garbage and litter, noisy neighbors, drug houses, landlord–tenant issues, and animal control problems.

NEON (Neighborhood Enhancement Operation Network) (Miami, Florida, Police Department). A roving force of 100 officers are used to "saturate" a quadrant of the city to fight severe crime problems for 30 days, then move to another location for saturation patrol.

In a letter from Assistant Chief Arnold Gibbs dated April 21, 1992, the program works like this:

> *Beginning August 23, 1991 a roving force of 100... Its primary objective is to educate and empower residents and allow them fuller participation in making their neighborhoods safer. The operation also involves the Department of Sanitation, Code Enforcement, the Fire Department, Nuisance Abatement, the Parks Department, Public Works, and the State Attorney's Office. On its first night of operation, 61 arrests were made, 220 citations were written, 24 cars were confiscated or towed, and 1 crack house was demolished.*

Combat Auto Theft (CAT) Program (Widespread Use, Many Cities). People who do not usually operate their personal vehicles between 1 and 5 A.M. volunteer to have a decal put on their vehicle and sign a waiver that gives an officer probable cause to stop such a vehicle because anyone driving it will most likely be a car thief.

Business Crime Watch (Metro-Dade Police Department, Miami, Florida). This program is similar to the neighborhood watch in residential areas, but the participants are neighboring business establishments. The idea is the same, looking out for the neighbor's property at all times, especially when the tenant is away from the place.

Drug Abuse Resistance Education (DARE) and ADAPT (Alcohol and Drug Abuse Prevention Training) (Many Agencies). Officers are placed in the schools and present intensive educational programs on alcohol and drug resistance in grades 5 and 6, in some cases in the lower grades, and then carried on through the junior and senior high school years.

Community Police Officer Program (San Francisco, California, Police Department). This is principally a goal-directed foot beat program designed to bring officers and public closer together so that they may discuss and attempt to work out mutual problems.

"Dear John" Letters (Des Moines, Iowa, Police Department). Residents in neighborhoods where there is considerable unwanted prostitution activity, with the prostitutes standing around waiting on the street to be picked up by their "Johns," take down license numbers of vehicles cruising the area and/or picking up male and female prostitutes. They secure names and addresses of car owners from the Department of Transportation and send "Dear John" letters to those owners.

> *Mr. and/or Mrs. _____ Your (Vehicle Description) was seen picking up a prostitute in the vicinity of (Area) in Des Moines on (Date) at approximately (Time). We hope you realize that by participating in such behavior you risk criminal prosecution, as well as exposing yourself—and possibly your family—to public humiliation and a host of diseases, including the deadly AIDS virus. Prostitution is unacceptable and it will not be tolerated any more in our neighborhood. A detailed description of your vehicle, complete with the license number, has been circulated to area residents.*

It is signed by "area residents" and copies are sent to the vice squad of the police department and the prosecuting attorney.

The Des Moines Police also have a unit called S.C.A.T. (Strategic Complement Against Thugs) consisting of nine officers who work from 8 P.M. to 4 A.M. and mainly work foot patrol in specific target areas where gangs are known to congregate. They keep themselves familiar with gang members and drug dealers with their "GOOD BOOK," a file of mug shots and bios on all known gang members, which they share with officers on the beat throughout the city.

Operation C.A.R.E. (Combined Accident Reduction Effort) (Kentucky State Police in Cooperation with Local Police). Accompanied by a media "blitz," a D-Day is designated when all agencies set up road blocks and sobriety checkpoints with a combined effort to remove alcohol- and drug-impaired drivers from the roads.

AT&T Language Line (Carmel, California, Police Department). In diverse communities of many languages, it is often difficult to find someone who can interpret when it is critical. In this community the agency has arranged for instant access via telephone to an interpreter in any language. Another resource not to be overlooked is the language department at your local college or university. Many language instructors are fluent in several languages other than the ones they teach, and many other faculty members travel widely and study languages.

Graffiti Busters (Costa Mesa, California, Police Department).
Business owners volunteer to sign agreements that they will have graffiti removed within specified periods of time after discovery and to report all graffiti problems. The city has purchased graffiti removal equipment, consisting of sand-blasters, chemical paint removers, and paint-over paints. Using volunteers and Explorer Scouts, the mobile graffiti blaster goes out into the community and removes the unwanted symbols and messages. Many cities provide graffiti removal services and attempt to remove the graffiti on the day it is reported.

Building Security Standards (Orange, California, Police Department). Written into their building codes are minimum requirements for locks, gates, doors, and security devices that must be installed for code compliance. Citations are issued for violators.

Cellular Phone and Citizen Band Watch (Many Agencies). People who have their vehicles equipped with these convenient devices are encouraged to call in anything they observe that calls for the attention of the police or any other agency in the city, including crimes, graffiti, accidents, lots overgrown with weeds, abandoned buildings, and other problem items.

"I've Had Enough" Coupons (Manteca, California, Police Department). Coupons are printed in the local newspapers and are to be clipped out and mailed to the police department with reports and complaints about drug and other activities in the neighborhood that the complainant is tired of putting up with. This is similar to the WE TIP telephone call-in programs, where a person may report activities and suspicious people anonymously to the police.

Project Cuddle (Many Agencies, including Highway Patrols).
Children who are victims of traffic accidents, child abuse, and other emotionally traumatic situations are taken aside for personal attention and given teddy bears or raggedy-ann dolls of their own to help ease the pain.

Crime Prevention Column in Newspaper (Many Agencies). Local newspapers are recruiting police and highway patrol officers to write columns addressing the problems of crime and accident prevention and to answer questions asked by the reading public. This is an excellent forum for the agency to use to get messages to the public about items of mutual interest.

Operation Identification (Many Agencies). This project provides the residents of the community with decals to attach to windows notifying would-be burglars that all valuable items inside are marked for quick identification, and assisting people in affixing those marks of ownership with labels and engraving equipment.

Operation Cul-de-Sac (Many Agencies). Streets that have heavy traffic through the neighborhood by people dealing in drug trafficking have been closed to through traffic by barricades or curbs to eliminate some of that traffic.

Coordinated Neighborhood Policing (Dallas, Texas, Police Department). Utilizing neighborhood police officers working with the community as discussed in other places throughout this chapter, Dallas describes their program thus: "The problem-solving approach represents a significant evolutionary step in helping law enforcement work smarter, not harder. Rather than approaching calls for service as separate unrelated incidents, problem-oriented policing emphasizes analyzing groups of incidents and deriving solutions that draw upon a wide variety of public and private resources. Law enforcement has evolved from a reactive process to a proactive process, and now to a coactive process."

SUMMARY

As you can see, policing in the United States is moving toward development of a partnership with the communities that we serve. As the cities grew and departments got larger, the trend was to draw away from the community in a stand-off position, a process of "Us serving Them," and never the twain shall meet. As time passed and budgets became skimpier, the police community began to realize that the better approach to the problems of increased criminal activity and decay of the moral fiber of our citizens was to get the community involved in a partnership. Hundreds of police and sheriff's departments have developed Community Policing Models, each with a different twist, but the common thread in the fabric has been this partnership that is so essential to our success. This is the wave of the future, and we shall see more of it as time goes on. Within a few short years, the old-timers will no longer recognize their police departments. You as a young "beginner" in the profession are in for the ride of your life as the whirlwind takes you into the twenty-first century.

EXERCISES AND STUDY QUESTIONS

1. Outline a five-point plan for your department's community relations program as you think it should be.
2. What is a trigger word, and what should be the police attitude toward usage of such words?
3. Why must a peace officer take an active part in nonpolice-related activities, according to the author?
4. What should your own personal policy be concerning acceptance of free refreshments and other handouts while on duty?

5. Prepare a police–press policy that you think would be most appropriate for your department.
6. Define *community-oriented policing*.
7. Name and describe at least five separate community policing models listed in his chapter.
8. What departments other than the police are involved in community policing programs?

REFERENCES

ADAMS, THOMAS F. *Introduction to the Administration of Criminal Justice*, 2nd ed. Englewood Cliffs, N.J.: Prentice Hall, 1980.

BENT, ALLAN E., and RALPH A. ROSSUM. *Police, Criminal Justice, and the Community*. New York: Harper & Row, 1976.

BRANDSTATTER, A. F., and LOUIS RADELET. *Police and Community Relations: A Sourcebook*. Beverly Hills, Calif.: Glencoe, 1968.

CROMWELL, PAUL F., JR., and GEORGE KEEFER. *Police–Community Relations*. St. Paul, Minn.: West, 1973.

HOLLINGSWORTH, DAN. *Rocks in the Roadway*. Chicago: Stromberg-Allen, 1954.

INTERNATIONAL ASSOCIATION OF CHIEFS OF POLICE AND ANTI-DEFAMATION LEAGUE OF B'NAI B'RITH. *The Police and the Civil Rights Act*. New York: International Association of Chiefs of Police and Anti-Defamation League, 1959.

KRETCH, DAVID, RICHARD S. CRUTCHFIELD, and EGERTON L. BALLACHEY. *Individual in Society*. New York: McGraw-Hill, 1962.

RADELET, LOUIS A. *The Police and the Community*. Encino, Calif.: Glencoe, 1980.

TROJANOWICZ, ROBERT C., and SAMUEL DIXON. *Criminal Justice and the Community*. Englewood Cliffs, N.J.: Prentice Hall, 1974.

INDEX

A

Abandoned vehicle abatement, 234–35
Abbreviations, in reports, 172
Access control, 22
Accident scene sketch, essential elements
    for, 287–88
Acknowledging a call, 139
Aircraft crashes, 326–29
    access hatches/rescue point/exits, how
        to use, 327
    military, 326–27
    reporting, 328–29
Airports, searches conducted at, 386
Alcoholic beverage control,
    investigation/enforcement, 232–34
Ambiguity, in reports, 172–73
Amphibian vehicles, 34
Animal control, 14, 242, 417
Apprehension of offenders, 7–8
Arrest, 20–21
    breaking into a building to, 377
    defined, 373–74
    diplomatic immunity, 379–80
    entrapment, 380–81
    force, use of, 371, 374–77
    investigative detention, 381–82
    laws providing for, 370–73
    procedures, 374–82
    resistance to arrest a crime, 377
    warrant arrests, 377–78
    warrantless arrests, 371, 378
    without warrant, 371
Arrest report, 175–77
Arson investigations, 288–89
Asset protection, 22–23
Assignments, See also Field assignments;
    Routine assignments
Attempted suicides, investigating, 298–99
Attractive nuisance doctrine, 72–73, 235–37
Automatic rifles, 411
Automobile patrol, 34
Auto surveillance, 76
Auto theft investigations, 289–90

B

Basic field procedures, 48–82
    district responsibility, 64
    patrol, 55–64
        hazards of, 72–73
        inspections on, 64–72
        preparation for, 49–55
        specialized patrol, 77–78
        surveillance/stakeouts, 73–77
        team policing, 79
Baton, 412–13
Benevolent/community services, 11–12

Bicycle patrol, 32–33
Bill of Rights, field officer, 3–4, 40–44
Binoculars, detailed descriptions of, 115
Biological fluids, 279–80
Boat patrol, 34
Body, reports, 169–70
"Body bubble," 122
Body-language communications, modes
    of, 121–22
Bombs/bomb threats, 329–32
Booking, 21
Broadcast procedures, radios, 138–39
Building inspections, 65–69
Burglary investigations, 290–91
Business security, 12

C

CAL-ID, 131
Calls for service, responding to, 13–14
Cameras, detailed descriptions of, 115
Car stops, 352–60
    approaching the suspect vehicle, 352,
        354–58
        one officer, 356
        removing suspects from vehicle, 358
        suspects in vehicle, 357–58
        two officers, 354–56
    legal considerations, 360
    location, selecting, 352–53
    traffic citations, 358–60
Celebrity protection, 23
Chain of evidence custody, 282–84
Chemical fire extinguisher, 412
Child molestation, investigating, 298
Civil and domestic disputes, 225–32
    domestic quarrels, 227–29
    landlord-tenant disputes, 229–30
    mechanics'/innkeepers' liens, 230–31
    repossession disputes, 231–32
Civil liability, 39–40
Clothing, detailed descriptions of, 107–13
Clover leaf pattern, 59
Communications, 119–47
    body-language communications, modes of,
        121–22
    communications media guidelines, 128–35
        facsimile (fax) and computer
            interface, 130–31
        hand signals, 128–29
        nightsticks, 128–29
        police radio, 135

recall signal devices, 129
        telegraph, 129
        telephone, 132–35
        teletype and computers, 129–30
        television, 131–32
        U.S. Mail, 128
        whistles, 128–29
    communications system, 122–24
    "in-progress" communications procedures,
        246–47
    interpersonal communications, 120–22
    intra-/interdepartmental communications,
        124–28
    radio operation guidelines, 135–45
    video data terminals in field units, 144
Community-oriented policing, 430–36
Community relations, 4, 419–37
    community-police partnership (CPP),
        427–30
    informants, 423
    intimidation, 422
    overfamiliarity with community members,
        421
    personal appearance/grooming, 421
    police department activities, 423–27
    policies, 42–27
    prejudice, 422
    units, 425
Conclusion, reports, 171
Consensual encounter, 373–74
Contacts, developing, 17–18
"Contact" situation, 373
Conviction of offenders, 7–8
Convoys, 74
Courtesy services, 239–41
Crime file, 185
Crime prevention follow-up, 69
Crime report, 177–81
    property description, 181
    suspect, 180
Crime scene investigator (CSI), 20
Crime scene sketch, essential elements for,
    287
Crimes in progress, 245–66
    field unit response, 247–49
    gang activity, 259–61
    general coordination/search, 261–62
    "in-progress" communications procedures,
        246–47
    plainclothes assistance, 263–64
    prowlers, 256–59

suspect, questioning, 255
tactics:
    crimes against person, 250–51
    crimes against property, 251–55
weapons, 255–56
Crime suspect:
  interviewing, 198–204
    confessions/admissions to private
      person, 204
    constitutional guidelines, 198–204
Criminal behavior:
  prevention of, 6
  repression of, 6–7
Crisis intervention, 332–34
  See also Disasters/unusual occurrences
Crowd control, 24
Crowd control formations, 321–26

D

Dead body calls, See Homicide
    investigations
Deductive reasoning, 271
Delinquent behavior:
  prevention of, 6
  repression of, 6–7
Delusion, 335
Detailed sketch, 285
Detention, 373–74
Diplomatic immunity, 37–80
Disasters, 11
Disasters/unusual occurrences, 303–40
  aircraft crashes, 326–29
  assignment of responsibility, 311
  bombs/bomb threats, 329–32
  crisis intervention, 332–34
  disaster control procedures, 305–8
  disaster response, 304–13
  federal troops, 310
  intelligence assignments, 311
  logistics, 308–9, 311
  martial rule, 309–10
  mentally/emotionally disturbed
    individuals, 334–37
  mobilization, 308–9
  mutual aid agreement, 309
  public information, 311–12
  riot control, 313–26
  staging area, 312
  victims, identification of, 312–13
Discovery rules, 22
Discretionary prerogatives, 35–39

operational guidelines for, 38–39
District orientation tour, 54–55
Disturbance prevention, 24
DNA (genetic fingerprinting), 276–77
Domestic quarrels, 227–29
Due process, 8
DUI (driving under the influence), 361–68
  DUI report, 366–68
  field sobriety tests, 364–66
  suspected DUI, stopping, 362–64

E

Entrapment, 380–81
Escorts, 349–50
Evidence, 273–82
  biological fluids, 279–80
  chain of evidence custody, 282–84
  collection/preservation of, 20, 272–73
  DNA (genetic fingerprinting), 276–77
  fabrics, 280
  fingerprint identification systems,
    274–75
  fingerprints, 274
  glass particles, 281–82
  gunpowder/shot pattern tests, 280
  marking, 282
  and odontology, 280
  paint identification, 281
  safe insulation, 280
  shoeprints, 277
  soil, 278
  tireprints, 277
  tool marks, 277–78
  wood identification, 281
Executive protection, 23
External factors, perception, 85–87
External relationships, 127–28
Eye contact, 121
Eyewitness identification, 94–100
  field identification, 95–96
  lineup, 98–100
  photographic identification, 96–98
  See also Witnesses

F

Fabrics, as evidence, 280
Facial expressions, 121
Facsimile (fax), 130–31
Felonies, 21
Female prisoners:
  control of, 393–94

transportation of, 395
Field activity reports, administrative
    evaluation of, 3
Field assignments, 24–29
    patrol deployment, factors determining,
        27–28
    patrol districts, designation of, 28–29
    policy decisions concerning, 25–27
    rotation of, 29
Field identification, 95–96
Field interrogation card, 207–8
Field interviews, 205–16
    approach on foot, 211–12
    field interrogation card, 207–8
    guidelines, 213–16
    interrogation, position of, 212–13
    location for, 211
    objectives of, 205–8
        identification, 205–6
        prevention/repression of crime, 206
        records, 206–8
    procedure, 211–16
    when to conduct, 210–11
Field notebook, 154–57
    entries regarding search, 389
    format of, 155–57
        chronological approach, 156–57
        narrative style, 155–56
        question-and-answer style, 156
    numbering pages in, 17
    person descriptions, 157
    sample of, 154
Field notes, 149–60
    defined, 150
    notebook, 154–57
    notetaking techniques, 157–59
    officer's daily log, 159–60
    retention vs. destruction of, 153–54
    value of, 152
    what to record, 152–53
    when to take, 150–52
Field officer:
    Bill of Rights, 3–4, 40–44
    civil liability of, 3–40
    defined, 1
    See also Officer survival
Field operations:
    objectives of, 4–10
        defense of life/property, 4
        identification/apprehension/
            conviction of offenders, 7–8

maintenance of order, 9–10
participative law enforcement, 4–6
prevention of criminal/delinquent
    behavior, 6
repression of criminal/delinquent
    behavior, 6–7
traffic control, 8–9
Field search, 38–85
Field unit response, 247–49
Fingerprint identification system, 131
Fingerprint identification systems, 274–75
Finger printing, genetic, 276–77
Fingerprints, 274
Firearms:
    detailed descriptions of, 115–16
    field officer's use of, 413–17
    officer-involved shooting, personnel
        services following, 417
    warning shots, 417
    when to shoot, 415–16
Fire scenes, 237–38
First aid, 238–39
First impressions, noting, 272
Fixed surveillance, 34
Fixed-wing aircraft, 33–34
Foot patrol, 31
    tactics, 56–59
Foot search, 262–63
Foot surveillance, 75–76
Force, use of, 371, 374–77
Forgery investigations, 295–96
Frisk, 382–83

G

Gambling, 296
Gang activity, 259–61
General orders, 125
General preparation, for patrol, 49–50
Genetic fingerprinting, 276–77
Gestures, 120, 122
Grounds sketch, 285
Gunpowder/shot pattern tests, 280

H

Hallucination, 335–36
Handguns, 412
Hand-saps, 412
Hand signals, 128–29
Helicopters, 33–34
Homicide investigations, 291–95

investigation guidelines, 293–95
signs of death, looking for, 291–92
Horse patrol, 31–32
Hot lines, 134
Hot sheets, 51
House inspections, 69–71

I

Identification of offenders, 7–8
Inductive reasoning, 271
In-field preparation, 53
Informants, 17-18, 423
Information services, 15–16
Infractions, 21
Innkeepers' liens, 230–31
Inspections, 64–72
    building inspections, 65–69
    crime prevention follow-up, 69
    house inspections, 69–71
    miscellaneous inspections, 71–72
Inspection services, 12–13
Interdepartmental communications, 127
Internal factors, perception, 87–92
Interpersonal communications, 120–22
Interrogation, position, 212–13
Interview/interviewing, 192–219
    art of, 193–94
    of crime suspect, 198–204
        confessions/admissions to private
            person, 204
        constitutional guidelines, 198–204
    field interviews, 205–16
        objectives of, 205–8
    general techniques, 195–98
        logical approach, 197–98
        operational suggestions, 198
        sympathetic approach, 197
    objectives of, 194–95
    See also Field interviews
Intimate space, 122
Intimidation, 422
Intoxication cases, 224
    civil and domestic disputes, 225–32
Intradepartmental communications, 125–27
Introduction, reports, 169
Inventory shrinkage, 22–23
Investigative detention, 381–82

J

Jewelry, detailed descriptions of, 103–7

L

Landlord-tenant disputes, 229–30
Leads, developing from informants, 17–18
Leapfrog, 263
Lineup, 98–100
Listening skills, 120
Locality sketch, 285
Location:
    car stops, 352–53
    field interviews, 211
    of stolen children, 23
Location file, 187
Logical approach, to interview, 197–98
Lost child assignments, 221–23
Luggage, detailed descriptions of, 114–15

M

Maintenance of order, 9–10
Martial rule, 309–10
Master index, 184–85
Mechanics' liens, 230–31
Mentally/emotionally disturbed individuals,
    334–37
Microphone technique, radios, 137–38
Military aircraft crashes, 326–27
Minor complaints, 13–14
Miscellaneous incident report, 175
Miscellaneous inspections, 71–72
Misdemeanors, 21
Missing persons, 223–24
Mob formation:
    stages in, 318–19
        See also Riot control
Motion, 122
Motorcycle patrol, 32
Muscle tone, absence of, as sign of death,
    292–93
Musical instruments, detailed descriptions
    of, 116
Mutual aid agreement, 309

N

Names, in reports, 171
National Crime Information Center
    (NCIC), 130
Neurosis, 336
Nightsticks, 128–29
911 telephone system, 134
Nonverbal communications, 120
Notebook, See Field notebook

Nuisances, 235–37

O

Observation, 10, 53, 83–118
  descriptions of persons, 92–94
  eyewitness identification, 94–100
    field identification, 95–96
    lineup, 98–100
    photographic identification, 96–98
  perception, 85–92
  property descriptions, standard formula
    for, 100–103
  witnesses, basic requirements of, 84–85
Odontology, and evidence, 280
Officer-involved shooting, personnel
  services following, 417
Officer's daily log, 159–60
Officer survival:
  dangerous situations/countermeasures,
    404–6
  firearms, use of, 413–17
  self-defense, rules of, 406–11
  stress, 399, 400–403
  weapons, choice of, 411–13
Order maintenance, 9–10

P

Paint identification, as evidence, 281
Parades/special events, 237
Paranoia, 336
Parking, police vehicles, 61–62
Participative law enforcement, 4–6
Patdown searches, 372, 382–83
Patrol, 3, 31–35, 55–64
  activities, 10–22
    animal control, 14
    arrest of offenders, 20–21
    benevolent/community services, 11–12
    business/property security, 12
    calls for service, responding to,
      13–14
    contacts, developing, 17–18
    evidence collection/preservation, 20
    information services, 15–16
    inspection services, 12–13
    preliminary investigations, 18–20
    preventive attendance at public
      gatherings, 10–11
    report preparation, 21–22
    routine patrol and observation, 10
    testifying in court, 22
    traffic control, 15
  automobile patrol, 34
  basic methods of, 55
  bicycle patrol, 32–33
  boat patrol, 34
  fixed surveillance, 34
  foot patrol, 31
    tactics, 56-59
  helicopters/fixed-wing aircraft, 33–34
  horse patrol, 31–32
  inspections, 64–72
    building inspections, 65–69
    crime prevention follow-up, 69
    house inspections, 69–71
    miscellaneous inspections, 71–72
  motorcycle patrol, 32
  patrol driving, 60–62
  patrol patterns, 59–60
  plainclothes patrol, 62–64
  preparation for, 49–55
    district orientation tour, 54–55
    general preparation, 49–50
    in-field preparation, 53
    prepatrol preparation, 50–53
  small-vehicle patrol, 32–33
  specialized patrol, 77–78
  vehicle patrol, tactics, 59–60
  vehicles:
    inspection of, 54
    parking, 61–62
    skidding, 61
Patrol deployment, factors determining,
  27–28
Patrol districts, designation of, 28–29
Patrol force distribution, 24–29
  field assignments, rotation of, 29
  patrol deployment, factors determining,
    27–28
  policy decisions concerning, 25–27
Patrol time, 3
Pawned object file, 186
Perception, 85–92
  external factors, 85–87
  internal factors, 87–92
Perimeter control, 22
Personal appearance/grooming, 421
Personal protection, 23
Photographic identification, 96–98
Photographs, 284–85
Plainclothes assistance, for crimes in
  progress, 263–64

Plainclothes patrol, 62–64
  recognition of officer on, 64
Police radio, 135
Police sketching, See Sketching
Postmortem lividity, 292
Preliminary investigations, 18–20, 267– 302
  arson, 288–89
  auto theft, 289–90
  burglary, 290–91
  deductive/inductive reasoning, 271
  evidence, 273–82
      collection/preservation of, 272–73
  first impressions, noting, 272
  forgery/suspect documents, 295–96
  gambling, 296
  homicides, 291–95
  photographs, 284–85
  prelude to, 268–71
  receiving stolen property, 296–97
  robbery, 297
  sexual assault, 297–98
  sketching, 285–88
  suicides/attempted suicides, 298–99
  traffic collisions, 299– 300
  witnesses, personal interviews of, 268,
      272
Prepatrol preparation, 50–53
Press relations, 429–30
Prisoners:
  control of, 392–93
      female prisoners, 393–94
  transportation of, 394–95
      female prisoners, 395
Private police activities, 22–24
  asset protection/inventory shrinkage,
      22–23
  disturbance prevention/crowd control, 24
  perimeter/access control, 22
  personal/executive/celebrity protection,
      23
  special-purpose police, 24
  stolen children, location/recovery of,
      23
Proactive patrol, 30–31
Processing, 21
Property descriptions:
  binoculars, 115
  cameras, 115
  clothing, 107–13
  firearms, 115–16
  jewelry, 103–7

  luggage, 114–15
  musical instruments, 116
  order for listing items in report, 102–3
  radios/televisions, 113–14
  standard formula for, 100–103
  tools, 114
Property security, 12
Prowlers, 256–59
Psychoneurotic condition, 336
Psychosis, 335–36
Public relations, 4
Public utilities/service agencies,
      assisting, 241–42
Pursuit and emergency driving, 341–69
  abandoning the pursuit, 347–48
  "code three" runs, 342
      guidelines for, 349
  escorts, 349–50
  legal aspects of, 351–52
  ramming, 348
  red light/signal, using, 343
  roadblocks, 346–47
  shooting at fleeing vehicle, 343–44
  transporting injured persons, 350–51

Q

Quadrant search, 59, 263

R

Radios:
  acknowledgment of calls, 139
  broadcast procedures, 138–39
  detailed descriptions of, 113–14
  general broadcasting rules, 140
  microphone technique, 137–38
  operating laws/regulations, 137
  operation guidelines, 135–45
  radio codes, 138, 140–44
  station broadcasting, 139–40
Rattle watch, 7
Reactive patrol, 30–31
Recall signal devices, 129
Receiving stolen property, 296–97
Records, 183–89
  crime file, 185
  field interviews, 206–8
  location file, 187
  master index, 184–85
  pawned object file, 186
  report files, 185

serial number file, 186
stolen object file, 186
uses of, 183–84
using the files, 187–88
Report files, 185
Reports, 148–91
  abbreviations in, 172
  ambiguity in, 172–73
  arrest report, 175–77
  body, 169–70
  conclusion, 171
  construction of, 169–75
  crime report, 177–81
  dictating, 173–75
  DUI report, 366–68
  field notes, 149–60
  miscellaneous incident report, 175
  names, use of, 171
  preparation of, 21–22, 165–68
    background preparation, 165
  purposes of, 163–65
    allocation of resources, 163–64
    information resource for other
  agencies, 164–65
    investigative source, 164
    policy changes, 164
  records, 183–89
  report writing, 160–83
  special reports, 181
  style of, 166–68
  synopsis/introduction, 169
  See also Records
Report writing, 160–63
Repossession disputes, 231–32
Rescue and first aid, 238–39
Rigor mortis, 292
Riot control, 10, 313–26
  crowd control formations, 321–26
  mob formation, stages in, 318–19
  operations, 313–14
  police purpose/objectives, 317–18
  psychological influences, 318
  unlawful assembly, 319–21
  warning signals, 314–16
Roadblocks, 346–47
Robbery investigations, 297
Rotation of field assignments, 29
Rough sketch, 285
Routine assignments, 220–44
  abandoned vehicle abatement, 234–35
  alcoholic beverage control,

  investigation/enforcement, 232–34
  animal calls, handling, 242
  courtesy services, 239–41
  fire scenes, 237–38
  intoxication cases, 224
  lost child, 221–23
  missing persons, 223–24
  nuisances, 235–37
  parades/special events, 237
  public utilities/service agencies,
    assisting, 241–42
  rescue and first aid, 238–39
Routine patrol, 10
Rumors, 126–27

S

Safe insulation, as evidence, 281
Schizophrenia, 336
Search, 261–62
  field search, 383–85
  foot search, 262–63
  frisk, 382–83
  leapfrog, 263
  legal considerations, 390–91
  notebook entries regarding, 389
  patdown searches, 382–83
  of persons at airports, 386
  of premises, 389
  quadrant search, 59, 263
  with search warrants, 391–92
  spot cover, 263
  strip search, 385
  techniques, 382–92
  vehicle search, 386–88
  where to search, 388–89
  of women, 385–86
Self-defense, rules of, 406–11
Semiautomatic rifles, 411
Serial number file, 186
Sexual assault investigations, 297–98
Shakedown searches, 372
Shoeprints, 277
Shotguns, 411–12
Shot pattern tests, 280
Signs of death, looking for, 291–92
Silence, as body language, 122
Sketching, 285–88
  accident scene sketch, essential
    elements for, 287–88
  basic rules for, 287–88
  crime scene sketch, essential elements

for, 287
    detailed sketch, 285
    finished drawings, 285
    grounds sketch, 285
    locality sketch, 285
    materials needed for, 285–86
    measuring methods, 288
    rough sketch, 285
Skidding, police vehicles, 61
Small-vehicle patrol, 32–33
Social space, 122
Soil, as evidence, 278
Specialized patrol, 77–78
Special orders, 125
Special-purpose police, 24
Special reports, 181
Spot cover, 263
Stakeouts, 73–74, 76–77
    basic guidelines for, 77
Stolen children, location/recovery of, 23
Stolen object file, 186
Stress, 399, 400–403
Strip search, 385
Stun guns, 412
Style, of reports, 166–68
Suicides/attempted suicides, investigating,
        298–99
Surveillance, 73–76
    auto surveillance, 76
    fixed, 34
    foot surveillance, 75–76
    loose, 73–74
    objectives of, 73, 74
    preparation for, 74–75
    stakeouts, 73–74, 76–77
Suspect, questioning, 255
Suspect documents, 295–96
Sympathetic approach, to interview, 197
Synopsis/introduction, reports, 169

T

Tasers, 412
Team policing, 79
Tear gas, 413
Telegraph, 129
Telephone, 132–35
Television, 131–32
    detailed descriptions of, 113–14
Testifying in court, 22
Tireprints, 277
Tool marks, 277–78

Tools, detailed descriptions of, 114
Traffic citations, 358–60
Traffic collision investigations, 299–300
Traffic control, 8–9, 15

U

Unlawful assembly, 319–21
Unusual occurrences, See Disasters/unusual
        occurrences
U.S. Mail, 128

V

Vehicle inspection, 54
Vehicle patrol, tactics, 59–60
Vehicles:
    inspection of, 54
    parking, 61–62
    skidding, 61
Vehicle search, 386–88
Victims:
    disaster, identification of, 312–13
    personal interviews of, 268
Video data terminals in field units, 144

W

Warning shots, 417
Warrant arrests, 377–78
Warrantless arrests, 371, 378
Warrants, search, 391–92
Weapons, 411–13
    crimes in progress, 255–56
Whistles, 128–29
Witnesses:
    basic requirements of, 84–85
    eyewitness identification, 94–100
    personal interviews of, 268, 272
    See also Eyewitness identification
Women:
    as police officers, 35
    search of, 385–86
Wood identification, as evidence, 281

Z

Zigzag pattern, 59